Adaptation to Life

Adaptation to Life

by George E. Vaillant

1837

Little, Brown and Company   BOSTON   TORONTO

D

The epigraph on page 351 is from the play *Equus* by Peter Shaffer. Copyright ©
1974 by Peter Shaffer. Reprinted by permission of Atheneum Publishers.

Library of Congress Cataloging in Publication Data

Vaillant, George E
  Adaptation to life.

  Includes bibliographical references and index.
  1. Adulthood — Longitudinal studies. 2. Defense
mechanisms. 3. Emotional maturity. I. Title.
BF724.5.V34   155.6   77-22475
ISBN 0-316-89520-2

BP

Designed by Christine Benders

*Published simultaneously in Canada
by Little, Brown & Company (Canada) Limited*

PRINTED IN THE UNITED STATES OF AMERICA

This book is dedicated to the members of the Grant Study. Their fidelity, their difficulties, and their solutions have inspired, touched, and guided me for the past decade. My life is vastly richer for having known them.

Acknowledgments

The Grant Study of Adult Development was conceived in 1937 when I was three years old. I did not join the staff until 1967. In writing this book, then, I have harvested a crop that for three decades many others have planted and devotedly tended. I am deeply indebted to the foresight of William T. Grant, Earl Bond, M.D., and Arlie V. Bock, M.D., for having planned the Study. I am equally indebted to Clark W. Heath, M.D., who guided the Study for the first seventeen years of its existence, and to the many social scientists, too many to list here, who worked with him and helped him to gather its data. I am particularly thankful to Lewise W. Gregory Davies, who is the only current staff member who has been with the Study since the beginning; for almost forty years she has provided the personal warmth that cemented living men to the abstraction of a study of adult development.

Over the years I have enjoyed many teachers whose guidance indirectly has helped to shape this book. Among the most important are Lee Robins, Peter Dews, Norma Haan, William Binstock, and most especially Elvin Semrad, who first conceived the hierarchy of defenses described in this book.

Over the decade that I have worked on the Grant Study there have been several men who have provided the intellectual climate and the institutional support needed to conceive, research, and write this book. My patrons have been Bert Boothe of the Career Investigator Grant Program of the National Institute of Mental Health and Douglas Bond and Philip Sapir of the Grant Foundation. My patient chiefs of service, Paul Myerson and then John Mack, and my institutional hosts, Dana Farnsworth, followed by Warren Wacker, have seen to it that I have had time and space in which to be curious. (In more material terms, the Grant

Foundation and grants MH-10361 and MH-38798 from NIMH provided financial support.)

There are many individuals who have helped me to write this book even more directly: Some have helped as research associates and as independent raters (Jane Brighton, Nancy Sobowale, Charles Ducey, Ana-Maria Rizzuto, Kenneth Robson, Eleanor Weeks, Henry Vaillant, and Eva Milofsky).

Some have helped me as intellectual critics (Leon Shapiro, Leston Havens, Norman Zinberg, Bennett Simon, John Mack, Jerome Kagan, George Goethals, Henry Grunebaum, and Stuart Hauser).

Some have helped me as editors (Clark Heath, Suzannah Vaillant Hatt, and especially Llewelyn Howland III of Little, Brown).

Phyllis Remolador deserves triple credit for serving both as a research associate and as editor, and, together with Ronnie Ventura and Liv Bjornard, uncomplainingly typing and retyping the myriad drafts that this book has undergone.

Two other people deserve special gratitude for playing multiple roles. The first, Charles C. McArthur, was director of the Study from 1955 to 1972. Without his devotion the Study might not have survived to maturity. Not only did he gather much of the data that comprise the Study, but also, in welcoming me into his "laboratory" and generously providing counsel and help, he created a climate in which my own efforts could prosper. Charles McArthur achieved the most difficult and the most selfless task of a mentor: he allowed me to feel that a work that would have been impossible without his help was my own creation.

The second is my wife, Caroline Officer Vaillant. Over the years she has made an invaluable contribution to this book as research associate *and* intellectual critic *and* editor. She has always shown an uncanny ability to ask the right questions and for years she has made time present the very best part of my life cycle.

Only the Grant Study men themselves have made a more critical contribution to the birth of this book.

G. E. V.

Contents

Tables and Figures

Cast of Protagonists

Chapter 1
David Goodhart — Son of prejudiced Detroit blue-collar worker; consultant to Ford Foundation for urban affairs. Adaptive style: altruism, humor, sublimation, and suppression.

Carlton Tarrytown, M.D. — Florida ear, nose, and throat specialist; lonely; Lotus-eater; an alcoholic with a poor childhood. Adaptive style: dissociation and projection.

Chapter 4
Frederick Lion — New York magazine editor, who used anger creatively. Adaptive style: sublimation.

Horace Lamb — Retired single ex-diplomat and book collector. Adaptive style: fantasy.

Casper Smythe, M.D. — University health service physician with two divorces and a not always satisfactory sexual adjustment. Adaptive style: repression and passive aggression.

George Byron, Esq. — Government AID lawyer, who had excellent marriage and a very satisfactory sexual adjustment. Adaptive style: dissociation, anticipation, suppression, and sublimation.

Chapter 6
Lieutenant Edward Keats — World War II combat pilot; subsequently an unhappily married social worker. Adaptive style: sublimation, reaction formation, and passive aggression.

Professor Dylan Bright — Pugilistic professor of poetry. Adaptive style: sublimation and dissociation.

Professor Ernest Clovis — Professor of medieval French whose wife, then his daughter, became chronically ill. Adaptive style: sublimation and suppression.

Chapter 7

Mayor Timothy Jefferson — Long Island politician whose daughter had cystic fibrosis, and who struggled to master anger. Adaptive style: suppression, anticipation, and altruism.

Dr. Jacob Hyde — A pharmacologist with a hypochondriacal mother; he beat swords into plowshares. Adaptive style: reaction formation and altruism.

William Forsythe — State Department troubleshooter. Adaptive style: anticipation.

Richard Lucky — The prototype of a happy childhood and a happy marriage; ran two corporations during the week and six miles on the weekend. Adaptive style: repression.

Eben Frost, Esq. — Vermont farmboy turned successful corporation lawyer. Adaptive style: suppression.

Chapter 8

Richard Lucky — Introduced in Chapter 7.

Richard Stover — Basketball captain who for years never had a date but who became a warm husband and father. Adaptive style: repression.

Dean Henry Clay Penny — Parsimonious, superstitious college dean. Adaptive style: intellectualization.

Samuel Lovelace — Lonely, gentle, loyal liberal with an unhappy marriage and few social supports. Adaptive style: intellectualization.

Russell Lowell, Esq. — Boston lawyer and Stoic. Adaptive style: intellectualization and suppression.

Vice-President Richard Fearing — Computer magnate with multiple fears as a child and conversion symptoms as an adult. Adaptive style: displacement.

Judge Conrad Spratt — Chicago probate judge who grew up in Manchuria and suffered osteomyelitis. Adaptive style: reaction formation.

George Byron, Esq. — Introduced in Chapter 4.

Carlton Tarrytown, M.D. — Introduced in Chapter 1.

Chapter 9

Harry Hughes — Trade book editor, who as a child learned initiative could be dangerous, and who experienced a prolonged

adolescence. Adaptive style: projection and reaction formation.

Francis Oswald — Virtuous as a marine, too strict as a father, and
gallant as a defender of the Florida Everglades. He suffered a
serious depression. Adaptive style: reaction formation, projection, and delusional projection.

Harvey Newton — Lonely but famous physicist who built an institute to solve the riddles of the universe. Adaptive style: fantasy.

William Mitty — Lonely astronomer who joined the Oxford
movement as a young man. Adaptive style: fantasy.

Robert Hood — Promiscuous alcoholic who almost became a
child batterer and instead became a celibate student of T.M.
Adaptive style: projection and acting out.

John Hart — Brilliant mathematician who developed heart pains
after his father died of a coronary thrombosis. Adaptive style:
hypochondriasis.

Lieutenant Edward Keats — Introduced in Chapter 6.

Thomas Sawyer — Rockefeller campaign aide who first was bullied by his mother and then by his wife. Adaptive style: passive
aggression and displacement.

Chapter 10

Robert Jordan — A college conservative who became a fifty-year-
old liberal.

Adam Carson, M.D. — Harvard physician who turned from research to clinical practice and illustrated the stages of the
adult life cycle.

Oliver Kane — Orphaned corporate executive with mature ego defenses and a barren personal life. Adaptive style: intellectualization, suppression, and humor.

Mayor Jefferson — Introduced in Chapter 7.

Harry Hughes — Introduced in Chapter 9.

Chapter 11

Robert Brooke — A sensitive bombardier who cured a wartime
neurosis through poetry. Adaptive style: evolution from repression and dissociation to sublimation.

James O'Neill, Ph.D. — Boston economist and statistician with
happy childhood; for years was diagnosed as an "inadequate

personality" due to chronic alcoholism, then recovered. Adaptive style: evolution from reaction formation and intellectualization to passive aggression and acting out, which in turn evolved into sublimation and altruism.

Francis DeMille — Hartford advertising man who when young was dependent on his mother and oblivious to women, but who matured into a competent husband and father. Adaptive style: evolution from repression and dissociation to sublimation.

Herman Crabbe, Ph.D. — An industrial chemist who matured through a fortunate marriage, from an eccentric scientist, overwhelmed by a mentally ill mother, into an effective leader of a research team. Adaptive style: evolution from projection and fantasy to displacement.

Godfrey Minot Camille, M.D. — A dependent, hypochondriacal, and suicidal medical student who through prolonged medical and psychiatric treatment became an independent and giving physician and father. Adaptive style: evolution from hypochondriasis through displacement and reaction formation into altruism.

Chapter 12

Steven Kowalski — Ebullient businessman who made a success of life and a virtue of aggression. Adaptive style: suppression.

Leslie Angst — Harried banker who drank too much, worried about his chronic failure, and did not enjoy his marriage. Adaptive style: displacement.

Chapter 13

Samuel Lovelace — Introduced in Chapter 8.
William Lucky — Introduced in Chapter 8.
Oliver Kane — Introduced in Chapter 10.

Chapter 14

Francis Oswald — Introduced in Chapter 9.

Chapter 15

William Forsythe — Introduced in Chapter 7.
Adam Carson, M.D. — Introduced in Chapter 10.

Chapter 16
Alan Poe — San Francisco poet, thoughtful conscientious objector and empathic iconoclast who illustrated that mental health
 is not simple. Adaptive style: sublimation.

Part I

The Study of
Mental Health:
Methods and
Illustrations

Introduction

There are thousands of studies of maladjustment for each one that deals directly with the ways of managing life's problems with personal strength and adequacy.

— Lois Murphy, *The Widening World of Childhood*

In 1937 a philanthropist, William T. Grant, met with the director of a university health service, Arlie V. Bock, M.D., and together they decided that medical research was too weighted in the direction of disease. They agreed that "Large endowments have been given and schemes put into effect for the study of the ill, the mentally and physically handicapped. . . . Very few have thought it pertinent to make a systematic inquiry into the kinds of people who are well and do well."[1] As a result, the philanthropist and the health service director agreed to select a small but healthy sample of several consecutive college classes for intensive medical and psychological study. Thus, there came into being a cohort of men who were chosen for study because they seemed healthy. This book will describe their lives over the thirty-five years that followed. The men of the Grant Study, as it came to be called, did not all live happily ever after, but their experiences have meaning for us all.

In a somewhat similar study, Frank Barron, a University of California psychologist, had studied healthy graduate students in great detail. A major conclusion of his investigation was that "no especially blessed individual turned up in this assessment; the luckiest of the lives here studied had its full share of difficulty and private despair. . . . The conclusion to which the assessment study has come is that psychopathology is always with us and soundness is a way of reacting to problems, not an absence of

3

them."[2] His conclusion will become the dominant motif of this book.

At the time that they were chosen for special study, all of the men in the Grant Study had achieved good academic standing in a highly competitive liberal arts college. Most of the men selected subsequently rose to the rank of officer and made distinguished records for themselves in the less academic atmosphere of World War II. There they were judged for skills other than intellectual achievement. Three decades later, as they pass their fiftieth birthdays, most are still alive and without disabling physical illness. Over ninety percent have founded stable families. Virtually all have achieved occupational distinction. *Yet there is not one of the men who has had only clear sailing.* Thus, over the years the focus of the Grant Study became how men adapt to life.

In his 1937 monograph, *Ego Psychology and the Problem of Adaptation*, Heinz Hartmann suggested that health and adaptation were inseparable. "The concept of adaptation," he wrote, "though it appears simple, implies . . . a great many problems. The analysis of this concept promises to clarify many problems of normal and abnormal psychology, among them our conception of mental health."[3] Hartmann was quite unaware of the Grant Study, and although his monograph eventually became a cornerstone of modern psychoanalytic thinking, the Grant Study staff were quite unaware of Heinz Hartmann.

At the time the Grant Study began, the staff consisted of internists, psychiatrists, psychologists, physiologists, and anthropologists. As specialists, these men recognized that each of their disciplines had been distorted by its focus upon the deviant or exceptional members of human society. The Study staff members were determined to pool their efforts and examine a group of healthy young men. In the mid-1940s, the first two books on the Study were published. *What People Are* by Clark Heath and *Young Man, You Are Normal* by Ernest Hooton provided few surprises.[4] These early publications were designed to summarize research already accomplished, and this they did. But even at the time, the original investigators realized that publication was premature. Hooton warned, "For one thing, it is not enough to cut two or three small cross-sections out of the young manhood of a tiny sample of our species; they must be watched and studied through their entire careers."[5] In the first year after its bottling, you cannot savor the true quality of a fine Bordeaux.

Thirty more years have passed, and the men continue to participate in the research with astonishing loyalty. As they have grown in stature, their study has become progressively more fascinating. The subjects have become bestselling novelists and cabinet members, scholars and captains of industry, physicians and teachers of the first rank, judges and newspaper editors. Yet all have displayed in abundance what Freud called the psychopathology of everyday life.

This attempt of mine to describe how these men adapted to life is a presumptuous task, and one beset by myriad difficulties. The greatest pitfall is that I try to suggest that some behaviors are "healthier" than others. Yet all definitions of health — especially of mental health — are relative. I have taken the position that since good health can get worse but not better, "average" or "normal" has no place in its discussion. Average eyesight, average life expectancy, even average I.Q. reflect the average amount of disease and incapacity present in the population. By definition, then, "healthy" will not be "average."

But from whose vantage point should mental health be judged? Mental health may be considered from the subjective viewpoint of the individual being studied (i.e., feeling good) or from the point of view of the group (i.e., nondeviant). But if "health" is judged by group consensus, then which group determines what consensus? "Health" can also be defined from the point of view of the clinician (that anything is healthy that does not interfere with the objective well-being of the organism). But then, as the psychoanalyst Edward Glover has suggested, cannot health merely be a form of madness that goes unrecognized because it happens to be a good adaptation to reality? Glover suggested an alternative measure of health, "behavior unaffected by conflict";[6] but cannot healthy behavior be the result of ingenious response to conflict? The possibilities for debate are endless.

To pose the question differently, what facet of a person's life should we examine in order to find health? Certainly, the more sophisticated and sensitive we become, the more unmeasurable become our criteria. Frank Barron's early studies of creativity postulated that healthy persons should manifest such traits as "a sense of humor," "personal courage," "a certain innocence of vision and spontaneity of action," "honesty of thought," "social responsibility," "acceptance of the past and no fear of the future," and finally, a capacity "to be able to contribute something of human love to the world."[7] I heartily agree with such criteria, but in what units do you measure them? Unfortunately, ideal definitions cannot be systematically applied to real people. Like beauty, the perception of such abstractions too often lies in the eyes of the beholder.

In providing mankind with a working definition of mental health, Leo Tolstoy, a patron saint of the counterculture, had anticipated Sigmund Freud's middle-class concept of *lieben und arbeiten* by half a century. Freud was only six months old when Tolstoy advised his almost-fiancée, Valery Arsenev, "One can live magnificently in this world, if one knows how to work and how to love, to work for the person one loves and to love one's work."[8] One of the soundest men in the Study agreed with Tolstoy; he wrote, "I am enthusiastic about the future because I have a good business to work at and a good family to work for." Another Grant Study member suggested that health could be estimated from a person's "dealings with other people." He believed that a healthy man would succeed in "reaching his own goals and helping those around him to reach theirs," while a misfit's life would consist of "making more enemies than friends and frustrating his own desires."

Rather than becoming bound to any rigid definition of health, I prefer to align myself with Roy Grinker, Sr., a psychiatrist who has contributed significantly to our understanding of psychological health. He suggested that "the articles and books written on [health] are numerous but highly repetitive. . . . Most of the discussions are theoretical and conceptual and . . . without operational referents."[9] So, adhering both to Grinker's suggestion and to Barron's quotation that *"Soundness is a way of reacting to problems, not an absence of them,"* I will confine myself to a discussion of concrete aspects of adaptation. In this book "health" will be defined in terms of objective clinical evidence. Men will be considered well adapted in terms of the number of areas in which they function well, rather than in terms of excellence within a special area. Finally, what a man does will be given more credence than how he says he feels: the robust hypochondriac, in this sense, will be considered healthier than a Christian Scientist who denies his brain tumor. Nevertheless, I hope to show that what humans do and how humans feel are closely related.

Because an introduction permits the writer certain liberties, I shall use it to orient the reader further to my theoretical bias. Since the focus of the Study is upon adaptation to life, much attention will be devoted to *ego mechanisms of defense.* Often such mechanisms are analogous to the means by which an oyster, confronted with a grain of sand, creates a pearl. Humans, too, when confronted with conflict, engage in unconscious but often creative behavior. These intrapsychic styles of adaptation have been given individual names by psychiatrists (projection, repression, and sublimation are some well-known examples). The generic term for such adaptive styles as a class is *ego mechanisms of defense.* In such context the word *ego* represents a reification of the adaptive and executive aspects of the brain. In this book the so-called *defense* mechanisms of psychoanalytic theory will often be referred to as coping or adaptive mechanisms. This is to underscore the fact that defenses are healthy more often than they are pathological. I shall be discussing defenses as actual behaviors, affects, and ideas which serve defensive purposes, rather than as theoretical constructs that attempt to describe mental functioning. Throughout, I shall try to infer what goes on inside a man by what can be outwardly observed. In reviewing modern approaches to the mind, Leston Havens points out that the objective-descriptive mode is not the only approach to the mind,[10] but it is the one that I have chosen.

At first the reader may find both my concepts and my nomenclature of adaptive mechanisms arbitrary and difficult. (To many, the birds that touch down at a feeder look remarkably alike, and their alleged classification seems unnecessary. But by attending to examples and permitting experience to accumulate, the observer gains pleasure and mastery by perceiving that nuthatches are truly different from chickadees.) I must acknowledge from the start, however, that defenses are far less tangible than birds. Indeed, the so-called ego mechanisms are metaphors, not biological species or pieces of clockwork. Readers should feel free to substitute their own taxonomy. What must be kept in mind, however, is that some sort of shorthand is needed to describe mental processes. I have found the metaphorical language provided by psychoanalysis to be serviceable.

In writing of mechanisms of adaptation, I am not writing about conscious avoidance of problems, or about willpower, nor do I mean perseverance or turning to others. These all serve as a means of handling problems; rather I am discussing a far more subtle and almost entirely unconscious process. Indeed, the ego mechanisms of adaptation went unrecognized until described by Sigmund Freud in his earliest psychiatric papers of 1894–1896.[11] Today, the majority of recent college graduates would probably recognize several of the following terms: sublimation, projection, repression, reaction formation, and displacement. Many could probably cite an example in the behavior of a perfectly healthy friend. But before the twentieth century, awareness of such mechanisms did not exist. Like the curvature of the earth, adaptive mechanisms have been always in view, but someone had to point them out before everyone could notice them.

Let me give a concrete example of unconscious adaptive behavior. A California hematologist developed a hobby of cultivating living cells in test tubes. In a recent interview, he described with special interest and animation an unusually interesting culture that he had grown from a tissue biopsy from his mother. Only toward the end of the interview did he casually reveal that his mother had died from a stroke only three weeks previously. His mention of her death was as bland as his description of the still-living tissue culture had been affectively colored. Ingeniously and unconsciously, he had used his hobby and his special skills as a physician to mitigate temporarily the pain of his loss. Although his mother was no longer alive, by shifting his attention he was still able to care for her. There was nothing morbid in the way he told the story; and because ego mechanisms are unconscious, he had no idea of his defensive behavior. Many of the healthiest men in the Study used similar kinds of attention shifts or *displacement*. Unless specifically looked for by a trained observer, such behavior goes unnoticed more often than not.

Another example of the ego's ingenuity was offered by a very gentle, idealistic lawyer. As a young man he had been bullied by his wife into taking divorce cases because such cases were so profitable; but when he came home at night from his work, the maid would often tell him his wife was out and that no supper had been prepared. Gradually, he realized that she had been going to the Lake Tahoe casinos with a boy friend whose gambling habit the lawyer was supporting. When I asked him what he did with his anger, he replied, "I tried to sweep it under the rug. I pretended it wasn't there." I waited for what else he might add. He was silent a moment; and, then, in an offhand manner he told me that he would often spend such evenings with an amateur theatrical group whose mission it was to put on comic plays. "It was a place people could sublimate in. It was sort of a family substitute." In this way, he was able to *dissociate* himself from his rage. The overt behavior of both the lawyer and the physician did not seem out of the ordinary to them, but their behavior did appear decidedly unusual to the outside observer. Such unconscious behavior allows us to go on about life's business without anxiety or depression — the overt hallmarks of intrapsychic conflict.

The reader may scoff at these examples and wonder how they could occur in the lives of healthy people. But ego mechanisms of defense imply a dynamic restorative process, and by no means connote the abnormal. Rather, defenses have much in common with the behavior of an opossum vigorously and alertly playing dead or with a grouse seeming to nurse a "hurt" wing in order to protect her babies. Such smoothly functioning actions are a sign of health.

By analogy, for centuries fever and pus were synonymous with disease, yet they are actually the body's adaptive response to invading bacteria. If complications do not occur, such responses are normal; it is the external infection that is unusual. So it is with ego mechanisms; they are normal responses to abnormal circumstances.

In more formal terms, ego mechanisms of defense describe unconscious, and *sometimes* pathological, mental processes that the ego uses to resolve conflict among the four lodestars of our inner life: instincts, the real world, important people, and the internalized prohibitions provided by our conscience and our culture.

Conflict may arise between just two or among all four of these sources of human motivation. Usually, ego mechanisms are employed:

1. to keep affects within bearable limits during sudden life crises (e.g., following a death);
2. to restore emotional balance by postponing or channeling sudden increases in biological drives (e.g., at puberty);
3. to obtain a time-out to master changes in self-image (e.g., following major surgery or unexpected promotion);
4. to handle unresolvable conflicts with people, living or dead, whom one cannot bear to leave (e.g., the lawyer's wife, the hematologist's mother);
5. to survive major conflicts with conscience (e.g., killing in wartime, putting a parent in a nursing home).

The psychologically sophisticated reader may balk at my use of the theoretical construct — *ego mechanism of defense* — to describe overt behavior. Such critics will be right if they say that I am really writing about adaptive styles rather than "mental mechanisms." But in turn, I remind them that the chronology of the book covers a lifetime and not a therapeutic hour. How long must a "mental mechanism" last before it affects life-style? Besides, the life study of adults may offer the investigator data similar in nature to what a child psychiatrist observes during play therapy. Because of their relatively high intelligence and education, the men in the Grant Study had a great deal of freedom in regard to both career choice and life-style. Thus, by the age of fifty, many of the men in this Study were in idiosyncratic careers of their own devising. These were often careers in which the men had to answer only to themselves and which had been in part shaped to solve conflict. As a student of their behavior, I knew little of the subjects' dreams, their unconscious fantasies, their slips of the tongue; but I knew a great deal about what they did with their lives.

Judging a man by his behavior rather than by what he says or feels is, of course, a perilous business. Nevertheless, it is easier to handicap a horse on his track record than by careful scrutiny of his appearance in the paddock. Similarly, by paying attention to a person's external behavior, it becomes much easier to validate clinical judgment. In looking for and interpreting adaptive styles, error is bound to occur and personal bias to show. In part, trying to fathom the adaptive purposes of unexpected behavior is like trying to interpret Rorschach inkblots — one's own projections take over. But the study of lifetimes protects the observer from many biases. For example, with Van Gogh's whole life before us, it is not hard to gain consensus of personal judgments of both his genius and his mental anguish. Van Gogh may be judged gifted because his paintings brought the world great pleasure, as evidenced by their sustained popularity and current cost; and he may be considered depressed and angry because he was psychiatrically hospitalized and he cut off his own ear.

Let me anticipate three criticisms. First, while describing the adaptive maneuvers of these men, I was repeatedly reminded that their lives were "too human for science, too beautiful for numbers, too sad for diagnosis, and too immortal for bound journals." Human beings need science. But science never does human beings justice. The Grant Study subjects deserve better than to be regarded as guinea pigs.

Second, I am a clinician, and the men's lives have been discussed with clinical candor. Any resemblance between the examples in this Study and persons living or dead is entirely intentional. However, I have deliberately selected examples that describe more than one member of this Study and, I hope, describe many others outside of it. I have taken pains to camouflage the actual details of the subjects' lives. If the clinical detail fits anyone of the reader's acquaintance too closely, anyone who might have been in college in 1940, it will almost certainly turn out that he has identified the wrong man. Even when the Study members recognize themselves, I suspect that they will be wrong as often as they are right; but I hope that through identifying they learn something worth knowing. (All the case histories presented in this book have been reviewed by the living protagonists and they have granted me permission to publish the disguised narratives.)

Third, the fanciful names like David Goodhart and Horace Lamb, assigned to the subjects, are neither intended to be facetious nor to make sport of human foibles. Rather, my intent has been to permit a busy reader to remember individual examples from one chapter to the next. Designations such as "Case 1" or "Dr. C.R." would be useful in a short paper, but not in a book.

Finally, let me offer a fourth caveat. This book is written through my eyes, through my limited experience, and must in part reflect the distortions of my own adaptive mechanisms. Readers are welcome to do their own editing, or, if they wish, to theorize about my own prejudices and adaptive distortions.

In order for the reader to fix me in social time and place and thus to gauge my biases, the reader is entitled to know a little of my background. I was born in New York City of academic, "WASP" parents. I was educated in "eastern" private schools and an Ivy League college, and I went on to Harvard Medical School, with the internalized injunctions that to teach and to serve were good and that business and private practice were bad. Politically, I believe that the *New York Times* is the source of truth, and I am a Republican who votes Democrat. I am divorced, happily remarried, and live in Cambridge, Massachusetts, with my second wife and four children. I suspect that on the "scales" that I provide of adult adjustment, defenses, and childhood environment, I fall about in the middle. As a psychiatrist, I pretend, like so many of my profession, to belong to no "school," but it may not take the reader long to realize that I am trained as a psychoanalyst and am a staunch admirer of Adolf Meyer and Erik Erikson. Less obvious, but important, I worked for two years in a Skinnerian laboratory and believe that as a means of uncovering truth the experimental method is superior to intuition.

Chapter 1

Mental Health

> SIR CLAUDE: If you haven't the strength to impose your own terms upon life, you must accept the terms it offers you.
>
> — T. S. Eliot, *The Confidential Clerk*

What is mental health?

I submit that health is adaptation, and adaptation is quite the opposite of the quote from Mr. Eliot. If you have not the strength to accept the terms life offers you, you must, in self-defense, force your own terms upon it. If either you or your environment is distorted too much in the process, your effort at adaptation may be labeled mental illness.

This book will examine specific ways in which men alter themselves and the world around them in order to adapt to life. The examples will be concrete; and, as I have indicated in the introduction, they will be drawn from the lives of men specifically selected because they demonstrate psychological health. (The absence of women in the Grant Study was an unforgivable omission, and an omission that will require another study to correct.) Since good psychological health becomes apparent only when the going gets tough, this book will focus on the difficulties that these men encountered. The terms *adaptation* and *defense* will be used interchangeably.

At the start, it is important to note that the ways in which people adapt to help themselves are quite distinct from the ways in which they conventionally receive help from others. A guiding clinical principle of Dr. Arlie Bock, the physician who conceived the Study on which this book is based, was that people in trouble need to be offered "a leg up" — assistance from others. Yet, in order to study health, Dr. Bock directed that the college sophomores selected for study be chosen for each man's capacity for self-reliance.

In a crisis, everyone may turn to friends, parents, teachers, or physicians for help. A child falls down in the park and cuts his knee. Hearing his cries, his mother picks him up, comforts him, and bandages his cut. His mother has given him "a leg up," and the terms life offers are accepted by him. Assisted by others, his unconscious ego has not needed to come to his aid.

But however valuable the help of others may be, there is much that humans must do for themselves. Consider the child's involuntary cries that brought his mother running, or the blood-clotting mechanisms that sealed his wound. These were ways that he took care of himself. Choosing a more complex example, consider that a broken love affair may lead one man to write great poetry and another to commit suicide. Both responses represent adaptive efforts on the part of the individual to alter pain so that it may be borne. Yet neither process is under anything like full conscious control.

Since most people consider writing good poetry to be healthy and suicide to be sick, it is tempting at this point to try to define mental health. But wait. Terms like "health" and "sickness" are merely useful abstractions. Although I use them in discussing adaptation, the reader will not always agree with my definitions. On the one hand, imaginary physical illness may lead to real hypochondriacal invalidism. Is such an individual sick or well? On the other hand, as in the case of Teddy Roosevelt's real asthma, John Kennedy's tangible back injury, and Franklin Roosevelt's crippling polio, serious physical illness may contribute to mastery of life. Thus, inner processes can either erase or magnify the effects of external illness. Health and the "ego" must be considered together.

But already the reader may be startled and mistrustful. As soon as the names of public figures are mentioned in such a context, the issue of the author's values arises. In our hearts, we each claim a special insight into the question "What is health?" If the reader sees Teddy Roosevelt as neurotically overcompensating, his cousin Franklin as an insincere socialist, or John Kennedy as merely a handsome opportunist, how can he continue to believe anything that I have to say about health? Perhaps the reader really prefers the gentle, self-effacing qualities of some invalid of his acquaintance to the strident qualities of these politicians who knew only how to win. *Psychological* and *health* are inflammatory words. *Health* is both metaphysical and a value judgment. Mistrust is inevitable. But I write principally about the processes by which adaptation is achieved; the ultimate judgment as to whether such adaptation is "good" or "bad" remains the reader's prerogative.

Let me start with two men who began life with the dice loaded against them. One man seemed to adapt skillfully and to succeed at many of life's tasks — in a most moral and self-effacing fashion. The adaptive devices of the other man repeatedly caused both himself and others considerable distress. For his devotion to the needs of others, I will call the successful man Mr. David Goodhart. For his self-indulgence, I will call the other man Dr. Carlton Tarrytown. (If these pseudonyms remind you of Bunyan's *Pilgrim's Progress*, so be it. My intention is to preserve the men's anonymity without obliterating those particular qualities of their lives that are most under scrutiny. The *spirit* of their lives and their techniques for surmounting life's difficulties will be reported as faithfully as possible. But the *letter* of their lives — the little facts that serve to identify a specific individual — I have altered as much as possible.)

When I interviewed the men, they seemed very different. Mr. Goodhart had the look of a worried college president, with slightly tousled hair, a rumpled raincoat, and an aristocratic bearing. His well-tailored suit and accent belied his Detroit working-class background. Having put himself to great inconvenience to keep the appointment, Mr. Goodhart went to special pains to buy me a cup of coffee. In manner he was easy, open, relaxed, and warm. Although he made little eye contact, I got no feeling that Mr. Goodhart was cold — only shy. "Everything that I do," he said, "depends upon a personal relationship." Emotionally, he was low-key, but during the interview there was a full range of affect. (By *affect* I mean feeling, color, instinctual heat, and emotional tone. We *think* ideas, we *feel* affects.) Mr. Goodhart's eyes filled when he discussed his marriage; he expressed broad enjoyment as he remembered the activities that he and his family shared on their last vacation. He claimed that he found it "hard to maintain a strong emotion for any length of time — anger or the good ones too." But in point of fact, he was unusually skilled in describing his feelings.

The interview with Dr. Carlton Tarrytown was painfully antiseptic. Tarrytown talked to me in his Fort Lauderdale living room, a room so meticulously decorated that it reminded me of a *House and Garden* advertisement — or, because the realities of the adult world were so excluded, of a nursery. At forty-seven he looked sixty. Tall and cadaverous, Tarrytown dressed immaculately, but he had lost the social patina that he had brought with him from private boarding school to college. Dr. Tarrytown said that he did not depend upon other people; rather, he boasted that his greatest satisfaction came from using his own head. He displayed a cooperative but hollow charm, and he was hard pressed to tell me how things were going with him. All his life he either had been utterly unaware of his feelings or had acted upon them so impulsively as to obscure their presence. I felt that he never perceived me as another human being — only as an anxiety-provoking stimulus to be warded off as graciously as possible. Although self-centered, he was without force; talking to him was like talking to a callow adolescent. (In contrast, despite his self-effacing qualities, Mr. Goodhart had kept me respectfully aware that I was talking to a man wiser and more experienced than myself.)

Their different modes of adaptation help to explain why these men were so different. Mr. Goodhart used *sublimation* and *altruism* to make life tolerable; Dr. Tarrytown used *dissociation* and *projection*. (These clumsy psychiatric terms are formally defined in Appendix A; in this chapter, argot will be translated into English.)

For troubled individuals, both sublimation and altruism can achieve the alchemist's dream of turning dross into gold. Mr. Goodhart had such a gift: he transmuted his emotional response to crisis into creative acts that benefited others and gratified himself.

Dissociation and projection, on the other hand, are both ways in which a person can disavow responsibility for painful feelings and events, and over the short haul escape the suffering involved. With dissociation, internal pain is ingeniously denied or anesthetized and a happier state put in its place. Dr. Tarrytown used a variety of anesthetics — mystical experience, tranquilizers, and impetuous abandonment of unsatisfactory love affairs for fresh infatuations. In projection, the inner feelings that a person has, but does not wish to acknowledge, are assigned to someone else, which is why the paranoid is a problem to everybody but himself. When Dr. Tarrytown was in trouble, he was the last to know. In contrast, Mr. Goodhart had written, "Although this appears a formidable collection of ills, their effect has been more noticeable subjectively than objectively."

The relevance of the choice of adaptive mechanisms to health can be appreciated through a step-by-step examination of the lives of Goodhart and Tarrytown. Initially, it may look to the reader as if the correlatives of healthy adaptation have become confounded with the tenets of Horatio Alger and the Boy Scouts of America. In time, however, the facts should speak for themselves.

Raised in a blue-collar background, Mr. Goodhart spent his life working for social agencies concerned with problems of the inner city. At forty-seven he was earning $35,000 a year. Throughout his life he had advanced steadily in responsibility, finally becoming an authority on urban affairs for the Ford Foundation. His occupational success surpassed that of his father by a wide margin and fully matched his own ambitions for himself. Besides his work, he devoted time and energy to other public service activities.

In contrast, despite a socially privileged youth and training in that lucrative profession, surgery, Dr. Carlton Tarrytown made half Goodhart's income. Dr. Tarrytown had given up his small private practice of general surgery and now worked as an ear, nose, and throat consultant to the State of Florida. His motivation was security, not public service. Not only was his occupational success inferior to that of his father, but he was also a failure in his own eyes. Outside of his professional duties, he had no responsibilities.

In fact, on an adjustment scale that rated the overall mental health of the men in the Study, Mr. Goodhart fell in the top fifth and Dr. Tarrytown in the bottom fifth. Reflecting the relative success of the men over the twenty-five years that had elapsed since college, the scale rated the four areas of occupational, social, psychological, and subjective medical adjustment. Like the definitions of the adaptive mechanisms, the formal scale of *Adult Adjustment* is relegated to the appendix; only the evidence that led to the relative ranking of Goodhart and Tarrytown will be described here.

For example, there were profound differences in their social adaptation. Mr. Goodhart's marriage was not good, but it had survived for twenty years. With tears in his eyes he had summed it all up: "There is a lot of substance to the relationship; it is not a cold marriage." His children had friends, succeeded in school, loved their father, and were loved in return. All his life his own mother and his older sister remained a source of pleasure. Although Goodhart had no hobbies and played no sports that involved other people, he had several close friends and shared his work with them.

In contrast, Dr. Tarrytown had been married three times, with many stormy affairs in between. His most recent marriage (to a social worker in a children's agency) appeared to be stable, but his wife played an almost parental role toward him. They had no children. Three children from his previous marriages had not fared well, and he was unperturbed that he was forbidden to visit them. Over the years Tarrytown had drifted apart from his family of origin. He had neither visited his parents nor shared responsibility for them when they were dying. When I asked him about his friends, Dr. Tarrytown replied, "I don't have any friends at the moment." A review of his life suggested that things had never been very different.

The psychological adjustment of the men showed the same contrast. Mr. Goodhart took enjoyable vacations and seemed to know how to play. Ever since college he had enjoyed his job. Although a heavy smoker, he drank in moderation and had never used tranquilizers. He had never sought psychotherapy, and the Study staff had never labeled him mentally ill. Dr. Tarrytown, on the other hand, had no interests beyond his work, and since college, the practice of medicine had been for him a chronic source of anxiety and dissatisfaction. He took no vacations, and instead, during crises in his life, would engage in spree drinking. He used all kinds of tranquilizing medication, always to excess. On three occasions he had required hospitalization for drug or alcohol detoxification. (No confidences are being betrayed; several doctors in the Study have had such difficulties.) Dr. Tarrytown's physicians had often labeled him mentally ill, and he had made over one hundred visits to a psychiatrist.

Although this book is primarily concerned with psychological well-being, it is impossible to discuss the relative psychological health of these two men without also comparing their subjective view of their physical health. Some facets of physical illness, of course, have little to do with psychological adaptation; but, in general, response to physical illness mirrored the men's style of adapting to other aspects of their lives. Since college, Mr. Goodhart had never been hospitalized. Although he did not always label his own health "excellent," he missed less than five days a year from work due to illness and was free from any condition for which he sought or required medical attention. Dr. Tarrytown, on the other hand, had been hospitalized twice for medical reasons; he did not usually perceive his health as excellent, and he regularly missed more than five work days a year due to illness. Although no ulcer was ever proven, he was plagued by abdominal complaints for which he sought frequent medical attention.

When I discuss the differences in their unconscious adaptation to life, I will examine Tarrytown's and Goodhart's backgrounds in greater detail. Neither socioeconomic discrepancies nor gross differences in home life can explain their different lives. In fact, a major thesis of this book is that a man's adaptive devices are as important in determining the course of his life as are his heredity, his upbringing, his social position, or his access to psychiatric help.

Mr. Goodhart came from a lower-middle-class family in Detroit and had been educated in urban public schools of indifferent quality. During the Depression, his father was often unemployed; but when Goodhart came to college as a scholarship student, his father was making $4,000 a year as a sales manager in a department store. He was able to contribute half the cost of his son's education. Despite inferior preparatory education, Mr. Goodhart graduated from college *magna cum laude* with an A— average.

Dr. Tarrytown grew up in an expensive suburb of Boston. His

father, a successful banker, sent him to first-rate schools. In college, Dr. Tarrytown wove his way in and out of disciplinary scrapes and, despite an interest in medicine, made a C average. Native intelligence was not a determining factor in the difference between these two men's college performances, for both were equally above the college average in verbal skills and below the average in mathematical aptitude.

Nor does the answer to Goodhart's and Tarrytown's different choice of defense lie in the realm of conscious will and morality. The little boy who falls down in the park does not deliberately choose to clot his blood; we would not blame him if he were a hemophiliac. Similarly, Dr. Tarrytown did not deliberately choose to use dissociation instead of altruism; nor can he be blamed for his use of projection. And we can never unravel the adaptive processes that an individual uses by asking him about them; they can be recognized only by an outside observer. The hypnotized subject can only rationalize his behavior; he is often not conscious that he is merely obeying a hypnotist's suggestion. In the same fashion, a person often explains his use of adaptive mechanisms by such remarks as "It seemed like a good idea at the time," or "I did what everyone does." Sometimes, like the lawyer in the introduction, he notes that he uses such mechanisms but labels them incorrectly.

The quality of their childhoods should be an obvious place to discover what differentiated Goodhart and Tarrytown. But I have chosen these men to begin a discussion of human adaptation precisely because both their childhoods left much to be desired. The childhood ratings of both men fell in the bottom fifth of the Study sample. (As with defense mechanisms and adult adaptation, the childhoods of all the men in the Study were rated by research assistants who were kept blind to (unaware of) other variables; several facets of childhood were assessed, and the more important findings will be discussed in Chapter 13.) In brief, both men had parents who, when compared to those of the other men in the Study, seemed ill-equipped to provide their children with either a sense of basic trust in the universe or a comfortable sense of autonomy. Both men were fearful, lonely children, and their parents had created home lives that, especially during their sons' adolescence, were filled with both covert and overt dissension.

An important difference between the two men lay in their un-
equal capacity to tolerate the reality of their parents' shortcomings. In adolescence, Mr. Goodhart was able to admit, albeit
reluctantly, that his mother was "very nervous, irritable, anxious, and a worrier." When he was twenty-eight, he reported that
she had long-standing personality problems; and the available
evidence supported his views. Dr. Tarrytown, however, never
wavered in his belief that his depressed and not always responsible mother "was too good to be in this world." In fact, as a college
sophomore whose own rampantly escapist behavior endangered
his welfare, Tarrytown tried very hard to take care of his sick
mother although she had, once more, abandoned him. Then and
thereafter, he thought everyone in the world was out of step except his mother and himself.

If retrospective vision is to be trusted, the mothers of both boys
"lived in a world of fiction." But Mr. Goodhart's mother, although inadequate, was physically present in a constructive —
not a destructive — way. She shared with her son her taste for
good literature. And Mr. Goodhart discovered through novels
that his parents' racial prejudices did not have to be his. In contrast, Dr. Tarrytown's mother had been very depressed at the
time of her son's birth; she had withdrawn and left him with
nurses. Later, when she reentered his life, she imbued him with
her only legacy, a private mysticism, which served to strengthen,
not weaken, his prejudices and escapist life-style. Thus, Goodhart
rejected and Tarrytown accepted his mother's fictional view of
life, but we can never be sure why.

Alcoholism was present in the fathers of both Goodhart and
Tarrytown. (As in the general population, alcoholism existed in
about a third of the families in the Study.) But again, there was a
difference. When he was drinking, Mr. Goodhart's father withdrew himself from the family, whereas Dr. Tarrytown's father
shared his drinking with his son and made it almost glamorous.
In adolescence, Tarrytown learned to use alcohol the way
Goodhart used books — to escape. Goodhart, frightened by his
drunken father, learned to use alcohol with care.

On the one hand, at nineteen Goodhart could admit that his
father was "unaffectionate," and at forty-eight he could recall
how he had feared his father's alcoholic anger and had tried to

overcome his fear. On the other hand, as a sophomore, Dr. Tarrytown had said of his father, "I like him as well as any man I have known; he is interesting and fun to be with."

After his parents' divorce, Tarrytown did not complain. He hastened to report his good fortune at having a father who could offer financial support when he needed it. Only in middle age did Tarrytown acknowledge a painful truth that was already clear to the Study staff when he was nineteen: "My and my father's entire life together had been a tortured relationship. We cordially hated each other." It is clear that the distortions produced by adaptive mechanisms may, over a period of years, become part of the individual's world view. Truth too awful to bear is unconsciously altered or postponed; *the altered truth then becomes subjectively true.* In other words, the men's adaptive styles affected their childhood environment as much as childhood affected choice of adaptation.

When the men were first evaluated as adolescents, neither Tarrytown nor Goodhart impressed the staff with his future potential. The differences in their future adaptation could never have been predicted in college. The staff had seen David Goodhart as a thin, pale, passive boy with excellent manners, but one who was "rather nervous and self-conscious, with cold, wet hands." At one point a psychiatrist evaluating Goodhart had said flatly, "I think this boy is neurotic." The overall evaluation included adjectives like "self-conscious, well-groomed, unaggressive, dependable, level-headed, sincere, and refined."

In college, Carlton Tarrytown received a paradoxical evaluation. One investigator saw him as an "attractive, well-poised, physically and mentally mature fellow. He seems headed for success if his health holds up. On the whole, I was quite pleased with this boy." On the other hand, another investigator was distressed by Tarrytown's chain smoking and daredevil drinking and driving. He felt Tarrytown "socially maladjusted, anxious, pleasure-seeking, erratic, undependable, and showing poor judgment." The explanation for the differences in opinion lay in the fact that Tarrytown's life-style lent itself to concealing, even to erasing, unhappiness. A staff member described him at twenty-five as "happy, well-poised, and seems to have more purpose in life." In fact, nothing was farther from the truth; but Tarrytown had succeeded in imposing his own terms on reality — for a price.

Having sketched in the background, let me now contrast the adaptive styles of these two men in greater detail. They had encountered many similar difficulties. First, both men had experienced chronic fear and anxiety due to the impulsive behavior of their alcoholic fathers. Second, when they formed their own families, each was haunted by his own experience of poor parental care; in both cases it may have contributed to unhappy marriages. Third, each experienced anxiety in his job. To master these difficulties, they seemed to use the same general style of adaptation that Goodhart described most succinctly: "I do what a child does: I turn my attention away." In adolescence, each had responded to his unhappy childhood by resolving to devote his life to helping others — Goodhart was to be a minister, and Tarrytown a psychiatrist.

But, over time, the modes of adaptation of the two men become easily differentiated. Goodhart's *altruism* and *sublimation* become distinguished from Tarrytown's *projection* and *dissociation*. For example, they defended against death differently. When Dr. Tarrytown's mother died, he left his medical practice and lost himself on a two-week bender, turning his attention away until the funeral and aftermath were over. In contrast, when Mr. Goodhart's best friend was lost in a sailing mishap in Maine, Goodhart stopped what he was doing and took part in the rescue operations. For days after reasonable hope for survival had been abandoned, he pressed for the continuation of the search. He, too, had turned his attention away, in the sense of not being willing to believe that his friend was dead; but his style of temporarily avoiding the pain of mourning was different. Hope and altruism mitigate, but they do not deny the unbearable.

When Dr. Tarrytown came into any kind of conflict with other people, he was devastated by social anxiety. Even the intimacy of normal friendship was more than he could comfortably bear. Thus, like many men who engineer multiple affairs and marriages, he felt most comfortable loving what he called "relative strangers." He found no trouble in admitting his abuse of sedatives and tranquilizers, but he was utterly unable to chronicle what it was that made him anxious or fearful. He could not personalize his emotions any more than a child could.

Tarrytown's own anger was an affect that he could never acknowledge. He was called by his mother "the greatest little liar that ever there was," but this was because in projecting his anger he saw himself perpetually surrounded by danger. He lied not because he was bad, but to survive. On one occasion he observed that "if you don't make people laugh, they'll kill you"; at another point in his life he believed himself to be in the desperate situation where, if he did not cheer up his mother, she would commit suicide. Tarrytown was plagued by multiple somatic symptoms — especially headaches and stomach spasms — but he could not say what caused them. He was a member of the John Birch Society and an enemy of all the Communists that he imagined were trying to take away his personal freedom. But he rarely voted and never demonstrated. He could not articulate the source of his terror, beyond stating that he had "a mild anxiety about everything." Remember, it took three decades for him to admit to the Study that there was ill feeling between himself and his father. At no time did he let himself act in an angry way — even on a tennis court.

Mr. Goodhart, too, had been terrified of his father, and as an adolescent had had great difficulty in sharing these fears with interviewers. But even at nineteen he was consciously curious about where his feelings were hidden and recognized that he "wore a mask" to hide them. "You could turn aside many a shaft if you could be clever," he said. Humor also lets one loose blunted arrows against others; and Goodhart had already discovered that writing for the college humor magazine provided an acceptable vent for *his* angry feelings. In his life's work, Goodhart soon engaged the problem more directly. He had grown up in a family where he was often caught between his embattled, prejudiced parents. Many poor white Southerners had migrated to his neighborhood, and racial prejudice ran high. In the army, as a white officer in a largely black division, he found himself facing "a very ticklish business to keep both superior officers and the men placated." After the war, he set about mastering this fear-provoking situation; hence, his life's work was spent in the urban ghettos of Detroit and in Chicago, devising ways to mediate between city officials and foundation executives, between hard hats and poor blacks. In a very real sense he was protecting his bigoted father from attack, even as he was openly and professionally combating his father's prejudices.

Compare Goodhart's ingenious altruism to Tarrytown's fears of murder and suicide. Compare Goodhart's covert but tension-relieving counterattacks to Tarrytown's anxious inactivity. And consider also three important consequences of Goodhart's adaptive style: first, that he enjoyed it; second, that the world saw his behavior as virtuous and worthy of remuneration; third, that successful adaptation allowed him to grow closer to, not more insulated from, his once-feared father.

As for Dr. Tarrytown, he did not enjoy either his intoxications or his prejudices. And, associated with his failure to acknowledge his anger was the fact that he abandoned his career in surgery; it became too dangerous. Last, Tarrytown's denial of anger led to a life of increasing isolation — from his mother, his father, from two wives and three children. Altruism is better than projection not because it is more moral, but because it is more effective.

The mentally healthy are by no means immune to anxiety and depression. This is because healthy adaptation requires an accurate perception of the universe, and accurate perception often evokes pain. When I asked Mr. Goodhart how he dealt with the growing rift in his marriage, he said that his first level of defense was "smoking." When I pushed him further, he acknowledged the fact that his marriage made him unhappy by saying, "I would rather not talk about it." But, in fact, he *was* able to talk about it; he identified his marriage as his greatest worry; he cried while discussing it; and he assumed full responsibility for his own role.

How did Tarrytown handle his own shattered marriages? He used dissociation in the form of sudden promiscuity or withdrawal into tranquilized oblivion. He would sleep ten hours a night, go months without feeling sexual desire, and engage in the solitary study of Yoga and Eastern religions. At no time did he ever tell the staff he was unhappy. Tarrytown was a master at imposing his terms upon life. He bested Goodhart in evading unhappiness. But while unhappiness reflects a failure of adaptive mechanisms, it is not, in itself, an indicator of poor psychological health.

There was a significant difference in the way the men used humor. Tarrytown's humor was clownish, almost masochistic; Goodhart's was a sublimated acknowledgment of his pain. At different periods in his life, Tarrytown had acquired among his friends a reputation as a clown, but the tragedy of the clown is that others must laugh *at* him. Goodhart was able to induce others to laugh *with* him. Through humorous verse, Goodhart had learned to show off before his friends in a self-effacing manner. He also used humor to master and to express the very real anxieties that plagued him while he mediated between angry urban factions. In short, Goodhart's stature was enhanced and Tarrytown's was diminished by their use of different sorts of humor. Since ironic humor better serves its practitioner than the masochistic pratfall, it becomes important to arrange such defenses along a continuum, yet where Tarrytown's dissociation ended and Goodhart's genuine humor began is a subtle distinction.

As with their dissociation and humor, Goodhart's empathic altruism and Tarrytown's projection bore similarities as well as differences; projection lies on a continuum with empathy. Each man perceived in other people a problem or an emotional state that was in fact his own. But Goodhart perceived his own problems in other people who, in fact, shared them, so that when he tried to ameliorate their problems they could appreciate his efforts. For example, at the height of the Cold War, Goodhart felt that if America went Communist, it would be due to inequities in our own system, not due to Russian meddling. He devoted his life to changing that system. Rather than seeking comfort in his father's prejudices, he fought for civil rights so well that at the age of forty the press singled him out as a national leader.

As the altruist accepts responsibility, the projector disavows it. Dr. Tarrytown's projection led him to see his own problems in those who did not share them. Thus, like a soul-saving priest of the Inquisition, he attacked the problems of others in ways that only he, *not they*, could appreciate. The period of the Cold War was a time of great personal turmoil in Tarrytown's own life, but he wrote to the Study as if nothing were wrong with him. "Something is awfully wrong in the whole value system with which we live," he wrote. "Americans are more disturbed and unhappy than anyone else." At the same time he told the Study that barbiturates serve "as a buffer against a reality I do not like too well (the worldwide trend toward collectivism in one asinine form or another)." His logic is hard to follow. Not only was everybody in America unhappy except him; but if, indeed, he *was* unhappy, then it was the Communists and not his own conflicts that were the cause.

In his adolescence, Dr. Tarrytown had as an ideal "helping people who needed help," but his altruism existed in fantasy, not in action. In reality, he gave up surgery lest he hurt someone, and as a government physician he worked as little as possible. Even his wish to reform the world in the model of the John Birch Society was confined to a fantasy level. Touting individual responsibility, he was an ardent enemy of the welfare state, but he was unable to offer sustained support either to his wives or to his children.

As he grew older, Dr. Tarrytown ignored public affairs by saying, "I don't read newspapers or listen to the radio." However, despite his withdrawal from knowledge of the real world, in 1968 he favored winning the war in Vietnam by military means "at the earliest opportunity." Despite a Bostonian upbringing that rejected the "red-neck" bigotry of Goodhart's parents, Tarrytown in 1968 supported Governor Wallace for president and advocated the defeat of Johnson's civil rights bill in order to "keep the Negro in his place." The anger he did not openly express was projected onto others. It came back to haunt him and add to his fearfulness. Paranoia is a defense of the truly desperate.

An outstanding feature of successful adaptation is that it leaves the way open for future growth. In this respect, Mr. Goodhart's altruism followed the pattern of his sublimation. As a child, he had used books just for escape, but by the time he reached college he was able to use reading about social injustice and his writing of ironic verse to free himself from escapism. At twenty-five Mr. Goodhart had written, "I used to think I am not my brother's keeper but I've now developed a social conscience." The rest of his life was an exciting search to gain for others what he had not received for himself. But Dr. Tarrytown became diminished with time. He became progressively less involved with his job and with other people. At nineteen he seemed mature; at forty-nine he was adolescent, almost a child. No wonder his Fort Lauderdale home resembled a nursery.

Before I leave Goodhart and Tarrytown, I will review the possible determinants of their differences. If the men's childhoods were similar, in the largest sense, there were also differences. A child psychiatrist, kept blind to the men's lives after eighteen, summed up their childhoods as follows. "Tarrytown was raised by a series of nannies." "Goodhart grew up in a home with a violent, murderous, alcoholic father. Mother's protectiveness and devotion to children appeared to give the subject ego strength." The psychiatrist had no way of measuring what she meant by ego strength, but the next thirty years supported her *impression*.

Goodhart's parents had been available to him during all of his formative years; Dr. Tarrytown, for one reason or another, had spent fully half of his childhood and adolescence separated from one or both parents. Tarrytown's mother withdrew when he needed her. She was most depressed at the time of his birth and then again during her divorce — the greatest crisis of her son's adolescence. In contrast, Goodhart's mother was most depressed when her son *left her* for college and again for the army. In some ways, Goodhart must have felt enhanced by a mother who minded his independence; Tarrytown must have felt diminished by a mother who failed to cope with his dependence.

The reliable presence of people who love us facilitates our perception and toleration of painful reality and enriches our lives. At age thirty, during a period of total sobriety, Tarrytown said of a woman with whom he was in love but did not marry, "She fulfills certain basic needs of mine to such an extent that it becomes both possible and desirable to devote more energies to creating an existence without alcohol." For a short time, Tarrytown functioned more maturely than he ever had before. The relationship ended, and Tarrytown resumed his escapism. In part, then, Goodhart's altruism and sublimation may have been a luxury derived from internalized human resources, a luxury that Tarrytown could not usually afford.

If any reader is tempted to stand in judgment over Tarrytown's bigotry, let him. But consider that it may be easy to fear people if your mother was absent during early childhood and if you have never had a real friend. If Goodhart seems more worthy of heaven, be forewarned that one of the hallmarks of healthy adaptation is that it often looks moral to outside observers. But, our adaptive mechanisms are given to us by our biological makeup, by internalization of people who loved us, and from other sources as yet unidentified; adaptive mechanisms are quite unconscious, and we can take no credit for them. If our defenses lead us not into temptation and deliver us from evil, we may offer thankful prayers either to our God or to our ego. (It all depends on whether we wish to project or internalize our ineffable saviors.)

In any case, Tarrytown was not a bad man; but he could not tolerate reality. When I visited him in Florida, he was a kind and gracious host. In failing in this chapter to render him respectable, I merely betray the limitations of my heart, and of my craft. I have tried to classify Tarrytown, to pigeonhole him, to be "objective" about him; in doing so, I have obscured a human being. I liked Goodhart much better. With more resourceful adaptive devices, Goodhart, in my eyes at least, courageously accepted the terms life offered. However, we must learn to divorce adaptation from moral judgment.

This chapter has introduced five motifs that will be developed and expanded through the book. First, it is not the isolated traumas of childhood that shape our future, but the quality of sustained relationships with important people. Second, lives change, and the course of life is filled with discontinuities. What at one point in time appears to be mental illness at another point in time may appear quite adaptive. Third, the key to making sense of psychopathology is to understand adaptive mechanisms; for much of what underlies psychopathology reflects a healing process. Such adaptive mechanisms can be differentiated from one another and arranged along a continuum — a continuum that correlates both with health and with maturity. As this book unfolds, it will become clear that one defensive style can evolve into another, allowing all personalities to appear dynamic and no life to follow an entirely predictable trajectory. Fourth, human development continues throughout adult life, and thus, truth about lives remains relative and can only be discovered longitudinally. Retrospective explanations are filled with distortion; and adequate explanatory truth about an event may not emerge for decades. Finally, positive mental health exists and can be operationally discussed in terms that are, at least in part, free from moral and cultural biases.

Chapter 2

The Men of the Grant Study

> The very act of being a participant, receiving and pondering the follow-up questionnaires, etc. . . . has made me more self-consciously analytical about my personal development, life choices, career progress, and the like. I am sure I have been affected, though in unmeasurable ways, by the knowledge that what happens to me becomes part of a long-range effort to learn more about human development and behavior. . . . Though I haven't been close to the Study except through sporadic written word and one follow-up interview, I would feel a considerable sense of loss if it were discontinued.
>
> — Excerpt from a Grant Study questionnaire

If the lives of specially selected college sophomores are to illustrate how human beings adapt to life, then the reader must know how they were chosen and how they compare with human beings in general. In all, 268 men were originally chosen, 66 from the classes of 1939 to 1941 and 202 from a seven percent sample taken from the classes of 1942 to 1944. The process of selection varied slightly from year to year, but ninety percent of the sample was chosen in the following fashion:

About forty percent of each class was arbitrarily excluded because there was some question of whether they would meet the academic requirements for graduation.

The health service records of the remaining sixty percent were then screened, and half were excluded due to evidence of physical or psychological disturbance.

Each year the names of the remaining thirty percent of the class were submitted to the college deans, who selected about one hundred boys whom they recognized as "sound." The deans had been instructed to choose those boys who seemed most independent and who were not likely to come to the attention of the health services.

In short, they chose boys who, in the words of Dr. Arlie Bock, Director of the University Health Services, were "able to paddle their own canoe" or, in the dean's own words, "boys that we were glad that we had admitted to college." About twenty men were chosen by chance factors: were self-referred (four percent), were the younger brothers of previously selected subjects (two percent), or were students of exceptional promise who had not been caught up in the standard selection net (four percent).

Of the men tentatively selected each year, one in five was not actually accepted into the Study due to his poor motivation toward the project. Reluctance to participate was usually the result of heavy laboratory or extracurricular commitments — varsity football, for example. Once accepted for study, the subjects were most loyal. During their college years only ten of the 268 boys finally selected dropped out. In those ten cases, the motivating force was usually parental.

Since the Study sample was not chosen to be representative, the fact that the selection process was not particularly systematic does not invalidate the results. Rather, the net was cast in such a fashion as to have a high likelihood of retrieving a large group of boys who would lead successful lives — regardless of the observer's bias.

However, quite apart from the sampling limitations inherent in a college sample, there were two serious biases introduced into the selection process. First, the emphasis was on choosing men at one end of the independent-dependent continuum. The college that the men attended was a difficult one, with competitive entrance requirements. Once in college only the academically successful were chosen. In later life, more often than not, the Grant Study men were the most occupationally successful of all their siblings. Put differently, the men had been chosen for their capacity to equal or exceed their natural intellectual ability. Happy-go-lucky but equally stable youngsters who felt less need to achieve were probably underrepresented. Capacity for intimacy was valued less highly than capacity for success.

The second bias is closely related to the first. The adaptive styles in this book will be overly weighted in the direction of the Stoics. As one of the most successful men in the Study said, what he enjoyed most in life was "being beholden to no one and helping others." Too many men in the sample lived up to the definition of normality offered by a staff member: "A healthy person is someone who would never create problems for himself or anyone else." Another net would have had to be cast to include the well-adapted hedonist. To return to the metaphor of the first chapter, when the Grant Study men skinned their knees, they tended to rely on themselves rather than on band-aids and mothers.

This book describes ninety-five men from the original 268. I derived this subsample in the following manner. First, the sample included only those men who graduated from the last three classes studied (1942–1944). By then, inconsistencies in the methods of investigation had been eliminated, and the data available on the members of these last three classes were highly standardized. Then, from 202 men who fell in this group, every man whose assigned case number ended in 1, 5, 6, 8, or 0 (these digits being selected by chance) was chosen for personal interview. There were 102 such men. Two of these 102 were among the ten who before college graduation had withdrawn from the Study. Current follow-up information on those two reveals that they are alive, stably married, raising children, and highly successful in business enterprises of which they are the head. Of the remaining one hundred men, five had died before their twenty-fifth college reunion. The causes of death were World War II combat, heart attack, auto accident, congenital kidney disease, and cancer. In college these five men did not seem to differ from the others in important particulars. This left ninety-five men. One of these men died of cancer just before he could be interviewed, but because his friends were interviewed he was included. Three decades after they had been selected for study, all the remaining ninety-four consented to see me and were interviewed for two hours. Thus, neither selective attrition nor geographic dispersion significantly altered the sample.

In trying to generalize from a sample of college men, the two biggest sources of bias are intellectual and socioeconomic. As measured by their Scholastic Achievement Tests (SATs), the academic achievement of the students chosen fell in the top five to ten percent of high school graduates, but their average score of

584 did not put them beyond the reach of many other able college students. Because one of the criteria for selection had been successful academic achievement in college, sixty-one percent of the Study subjects were graduated with honors in contrast to only twenty-six percent of their classmates. Seventy-six percent went on to graduate school compared to sixty percent of their college classmates. In tested intelligence, however, the Study subjects were only slightly superior.

Physically, the subjects were very much like college men anywhere. Seventy inches tall and 160 pounds in weight was the average both for the men in the Study and for their classmates. But compared to their classmates, twice as many of the Study subjects were mesomorphs (solidly muscular builds), ninety-eight percent were right-handed, and their posture was rated as slightly better than that of their classmates.

Socioeconomically, the Grant Study men were drawn from a privileged group, but not exclusively so. In 1940 a third of their fathers made more than $15,000 a year, a third made less than $5,000, and one in seven made less than $2,500. One-third of their fathers had had some professional training, but half of their parents never graduated from college. Almost half of the men had had some private education, but during college an equal proportion was on scholarship. While college was in session, half of the subjects worked in order to pay a significant part of their educational expenses. Significantly, at the end of thirty years, the relatively broad socioeconomic differences among the subjects upon college entrance had *no* correlation with any of the outcome variables. Initiative, a good education, and, particularly, the lapse of a quarter of a century erased all statistical differences.

The men came from families that were relatively stable. By the age of nineteen only fourteen percent had lost a parent by death and only seven percent had lost a parent through divorce. But, except for a slightly lower rate of parental divorce, these figures did not differ appreciably either from the college as a whole or from the American middle class in general. Oldest children were definitely overrepresented. Forty-one percent of the subjects were the oldest in the family, and eleven percent more were only children. Only twenty-one percent were the youngest in their families.

The sample was drawn from the very restricted population

who attended private colleges in the northeastern United States in 1940. Eighty percent of the subjects were Protestants, ten percent Catholics, and ten percent Jews. Most of their ancestors had been in America since 1850, and the Study contained no blacks. Eighty-nine percent of the men came from north of the Mason-Dixon line and east of the Missouri. (Twenty-five years later seventy-five percent of the sample remained within these boundaries, and sixty percent of the total sample had migrated to the five urban centers of San Francisco, New York, Washington, Boston, and Chicago.)

But the historical accident of World War II forced these men into a common experience that permitted them to be compared with their fellow men on grounds other than academic excellence and social good fortune. Although selected for success in the ivory tower of academia, they demonstrated common sense and courage on the battlefield. In his book about the Grant Study subjects, *College Men at War*, Dr. John Monks provides many useful comparisons.[1] Only eleven Grant Study men, instead of a statistically expected seventy-seven, were rejected for service on physical grounds. Instead of an expected thirty-six, only three were rejected for psychiatric reasons. A third of the men were in sustained combat for ten days or more, and the proportion wounded and killed did not differ from that of the armed forces as a whole. Under severe battle danger, however, the men reported far fewer symptoms of nausea, incontinence, palpitations, tremor, and giddiness than had been reported in other studies of men under acute battle conditions. The 230 subjects in uniform won twenty Bronze Star Medals, three Legions of Merit, three Distinguished Flying Crosses, and one Navy Cross; yet, because of their youth, most of the men did not see combat until the last year of the war.

In terms of advancement within the military, their adjustment was hard to fault. Only ten percent went into the army with commissions, but seventy-one percent were officers when discharged. Forty-five percent of those joining the navy entered with commissions, and forty-five percent more were commissioned during service. In fifty-two percent of the men's efficiency reports, their commanding officers said that they "particularly desired" these men to be in their command and in forty-one percent more their commanders acknowledged that they would be "pleased" to have them. In only seven percent of the efficiency reports would their commanding officers have been merely "satisfied" to have the men in the Study serve under their them. Less than five percent had difficulty in adjusting to postwar civilian life.

At forty-seven, the average man in the Study had the income and social standing of a successful businessman or professional and had the political outlook, intellectual tastes, and life-style of a college professor. Although their average 1968 income was about $30,000 a year, less than five percent drove sports cars or expensive sedans. Despite their economic success, the men voted for Democrats more often than for Republicans, and seventy-one percent viewed themselves as "liberal," not "conservative." In 1954 only sixteen percent had sanctioned the McCarthy hearings. In 1967 ninety-one percent were for de-escalating our involvement in Vietnam; this was true of only eighty percent of their classmates. Had the Grant Study subjects had their way, McCarthy and Rockefeller would have been nominated in 1968, not Humphrey and Nixon. Like so many liberal members of their generation, these men were "for equal rights." They applauded the Supreme Court decisions and civil rights legislation after they occurred, but only a few took an active role in bringing about racial equality.

A table of data gathered from questionnaires answered at their twenty-fifth reunion compares forty-four of the forty-eight Grant Study men in the class of 1944 with seventy percent of their classmates. (Only four Grant Study men, as opposed to thirty percent of their classmates, failed to respond to the reunion questionnaire.) Despite the pains taken in selecting the men, in many respects the differences between the Study sample and their classmates were not large. In 1969 one Grant Study man in four made more than $40,000 a year and one man in four (mostly those in the teaching professions) made less than $20,000. This range of income did not significantly differentiate the Grant Study man from his classmates, but compared to their classmates, four times as many continued to hold class offices. The divorce rate and reported marital instability were about the same for both groups. Twenty-five years out of college, roughly ninety-five percent of both groups had married, and fifteen percent of both groups had been divorced. A quarter of the class became lawyers or doctors;

fifteen percent became teachers, mostly at a college level; and twenty percent went into business. The remaining forty percent were distributed throughout other professions like architecture and accounting, or engaged in advertising, banking, insurance, government and engineering. The proportions of Grant Study men in each occupational subgroup was no different from their classmates. However, men who enjoyed smooth sailing in the areas of mental health, marital stability, and occupational success were more likely to complete reunion questionnaires. Since almost all the Grant Study subjects completed the questionnaire, they are probably being compared to a sample of seventy percent of their classmates self-selected for health.

What *was* different about the Grant Study subjects was that they were happier. Many more of them called their work "extremely satisfying." Significantly more Grant Study subjects described their health as excellent, and they took significantly less sick leave. At age forty-seven only eighteen percent of the men were even twenty pounds over their optimum weight, and only

TABLE 1
Responses to a Questionnaire at the Twenty-fifth College Reunion

	44 Grant Study Members	590 Classmates
1. Responded to reunion questionnaire	92%**	70%
2. Graduated from college with honors	61%**	26%
3. Went on to graduate school	76%*	60%
4. Feels job is extremely satisfying	73%*	54%
5. Occupationally less successful than father	2%**	18%
6. Takes less than 2 days sick leave a year	82%**	57%
7. Considers current health excellent	64%*	43%
8. Believes our involvement in Vietnam should decrease (Winter 1968/9)	93%*	80%
9. Attended public high school	57%	44%
10. Ever divorced	14%	12%
11. Never married	7%	6%
12. Current marriage unstable	16%	12%
13. Often attends church	27%	38%
14. Does not now use cigarettes	74%	71%
15. Never drinks	7%	20%
16. Drinks 4 shots (6 oz.) of liquor or more daily	7%	9%
17. 10+ visits to a psychiatrist since college	21%	17%

*Probably significant difference (p <.05 — a difference that would occur by chance only 1 time in 20)

**Significant difference (p <.01 — a difference that would occur by chance only 1 time in 100)

thirteen percent of the men averaged five days or more sick leave a year. These figures are much lower than those experienced by the general population. Most important, their mortality was fifty percent less than their classmates.

It is not particularly illuminating to compare the men in the Study with the population as a whole, for the Grant Study subjects comprise such a select sample. Every man in the Grant Study enjoyed some measure of occupational success; and, thus, unless they are compared with each other, occupational impairment is invisible. At some point fourteen percent became problem drinkers, but only four percent — significantly less than the national average — were even minimally disabled for more than two years.[2]

Psychologically, the Grant Study subjects in adult life fared better than the population as a whole, but it is hard to say how much better. Originally chosen for good health, there were none who experienced difficulties too severe to master; but there were also none who had survived the game of life without pain, effort, and anxiety. Comparison of the Grant Study sample with other groups is difficult when the groups being compared are not judged by the same investigators in the same manner. For example, under the criteria of mental health that Srole and associates used in their survey of the mental health of urban Americans, seventy to ninety percent of the Grant Study men would have fallen in the eighteen and a half percent of New Yorkers that Srole and associates considered "well."[3] On the other hand, the psychiatrists who interviewed the Grant Study subjects in college had felt that over half of the sample could have benefited from psychiatric consultation. By the time the subjects were thirty, ten percent had seen psychiatrists; and by age forty-eight the number had increased to forty percent. In Srole's random sample of New Yorkers only thirteen percent of the subjects age twenty to fifty-nine had ever seen a psychiatrist. Unfortunately, outpatient psychiatric care has more to do with privilege than with need.

Perhaps the only sample that is really comparable to the men of the Grant Study is from Terman's longitudinal study of 1,000 gifted California school children.[4] This group was chosen from socioeconomic circumstances that were roughly similar to the men of the Grant Study. In tested intelligence, Terman's men and women, representing the top one percent of the population, were more intellectually gifted than the Grant Study subjects. However, since Terman's subjects were selected for ability, not performance, only seventy percent graduated from college. An equal number of the Terman and Grant Study men (ninety-four percent) married, but more of the Terman marriages (twenty-three percent) ended in divorce. Men in the Terman sample had fewer children than those in the Grant Study — two instead of three — but some of their child-rearing years coincided with the Depression. In both samples, the incidence of homosexuality was between one and two percent.

Psychiatrically, nine percent of the Terman sample had shown "serious maladjustment," and three percent had been psychiatrically hospitalized. Allowing for semantic variation, these proportions would hold true for the Grant Study population. At some time in their lives fifteen percent of Terman's sample drank to excess; this was true for fourteen percent of the Grant Study subjects. In adult life criminal convictions were nonexistent for both the Terman and the Grant Study men. For both groups, the mortality rate was less than what would be expected for white Americans of similar age.

Grant Study men were more apt to have pursued graduate degrees, but their graduate work was less distinguished than that of the Terman men. At an average age of forty-five, roughly eight percent of the Grant Study men were in *Who's Who in America*, as opposed to seven percent of Terman's group. By age fifty, twelve percent of Terman's group were in *American Men of Science*, as were twelve percent of the Grant Study members. Because the Terman men are ten years older than those of the Grant Study, comparison of incomes is difficult. In 1964, forty percent of the Grant Study members were making $25,000 a year at an average age of forty-three. In 1954, at roughly the same age, only ten percent of the Terman subjects were making a comparable income; but in that period salaries were relatively lower.

A legitimate, if difficult, question can be posed: How did thirty years of continued study alter the lives of the Grant Study men? The men did not know who else was in the Study, and Study members never formed a campus subgroup, but they were all given copies of the early scientific reports. Recently, the men were all asked what effect the Study had had upon them. Aside from encouraging a sense of self-confidence and a habit of reflecting upon their lives at frequent intervals, the men did not *feel* that the Grant Study had profoundly influenced them. In reviewing their lives I have speculated that one result of their being studied was that they felt freer than their classmates to seek psychiatric help. However, there were many more dramatic and continuing forces shaping the lives of these men than the fact that occasionally they came under the scrutiny of social scientists. Their lives were too complex and interesting for them to spend much time ruminating on the fact that they were Grant Study guinea pigs. (It is also important to note that no material on the men's *adaptive styles* was published until the data for this book had been gathered. Nor had questionnaires been structured to draw the men's attention to this aspect of personality.)

As one man expressed the effect of the Study, "After this many years, the Study acquires a kind of sober, steady, durable, benign, dependable character in this changeable world, and I can see myself trusting with relief things that it might say. Obviously, this is a kind of slightly querulous request to 'tell me that I'm all right; reassure me that my course is reasonable and should lead somewhere; be the kindly authority figure, sage and approving.'" Another man said, "Frankly, when I committed myself to the Grant Study in 1939 I expected a lot more career guidance than I have received. I admit to pride in being one of the 268 guinea pigs and have on occasion publicly boasted of it. Overall, I have a feeling that your feedback leaves much to be desired."

From my own involvement in the Study, I can say that there was no man in the Study whom I did not respect. I regretted that my role as investigator made my contact with them so formal and evanescent; and yet I relished the role because there was no other way that I could have been able to know intimately, if only briefly, ninety-four such interesting men. In no sense are the Grant Study members supernormal or exotic, but as a group they reflect a broad view of what is healthy and valuable in one cultural segment of humanity. Sheltered as they were from the impediments of prejudice and childhood deprivation, allowed as they were to stand at the head of the line in occupational advancement, their lives are not representative of most of America. But it is precisely their position of relative privilege that makes them suitable for the study of human adaptation. The growth of flowers can best be studied under optimum conditions; humans can reveal themselves in their full flower only when they have free choice.

Chapter 3

How They Were Studied

> Doctors traditionally have dealt with their patients after troubles of many sorts have arisen. The Department of Hygiene . . . proposes to revise this procedure and will attempt to analyze the forces that have produced normal young men. . . . All admit that the sick need care, but very few apparently have thought it necessary to make a systematic inquiry as to how people keep well and do well. . . . A body of facts is needed to replace current supposition. All of us need more do's and fewer don't's.
>
> — Arlie V. Bock, M.D.,
> press release, September 30, 1938

The Grant Study of Adult Development vies with Berkeley's Oakland Growth Study for the distinction of being the longest prospective follow-up of adult development in the world. Set off by itself in a small brick building, the Study was a warm and friendly place; the staff, from the secretaries to the medical director, were kind and receptive, not analytic and austere. The Grant Study subjects were examined with their full consent and awareness, but they could not volunteer — a condition that helped exclude the quirks of would-be guinea pigs. Because the men were chosen on the grounds of mental health, membership was regarded as a mild honor. Because the staff were interested enough in the men to know when they hurt, the staff were often called upon to give help when it was needed. Thus, a strong alliance was forged that has survived for four decades. Most of the men found being part of the Study entertaining and valuable; they acknowledged this freely. A few parents even thought that participation in the project was the most valuable experience that occurred during their son's college career.

However, participation in the Grant Study was a demanding college commitment. It took up at least twenty hours of each man's time. After being accepted into the Study, each subject had eight interviews with a psychiatrist. These interviews focused on the men's families and on their own career plans and value systems. The psychiatrists made a special effort to get to know the men as people, not patients. No effort was made to look for pathology or to interpret the men's lives psychoanalytically.

Subjects were also seen by a social investigator, Lewise Gregory (now Mrs. William F. Davies), who is the only original staff member to remain with the Study in 1976. A warm and perceptive Virginian, Mrs. Davies was selected for the job by virtue of innate talent rather than professional training. Not only did she take a careful social history from each sophomore subject, but she also traveled the length and breadth of the United States to meet their parents. (When years later I encountered by chance some of these men's parents, they could still recall her visit with the greatest pleasure.) In each man's home she took a family history that included descriptions of grandparents, aunts, uncles, and first cousins. She also obtained from the mother a history of the early development of each subject and a history of mental illness, if it existed, in any relative. She inquired about the problems that had arisen in each boy's upbringing. The effect of these family interviews was to accentuate the positive. Not only did this foster the alliance between the subjects and the Study, but it also meant that when, in the social histories, pathological details were noted, they were usually significant. Too often, the usual psychiatric social history with its emphasis upon pathology makes all of us fugitives from a script by Tennessee Williams.

Dr. Clark Heath, director of the Grant Study from 1938 to 1953 and an internist by training, gave each man an unusually complete two-hour physical exam. This included a careful record of his daily habits, past illnesses, and his physical responses to stress. Each subject was studied by a physiologist, who measured his insulin tolerance, his respiratory functions, and the physiological effects of running on a treadmill for five minutes or until near exhaustion. These tests were made at the university's Fatigue Laboratory, then under the direction of Dr. Bruce Dill.

Each man was studied by Frederick Wells, Ph.D., a

psychologist unusually skilled in evaluating young men. He had played a major role in developing the army screening tests for mental intelligence — the Army Alpha Tests. He and his assistants gave each man psychological tests designed to reflect native intelligence (the Alpha verbal and Alpha numerical), a vocabulary test, a shortened Rorschach test, and a block assembly test designed to assess manipulative dexterity and the comprehension of spatial relationships. For most men, the Scholastic Aptitude Test (SAT) and the Mathematical Attainments Test (MAT) scores were also available.

The Study was limited by the prejudices of its era. For example, an electroencephalographer recorded each man's brain waves and, as was the fashion in those distant days, tried to deduce each man's personality from the squiggles of the recording pen. (No, the electroencephalographer's predictions were not borne out, but we have no right to mock her efforts. In 1937, the electroencephalogram had only begun to prove its usefulness, and students of personality had great hopes for it.)

Somatotyping was another ill-fated effort to use the project to advance a new science. Each man was studied by a physical anthropologist who literally measured him from head to toe and recorded his somatotype and other physical variables thought to be related to personality. At that time, influenced by the work of the German psychiatrist Ernst Kretschmer, William H. Sheldon believed that human personality was significantly correlated with the ectomorphic, mesomorphic, and endomorphic components of body builds. A third of a century later, the findings from the study suggest that neither the crude encephalography nor the sophisticated somatotyping of that era were particularly illuminating in the study of these subjects' personalities.[1]

Unfortunately, the work of four other innovative students of personality in the 1930s was ignored. I say unfortunately because the work of these four men and women have affected my interpretation of the results of the Study. Erik Erikson, Anna Freud, Harry Stack Sullivan, and Heinz Hartmann all significantly influenced modern understanding of personality; but in 1937–1942 their work was still too novel to shape the early design of the Grant Study.

By 1940 Harry Stack Sullivan had begun to revolutionize the

psychodynamic theory of personality.[2] Slowly, Sullivan and his British counterpart, Melanie Klein, led psychiatrists to realize that *inter*personal relations played as important a role in shaping personality as did the *intra*personal relations between ego, conscience, and instinct, but not before the Grant Study was well under way. For example, although in college the psychiatric interviews had included a careful history of adolescent sexual development, the Study psychiatrists did not inquire into the boys' friendship patterns, or their efforts at heterosexual intimacy. Not until 1950, really, did the Grant Study begin to pay close attention to the men's relationships with other men and women.

In 1937 Anna Freud first published in English *The Ego and the Mechanisms of Defense*,[3] and Heinz Hartmann had presented in German *Ego Psychology and the Problem of Adaptation*.[4] Not until 1967 did the Grant Study focus on these men's styles of psychological adaptation.

In the late 1930s at the University of California Erikson had begun the work that in 1950 was to culminate in *Childhood and Society* — providing convincing evidence that adults mature as well as children.[5] During the same period, the Grant Study staff, like their colleagues elsewhere, saw psychodynamic maturation as being largely completed by adolescence.

Despite the conceptual limitations that surrounded its birth, the Study survived and by 1950 had changed its name to The Study of Adult Development. After college graduation, the men of the Grant Study were followed until 1955 by annual questionnaires. After that, they were sent questionnaires every two years. These questionnaires paid special attention to employment, family, health, habits (e.g., vacation, sports, drinking, smoking, etc.) and political views. After 1950, these questionnaires were largely under the direction of Charles MacArthur, Ph.D., a gifted clinical psychologist and director of the Grant Study from 1955 to 1972. Through his extraordinary perseverance, the Study remained alive during an era when both government and foundations turned their backs on longitudinal studies. Funding agencies, like developmental psychologists, could not believe that the maturation of a human being might take a lifetime.

Unfortunately, too, although the men had been informed that it was the intent of the Grant Study to follow them for many years after graduation, no one anticipated quite how long the Study would continue, and many questions which later would be relevant to the vicissitudes of middle life went unasked.

Because the Grant Study members were literate and the questions open-ended, the questionnaires elicited a great deal more information than they manifestly requested. Not infrequently, the men responded with short essays. One man wrote, "As a rule, I have always written a little more than the questionnaire asked for, largely because of my gratitude toward the Study for helping me understand myself."

Characteristics that colored many other aspects of a man's life were mirrored in their idiosyncratic responses to standard questions. As one man admitted, "We reveal ourselves whenever we say anything." One man sent in a questionnaire two years late; he had just found it — under his bed! Another example was a man who had overcome polio to make the university football team; at age forty-three he wrote, "Your questionnaires help me; how can I help you?" This capacity for turning hardships into assets pervaded his whole life.

In contrast, despite great success, another man always regarded himself as a failure. He was critical of the Study for admitting him and felt it "very disturbing to write a self-appraisal of myself." He protested "at being pursued for so long . . . the Study demanded too much and gave too little." Self-doubt, pessimism, and passivity, traits that plagued the second man all his life, were never observed in the first.

Even responses to multiple-choice questionnaires could be revealing. With regard to his sex life, one man checked the answer "satisfying," commenting, "There is a 3/1 difference in the frequency of desire, but we adapt quite well." Then, since the other answers regarding his marriage were checked off in the most favorable terms, he saw fit to add at the end, "The above sounds uninteresting, but I think it is true. Maybe there is yet hope for the excitement of domestic conflict." The inference that this was a tranquil but highly intellectualized marriage was confirmed when I later interviewed both the subject and his wife.

Questionnaires also revealed the men through slips of the pen. In an effort to elaborate on his assertion that material things were *not* important to him, one young businessman assured the Study, "I do want to be fabulously wealthy"; he had forgotten to write in "not." Evidence that the slip was not accidental was the fact that this young man, at great personal cost, went on to make more money than any other member of the Study.

During 1950–1952 all the men in the Study were reinterviewed by Margaret Lantis, Ph.D. Trained and experienced as a social anthropologist, she traveled around the country to interview the men in their homes. During her interviews, she took careful developmental histories of their children and recorded their lifestyle, just as she might had they been Eskimos or Samoans. Often she also administered the Thematic Apperception Test, a projective test that uses interpretation of ambiguous pictures to assess personality.

Thirty years after the Study began, I interviewed all the ninety-four surviving men in the subsample of one hundred that I had chosen. In my request for interview I made it clear that I was a psychiatrist interested in what had gone right in their lives — not in what had gone wrong. I said I would come to whatever place was most convenient to the men. Although I was thirteen years younger than they, the experimental set of their college days held. I could not forget that I had been in first grade when they had entered adulthood, but invariably they treated me as students treat a college physician. I met no condescension.

Before interviewing the men, I usually completely reviewed their records, which consisted of several hundred pages of questionnaires, research protocols, tests, and correspondence. In only one case had I met any of them before. The interview was semistructured; the same open-ended questions (see Appendix B) were asked every man. Thus, the interview was conducted under circumstances where my knowledge of the men, my initial approach to them, my own personal foibles, and the questions that I asked were held relatively constant. In large part variations in the evolution of the interview could be attributed to the idiosyncrasies of the men.

Their individual responses to the interview were indeed very different. Only one man appeared overly reluctant to be interviewed; but he then let the interview be extended through his lunch hour and provided me with a lengthy, exciting, and startlingly frank account of his life. In contrast, several men who readily agreed to see me imposed ingenious obstacles. Two men used every opportunity to interpose their large families between themselves and me. Another man, having evaded the first few questions I had asked him, turned on me and said, "Well, let's hear about you!" At first I wondered if I had merely been inept, but upon rereading the psychiatrist's notes of thirty years before, I was reassured. The 1938 record read, "This boy is more difficult to interview than any I have encountered in the group."

With some men the interview was very like a psychiatric consultation, with some like a newspaper interview, with others more like a talk with an old friend. In a few cases when I asked a man how things really were with him, he anxiously signaled for me to discuss more neutral subjects. I learned to associate the capacity to talk of one's life frankly with mental health. Almost always the ways that these men responded to me paralleled the ways that they related to people in general. One of the warmest, richest personalities in the Study saw me at 7 A.M. at his home for breakfast, offered to cook me an egg, and then extended the interview well past the two hours that I had requested. This was in spite of the fact that he was working a sixteen-hour day, in two weeks was about to move his entire household to New York, and had just suffered a devastating business reverse that put his plight on the front page. Far less busy but more socially isolated men would put me off for a week and then meet me in the most neutral setting possible. Two of them chose airports.

Some men came to Cambridge to be interviewed, but in most cases I went to them — south to Florida, west to Hawaii, north to the Canadian border, and down east to the Maine coast. The fact that all of the living Study members would consent to a psychiatric interview after thirty years attests to the extraordinary tact and warmth of the men and women who initially conducted the Study. It also speaks to the equally remarkable loyalty and generosity of the men involved.

All of the New Yorkers and most of the New Englanders saw me in their offices and few offered me a meal. Virtually all the mid-westerners saw me in their homes and invited me to dinner. The Californians were evenly divided. Some men pushed their families forward to meet me and insisted that I spend time with them. Other men carefully hid their families until I was safely out of sight. Several wives were openly suspicious and made it clear that they refused to see "that shrink" under any circumstances. Another wife, after giving me a superb dinner, insisted that I take a homemade pie back to my wife, who was sick in bed.

Because I knew so much about the men and because even the reluctant members were so loyal, the interviews were consistently exciting and exhausting. Only from patients whom I have seen over a prolonged period of time have I been able to learn so much so quickly. There was an intensity to many of the interviews that was gratifying, yet surprising. Talking with the subjects was often like resuming an old friendship after a period of separation. It made me feel a little guilty, for I had done so little to earn the warmth and the trust that I received.

I soon discovered that whether the men liked me or I liked them had far more to do with their lives than with mine. The men who had always found loving easy made me feel warmly toward them, and led me to marvel at both my tact and my skill as an interviewer and at their good fortune to belong to such an enjoyable project. I left the office of one such man feeling ten feet tall; but he had had the same effect on others all of his life. In contrast, men who had spent their lives fearful of other people and had gone unloved in return often made me feel incompetent and clumsy. With them I felt like a heartless investigator, vivisecting them for science. During his interview one such man had confessed that he was afraid of dying and leaving nothing of worth to the world. Afterwards I, too, felt drained and depressed, as if I had done all of the work in the interview while he took much and gave nothing.

In order to orient the reader to the rest of this book, I shall also use this chapter to sketch the methodology by which I studied the lives of the subjects. The reader who prefers clinical detail to abstract exposition may skip to the next chapter.

First, since health is relative, the men are only compared with each other. To argue about the comparative mental health, maturity, and ability to adapt of Fëdor Dostoevski and Richard Nixon would be a fruitless project. It would be fruitless both because long before analysis of data, celebrities are prejudged, and because points of available comparison and sources of biographical data are so profoundly different. With regard to the men in this book, the sources of data were uniform. In terms of intellectual achievement, culture and historical epoch, as well as in their selection for physical and mental health, the men were already matched. They all had had the experience of the Great Depression as a reality in their past, and the active participation in World War II as a fact in their future. I had equally detailed information on each one. How these men would compare with Formosan fishermen, with Parisian housewives, or even with their Victorian parents or their post-Spock sons and daughters, I make no attempt to fathom. The subjects must serve as foils only to each other.

Second, an effort was made to reduce the outcomes of the men, their childhood adjustment, their character type, the adequacy of their defense mechanisms, even their marriages, to numerical scores (see Appendix C). Clearly, expressing such complex variables in numbers smacks of pseudo-scientism. But when they can be systematically derived, numerical scores serve to codify value judgments so that they cannot be subsequently altered and reinterpreted to suit the investigator's whim. Numerical scores also offer a simplified means of identifying men who fall at the extremes on a spectrum of values. If we walk into a crowded room and rank the men and women from 1 to 20 according to beauty, whether number 9 is more attractive than number 11 is a matter of opinion, but a reasonable consensus may be obtained that number 2 is more attractive than number 19. Yet beauty is hardly a variable that we ordinarily conceive of in numerical terms. The purpose, then, of assigning scores and systematically rating the subjects in the Study was not because childhoods and adult adjustments can be rated with the precision of weight and blood pressure, but only because numerical scores facilitate systematic comparison.

I further submit that health, like intelligence or athletic ability, reflects the integrated function of a number of skills. A good vocabulary or a knack for mental arithmetic does not make a man intelligent. But someone who scores well on many such subtests will appear intelligent to most observers regardless of their bias.

Similarly, it is hard to imagine a bad athlete obtaining a high score in the decathlon. Thus, a variety of traits and outcome criteria reflecting different facets of health were systematically searched for in each subject. Men who were successful in many areas were called healthier than men who were successful in only a few.

Third, although statistics, numbers, "controls," "blind" ratings, are tedious, they are necessary in order to combat the distorting effects of preconception. Health is a value-laden concept; statistical association and the experimental method help filter value judgments from fact. For example, whether epileptics were holy men, whether the tuberculous were more creative than the uninfected, whether marijuana use enhanced the performance of good jazz music, are all value-laden questions which in the past were answered in the affirmative by many reasonable observers. Today, each thesis has been answered in the negative by formal experimentation (i.e., controlled comparison of matched groups by blind raters). But even when disproven, a value judgment may still apply to a given individual. John Keats and Eugene O'Neill were not only tuberculous but were highly creative men.

In examining the Grant Study men, I have drawn conclusions in terms of evidence that is statistically valid but which may have little importance to a given individual. For example, since, statistically, divorce occurs more frequently among people who are poorly adapted in many other areas of their lives, it can serve in our culture as objective evidence of poor adaptation.[6] Yet in the case of one subject, to have stayed married might well have been suicidal, and after divorce another man achieved one of the best and most enduring marriages in the Study.

Inevitably, the statistical methods of this book lead to predictive statements; and often, prediction of human behavior seems blasphemous or dangerous. Many of us share the magical belief that prediction may unjustly determine the course of human lives, and therefore must be avoided. But, consider horse racing. Certainly, the odds on the toteboard have never yet kept a long shot from winning a race or insured the success of a favorite; but what serious horseplayer is willing to ignore the odds?

Fourth, the sample is patently drawn from a narrow spectrum of the population; in no sense is it representative. The members of the Study have been preselected on the basis of intelligence, stable family background, physical health, intellectual ambition, high performance, and socioeconomic security. But the purpose of the Study was not to observe "normal" in the sense of *average*, but "normal" in the sense of *best possible*. If one wishes to study the natural healing processes of fractures, a healthy young person is a more suitable subject than is an eighty-year-old with poor nutrition and heart disease. If one wishes to study adaptation to emotional stress it seems wise to start with a privileged population. When things went wrong in the lives of the Grant Study men, they had an optimal chance of setting them right. We shall see in these men many of the defenses that we associate only with the mentally ill, but the Grant Study men illustrate that these processes can lead toward health.

Choosing a relatively homogeneous group also greatly facilitated intragroup comparison. In studying the eating habits of human beings, we would want to study as many different cultures as possible. In studying human digestion, however, we might want to hold diet and culture constant. Since this book studies psychological adaptation, it seems legitimate to try to hold sociological, cultural, and intellectual variables relatively constant. Obviously, to complete our understanding, the same adaptive mechanisms must also be studied in women, in other cultures, and in other epochs.

Fifth, these men have been studied by the techniques of long-term follow-up. At a single moment in time, no single test, not even the most intuitive interviewer, can reliably determine beauty or honesty. These virtues are unsuited to simple definition. In part, a woman's beauty is defined by how many people view her as beautiful and for how long. We judge her honest only if we have often experienced her to be so. In long-term follow-up the key to certainty is not depth of examination but redundancy. This, of course, is also the essence of biography. Lincoln's mercy, John Kennedy's charm, Hamlet's indecision are not certainties because of single dramatic incidents, but because examples of these traits recur again and again. In this Study character traits and adaptive styles were weighted by how frequently, not how dramatically, they occurred. If a trait is seen often in one man and seldom in another, the men were called different along that dimension. At nineteen, the men were interviewed by three different observers, at thirty-one by still another, at forty-seven by me. No single interview was adequate, but the mosaic interview produced by several observers was more accurate than one could be alone. For example, one member of the Study was always seen as dynamic and charismatic by the female staff members and as a neurotic fool by the men. A shy man from a very privileged background was seen as charming by a staff member from a similar milieu, and as a lifeless stick by a staff member from a working-class background.

When the Study members were followed long enough, concealed truth often emerged. A reticent member of the Study was thirty before he revealed that his mother had had a postpartum depression following his birth. This fact had not emerged either from his psychiatric interviews at nineteen nor from the family interview. This young man was also well into his adult life when he revealed that he had been deeply in love during his freshman year. With great satisfaction he confessed, "Dr. W. [the Study psychiatrist who had seen him for eight research interviews] never found out. . . . I just wanted to see if I could successfully conceal information from a psychiatrist."

Finally, longitudinal follow-up and multiple interviews permitted some control over the halo effect that makes the best outcomes look better and the worst outcomes look worse than they really are. Longitudinal study permitted facets of the men to be evaluated by observers kept blind to other important variables.

But enough talk of methods. Let us return to the protagonists.

Chapter 4

Health Redefined —
The Joyful Expression
of Sex and of Anger

> W. C. Fields' secretary once asked her boss
> how she should respond to a particularly
> troublesome and insistent visitor who
> wished an audience with the actor. Mr.
> Fields allegedly replied, "Oh, give him an
> evasive answer. Tell him to go fuck himself!"
>
> — Anecdote from a Grant Study interview

> 1. How stable do you think your marriage
>   is?
>   QUITE STABLE
> 2. Sexual adjustment is, on the whole . . . ?
>   VERY SATISFYING
> 3. Separation or divorce has been consid-
>   ered: Never, Casually, Seriously? [The
>   multiple choice answers were ignored
>   and replaced by a message written boldly
>   in black ink]:
>   WE'VE NEVER THOUGHT OF DIVORCE,
>   BUT MURDER? YES!!
>
> — Excerpt from a Grant Study
> questionnaire

In the first chapter, Tarrytown's absence of mental health
seemed linked with his inability to express anger and sexuality. Yet, since many of society's taboos are directed toward keeping people from being too lustful or too angry, should not mental
health reflect the control of these two troublesome instincts? It is
not that simple. When Freud was asked for a definition of mental
health, he replied that health was the capacity to work and to
love. By showing how healthy coping mechanisms harness sex
and aggression in the service of working and loving, this chapter

will try to resolve the paradox that I have posed. For example, like lust and rage, both the quotes that begin this chapter, if taken literally, seem crude and harsh. My experience, however, with both vignettes is that listeners respond not with shock but with laughter. The first quote was the credo for one of the hardest working and most morally concerned men in the Grant Study. The second quote was excerpted from the questionnaire of a wife who had deeply loved her husband for twenty years; at last follow-up, both are still alive and well and happily married.

The lives of two contrasting men, Frederick Lion and Horace Lamb, shed light on the relationship between aggression and successful working and loving. Mr. Lion was an angry man. As a young adolescent he had come to physical blows with both parents. In college he was one of the few Grant Study men put on disciplinary probation. In the air force, some superiors saw him as irresponsible; and he consistently got his lowest marks for military bearing. Nevertheless, other military officers had described him as "outstanding." Later in life, with the self-image of a "barracuda," he enjoyed crusading for unpopular journalistic causes. As an editorial executive, he was known by some of his underlings as a demanding and explosive "bastard," but his magazine flourished.

If Mr. Lion was three times as abrasive as Mr. Lamb, he also was able to give far more of himself to the world. Despite day-to-day responsibility for publishing a fortnightly magazine, Mr. Lion saw me on twenty-four hours' notice. He met me in a diner, his bright yellow shirt sleeves rolled, his puckish face lined but smiling. He radiated a sense of to-the-manner-born, but so tempered it with enthusiasm and emotional honesty that I felt constantly included in everything he said. He combined dignity and arrogance with infectious warmth — a rare gift.

I shared breakfast with him, and then we went on to his office. The office was filled with many personal items that revealed both the man and his battles. Most mementoes were clearly of a sentimental value, and none was boastful. He did not capitalize on his associations with the famous and powerful. His bookshelves were filled with historical works and sociological books on the current American scene that looked as if they had been read. As I left my interview with the potentially angry and self-aggrandizing Mr. Lion, I was excited, filled with warmth toward the man, and delighted that he had given me so much.

Mr. Lamb was never in any trouble at all. As a child he had had a few tantrums, but his mother later boasted that "he was quickly disciplined out of them." There was no subsequent evidence that he was ever angry again. Instead, his mother called him "clinging," and his motto for mastering air force discipline became "You have to be polite and take it." At forty-five, his technique for dealing with unfair superiors was to "toe the mark."

Although his job entailed no responsibility, Mr. Lamb had trouble finding time to see me at work; finally, on two weeks' notice, he consented to see me at home. Horace Lamb's presence was commanding. His dress was immaculate, but gray. He kept his jacket on throughout. His face was unlined; his accent was affected but without inflection. A man hid behind his mask, but I never met that man. My clinical guess was that Horace Lamb was scared, not empty.

His apartment was spotless, but devoid of any personal articles except for the neatly bound stamp albums that he had filled as a boy. His bookcase revealed many books on china, porcelain, and a few choice first editions. Some of these were kept sealed under glass so that they would not deteriorate, but they also would never be read. After leaving Mr. Lamb, I felt depressed and frustrated. Talking to him about his past life was like being caught up in a surrealistic movie; nothing mattered or was real; none of the people had faces; and perhaps none of it had ever really happened.

Although permitted no outlet, hostility still troubled the inner life of Mr. Lamb. At thirty, he was given the Thematic Apperception Test — a test in which the subject is asked to provide spontaneous plots for ambiguous pictures. One card in the test is blank; and on that white expanse of cardboard, Mr. Lamb told the following story:

"This is a blank piece of paper with a number on the back. Well, this might be a picture of the latest wreck on the Pennsylvania Railroad. . . . I'd say the picture was taken at night and you see all the flood lamps, the ambulances . . . you see them trying to extricate some of the bodies from the wreckage and then you see all the crowds of morbid onlookers watching the whole thing. . . . I think of all the trains that this wreck is probably holding up." At forty-seven, when Mr. Lamb was asked if he had any questions about the findings of the Grant Study, his only question was how had the deceased subjects died. But Mr. Lamb was never to show hostility in real life; only his spontaneous associations and fantasies revealed his secret concerns about disaster.

In ultimate outcome, the lives of Mr. Lion and Mr. Lamb were very different. Frederick Lion raised a successful family; he had an exciting pattern of close friendships; and he held a very responsible job that won him self-respect, a high income, and a reputation for serving humanity. Horace Lamb was without children, close friends, or a job that he or the world found very useful.

Despite these differences in outcome, the childhoods of the men had much in common. In both families, there was a good deal of neurotic illness among the relatives. Both of their fathers were poor businessmen viewed by their sons as failures. Like many fathers in the Study they had lost their money during the Depression. The less typical consequence was, however, that both fathers depended upon their wives and their in-laws for support. Thus, both Lion and Lamb grew up seeing their mothers as the powerful figure in the family.

Both men were educated first in private day schools and then sent away to St. Paul's, a socially narrow but prestigious boarding school. Both men came to college wearing the political blinders common to the anti-Roosevelt, Atlantic seaboard, Episcopalian, upper-class families of that era. Mr. Lion put it with typical bluntness: "Before the war, I gave a shit about nothing." In college, the men were distinguished neither by their native intelligence nor by their academic records — straight C average. In their sophomore years, when first interviewed by the family worker and the internist, both men were seen as cooperative and attractive. The psychiatrist and the psychologist, however, noted marked differences between the two. Mr. Lion was seen not only as "well-mannered," but also as having "the confident manner of one who knows how to deal with people." The psychiatrist added, "He seems deeply affected by any emotional event." Indeed, Lion seemed to have "rather an excess of energy." In contrast, after describing Mr. Lamb as "tall, good-looking, and very much at ease," the psychiatrist added: "Generally speaking, I'm not very impressed with this boy. . . . He does not seem to have any drive." Later he called Lamb "bitter, blaming, and insincere." The psychologist noted that Lamb's tests did not "convey energy output or aggressiveness." A decade later, when the Study anthropologist interviewed the two, she called Lamb "a neat young man in a conservative suit," but was struck with Lion's "vigorous manner."

Although their military careers had not distinguished the two — both served as air force officers in noncombat positions — few would disagree that by age forty-seven Mr. Lion was healthier than Mr. Lamb. However, it was not in the areas of physical or psychological health per se that these men differed. In assessing Mr. Lamb's psychological adjustment at midlife, the rater noted that he was rather too calm and unemotional. Although he had never required psychiatric help, he did not always use his full vacation time; what vacation he took was spent in dutiful visits to his mother. On the other hand, although Mr. Lion enjoyed lengthy, imaginative vacations and was anything but unemotional, unlike Lamb he had made fifty visits to a psychiatrist. Neither man disliked his work, misused drugs or alcohol, or had ever been regarded as mentally ill or incapacitated.

For half a century, each of the men enjoyed excellent physical health. In childhood, Lamb's hay fever was perhaps a little worse than Lion's, but characteristically Lion was always having accidents and on three occasions was knocked unconscious. In adult life, neither man had any chronic illnesses, missed more than two days a year from work, or spent more than a few days in the hospital. The only difference was that Lamb would describe his present health only as "good" and under stress was beset by a wide variety of physical symptoms. Although he was without manifest emotion, he took medicines for hay fever, stomach upsets, and headaches. In contrast, although Lion was a passionate man, he experienced few physical symptoms under stress. "My health," he exclaimed, "is sensational." Lion was like another man in the Study who explained, "I've never had an ulcer; I just cause them!"

It was in the areas of working and loving that the differences between the men were striking. Mr. Lion had spent his adoles-

cence vigorously and successfully engaged in contact team
sports, and as an adult played golf for friendship and tennis for
competition. In his career, Mr. Lion received steady promotions,
was in *Who's Who in America*, and made $60,000 a year. But this
rebellious, emotional man achieved his "middle-class" success as
innovative editor of a liberal magazine. It was a job he vastly
enjoyed, and it fulfilled his own expectations for himself. Years
before he had written to the Study, "Anything that absorbs me
and at the same time generally furthers the well-being of mankind, that will I do."

In college, Lion said that he "fell in love with a new girl every
day"; and in fact, he had done so four times in the same year. He
had himself tattooed; he cried openly in the movies; and he
wanted to be a foreign correspondent because he thought it
would be "romantic." Under difficult circumstances, Mr. Lion
had had to win his wife from another man. As he confided to me,
"It was a hell of an ambitious project." When I met him, Mr. Lion
had been married to this wife for fifteen years and he still described his marriage as "completely challenging and completely
exciting." At times, however, he had described his relationships
with his closest friend and also with his wife as "too intense."
Lust and rage are not without risks.

Lion was extremely proud of his four children and despite their
eccentricities he had maintained warm relations with his parents
and siblings. He always had had a number of close friends who
had shown the capacity to come to his aid at times of need and to
whom he devoted a great deal of himself.

In sharp contrast, Mr. Lamb in his youth had engaged in sailing
and golf with indifferent results; as an adult, except for solitary
jogging, he withdrew from athletics altogether. For twenty years
he was modestly successful in the diplomatic service, but his
advancement was too slow, and he had been required to retire on
pension. His present job, very much below his previous one, by no
means met or seemed likely ever to meet his career expectations.
He was less successful than his father had been at the same age.
"Security," Lamb said, "is the motivating force in my life's work."

Not only had Lamb never married, but he never admitted to
having been in love. Unduly shy with women in adolescence, at
forty-seven Mr. Lamb was still put off by "eager women" and still

found "sex distasteful and frightening." He had gone through life without close friends of any kind, male or female, and at forty-five he still found it difficult to say good-bye to his mother.

There was also a marked difference in how each man viewed the world. Mr. Lion had broadened his narrow adolescent view until he could function as a spokesman for the liberal press. As a young man he had once driven 500 miles in order to vote, and at thirty-one, when he was asked what he would do if he was given a voice in shaping foreign policy, he responded with characteristic candor, "I'd remove Joseph McCarthy's vocal cords." Fifteen years later, his interview with me was filled with profanity; but he used four-letter words not from reflex but for emotional nuance. He did volunteer work in the inner city, and he was intimately involved with the political passions of his time.

At forty-seven Mr. Lamb confided to me that his social views had broadened; he illustrated the point by explaining that his brother's children could get a good education outside the Ivy League! He was quite serious. In the 1948 election, Mr. Lamb had not bothered to go to his neighborhood polls. His current participation in public affairs did not extend beyond giving blood to the Red Cross and collecting for the Heart Fund. In 1954, Mr. Lamb had been an admirer of Joseph McCarthy, and the only four-letter adjective that occurred in my interview with him was his repetitive use of "nice." Unlike W. C. Fields and Frederick Lion, Lamb was always afraid to tell people what he really thought; and thus, he truly gave mankind an evasive answer.

The point of relating these events is not to caricature the two men or even to show that Mr. Lion was healthier than Mr. Lamb. Rather, the purpose is to set the stage for demonstrating the ingenuity with which unconscious adaptive techniques can turn defensive behavior either into virtue or into ironic, sterile crucifixion.

Under stress, Mr. Lion used *sublimation,* and Mr. Lamb employed its primitive ancestor, *fantasy.* It should be clear that the sublimation of the artist necessitates fantasy, but sublimation also adds a critical quality that in part can explain the difference between Lion and Lamb. For instance, in college Horace Lamb dealt with his very real fear of people by being a solitary drinker. He enjoyed listening to the radio by himself and found math and philosophy his most interesting courses. Although afraid to go out with girls, he was very particular about his appearance; and paradoxically, this timid boy dreamed of the day that he would command his own submarine. Dr. Charles McArthur had the following to say of the Thematic Apperception Test that Lamb had taken (at age thirty): "It was as if he was in a world he felt he had never made. Instead of being burned, he has taken refuge in his peripheral vision."

Thirty years later, Lamb was less interested in clothes, but had become terribly preoccupied with keeping fit. He admitted that in his life "things had taken the place of people" and that he loved to retreat into the "peace and quiet of a weekend alone." Approaching old age with no family of his own, he daydreamed of leaving his rare book collection to a favorite young cousin; but he had made only a small effort to get to know this cousin personally. Mr. Lamb related that his principal "activity over rough spots" was to go to sleep and that he felt that his "personal philosophy" was more important than his "relationships with people." Of all the men I interviewed, he alone confused the two strikingly different women who, a decade apart, had interviewed all the men in the Study. One was a very outgoing Southerner who tried to make friends with the world; the other a reserved, careful intellectual, who "studied each subject."

For Lamb, fantasy served a definite purpose. For children, daydreams can become a major substitute for people; adults, too, can replace people with fantasy. The loneliness of Dr. Tarrytown evoked sadness in me; but when Mr. Lamb said, "Maybe I am self-sufficient," I believed him. Without fantasy, Mr. Lamb might have become seriously depressed or engaged in a frantic self-destructive search for gratification through alcohol and gambling. He might have pursued Tarrytown's promiscuous quest for intimacy. Instead, Lamb lived a life of staid tranquility. But the price he paid was high. For, not only does fantasy prevent any outward show of aggression; it also leads to an absence of pleasure. Mr. Lamb's life could be summed up in his simple statement to me, "I don't have any stress, I don't get that involved. By the same token, I don't have any great happiness." In lieu of anyone else to love, Lamb survived only for himself. Throughout life our internal lives are enriched by the people that we have permitted to touch us. Lamb seemed too well protected by his outer shell.

But we cannot will our choice of defenses, and Frederick Lion had not been born able to sublimate. That facility had to evolve from earlier defensive styles like fantasy. In college Mr. Lion, too, had been an escape artist. When depressed over academic life, he had run off to New York and had tried to enlist in the marines. When he was in danger of being permanently crippled from a diving accident, he remembered feeling no fear; it was as if the danger of paralysis did not exist.

As an adult, however, there was a shift in Lion's style. When he became too depressed by the responsibilities and the angry accusations that accompanied his job, Mr. Lion would retreat to his Vermont farm. There, with the telephone unplugged, he would help his wife with her hobby of raising roses. Escapist, yes; but as an adult he managed to turn his fear and despair into something beautiful in the presence of someone he loved.

The night after one of his closest friends had been killed in a hunting accident, Mr. Lion spent the night, tears running down his cheeks, writing the best poem of his life. In the poem, of course, his friend was not dead; and Lion's angry grief was transmuted into a hymn of praise. Later the poem won him a prize, and at the close of our interview he gave me a copy as a souvenir of my visit. (Rather than do what my conscience dictates, and make it part of the Study archives, I still retain that poem as a personal possession.) Like the fantasy of any artist, Lion's sublimation permitted the communication of dreams. Now his friend lives on in my heart, too.

To soften an unbearable reality, both Lion and Lamb had created worlds within their own minds. But Lion's world was rich in appropriate feelings that could be shared. Like a good camera, Lion's mature adaptive mechanisms brought emotional events into sharp focus, whereas like the mirror at a fun fair, Lamb's and Tarrytown's fantasies distorted reality beyond belief. Mature defenses can turn something as intrinsically unmarketable as despair into a commodity that others can cherish; but almost invariably, immature defenses, like fantasy and projection, waste more than they preserve.

The origins of effective adaptive mechanisms are clouded in mystery. The reasons for the differences between Lion and Lamb are uncertain, but hindsight permits certain speculations. In early adolescence, Lion had won the respect of each parent on separate occasions by physically fighting with them. He had risked the loss of their love by asserting his independence, but his parents regarded his rebelliousness as spunky and loved him for it. As we shall see, this was true of the families of many successful men in the Study. Lion had also been born with a gift of superb physical coordination — one of the early consequences of which is that a boy gets praise for using aggression in a skillful but controlled manner. Indeed, perhaps it was the grace experienced on the playing field that permitted Lion to defy his parents in a physical but "playful" manner that they could respect. With maturity, his physical prowess became displaced into the mental sphere. But the grace remained. Mr. Lion became rich while crusading for the poor, a balancing act rivaling that of Goodhart's. Perhaps, for anger to be effectively employed, its use needs to be channeled *and* the user loved.

Mr. Lamb's mother did not tell the Study that she admired her son. Instead, she told the Study that he had trouble getting on with people — perhaps another way of saying that she had trouble getting on with him. She viewed Horace as clinging and unconfident. She showed concern over his eating, but there is no evidence that she taught him anything else. Certainly, she forbade him to show anger; but to control aggression, Mr. Lamb was left only with the primitive mechanisms of childhood and the excellent manners that he had been taught.

The evidence from the Study did not support the idea that good or bad defenses run in families. Family trees "tainted" with mental illness did not lead to inferior defense choice. Perhaps it is not just coincidence that Lion had a brother — less preferred — who turned out like Mr. Lamb; and Mr. Lamb had a preferred brother who turned out more like Mr. Lion. Sublimation and altruism are not hereditary. My suspicion, then, is that the internal controls over anger that served Mr. Lion so well came not only from his constitutional talent of coordination, but also from his acceptance by crucial individuals; but such individuals need not be parents.

We cannot be taught self-esteem; we absorb it. Similarly, conscious learning plays no part in the acquisition of defense mechanisms; rather the response of people outside of us — not just events — shapes our modes of adaptation. A great violinist's style owes as much to his incorporation of dedicated and gifted teachers as it does to his own innate talents and idiosyncrasies or to his rote learning of notes and scales.

Finally, the larger social system also plays its role. As we shall see in Chapter 8, coping is facilitated by being in the right place at the right time. In a more rigid social structure, Mr. Lamb might have been able to capitalize on his aristocratic heritage and mannered emotions. If Lion's brand of journalism had been tried out, say, in Franco's Spain, his God-given sense of balance might have gone for naught and his aggression, however graceful, might have led him to the firing squad.

The lives of George Byron, Esq., and Casper Smythe, M.D., illustrate two very different styles of adapting to sexual expression. Over a period of twenty-five years, Mr. Byron enjoyed several affairs and yet sustained a close relationship with his wife. This feat was facilitated by deft and idiosyncratic use of adaptive mechanisms; like Lion and Goodhart, Byron's adaptation required a certain finesse. In contrast, Dr. Smythe, although not crippled by Lamb's fear of intimacy, was sequentially involved in two marriages and one affair, each causing as much pain as pleasure. At age fifty, he finally admitted what the Study staff had known for some time: He had serious problems with sexual expression.

In terms of psychological soundness in college and prospects for future success, both Byron and Smythe had been rated average by the Study staff. The adjectives used to describe both included "over-confident" and "blasé." Twenty-five years later, however, Byron's efforts at sophistication proved enduring, whereas those of Dr. Smythe, like those of Dr. Tarrytown, proved evanescent. In fact, profound differences in their social class had been reversed. Casper Smythe was born into an upper-class family, blessed with a trust fund, and sent to an excellent preparatory school. At forty-seven, in a rumpled suit, Dr. Smythe resembled a harried door-to-door salesman who needed longer vacations and a better tailor. Mr. Byron grew up in a "lace curtain Irish" neighborhood, attended an urban public high school, and yet, at forty-seven, seemed blended with the California upper-middle class. Dressed in a Hawaiian shirt, no coat, and well-pressed slacks, he welcomed me into his inner office. He was tall, smooth, tan, and relaxed. He seemed more at home in a country club than in a government office.

Unlike the previous men, however, there *was* a profound difference in the early childhoods of George Byron and Casper Smythe. Dr. Smythe's childhood received one of the lowest ratings in the Study. He was born of a difficult delivery, raised and bottle-fed by a variety of surrogates, and eventually went to live with an elderly aunt and uncle. They were old and did not enjoy the challenge of dealing with an energetic young boy. Throughout his infancy, Smythe's mother was ill with tuberculosis, and she died when he was eighteen months old. Smythe's father, due to his own ill health and his diplomatic career, had very little more to do with his son. He died when his son entered sixth grade. As a young child, Casper had been a head-banger; and at puberty, he withdrew from his modest success in the schoolyard to become, in his own words, a "lone wolf." At forty-seven, he was one of the few men who saw the ages one to thirteen as the unhappiest in his life.

In contrast, the blind raters had scored Byron's childhood as one of the sunniest in the Study. His mother had no trouble breastfeeding him; his family was unusually close; and his early childhood health was excellent. As Byron grew older, he was, like Frederick Lion, a very aggressive boy; and his mother loved it. In high school and college, he always had intimate friends and was skilled at winning the acceptance of strangers.

As with Lion and Lamb, the differences between Byron and Smythe could only be documented in the areas of working and loving. In terms of the formal indicators that this Study used to identify psychological and physical health, both men were equal. They enjoyed their jobs and never sought psychotherapy. They neither required psychiatric hospitalization nor were they ever diagnosed mentally ill. They took sleeping pills only occasionally, and only their wives believed that they drank too much. In terms of physical well-being, both men tended to view their health as excellent and each missed less than two days a year from work. Dr. Smythe had had only one adult hospitalization, but had sometimes required medical attention for his ulcer. Largely as a result of his adventurous life-style and travel, Byron had had seven brief hospitalizations, but was currently in good health.

Like Goodhart and Lion, Byron managed to achieve great occupational success while engaged in idealistic activities. After law school he shunned private practice, and instead alternated between working in the Department of Health, Education and Welfare and (because he loved to travel) in foreign aid programs (Point IV and AID). He advanced steadily, was more successful than his father, and is currently earning $35,000 a year. In important ways, he was involved in community affairs outside of his job, and his career fulfilled his expectations for himself.

Mr. Byron has been married for over twenty years, and overall the marriage has been harmonious. In most of the stable marriages, after two decades sexual adjustment was rated only "satisfying"; for the Byrons, despite his affairs, it was still described as "very satisfying." Byron enjoyed and remained close to his parents and siblings, and all of his five children have made stable adjustments. With ingenuous pleasure, he showed me photographs of his wife and five children. Byron often engaged in athletic activities with his friends.

In contrast, for twenty years Dr. Smythe had failed while trying to grow rich. He worked in a large university health service and continually complained that the job was not challenging. But he had neither been bold enough to accept offers to run another college health service by himself nor had he received the promotions that he expected. Although he was decidedly interested in money, as a physician he made only $18,000 a year. He had not equaled the success of his father and was not currently engaged in any public service. (In college, Byron had achieved a B+ average; Smythe, with similar intellectual endowment, made a C− average that included several E's.)

Dr. Smythe had been divorced twice and his children had suffered accordingly. In midlife, this orphan made no effort to see his twenty-year-old son — the relative who was probably closest to him in the world — because the son had not tried to see Dr.

Smythe. On questionnaires that reflected the early years of each of his two marriages, he had described his sexual adjustment as "not as good as wished." Although at times Smythe had participated in community organizations, he seemed not to have acquired close friends.

The sexual adjustment of the two men elucidates important differences in their adaptive styles. By eighteen, Dr. Smythe claimed to be very interested in girls; "I feel much better," he said, "when I'm in love." But it appeared to the Study staff that to Smythe being in love meant having someone "to care for him." At nineteen, his Rorschach was remarkable because it suggested frank fear of sex. During the first year of his first marriage his frequency of intercourse was once a month. His wife volunteered, "I wish he'd be analyzed, not only for our sex life but for his ulcer and to give me someone to talk to." At twenty-three, Dr. Smythe saw keeping his wife sexually satisfied as one of his greatest problems. Later on, he tried to tolerate his wife's affairs with rationalized good humor. At twenty-eight, he wrote that he could "not keep up with her due to the extracurricular activities I've been roped into." That this, too, was rationalization was evidenced by the fact that on vacations he engaged in compulsive spree drinking which obviated sexual relations. Repeated physical examinations provided no medical reason for poor libido; he had no difficulty fathering children; and at forty-two, he boasted that he was "enjoying sex for the first time." But even at fifty, Smythe still thought that "sexually, most people are animals," and wrote that he would have preferred "an asexual marriage."

In contrast, Mr. Byron's wife tolerated *his* affairs with stoical acquiescence. During adolescence, like several Catholic boys in the Study, Byron had felt masturbation was too great a sin to commit. Undaunted, he worked out ingenious techniques for securing a seemingly limitless supply of girls with whom to have intercourse — hardly the usual coping pattern for the Grant Study members. With equal but quite unconscious ingenuity, Byron dissociated this behavior from his Catholic conscience.

After Byron married he continued to have occasional affairs, but these were with women whom he had known for a long time. Unlike the affairs of Dr. Tarrytown, those of Byron were based upon mutual interests and respect. But the reason that his case is noteworthy is not only for the quality of his love affairs but also for the quality of his marriage. In 1950 after interviewing both Byron and his wife, the Study anthropologist had remarked, "They depend on each other almost exclusively for emotional support." Twenty years later Mr. Byron wrote to the Study, "My wife is my best friend."

The differences manifested in the interpersonal relationships of these two men were also reflected in their character styles. Mr. Byron exhibited many so-called hysterical character traits, such as aggressiveness, sexual provocativeness, exhibitionism, and emotionality. From his orphaned childhood, Dr. Smythe showed many of the features of the so-called oral dependent character — pessimism, passivity, self-doubt, and fear of sex. On one hand, Dr. Smythe wrote, "I long for bigger things, travel, more exciting settings," but he never left the safety of his midwestern university sinecure. On the other hand, Mr. Byron traveled around the world and, in directing international philanthropy, accepted ever bigger responsibilities.

It is a truism of the Grant Study that men who are comfortable with their own aggression respond more lovingly to the world in general. Mr. Byron's mother called her son a Tartar, and added, "He was a great tease, but never unkind." In 1967, the pugnacious Mr. Byron wanted gradual withdrawal from Vietnam; in 1970 he was for stopping the war outright. In contrast, in 1947 the more passive Dr. Smythe had wanted to start preventive war with Russia. "Let's go all out and get it done," he said, but he could also tell the Study that "Security was the brightest part of my job. . . . I haven't the guts to go out on my own as a man of the world." In 1967 he blustered, "Hydrogen bombs must be used in Southeast Asia. . . . It is inconceivable to me that we have sunk so low as to let a little satellite of Russia bring us to our knees."

Our task is not to judge politics but to compare the way in which these men, as adults, coped with life. But often in this Study, the men's political beliefs toward the external world seemed to parallel their ego's efforts to organize internal turmoil. Perhaps one explanation for the difference between Smythe's and Byron's politics was that in his marriage Mr. Byron felt in control while Dr. Smythe described the experience of his faltering second marriage as similar to "being surrounded by Viet Cong." The most conspicuous difference between the two men was that Mr. Byron used anticipation and suppression to control his instincts, and Dr. Smythe used a passive-aggressive life-style that turned his anger against himself as well as against his imagined enemies. Throughout life, George Byron put off gratification until he was fully ready. While reading marriage manuals and actively plotting how best to seduce young ladies, he had denied himself masturbation. Fully prepared he set out on the most promiscuous college career in the Study. Entangling alliances, conception, and venereal disease were all anticipated and avoided. As he worked his way through law school, the quality of Byron's future life was continually in the forefront of his mind. He read the lives of great men with interest, and twenty-five years later could point with pride to a fulfilled life plan. "Because I knew I could not bear to send people bills," he did not go into a private law practice. But he had so prepared himself with postgraduate courses that attractive jobs in domestic government, then in Point IV and in AID were not long in coming. Although he had led an exciting life, he was a thrifty and a shrewd investor. Thus, at forty-seven, like several anticipators in the Study, he had acquired an independent income as large as the one with which Casper Smythe was born. (Despite a rising stock market, Smythe was no richer from his inheritance at forty-seven than he had been at twenty.)

Knowing that he was impetuous, Byron always planned where he would work next in case his present job went awry. In Washington he became so furious with his boss that he went on a self-imposed vacation lest he physically attack his superior; but he was fully in tune with his fury. His adult love affairs seemed equally well planned.

Dr. Smythe dealt with gratification in a very different manner. Even before college, regardless of the consequences to himself, he had tried to free himself from his strong-minded aunt by doing just the opposite of what she wanted. Over rough spots his philosophy was "I don't give a damn." Unlike George Byron, in college Smythe managed to acquire the reputation of a ne'er-do-well — but without any of the fun. He was on probation twice; the first time for academic failure and the second time when his drunken driving resulted in a serious accident. When his girl friend broke up with him, he went on a two-day drinking binge.

He did the same thing when he was rejected for pilot training. His verbal response was "It doesn't bother me; I think it's rather silly"; but the concrete result of his second binge was a broken leg. After one drunken, sexually inactive vacation, he wrote the Study that his vacation had been "wonderful." His wife called the same vacation "a terrible failure." The upshot of Smythe's passive-aggressive style of mastering conflict was that this marriage foundered on his wife's infidelity.

To summarize, by instinctively planning each move far in advance, George Byron wrested great pleasure from an impulsive nature. He could remain aware of passion and not act. Although by nature less passionate, Dr. Smythe acted on his feelings thoughtlessly but ambivalently. The end result was the same as it is for the man who spits to windward.

A second major difference in adaptive technique was that Byron, like Lion, was skilled at *sublimating* his instinctual wishes and conflicts. Casper Smythe tended to "forget" or *repress* his passions. Sublimation channels emotions; repression dams them. Byron, sure that the knowledge would come in handy, read Freud for pleasure. Smythe failed Introductory Psychology; it was easier not to remember such things. In college Smythe had seen in the inkblots of his Rorschach terrifying percepts of insects and spiders; when asked about the test years later, he remembered seeing nothing but butterflies. After his serious automobile accident, Smythe arrived at the hospital feeling unusually calm. Twenty-four hours later, without physical cause, he started to vomit uncontrollably, but he could not imagine why. During a time when he was having difficulty assuming a masculine role in his marriage, Smythe wrote to the Study that he belonged to the "University Alumnae Association." Later, as his marriage was falling apart, he wrote as an aside "I have doubts about the real value of marriage . . . the state of my own marriage (which is excellent) has nothing to do with my philosophizing." Like the householder in the song of "The Arkansas Traveler," Smythe could never fix his roof because as soon as the sun came out, he forgot that it had a leak.

Emotional conflict made Byron remember — not forget. George Byron transformed his adolescent promiscuity into a stable marriage on the one hand, and into a passionate interest in aesthetics and Renaissance painting on the other. He devoted his manipulative energies into arranging philanthropic jobs for himself in Rome, Paris, and Tokyo. He reveled in the sophistication of foreign countries, but he traveled with his wife and five children in a responsible and convivial manner. Although he rejected the strict Catholicism of his childhood, he noted, "I return to church whenever they play my favorite composers." He vented anger by bullying foreign bureaucracies into paying attention to their disadvantaged citizens, and unashamedly indulged himself in the "perks" that went with his job. While living in Rio de Janeiro, he reveled in the warm climate, the beach, and his two servants.

Dr. Smythe's repression made him like an unconscious voyeur who gets arrested for accidentally walking into a woman's public dressing room. He was always guilty, but he never could remember why. Mr. Byron's sublimation would have permitted such a voyeur to become an artist and wax rich painting nudes.

Real sophistication, like real courtesy, however, reflects more about a person than just the constricting manners of the rich. Sophistication reflects knowing how others feel; it involves the acquisition of a variety of skills; it is epitomized by knowing how to play. Sophistication is Goodhart's graceful capacity to satisfy his own needs and yet rarely inconvenience others; sophistication is Lion's capacity to make one feel proud to have known him. Mr. Byron from the wrong side of the tracks became a sophisticate in midlife; and by comparison Dr. Smythe from Park Avenue seemed a little boorish. Back we come, then, to the question: Why? What accounts for differences in adaptive styles?

In accounting for the differences in adaptive styles between Smythe and Byron, the importance of internalized people seemed to outweigh sociological factors. Byron benefited from loving, accepting parents who cared enough to educate their young; such parents stay with their children when they are upset so they may learn the capacity to bear and plan for pain; and they encourage both playfulness and roughhousing. Lamb and Smythe lacked such parents. The morals of a rake and the socioeconomic accoutrements of the godless upper class could not free Smythe from his fear of sexuality. As an orphan, he had learned of his universe from distant, inhibited relatives. With few cultural inhibitions but an early development marred by a lack of fondling and love, Smythe found self-gratification easier than a sexual relationship with another person. With neither siblings nor parents to teach him to play, he knew no social forms of recreation. Yet without recourse to play, the lesson of bearing conscious pain is difficult to learn; Smythe learned only to escape. Then again, Dr. Smythe always married women as needy as himself. Each looked for but could not give parental support. Smythe always pretended that he sought a sexual object; he could not admit the truth that he longed for his lost parents. However, without an internalized mother, he did not develop the adaptive skills to turn his strong wish for a mother into anything but just that.

In contrast, Byron's culture had taught him to believe that hellfire was literal and that Protestants and masturbaters would be eternally damned. But his mother had also loved him and had thought her son's temper admirable. With this foundation, sublimation permitted Byron to enjoy mature sexual relationships and to acknowledge unabashedly the fact that he had "married both a wife and a mother." Since he and his wife had both had happy childhoods, they each could provide parental support for the other.

In sum, it appears that close relationships, not our culture, shape our adaptive resources. In turn, good adaptation further enhances close relationships. As the lessons of Harry Harlow's isolated infant monkeys have suggested, we need close and loving associations as children, if we are not, like Smythe, to fear sex when adult. In the Study, sanguine childhoods had little effect upon the men's careers; rather the importance of their upbringing was seen in its profound effect upon their capacity for loving. This broad generalization will be developed in Chapter 13.

Part II

Basic Styles of Adaptation

Chapter 5

Adaptive Ego Mechanisms
—A Hierarchy

> Our language, in fact, is only approximate;
> and even in science it is so indefinite that if
> we lose sight of phenomena and cling to
> words, we are speedily out of reality. We,
> therefore, only injure science by arguing in
> favor of a word which is now merely a source
> of error, because it no longer expresses the
> same idea for everyone. Let us therefore
> conclude that we must always cling to
> phenomena.
>
> — Claude Bernard, *An Introduction to the
> Study of Experimental Medicine*

In examining the adaptive styles of the six men looked at so far, I have already described several ego mechanisms. I have suggested that Mr. Goodhart's altruism and sublimation were more adaptive than Dr. Tarrytown's dissociation and projection. Dr. Smythe's passive aggression seemed less effective than Mr. Byron's anticipation, and Mr. Lamb's fantasy led to loneliness while Mr. Lion's sublimation was intrinsic to his loving. The intent of this chapter will be to organize eighteen such mechanisms into a formal framework. I do this both to facilitate understanding of the rest of the book and to provide a possible scheme for understanding unconscious adaptive response. Like Chapters 2 and 3, this one may be skipped by any reader who has grown tired of explanatory words and prefers to view Claude Bernard's phenomena.

The concept of unconscious adaptive mechanisms brings forth a variety of questions. First, how do you identify and measure a defense mechanism? Second, do such mechanisms really exist, or, in order to perceive them, must you have the faith of a devout

Freudian? Third, how many defense mechanisms are there? Fourth, what is the difference between pathological defense mechanisms and adaptive coping mechanisms? Are defense mechanisms ever healthy? Fifth, what are the practical consequences of the defense mechanisms that we use? Sixth, are defense mechanisms immutable or do they change with maturity? Finally, what should you do if you perceive your friend or child using a particular defense?

Let us begin with the first question, how do you identify defenses? Unfortunately, our knowledge of defenses is analogous to knowledge by nineteenth-century astronomers of the planet Pluto. Pluto could not be directly visualized, measured, or even identified as a single planet. Nevertheless, the tangible reality of Pluto could be appreciated by its systematic distortion of orbits of planets that were visible. In similar fashion the observer identifies a user's invisible defenses by noting systematic distortions. The problem of the measurement of defenses is even more difficult than that of unseen planets; for defense mechanisms refer to unifying processes rather than discrete entities. Like our recognition of a symphony as a unitary whole, our perceptions of a single defense mechanism actually reflect the merging of many discrete processes acting in concert over time. Recognition of defenses is still further hampered, for to learn too much about our individual defenses is to risk experiencing personal discomfort. Identification of defense mechanisms, then, is always an approximate process.

Before we can consider a formal listing of defenses, the second question also demands an answer: Are defenses figments of psychoanalysts' imaginations? Certainly, when Freud originally identified them, defenses reflected human phenomena that had not been previously recognized. Not Aristotle or Hippocrates, not Sophocles or Shakespeare, not Montaigne or Janet had anticipated Freud in recognizing even such simple psychological mechanisms as isolation and projection. Freud not only established that upsetting *affects*, not disturbing *ideas*, underlay psychopathology; but he also established that much of what is perceived as psychopathology reflects a potentially healing process. In 1894 Freud observed that not only could *affect* be "dislocated or transposed" from ideas and objects (by what Freud would later call dissociation, repression, and isolation) but affect could be "reattached" to other ideas and objects (by displacement and sublimation).[1] These were revolutionary ideas; and, indeed, perhaps the concept of unconscious defense mechanisms was Freud's most original contribution to man's understanding of man. During Freud's lifetime, however, both he and his students tended to ignore the importance of defense mechanisms. It took James Strachey, Freud's final editor, and Freud's daughter, Anna, his intellectual heir, to appreciate and to emphasize what Freud often chose to ignore — the variety and the power of his discovery, ego mechanisms of defense.

Over a period of forty years, Freud recognized most of the defense mechanisms that we speak of today and identified five of their most important properties: (1) Defenses were a major means of managing instinct and affect. (2) They were unconscious. (3) They were discrete from one another. (4) Although often the hallmarks of major psychiatric syndromes, defenses were dynamic and reversible. (5) Finally, they could be adaptive as well as pathological.

During the first decade after he had postulated their existence, Freud described the separate mechanisms of humor, distortion, hypochondriasis, dissociation, displacement, repression, suppression, fantasy, and isolation. After 1905, however, the term defense *(Abwehr)* no longer figured prominently in his work and was replaced by " 'repression' (as I now began to say instead of 'defense')."[2] For twenty years, distinctions between ego mechanisms remained blurred. In 1936 Freud advised the interested student, "There are an extraordinarily large number of methods (or mechanisms, as we say) used by our ego in the discharge of its defensive functions . . . my daughter, the child analyst, is writing a book upon them."[3] He was referring to his eightieth birthday present from Anna — her historically important monograph, *The Ego and the Mechanisms of Defense.*[4]

It is probably no accident that Anna Freud, by standing, as it were, on her father's shoulders, was able to see clearly two facets of psychological function that had been obscure to him. She saw not only that defenses could and should be sharply differentiated from each other, but also that aggressive instincts, against which so many of the defenses are erected, were potentially useful and constructive.

Although Freud never bothered to label all the mechanisms that Anna Freud was to catalogue twenty years later, or to bring them together in a single paper, he sometimes hinted that they bore a hierarchical relationship. Denial, distortion, and projection were the defenses of psychosis, and at the opposite end of the continuum, sublimation, altruism, humor, and suppression were the defenses of maturity.

Recently the psychoanalyst Robert Wallerstein outlined an important focus for future research. "In development the individual ascends an epigenetic ladder toward a more mature and reality-adequate mode of adaptation. Each rung represents the hierarchy of defenses appropriate for that developmental phase."[5] But in 1905 Freud already had introduced this tremendously important concept — the ontogeny of defenses. He wrote, "The multifariously perverse sexual disposition of childhood can accordingly be regarded as the source of a number of our virtues, insofar as through reaction-formation, it stimulates their development."[6] Delinquency could evolve into altruism.

For Freud conceived of a class of defense mechanisms that could transmute libido, not into a source of neurosis but into culture and virtue. "The sexual life of each one of us extends to a slight degree — now in this direction, now in that — beyond the narrow lines imposed as the standard of normality. The perversions are neither beastly nor degenerate in the emotional sense of the word. They are a development of germs, all of which are contained in the undifferentiated sexual disposition of the child, and which by being suppressed or being diverted to higher asexual aims — by being 'sublimated' — are destined to provide the energy for a great number of our cultural achievements. . . . Sublimation enables excessively strong excitation arising from particular sources of sexuality to find an outlet and use in other fields, so that a not inconsiderable increase in psychical efficiency results from a disposition which in itself is perilous."[7] Later he wrote, "Humor can be regarded as the highest of these defensive processes. It scorns to withdraw the ideational content bearing the distressing affect from conscious attention as repression does, and thus surmounts the automatism of defense."[8] However, the similar yoking of aggression with creative results, rather than to what Freud often perceived as death and destruction, had to wait for his daughter and her clearer cataloguing of the mechanisms of defense.

It should not surprise us that popular acceptance of the concept of unconscious defense mechanisms has taken time. That the earth is round, that our planet revolves around the sun, and that our ancestors were apelike were concepts originally perceived as heresies. Freud's concept of unconscious mechanisms of defense was similarly dismissed. Each of these ideas had to become part of the belief system of a limited number of people before each idea could be accepted as part of the established body of scientific fact. That unconscious psychological defenses exist (in a metaphorical sense) is no longer confined to the belief system of those who religiously adhere to psychoanalysis. Heads of state are aware of projection; ethologists speak freely of displacement; sublimation and repression have long been clear to biographers and more recently to social historians.

Nevertheless, to prove that a given behavior is defensive and "not just coincidence" is not simple. To identify a given defense in a given individual is a time-consuming process. It involves the same kind of inference and data collection that we associate with the identification of the murderer in mystery stories. Longitudinal methods of study facilitate the appreciation of defenses as human *phenomena* and not psychoanalytic notions. It is no accident that this book uses data gained from a thirty-year study of lifetimes rather than from the consulting room.

The answer to the third question, "How many defense mechanisms are there?" is "As many as the number of angels who can dance on the head of a pin." There are as many defenses as the cataloguer has the temerity to imagine. I have selected eighteen mechanisms to discuss; these have been chosen from the compilations of defenses produced by six important contributors to our knowledge of the adaptive mechanisms (Percival Symonds,[9] Anna Freud,[10] Arthur Valenstein,[11] Elvin Semrad,[12] Otto Fenichel,[13] and Lawrence Kolb[14]). Any limited selection, however, must be arbitrary and idiosyncratic. In his summary of psychoanalytic theory in 1932, Freud mentioned only four defenses; Valenstein describes forty-four.

I have grouped the eighteen defenses that I selected according to their relative theoretical maturity and pathological import.[15] In Table 2 they are arranged in four general levels — psychotic, immature, neurotic, and mature. Such ordering underscores lessons already suggested by the lives of Lion and Goodhart — that the maturation of human beings is accompanied by the evolution of their adaptive processes from those of Level I into Level IV. A child's denial of reality (a "psychotic" defense) can evolve into the fantasy of a Lamb; in adolescence, fantasy can then merge with the dissociation of a Tarrytown, and become in maturity the sublimation of a Lion.

In Appendix A, the eighteen mechanisms in the table are formally defined; in this chapter I merely want to offer enough synonyms so that readers can integrate my terminology with their own. But before proceeding, let me make one caveat. The phenomena of unconscious defensive behavior exist, but the reification of these phenomena is metaphorical. Their classification in this chapter is only for convenience.

TABLE 2
Schematic Table of Adaptive Mechanisms

Level I —	Psychotic Mechanisms (common in psychosis, dreams, and childhood)
	Denial (of external reality)
	Distortion
	Delusional Projection
Level II —	Immature Mechanisms (common in severe depression, personality disorders, and adolescence)
	Fantasy (schizoid withdrawal, denial through fantasy), cf. Lamb
	Projection, cf. Tarrytown
	Hypochondriasis
	Passive-Aggressive Behavior (masochism, turning against the self), cf. Smythe
	Acting Out (compulsive delinquency, perversion), cf. Tarrytown
Level III —	Neurotic Mechanisms (common in everyone)
	Intellectualization (isolation, obsessive behavior, undoing, rationalization)
	Repression, cf. Smythe
	Reaction Formation
	Displacement (conversion, phobias, wit), cf. hematologist in Introduction
	Dissociation (neurotic denial), cf. Tarrytown
Level IV —	Mature Mechanisms (common in "healthy" adults)
	Sublimation, cf. Lion
	Altruism, cf. Goodhart
	Suppression
	Anticipation, cf. Byron
	Humor, cf. Goodhart

At Level I, the most primitive end of the continuum, I have included the so-called psychotic defenses of delusional projection, psychotic denial, and distortion. Often, these mechanisms can be identified in normal individuals before the age of five. They are common in the dreams and fantasy life of adults. At times ghosts and demons intrude into our consciousness; the Walter Mitty in us all can bring the dead to life, and effect heroic political change. For the *user* Level I mechanisms rearrange external reality, but to the *beholder* the user of such mechanisms appears crazy. Thus, our thoughts while waiting for traffic lights or leafing through pulp magazines are often best kept to ourselves. When Level I mechanisms cease to be private and affect everyday behavior, this behavior cannot be altered by conventional psychotherapy, reason, or threats. The insane, the dreamer, and the outraged two-year-old are all omnipotent. Only alteration of external reality or alteration of the user's nervous system (e.g., with tranquilizers or through maturation) can breach psychotic defenses.

Delusional projection involves frank delusions about external reality, usually of a persecutory type. It is a dominant adaptive mechanism in paranoid schizophrenia, in delirium tremens, and in organic brain syndromes. Denial involves the literal denial of external reality. Although denial is a prominent feature of psychosis, to ignore reality may be quite adaptive for a patient who is dying. Distortion grossly reshapes external reality to suit inner needs. It is a common element of both manic delusions of grandeur and adaptive religious belief.

Since in the waking behavior of healthy adults these three mechanisms rarely occur, the few examples that I observed in the Study will be cited now. During one man's adolescence, distortion was a harbinger of the fact that he would continue to use relatively maladaptive mechanisms all his life. At sixteen, he sincerely believed that if he did not obsessively wash the germs off his drinking glass before each use, he would be guilty of the sin of suicide. Whereas the neurotic obsessional perceives that his obsessions are bizarre, this man saw his behavior as quite appropriate. As a highly sophisticated and well-read college sophomore, he was fearful of the consequences of sexual activity. In fact, he adhered to the belief that masturbation led to mental illness. At twenty-three, during basic infantry training, this shy intellectual wrote to the Study, "I'm the happiest fellow in camp"; such happiness must truly have been delirious.

Other examples of distortion in the men's lives occurred in more specialized settings — childhood, religious belief, and insanity. At three, one man had two imaginary friends and a dog; these were unusually vivid companions and required places set for them at the family table. At sixteen, another man accepted the truth of modern religious miracles so unquestioningly that the principal of his parochial school thought it abnormal. In the third instance, a sophisticated biochemist refused to admit that he had diabetes. Despite positive tests for urinary sugar that were tangibly visible to him, he refused to take appropriate medicine. But he manifested such behavior only during the acute stages of a depressive psychosis. When his psychosis was treated, he felt sufficiently in control of his life to acknowledge his diabetes.

During this psychotic episode, the same man showed the only adult example of delusional projection. Over the telephone he told me at length that as a suspected Communist spy he was being tailed by the FBI. In reality he was tailed by self-doubts and guilty recriminations regarding his competence both as a scientist and as a father. He was subsequently hospitalized.

The only other recorded example of delusional projection occurred during the early childhood of the Grant Study's only juvenile delinquent, but had events from the men's early childhood been collected in greater detail, such examples would be more common. At five, he had believed his nurse's punitive threats that the chips on his bathtub were bugs; he responded with terror. At seven, he had had to leave a marionette production of Hansel and Gretel because the puppet act became too vivid. Such an episode illustrates the task that confronts every child's ego. How can a child play out his fantasies and resolve family conflicts in fairy tales and yet never confuse dream with reality? It is only during nightmares and night terrors (delusional projection) that a child's occasional anger toward and mistrust of his mother becomes painfully overt — only then is fantasy mistaken for reality. Usually, the conflict can be ingeniously resolved by cuddling close to good *mummy* while she regales the engrossed child with stories of bad witches who get cremated (e.g., Hansel and Gretel) or bad *stepmothers* who get crushed (e.g., Snow White).

The only clear example of psychotic denial was a businessman who was unable to admit either to himself or to his doctor that he was addicted to sedatives. As a result, to rule out suspected neurologic disease that was in fact barbiturate intoxication, he permitted unnecessary diagnostic surgery to be performed on his brain. Although this episode was atypical for this man, it reflects the clinical fact that in nonpsychotic adults, denial of external reality is most often encountered in addiction.

Unlike the psychotic mechanisms, Level II, or "immature," mechanisms (projection, fantasy, hypochondriasis, passive-aggressive behavior, and acting out) were frequently seen in the behavior of members of the Study. Immature mechanisms are common in childhood and adolescence. They are also common in adults with depressive illness, addiction, and "character disorder."

Immature defenses may also be mobilized by physical illness and genetic vulnerability. The deaf, the mentally defective, and the delirious become paranoid. The nearly blind and severely alcoholic retreat into fantasy worlds to deny their affliction. Hypochondriasis is most common in the physically ill, and there is a genetic disorder where afflicted individuals masochistically devour their own fingers. Finally, epilepsy leads some people to act out their impulses without conscious awareness.

During adolescence most of the subjects displayed Level II mechanisms, and some men continued to use such mechanisms when adult. For the *user* these mechanisms usually alter distress caused by other people — either their presence or their loss. When these defenses are used to resolve conflict among conscience, reality, and instincts, the integration is imperfect. Anxiety may be avoided; but for the *beholder*, immature mechanisms appear socially undesirable, profoundly inconvenient, and may be labeled misbehavior. The *user*, however, is rarely aware that he has problems. It is a rare paranoid who comes to a psychiatrist and complains of his projections.

Reason, interpretation, and threats fail to alter immature defenses. For example, the student who is perennially late for lectures will not respond to being given an alarm clock or demerits. However, these defenses may be breached through improved personal relationships (e.g., a more concerned teacher or a girl friend's auditing the course), through repeated confrontations (especially by peers), or through showing the student rather than just telling him (e.g., the reality of expulsion).

We should not be surprised that a chronic user of a specific immature defense can often understand another user with similar problems. Perhaps the reason that both adolescents and adults with character disorders can find love and comfort through peer self-help groups is that such groups can forgive, see through, and confront the immature defenses common to the group. The average human is not so gifted; we often condemn and thereby enhance the impregnability of immature defenses.

Level III includes "neurotic" mechanisms (intellectualization, repression, reaction-formation, displacement, and dissociation). Although these mechanisms underlie the symptomatology of neuroses, they are also common in normal individuals from childhood to senility. They were as frequent among the Byrons and Lions as they were among the Smythes and Lambs. These mechanisms are most often used in mastering acute conflict. Unlike the immature defenses, which usually are adaptations to *inter*personal conflict, the neurotic defenses are more often employed against purely *intra*psychic conflict. For the *user* these mechanisms alter private feelings or instinctual expression and, unlike immature defenses, these mechanisms cause the *user* to seek out psychiatrists. To the *beholder*, they appear as individual quirks or neurotic hang-ups. Often neurotic defenses can be dramatically changed by brief psychotherapeutic intervention.

Indeed, among those who seek out psychotherapy, neurotic defenses are often more prominent than immature mechanisms, not because the need for intervention is greater but because these relatively more adaptive mechanisms are more likely to produce conscious discomfort than the less adaptive *immature* mechanisms.

Level IV or mature mechanisms include altruism, humor, suppression, anticipation, and sublimation. These mechanisms are common among "healthy" individuals from adolescence to old age, and they can be conceptualized as well-orchestrated composites of less mature mechanisms. For the *user* these mechanisms integrate the four sometimes conflicting governors of human behavior — conscience, reality, interpersonal relations, and instincts. To the *beholder*, mature mechanisms appear as convenient virtues, and there is usually no therapeutic reason to alter them. The chief danger to their adaptive use is that they will be used not wisely but too well. Unfortunately, although closer to consciousness than the mechanisms previously described, mature mechanisms cannot be acquired by a conscious act of will. There is nothing more transparent than someone *trying* to use humor or altruism; there is no one more angry-looking than someone consciously trying to hold back rage. Under increased stress mature mechanisms may revert to those that are less mature.

Having arranged the defenses along a continuum, we may address the fourth question: When is a given adaptive mechanism coping and when is it pathological? For by now it should have become clear that much of what is called mental illness is in fact the manifestation of an individual's adaptive response. It is not the defenses themselves that are pathological but the conflicts and disordered events that call them forth. In evaluating the significance of a given defense, both context and flexibility become exceedingly important. If a defense is used in a rigid, inflexible way, if it is motivated more by past needs than by present and future reality, if it too severely distorts the present situation, if it abolishes rather than limits gratification, or if it dams rather than rechannels the expression of feelings, then it is likely to be maladaptive.

The context is also important. A man with cancer might dream that he is well and so *deny* the reality that he is fatally ill. Clearly, the comfort gained from denial in dreams has no harmful consequences. But let us suppose that this man persisted in his denial. If he went to a faith healer to escape the pain of surgery, some might label him crazy, and he might compromise his biological adaptation to his cancer. But if under special circumstances, let us say *after* he was in the hospital receiving optimal care, he were to deny that there was anything more wrong with him than a bad cold, denial might once again become adaptive. He might facilitate his own and his family's enjoyment of his last days. We cannot evaluate the choice of a defense without considering the circumstances that call it forth and how it affects relationships with other people.

Equipped with a schematic hierarchy, it also becomes possible to answer the fifth question: If our defenses are flexible, mature, and coping, how does that help us? The answer to this question is a major focus of this book; but in general terms, an answer is given by the striking contrasts in Table 3.[16] In gathering the data for Table 3, blind raters were used. The rater who judged the men's adjustment was ignorant of their use of defenses. The raters who judged the maturity of the men's defenses were ignorant of their external adjustment. The twenty-five men who used predominantly mature defenses are contrasted with thirty-one men who used the most immature. (The scheme for judging maturity of defenses is explained in Appendix C.)

The positive association between theoretically mature adaptive mechanisms and tangible success in many aspects of life is dramatic. Even happiness was four times as frequent among men with mature defenses. ("Happiness" was defined by four or more of the following self-judgments being true — job is enjoyable, job meets personal expectations, health feels excellent, marriage is enjoyable, the present is the happiest period, and the present is *not* the unhappiest period in life.)

As the case histories have suggested, men with mature defenses were far better equipped to work and to love. Friendship and mature defenses went hand in hand. More than half of the men with immature defenses were called mentally ill, and most seemed unable to play. Conversely, no man with mature defenses sought out psychotherapy or received a psychiatric diagnosis. Surprisingly, the use of immature defenses could be shown to precede rather than follow the development of chronic physical illness. All of the men who showed mature defenses at forty-five continued to enjoy good physical health at fifty-five, as assessed by a recent physical exam by independent physicians. In contrast, a third of the thirty-one men who deployed the most immature defenses between twenty and forty-five developed chronic physical illness or died during the next decade.

Equally important is the fact that sudden regression of defense

TABLE 3
A Comparison between Men Who Used Mature Adaptive Mechanisms and Men Who Used Immature Adaptive Mechanisms

	Predominant Adaptive Style		
	MATURE	IMMA-TURE	Statistical Significance
	n = 25	n = 31	of Difference
Overall Adjustment			
1) Top third in adult adjustment	60%	0%	***
2) Bottom third in adult adjustment	4%	61%	***
3) "Happiness" (top third)	68%	16%	***
Career Adjustment			
1) Income over $20,000/year	88%	48%	**
2) Job meets ambition for self	92%	58%	***
3) Active public service outside job	56%	29%	*
Social Adjustment			
1) Rich friendship pattern	64%	6%	***
2) Marriage in least harmonious quartile or divorced	28%	61%	**
3) Barren friendship pattern	4%	52%	***
4) No competitive sports (age 40–50)	24%	77%	***
Psychological Adjustment			
1) 10+ psychiatric visits	0%	45%	**
2) Ever diagnosed mentally ill	0%	55%	***
3) Emotional problems in childhood	20%	45%	*
4) Worst childhood environment (bottom fourth)	12%	39%	*
5) Fails to take full vacation	28%	61%	*
6) Able to be aggressive with others (top fourth)	36%	6%	*
Medical Adjustment			
1) Four or more adult hospitalizations	8%	26%	
2) 5+ days sick leave/year	0%	23%	*
3) Recent health poor by objective exam	0%	36%	*
4) Subjective health consistently judged "excellent" since college	68%	48%	*

***Very significant difference ($p < .001$ — a difference that would occur by chance only one time in a thousand)
 **Significant difference ($p < .01$)
  *Probably significant difference ($p < .05$)

mechanisms plays an intrinsic part in the process we call mental illness. For example, when the theoretic framework of this chapter was applied to twenty-five hospitalized psychiatric patients, it was difficult to identify a time in the lives of these patients when they had manifested those mature, Level IV mechanisms so commonly used by the men in Table 3 who seemed immune to psychiatric diagnosis. Rather, when not in hospital, adaptive mechanisms used by the twenty-five hospitalized patients (and the thirty-one more troubled Grant Study men in Table 3) had been drawn from the neurotic and immature levels. When hospitalized, half of the patients showed evidence of Level I defenses — psychotic denial, distortion, and delusional projection. Thus, the hierarchy in Table 2 reflects not only a continuum from child to adult but also from sickness to health.

Several years ago Norma Haan and Theodore Kroeber at the Institute of Human Development at Berkeley developed a hierarchy of defenses very similar to this.[17] Using blind raters they also found that defense choice among men was powerfully associated with mental health and maturity and that the same hierarchy held for women. Haan demonstrated that during adult life mature defense choice led to upward shifts in intelligence and social status.[18] Although some studies have suggested that defensive style is a result as well as a determinant of social class,[19] review of existing research supports the idea that adaptive choice determines social mobility at least as much as it is affected by it.[20] In an exhaustive study of the mental health of a cross-section of urban adults, Langner and Michael observed that the upwardly mobile tend to be obsessive, utilizing the mechanism of inhibition or repression.[21] "The downwardly mobile," they wrote, "tend to be alcoholics and to have character disorders, particularly the suspicious and passive-dependent varieties. These involve both acting out and the more severe withdrawal devices, alcoholism in particular being associated with self-destructive tendencies. The low SES [socioeconomic status] stratum, then, tends to accumulate people who have used these relatively maladaptive or impairing devices in an unsuccessful attempt to solve or relieve their stress situation."[22]

What is the effect of maturation upon our adaptive mechanisms? This sixth question cannot be answered with certainty. It seems likely, however, that both as a result of a maturing nervous system and as a by-product of successful identifications with other people, "mature" mechanisms evolve during adolescence. As in the development of any skill, the growth of mature defenses requires both biological readiness and suitable models for identification. Jean Piaget, a brillant Swiss student of human development, has documented that as children mature, the harsh talion law of the Old Testament gives way to the more merciful and flexible precepts of the Golden Rule.[23] Piaget has gone on to show that an increasing capacity for complex mental integration accompanies adolescence.[24] In parallel fashion, biological capacity to use the more mature mechanisms of adaptation may evolve in harmony with adult development.[25]

For example, it is not until about age seven that a child can describe the physical geography of a room as it might appear in the perspective of another observer seated in a chair opposite the child. Perhaps projection of feelings cannot be given up for repression or displacement of feelings until a child is neurologically as well as emotionally capable of recognizing that others do not necessarily share his perceptions. Certainly, anyone who has raised small children is familiar with the fact that impulsive behavior is often suddenly replaced by strict prohibitions (reaction formations) such as "boys never cry," or "eating between meals is always bad for you." Less familiar because it occurs in "us" not "them" is a process occurring during adulthood; in this process the child's maturing morality permits the replacement of pleasureless reaction-formation with more gratifying altruism or sublimation. Again, over the life cycle the evolution of children's jokes from masochism to displacement to humor is linked both to cognitive maturation and to the evolution of impulse control.

In considering the fact that defenses evolve from less mature to more mature, it is also important to realize that the world of the adult is safer and more predictable than that of the child. Considerable time has already been spent developing the reasons why sublimation of aggression for a man like Lion could be facilitated by living both in a family where the members respected autonomous behavior and also in a country that rewards a free press.

Psychotherapy, if defined broadly, is a final factor that affects shifts in defense level. During the course of psychoanalysis rigid defenses are abandoned and replaced by more flexible means of coping. During an alcoholic's experience in Alcoholics Anonymous, altruism and reaction formation replace acting out and projection. A good teacher, coach, or spouse also facilitates the evolution of flexible coping patterns.

The final question posed by this chapter is: What should you do if you see your friend or child using a maladaptive defense mechanism? While a cut-and-dried answer is, of course, impossible, I have been asked the question often enough to offer some guidelines. First, a person is naked without adaptive mechanisms. Therefore, you should remove or point out a person's mechanisms of defense with the same tact and respect for individual choice and privacy that you would use in removing a piece of somebody's clothing. Second, never try to challenge or interpret a defense unless you have the time, the love, and the patience to share responsibility for the consequences. A person can often surrender some defenses if another person is willing to volunteer him- or herself as a partial buffer. Third, the attempt to remove a defense will usually fail unless you are prepared to offer the opportunity for an alternative mode of coping. Defense mechanisms evolve into other mechanisms. They do not disappear. Last, remember that defenses are unconscious. Trying to reason with or to discipline adaptive mechanisms is likely to prove as effective as trying to stop the wind.

The next four chapters will try to amplify on the hierarchy of defenses described in Table 2 and to illustrate how in combination defenses become the building blocks of psychopathology.

Chapter 6

Sublimation

> What men or gods are these? What
>   maidens loth?
> What mad pursuit? What struggle to
>   escape?
> What pipes and timbrels? What wild
>   ecstasy? . . .
>
> More happy love! More happy, happy love!
> Forever warm and still to be enjoy'd,
> Forever panting and forever young;
> All breathing human passion far above,
> That leaves a heart high-sorrowful and
>   cloy'd.
> A burning forehead, and a parching tongue.
>
> — John Keats, "Ode on a Grecian Urn"

The task of a successful defense is to resolve conflict. As the lives of the Grant Study men illustrated, ideal resolution is never achieved by sweeping distress under the rug, nor by arbitrary compromise between instinct and conscience, or by cowardly purchase of intimacy with masochistic sacrifice. No, the sign of a successful defense is neither careful cost accounting nor shrewd compromise, but rather synthetic and creative transmutation. John Keats conveys a miraculous concept: "More happy, happy love! / Forever warm and still to be enjoyed." With a control of language that defies description, he turned lust, perhaps even imminent rape, into the most beautiful of games. Upon an inanimate Attic vase he discovered — and shared — an attenuated, yet still passionate sexuality. A less poetic Grant Study subject described the same process in mundane language. He wrote, "I have twice the sex drive of my wife. We adjust ourselves by varying our sex play to suit each other. We believe that lovemaking should be practiced as an art!"

To solve important human crises, such creativity is critical. To use a very different example — the tragedy of the Potsdam and Yalta agreements was that each Great Power got exactly one quarter of Berlin. To cure the suspicions and jealousies that each Great Power engendered in the other, mere compromise was not enough. Perhaps only if each country had received more than it gave could the crises of the Cold War have been averted. So it is with intrapsychic conflict. The miracle of the human ego is that sometimes it can supply to the embattled forces within an individual the alchemy that international politics lacks. Frederick Lion in great grief could write good poetry. David Goodhart in anger could heal racial wounds. At thirty-one, a suicidal but only partially deaf Beethoven had written of his loss of hearing, "Oh, if I were rid of this affliction, I could embrace the world." At fifty-four, an utterly deaf Beethoven immortalized Schiller's *Ode to Joy*, "Be embraced all ye millions with a kiss for all the world," in the lyrical, life-affirming chorus of his Ninth Symphony.

The adaptive process to which I allude is often called sublimation. Its synthetic process is mysterious; for no artist creates, no child plays by conscious will alone. Perhaps the life of Lieutenant Edward Keats exemplified this mystery better than that of any other man in the Grant Study. Since sublimation is not something that just happens, his story will require a little time in the telling.

Edward Keats was like the storybook rich boy. He possessed everything that all other boys wished for — except freedom. Allegorically, he lived in a mansion behind the great wrought-iron fence of the conscience that his parents had bequeathed him. Since he could not escape, he had to discover games with which to entertain himself. For a while, these worked. Keats had grown up in a family environment that received one of the highest childhood ratings in the Study. Everyone conveyed to Keats the fact that he was loved; his mother boasted, "The servants and his sisters adore him," and added that he was "the most satisfactory sort of child." At the time the Study began, both research staff and classmates felt that Keats was special. Indeed, even in midlife, by which time he had become emotionally crippled, he was still beloved by many friends.

In college, the research psychiatrist had seen Ed Keats as

having no conflict with family members and described him as "pleasant, warm, open, with a sense of comfortable well-being — without euphoria." Keats was seen as "a swaggering, muscular, athletic fellow" but also as "sympathetic, unself-conscious, generous, forgiving, and natural — the most normal so far." At twenty-five his commanding officer said of Keats, "He has a cheerful and pleasant disposition. His fine sense of humor has a favorable effect on the morale of his associates. He performs his regular and additional duties in an outstanding manner." At thirty a close college friend described Keats as someone who was "always good-natured, cheerful, smiling, and did not grumble or criticize." In fact, he never complained or got angry at others. When he was forty-seven, a physician and close friend remarked that Keats was "vigorous, solid, and had impact. He had an actor's ability that was always entertaining. . . . He struck people as well put together and at ease in a relationship." In short, Lieutenant Keats trusted the universe.

What went wrong was that Keats's parents raised him *too* well. If their parents have been unworthy, many children learn in adolescence, as Goodhart did, to cast off parental shackles. The admonitions of loving parents are harder to abandon. By one year of age, not only was Lieutenant Keats fully toilet trained, but aluminum mittens had broken his habit of thumbsucking. By age eight, he was able to take over his own policing from his parents. At that age he made a vow never again to fight with his younger sister, and he never did. His reward was that he grew up beloved by his parents, who took delight in his "marvelous sense of humor" and "sweet nature."

Not until college did the outline of real conflict emerge. How could Keats get close to real people in a real world without losing the love of internalized parents who — so he thought — had forbidden him ever to soil his hands? At twenty, he told the Study staff that dirty jokes were fine, "because they are not accompanied by sexual feelings." But he did not believe in kissing girls because such behavior was "immature and disrespectful." He perceived the male genitalia as "ugly."

Yet in his moral prison Keats was not without resources. As an adolescent he had already begun to seek out ways to reconcile his vigorous instincts with his internal prohibitions. If he found the male body unattractive, he was fascinated by human physiology and reveled in the feel of his own body in hard athletic play. If he dated little and maintained that the bodies of women were sexually unexciting, he found paintings and sculpture of nude women objects of great beauty. If tangible romances were denied him, the Romantic poets were his favorites.

When at nineteen he gave up the game of football as being too aggressive, it looked as if the conscience of this "swaggering, muscular, athletic fellow" might have gone too far. But Keats took up flying as a substitute, and briefly fate smiled on him. The fortuitous events of World War II led to his becoming a fighter pilot. He piloted Thunderbolts — stout, Jovian, high-performance pursuit planes that could also unleash a ton of bombs. Performed under less special circumstances, his activities would have evoked great guilt. Instead, Lieutenant Keats found being a fighter pilot immensely exciting. At twenty-three, he wrote home, "I have always liked flying, and just being in the air is very enjoyable. There are two things that appeal to me especially — the first is shooting at a towed target, and the other is being able to maneuver a small fast plane about at will." If Keats had to wait until he was thirty-one to extend his sexual adventures beyond even light petting, piloting Thunderbolts must have been an intriguing substitute. Students of the psychology of flying have been impressed that many normal people in dreams, and many pilots, equate flying with intercourse.

Having served as a fighter-bomber pilot in Italy and then in France, Keats wrote, "As far as fighting the war goes, I can't imagine a more satisfactory job. Flying in itself is always thrilling, and fighting from the air is more so. . . ." He then added the caveat, "Without the present goal behind it of winning the war, flying in my case would be selfishness." Through sublimation he could vent aggressive instincts and still win praise from the society (or conscience) that he wished so much to please. On three occasions he was awarded the Air Medal.

The external dangers of war were of minimal importance to Lieutenant Keats. He wrote, "I can remember saying to myself as I taxied back to the line after an hour of combat 'these are the most exciting days I'll ever live in.' I had cause to repeat that statement many times thereafter. The duty of a fighter pilot was absolutely beyond compare. . . . Once in and up in the air, it was always thrilling. . . . Anti-aircraft fire always disturbed me; aerial combat was very exciting. . . . In a way, the duty I had was like college life, so that the adjustment was not difficult. Being detached from the destruction one was causing a thousand feet below, we had very little contact with the horrors of war. The whole thing was like a game (awful admission to make!)." Football may have seemed too aggressive, but for Keats, fighting Nazis as a combat pilot provided both the distance and the *raison d'être* to transform murder into sport. What mad pursuit! What wild ecstasy!

After the war the flak from his conscience caught up with Lieutenant Keats. Thus, in 1946 Keats wrote the Study, "We have had a very exciting and comfortable bit of duty during this war . . . but I feel guilty when thinking of the infantry slogging through the jungle and living in the mud, while we got the best of everything. Our fighting was detached. We sat thousands of feet in the air shooting at a target, but never seeing people dying or fighting in hand-to-hand combat with them. . . . To be decorated for having had the privilege of being in the most exciting branch of service with no routine and superb living accommodations is almost immoral."

Yet this later distress merely underscored the elegance of his wartime adaptation. Perhaps part of his later difficulty was that, except in games, Keats could *never* tolerate his own assertiveness. Perhaps part of his difficulty was that after the war he began to become conscious of his defenses, and so he lost their protection.

After the war, Keats attended graduate school and then became a social worker. He tried to throw himself into altruistic endeavor; but he did so with such selflessness that little pleasure remained for himself. Within the framework outlined in this book, such behavior was more in keeping with *reaction formation* than altruism. With the world at peace, he returned to Germany to help atone for the pleasure he had achieved in its destruction. For a while, it looked as if Keats was once more to get sublimation to work for him. He was assigned to Heidelberg — not exactly a hardship post. However, he was unable to flower behind the walls of his conscience, and he found that "communication barriers" kept him isolated from the Germans themselves.

At thirty-one Keats wrote the Study, "The most important element that has emerged in my own psychic picture is a fuller realization of my own hostilities; I used to pride myself on not having any." He never mastered this self-revelation. He became increasingly estranged from his job, his wife, and the Germans. When he returned at age forty to the United States, he returned in defeat. He moved to Boston and devoted himself to encounter groups — giving others the freedom to enjoy the emotional expression that he denied himself. From behind the iron bars of his psychological prison he practiced philanthropy; but there remained little pleasure for himself. As a physician friend remarked, "In midlife he retained his charm, but he had lost his energy and effectiveness."

Although in this book I stress the fact that ingenious egos were more important than good luck in determining the course of these men's lives, circumstances do play their part. Thus, the peculiar rules of World War II, coming when they did, permitted Keats a graceful reprieve. As might have been expected, his response to the Vietnam war was very different. He saw it as an unjust and shameful war. He opposed it as he had his own unforgivable hostility — by passive aggression. He organized sit-down strikes against the draft and was arrested, not decorated, for his pains. Contrast this with Frederick Lion who was highly paid and admired for his far more active efforts to end the Vietnam war through overtly aggressive journalism.

Keats illustrates that it is possible to suffer with "mature defenses," just as it is occasionally possible to master life with immature mechanisms. Like an overtrained German shepherd, he brought pleasure often and inconvenience seldom to those who knew him, but he never knew freedom.

It is also possible to argue that his sublimation, unlike that of Beethoven, was unstable, and therefore faulty, or maybe it was not sublimation. Significantly, episodes I have called sublimation (a mature defense) three independent raters labeled displacement, reaction formation, and intellectualization (neurotic or Level III defenses). I had followed Keats's life through the serial questionnaires; I had rated each episode as it occurred; thus, his end surprised me. But perhaps because the raters judged the serial episodes as a single cluster (at the beginning they knew the end of his story), their perception of Keats and his defensive style differed. Just as reaction formation can evolve into altruism, so can displaced instinctual expression become transformed into a sublimated interest that many will appreciate. Defenses are relative and susceptible to mutation. Aggression may be sublimated, displaced, or turned against the self. Lieutenant Keats did all three.

But sublimation does more than make instinct acceptable; it also makes ideas fun. Displacement, which separates emotion from its object, and intellectualization, which separates emotion from ideas, can lead to arid lives unless they evolve into sublimation; for sublimation permits idea, object, *and* attenuated emotion to remain together in overt behavior.

Not surprisingly, then, sublimation became a major mechanism of adaptation in men who achieved recognition and pleasure in academic life. For example, of the seventeen men in the sample who went into teaching, all were intellectual overachievers. In college their grades were better than their native endowment seemed to warrant, and as adults all had coped with the hurly-burly of reality by retreating into the pleasures of the mind. Many continued to value ideas more than feelings. But although intellectualization may make for a brilliant academic record in high school, in adult life it must be tempered by a more flexible defense system — one that lets instinctual pleasure peek through. Thus, when compared to the eight men with relatively unfruitful academic careers, the nine men whose university lives were most productive used sublimation three times as frequently (in terms of the system of scoring used by the Study). The professors who could not sublimate had sterile marriages, students whom they did not respect, and far more emotional illness. In terms of their tested intellectual aptitudes in college, the men with the most successful academic careers were not more intellectually gifted than the others, but they were far more comfortable in coloring their ideas with the pigment of emotion.

Professor Dylan Bright provides a vivid illustration of the coping potential of sublimation. Although he was less intellectually gifted than the average member of the Study, an exciting luminescence surrounded his life. As soon as I walked into Professor Bright's office, he put his feet up onto the desk and started talking nonstop. He looked like a prize fighter, not an English professor. Although I was moved by his affective richness, initially I was not quite sure that I liked him. His first response to my request for an interview was "Christ, that kills the afternoon!" His barely tamed aggression verged on the abrasive, and only his charm kept me from regarding the encounter as a pitched battle. He graphically described his worries and then growled, "If they get out, I'll kick your teeth in."

Bright, you see, was a football lineman and a champion wrestler who, almost as an afterthought, became a professor of poetry. In high school he was a rebellious D student, and at one point was nearly expelled. He greatly preferred the excitement of athletics to the dreary world of class. Nevertheless, his headmaster saw Bright as "vibrant and ardent in his beliefs"; and the Study staff perceived him as "an eager, enthusiastic, attractive youngster with an outgoing personality. . . . All of his mother's exuberance and ready charm." Bright's intensely competitive spirit, although eventually leashed and sublimated, was never extinguished. In fact, his energy, his extraordinary capacity to win close friends, and his knack for engaging in exciting hedonistic activities made him one of the most dramatic members of the Study.

Unlike suppression and anticipation, the use of sublimation was not associated with particularly happy childhoods. Like Goodhart, Professor Bright grew up in a family filled with turmoil. His emotionally unstable, alcoholic father was rarely at home. Early, he tasted both the triumph and the danger of figuratively taking the place of his father in his family. As a child, Bright had seen his parents' marriage destroyed by fighting; and if Bright's father at times was a weakling, he was also a moody man whose hobby was hunting. His mother was a large and energetic woman who, even when her son was adult, was three inches taller than he was. As a child, Bright conceived of God as "a person looking down on me, ready to conk me on the head with a thunderbolt." Perhaps this is why he, his mother's favorite, was such a frightened child. He clung to his mother's skirts, he feared the dark, and his mother told the Study, "Since Dylan has been old enough to think, he has been afraid of death."

Professor Bright was also frightened of his own energy. His difficulty in controlling his instincts dated back before his near expulsion from high school. From the beginning, his mother had taught him to beware of instinctual pleasure. Like Lieutenant Keats, before his first birthday Bright was cured of thumbsucking, bedwetting, and soiling himself. At two, his mother made him wear mittens to bed because "of his perfectly revolting habit of masturbating."

In his lifelong quest to conquer fear, Dylan Bright first left his mother's skirts to become a daredevil quasi-delinquent. As a youth he got more cerebral concussions than anybody else in the Study. Then, with the passage of time, his mastery became more graceful. After eighteen, he learned to do what he called "responsibly adventurous things"; and there were no further injuries. From an all-state football lineman in high school, he became a fiercely competitive college wrestler. Playing tennis for blood, he shunned doubles for the joy of single combat. After college, his fierce devotion to tennis and wrestling was replaced by an equally fierce devotion to poetry; but he was still out to win. Despite average intellectual equipment, he raced through Yale graduate school with absolutely top grades. He accepted an appointment at Princeton for the prestige and a few years later exulted in his early acquisition of academic tenure.

The capacity of Bright's ego to discover creative solutions had not always been so remarkable. His first efforts at overcoming his fears had been through passive-aggressive rebellion, reminiscent of Dr. Smythe's whole life or of Lieutenant Keats's middle-aged regression. As he matured, Bright replaced rebellion with *reaction formation*. Suddenly, Bright found the first girl with whom he had slept "revolting." Unconsciously, he had chosen the same word that his mother had used to condemn his sexual experimentation in infancy. Ascetically, he gave up intercourse with his next girl friend "just to see if I could." In college, the once-delinquent Bright seriously considered undertaking a career in law-enforcement, and as a young and lusty English instructor at Princeton, his devotion to enforcing the parietal rules irritated the student body and surprised the administration. Even in middle life, Professor Bright had conceived of his success in terms of rigid control: "If a person does not have self-discipline," he cautioned me, "he can go to rot so fast."

However, Bright was wrong. With rigid defenses, his life would have been a disaster. It was when sublimation replaced the reaction formation of his youth that Dylan Bright caught fire. When he risked his amateur standing by wrestling in exhibition matches, he would consecrate his illegal fee by investing it in violin lessons. When at nineteen he resolved to abstain from further sexual intercourse, he quickly substituted a close and exciting intellectual friendship and made his first discovery of poetry. He fought to be first in his graduate school class, but he gentled his ambition by writing his Ph.D. thesis on the poetry of Shelley.

The critical period in Bright's life occurred at age thirty-five when, at his wife's initiative, what had been a very close marriage began to break up. This failure occurred at the same time that he became aware that his scholarship, although adequate to win tenure at Princeton, would never win him national recognition. Faced by these two very real defeats, he lost himself in alcohol, careless affairs, and stock car racing — the poetry professor regressed to adolescent acting out. As in college, Bright quickly replaced these adult delinquencies with more graceful quests for excitement. Although he remained close to all his children, he went scuba diving off the Barrier Reef and mastered Australia's most challenging surfing beaches. In the company of a close friend he plunged into the Amazon jungle to hunt for orchids — the most sensual of flowers. With great delight, he described that he and his friend had discovered an entirely new species of orchid. "Oh," he told me, "that was a heady experience!"

Professor Bright's adaptive responses were ingenious indeed. His withdrawal from marital defeat brought him into close friendship with another person. His withdrawal from academic defeat involved him in activities that permitted him to master danger with minimum risk, and at the same time to anesthetize grief with real excitement. Sublimation not only facilitated the efficient expression of his instincts, it also permitted Bright to avoid the labels of "neurotic" or mentally ill. Like Dr. Smythe, Bright had described himself as a "laughing man. I just let things slip off my back. I laugh at trouble." But unlike Smythe, Bright did not permanently drown his troubles in alcohol or in self-destructive chance-taking. Twice in his life, in order to control incipient alcoholism, Bright had had to go on the wagon; and after his father died, a staff member had described Bright's response as "hypomanic" — a clinical term implying a tendency to frank mania. But in each case Bright's dissociation from painful affect was only temporary. Sublimation enabled him to accept the terms life offered. He remained in touch with his feelings while softening them with excitement, laughter, and people. Bright was asked if he had ever seen a psychiatrist. Referring to his best friend and to his second wife, his reply was, "Professional assistance would be a pale shadow compared to these companions." Like art, intimacy is an act of creation, but intimacy far surpasses art as a cure for emotional suffering.

A final and very important facet of sublimation is that it permits the counterfeit fantasies of a Mr. Lamb to achieve real currency in everyday life. The artist is a man who can peddle his most private dreams to others. Although this skill was present in all the successful academicians, it was best exemplified by Professor Ernest Clovis. What was so striking about Professor Clovis was that of all the men in the Study, he had perhaps suffered the most personal tragedy; yet at midlife he could write, "Perhaps I have not struck any particularly rough spots." Unlike Bright, he did not seek comfort through exciting laughter. He did not have Keats's facility to turn all life into a game; rather he had survived by removing himself to the world of medieval France.

I interviewed Professor Clovis in the stacks of Sterling Library at Yale. His was a cramped, almost monastic cubicle filled with old books and manuscripts, and yet enlivened by one bright contemporary print. Clovis himself was a pleasant, good-looking man, his somber gray suit unexpectedly brightened by a flamboyant orange tie. As he talked to me, he often looked away; and initially, I experienced him as cold. But his self-discipline impressed me more than his emotional rigidity, and I soon realized that he was a very private and self-contained individual whose banked emotional fires provided inner light. I learned that talking about people depressed him, but that the discussion of ideas would bring a smile to his face.

Nevertheless, I was often deeply moved by what Clovis said;

and if his scholarship was at times a means to master chronic depression, he had much to be depressed about. When he told me of his father's death four years previously, his eyes filled with tears. As he hastened to assure me, "At the time of my father's death I had to suppress my feelings." When he talked of the tragedy of his first wife's illness, he became distant, acutely anxious, and distressed. When he talked of his happier second marriage, he became warm and maintained eye contact.

An only child, Clovis had grown up in an austere, religious farming community. He alleged that he had achieved an enjoyable relationship with both his parents, but if his parents seemed spiritually generous, he also felt them to be emotionally constricted. He grew up without any physical affection, and his mother revealed to the Study staff that "very early Ernest developed qualities of self-reliance." In college, he had impressed observers as showing very little emotional color. In those years the bright necktie that caught my eye was not yet visible. Some men with childhoods similar to Clovis's had become emotionally frozen adults. They worked in fields that concerned the physical sciences and led rigid lives devoid of observable pleasure. Instead, Clovis was to become not only a distinguished medievalist, a first-rate squash player, and a good father; but after fifteen years of marriage he and his second wife agreed that they still enjoyed "a very satisfactory" sex life.

As a child, Clovis had found comfort in fantasy. Since his family permitted selfishness in none of its members, he acquired an imaginary playmate whose outstanding trait was selfishness. Not only did this imaginary companion provide friendship to a geographically isolated little boy, but also the playmate had the marvelous knack of always getting one up on the boy's dominating father. As he grew up, Clovis found fresh ways to bring pleasure into a cerebral life. Real games took the place of fantasy. He learned to beat his father in tennis, and through this sport they became close. In college many of the more inhibited scholarship boys rationalized their lack of dates by pleading lack of money. In contrast, the equally impecunious Clovis was very successful with the opposite sex. He entertained his dates by taking them to art museums, which were free.

During World War II Clovis had fought with Patton's army

through France, and afterward he felt an emotional pull to the people and the culture. Unlike several classmates, he did not become involved in tangible postwar efforts to rebuild Europe. Instead he became a scholar of the France that once had been. He enjoyed plowing through medieval manuscripts, mastering archaic languages, and reconstructing an imaginary world that was no more tangible than his childhood playmate. But he also managed to connect his fantasy with the real world. From the flintstone of his intellect, he struck sparks of marketable excitement. In so doing, Clovis illustrates a critical aspect of the creative process. For there is no one lonelier than the artist whose work speaks to no one, and no life is less appreciated than that of the scholar who cannot relate his facts to life.

Clovis always received the most prestigious scholarships for his graduate work, the warmest accolades of his instructors, and offers of tenure from great universities. He could also say, "I have developed a sense of mission that I may contribute to this country a better appreciation of France's social and political values — not just of her literary and historical contributions." As a teacher, an author, and a scholar, his career was an unqualified success.

Despite vocational victory, disaster struck. His first wife was stricken with encephalitis, which distorted her personality and rendered her permanently bedridden. As a Catholic, he felt divorce was forbidden; and yet his marriage became progressively and mutually more painful. Since neither parent had ever shown emotion, Clovis had learned early that emotions were private. Stoically, he wrote to the Study of the "minor frustration caused by my wife's encephalitis . . . to discuss it further with my parents would only make them unhappy. . . . I sometimes feel desire to discuss these problems with some of my wife's women friends, but I have never done this because it would seem like complaining." But he mastered his reserve. He did form close substitute relationships with women, and after his wife's death remarried happily.

Before his wife's illness, contemporary theater had been a shared hobby for the Clovises. When through her illness Ernest Clovis was forced to attend plays by himself, he became passionately interested in classical French dramatists. Early in his wife's illness Clovis had been on the verge of a divorce that his conscience would not countenance. It was at that point in his life he chose to translate from the French "the romantic tragedy of the hopeless love of a married man and a prostitute, both of whom chose to commit suicide rather than to be false to their love." This ascetic professor, who in the light of day could not permit himself tears, found himself weeping in darkened theaters at plays which to most English-speaking people were of only historical importance. "I cry along with the old ladies," he confessed, "and feel thrilled by the experience." But unlike Dr. Tarrytown, Clovis did not keep his source of comfort secret. At Yale he brought the French theater vividly to the awareness of all his students.

Five years ago Clovis's daughter became afflicted with lupus erythematosus, a poorly understood disease which causes arthritis, irreversible kidney damage, and episodic emotional instability. He was affectively aware of his daughter's peril and the awful years with his first wife were again before him. But Clovis had developed at least one area of his life where he could always maintain control. He wrote that he felt "enthusiastic" about the future because of the scholarly writing he had planned. He added, "The language of the material you read has an emotional, aesthetic satisfaction."

In my own interview with Clovis, I felt that the only disaster that could crush this man would be the failure of his intellectual creativity. Unable to communicate his secret world of medieval France to others, he might have become deeply depressed. However, as long as he could maintain sublimated scholarship, he could also retain his animal vigor and *joie de vivre*.

Professor Clovis, Lieutenant Keats, and Professor Bright were not among the best outcomes in the Study. A psychiatrist could see psychopathology and the student of healthy adjustment could find flaws in all. Each man showed personality traits that could have brought despair to himself or made him appear neurotic to others. Nevertheless, each, at least for a while, transformed his shortcomings into behavior that brought sensual pleasure — but pleasure that conformed with the realities of the universe. John Keats, the poet, put it differently: "Beauty is truth, truth, beauty — that is all ye know on earth and all ye need to know."

Chapter 7

Suppression, Anticipation, Altruism, and Humor

> Maturity is the ability to postpone gratification.
>
> — Attributed to Sigmund Freud

Adaptation to life means continued growth. If some styles of coping are to be judged relatively healthy, they must contribute to the continued development of the individual. There were six men who were seen as psychologically very sound in college but who subsequently made poor adult adjustments; all used many immature defenses. Conversely, four men perceived as psychologically very vulnerable in college enjoyed excellent life adjustments; all of these men used predominantly mature defenses.

The example of Grant Study subject Mayor Timothy Jefferson illustrates the interrelationship between mature adaptation and continued growth, for Jefferson was a man who improved and mellowed like a good wine. Originally, the deans had recommended him to the Study on the basis of his high school letter of recommendation: "Tim is a boy who knows where he is going and how to get there." When they actually saw him, the Grant Study staff were not impressed. They saw a youth who was "conscientious, reserved, and lacking in charm." The internist called him "tense, stiff, colorless, cold, immature, . . . a just-so person."

At nineteen, Timothy Jefferson neither smoked nor drank; he seemed incapable of getting angry, and his bland psychological adjustment had been judged only average. At first meeting, the psychiatrist saw him as "extremely inhibited, passive . . . he prefers abstract ideas to people." Three years later, the internist relented a little and called Jefferson "emotionally stable, internally content, and externally successful." But he still felt Tim was too serious and that he lacked a sense of humor. Five years later, the picture changed further; the law school dean summed Jefferson up as displaying "an abundant amount of energy." Two more years passed, and another Study internist familiar with Jefferson's case record wrote, "considerable change in him, because he is now definitely outgoing, easy to talk with, and has an extremely pleasant manner."

Almost every questionnaire asked the men what they liked best about their jobs, and the sequential change in Jefferson's answers to these questions underscored his maturation; over the years, he moved from valuing things toward valuing people. At twenty-five he had said that he liked "solving problems" best. At thirty he liked best "doing what has to be done." At forty it was "administration" that he liked. And at forty-seven it had become "working with people." Without having lost his earlier qualities of justice and perseverance, this colorless teenager had grown into a humane, clear-thinking politician.

The same family worker who had found the adolescent Jefferson "reserved and lacking in charm" wrote when he was forty-five, "I had a delightful talk with Timmy; we laughed at length over his failure to complete the questionnaire."

In 1969, when I interviewed him, Jefferson was the mayor of a Long Island suburb. In keeping with his previous personality, he arrived at my office within sixty seconds of the appointed time; but he now wore a well-tailored suit and a distinguished, graying mane. He looked far more like a political fat cat than a boy scout grown up. His manner was easy, and the former ascetic was now a man who dearly loved his pipe. Except for moments when he would close his eyes, pinch his nose, and appear deep in thought, he maintained eye-to-eye contact. Although still serious, he was now very much aware of the world and open to it. He appeared solid, confident, articulate, and yet sensitive toward others. There was no longer an aura of the abstract about him; instead, he saw the world as Mr. Goodhart did, entirely in terms of people. The adolescent blandness was gone. When amused, he was now able to laugh wholeheartedly; and when he was sad during the interview, he had to blow his nose because of tears.

However, what impressed me most about Jefferson was his capacity to meet adversity directly. In adult life, the two greatest obstacles he had had to surmount were the rigidity and emotional constriction of his early character and his daughter's affliction with cystic fibrosis, a disease that greatly shortened her life expectancy. To master these difficulties, he used *altruism, anticipation*, and *suppression*.

Jefferson's mother had confessed to the Study that she had been unable to tolerate any aggression in her children; as a result, she had ridiculed her son's anger whenever it occurred. The mother of Lieutenant Keats also could not tolerate hostility, and her son had had lifelong difficulty with anger. In contrast, Jefferson responded more flexibly. His first adaptive maneuver, like that of Keats, was *reaction formation* (see Appendix A). For example, in college Jefferson had told the Study that he never got angry; immediately, he followed this remark with a revealing anecdote. That afternoon he had seen a policeman angrily strike a boy; he had come home and let loose a tirade to his family about what he had seen. He added that the only people that he hated were aggressive people. In other words, he hated hating.

As soon as Jefferson discovered how to inject pleasure into reaction formation, it evolved into the more mature defense of altruism. For example, he was unwilling to give up his strict Kansas Baptist background, and throughout his college years he went regularly to church. But he found that regular church-going provided a shy midwesterner the opportunity of making and maintaining college friendships. Church socials became a reliable source of new girl friends.

At thirty-one, Jefferson wrote that the greatest pleasure from his work came from the "worthy contribution of my abilities to a common purpose, and it is recognized by some, at least, as such." At forty-seven, he perceived his greatest achievement was "to get the citizens to run the town, and the town is better for it." He could say this despite having always been a man who relished control, and having enjoyed twenty years of vested interest as the town mayor. This might have been less remarkable had Jefferson himself not been denied independence in childhood.

The blind raters had been so appalled by the rigidity of Jefferson's Kansas parents that they had ranked his childhood in the bottom half of the Study. At nineteen, had he not complained that his mother had been overly strict in regulating his bowel movements? Had she not made him look foolish when he tried to be aggressive? Nevertheless, in middle life, a period when for the first time many men saw their childhoods without rose-tinted glasses, Jefferson described that underneath his mother's stern Great Plains exterior was "a genuine warmth," and his career suggested that he had absorbed from her at least two things. First, in reaction against his upbringing, he had modeled himself on Oliver Wendell Holmes, "because he showed courage, love of truth and humor, and because [unlike Jefferson's mother] he respected the independence of others." At the same time, in creative identification with his overly fastidious mother, Jefferson reported that his greatest source of pride was that he had provided his town with a first-class sewage system.

As a coping mechanism, anticipation permits the user to become affectively aware of an event before it happens and thus attenuates associated anxiety and depression. In some ways, anticipation is synonymous with what psychiatrists call insight. Even at fourteen, Jefferson had the capacity to view himself as others saw him. He made a conscious effort not to be so shy. At eighteen, he decided not to have sexual relations before marriage "because it would upset me a great deal." Many of the members of the Study unconsciously felt as he did; but in contrast to Jefferson they placed the blame for their fears outside themselves and cited as their chief emotional stumbling blocks their fears of pregnancy and of venereal disease. At twenty-seven, Jefferson was one of the very few men who could candidly admit to the Study that he was frightened of getting married. His style of mastery, however, was to spend all his spare time preparing for marriage; he did all the carpentry and the painting in the apartment in which he and his bride were to live. Like Mithridates protecting himself against poison, Jefferson prepared for marriage by a regimen of small anticipatory doses. He said that his reason for remaining a small-town mayor was that early in life he realized he was both too ethical and too fearful of aggression for competitive political life. However, he wished to work in government because that would balance his introversion and let him work with people.

Throughout his life, Jefferson has remained an overqualified big frog in a small but appreciative pond; for his capacity for anticipation offered Jefferson more than just insight into his emotional vulnerabilities. This mode of adaptation permitted him throughout life to be overprepared. With both a Harvard law degree and a master's degree in public administration, he was the best-trained mayor on Long Island. As a means of resolving difficulties with others in town government, he practiced listening to his employees, and he systematically utilized his graduate courses in labor law. The increasingly generous salary voted him by the taxpayers gave testimony to his success.

Mayor Jefferson was also the master of *suppression*. As he got to know the Grant Study staff better, Jefferson confessed that he was not devoid of the anger that his mother proscribed; rather, although nobody ever saw him angry, "I bubble and boil inside." (Compare this to Dr. Tarrytown, whose life was filled with angry acts, but who never consciously felt the emotion.) During the war Jefferson knew that he did not like the navy, but he never complained. On one occasion Jefferson knew that he was so angry at a superior officer that he was likely to strike him. He kept his peace, but later consciously shared his anger with a fellow officer. In other words, he held on to his anger until he could release it safely. Another time he watched an enemy torpedo glide into his ship. With a composure that amazed his enlisted men, he put his energies into restoring order and then slept well that night. Jefferson was quite conscious of anticipatory anxiety before his marriage, and accordingly refused to answer a Grant Study questionnaire; he wrote, "I would like to defer answering this . . . the matter has become of serious concern to me so very recently that my thoughts are currently in a state of flux." But later, Jefferson remembered to tell the Study how he had felt. In contrast to suppression, both repression and passive aggression indefinitely postpone the unpleasant.

When I asked Jefferson at forty-seven what was most difficult about his job, his characteristic response was, "I'm not sure what you mean. I hope I'm not immodest, but nothing is difficult in terms of competence to deal with the problem. I don't find myself facing that kind of situation." When I asked him about problems at work, he told me first what wonderful employees he had. Then, he summed himself up by saying that he had a "strong streak of patience. I can go a long way with people before I lose my cool."

I asked him about his children, and he told me that his daughter had cystic fibrosis. He said, "No one is willing to predict the course of her affliction." I asked him how he had mastered the discovery of his daughter's diagnosis. "It was a pretty rough blow to learn about it." Blowing his nose, he added, "I took it harder than my wife. We were fortunate in having an excellent doctor. He was great in showing us how to handle the disease. My wife gets all the credit. We decided not to treat it as a problem." In other words, while acknowledging the dangers and his own emotional upset and without fending off my questions (as members of the Study often did), he had nevertheless told me the bright side. There was a treatment plan that could be followed for cystic fibrosis, and the people by his side were wonderful. He *said* he did not treat it as a problem, but in fact, the way he *behaved* was perfectly realistic. Jefferson was at peace with his conscience, his instincts, his reality, and the people who mattered to him. He saw the terms life offered clearly and he accepted them.

As he left the interview, Jefferson confided to me with ingenuous pleasure the fact that at last he had learned how to fight with his wife. "Surprisingly," he reported, "fighting has improved our sexual adjustment." From twenty-five years of observation, it had already been clear that he had built one of the most stable marriages in the Study. Now he had learned to enjoy it.

By turning to the lives of other men, it is possible to examine in depth the four mature mechanisms: altruism, anticipation, suppression, and humor.

Altruism involves getting pleasure from giving to others what you yourself would like to receive. It is an adaptive outgrowth of reaction formation, a defense mechanism that allows a user outwardly to steer a course exactly counter to some inner unconscious passion. Rarely an unalloyed virtue, altruism nevertheless provides a protective filter for the most searing emotions. Many Study members who had defensively denied themselves pleasure when young never became completely comfortable with their own passions; but they learned to derive pleasure from helping others enjoy the very instincts that made themselves uneasy.

Dr. Jacob Hyde illustrated this relation between altruism, inner turmoil, and reaction formation. Dr. Hyde was a paradoxical man, and the source of this paradox arose from his extensive use of reaction formation. The very passions that raged strongest in him were the ones that he kept under most rigid rein. Interviewing this intense, balding, powerfully built man was like making small talk with a smoldering volcano. A slow-burning cigar was never far from his Churchillian jowls. A problem for Jake Hyde, as for other altruists, was that he knew so much more about the warmth and richness of life than he could participate in himself. Originally, the Grant Study summary had described Hyde as "lacking energy . . . pathetically serious-minded and unimaginative," and his medical school dean had referred to him as "a rather colorless personality." In contrast, the Grant Study internist who really knew him suggested that "more goes on under the surface than one sees"; and a skilled clinician who had given Hyde extensive psychological tests wrote, without equivocation, "Hyde is a passionate man."

There was more overt mental illness in Hyde's family than in almost any in the Study, and the blind raters gave the childhoods of only ten other men a lower rating. At six, Jake Hyde had sadistically mistreated cats; but by the time he was fifteen, he was condemning his father, "a great big fellow, and pretty forceful," for mistreating a hunting dog. At the same age, however, Hyde's own earlier cruelty was only barely leashed. Thus, he chose to spend the summer in a slaughterhouse to ensure that the work was done as painlessly as possible.

His life was filled with risk-taking. He exclaimed, "I love storms, and would go out in the worst of them!" Then, when he came to college, his risk-taking suddenly vanished from sight. Jake Hyde was one of the very few boys in the Study to take no part at all in college athletics, and he assured the Study that he had never been hurt. (In fact, in his early teens he had been rather badly bitten by a German shepherd that he had unwisely provoked; but as Hyde said, "I make it a point to forget unpleasant things.")

The underlying conflict that elicited Hyde's anger and his subsequent reaction formation against that anger was the fact that in many ways he had suffered under his mother, who in turn, as in Greek drama, had been tortured by her mother. In college this conflict was so secret that Hyde's overt filial devotion led to the comment, "His attachment to his mother is as reverential and enduring as that of any subject examined in the clinic." Allegedly, Hyde's mother had a "radiant personality," and "bore pain without murmuring." But the Study staff never got to meet her face to face; she was in too much pain to come downstairs to meet the social investigator. After her home visit to Hyde's father, the family worker had written, "I felt there must be a problem somewhere, but I could not unearth it."

The problem was that there was no good evidence that Mrs. Hyde's "pain" was ever real. Mrs. Hyde had led her son to believe that his birth was the cause of her infirmities. In her son's eyes, these ills were of such magnitude that he revealed, "Ever since I was a kid, I've wanted to be a doctor and fix her up." In adolescence Hyde engaged in religious rituals in order that his mother should not die. In the eyes of the Study physicians, however, her ills were so patently hypochondriacal that even in absentia she was diagnosed as neurasthenic. At forty-five, Dr. Hyde wrote, "My mother's health is as good as ever." In midlife he had insight into the fact that she had used her many imagined ills to establish a tyrannical control over all her sons.

Before his marriage, Hyde had used reaction formation against more than just anger. In college he said he "lost all respect for people who drank." In part, he was drawn to medicine to mother a mother who had not mothered him; and in part because, he said, "Doctors [in sharp contrast to his father and himself as a child] do not hurt people." The staff, however, feared that his earlier sadism might continue. The internist had written, "If given power, which I doubt he would be, I think Hyde could be stubborn and even dangerously aggressive."

Due quite probably to Hyde's capacity to transform reaction formation into altruism, the internist's fears proved groundless. Instead, Hyde spent his life devoted to his family and to the service of man, and the potential for Sophoclean tragedy was averted. But to achieve this, the ingenuity of Hyde's ego was sorely taxed; for until the user has something for which to be genuinely grateful, altruism proves too difficult a psychological balancing act. (As an adolescent, Dr. Tarrytown had tried to become an altruistic psychiatrist without having been first given a "leg up," and succeeded only in fantasy.) Ostensibly, Dr. Hyde had gone into medicine to mother his mother; but not until he himself finally married a nurse was Dr. Hyde's anger truly replaced by altruism. Miraculously, after Hyde's marriage the interviewer could remark that he and his wife "seemed the gayest couple interviewed so far." And, after his marriage Hyde himself was able to write, "I owe the world so much more than it owes me; I only hope that I may repay some of this tremendous debt." In short, at nineteen, Hyde tried to atone for his sins; at twenty-five, he offered to pay for his blessings.

After completing his medical training, the paradoxical nature of his life became further revealed. Hyde withdrew from the practice of medicine in order to obtain a Ph.D. in pharmacology — allegedly to serve the world in the laboratory rather than at the bedside. But after obtaining his degree, he accepted a position at the Edgewood Arsenal in Maryland. Here the army was hard at work on "nerve gases," which could kill invisibly, odorlessly, and almost instantly. Dr. Hyde found this laboratory a good place to pursue his own research in acetylcholine, the chemical transmitter of impulses from nerve to nerve and from nerve to muscle. He took careful, perhaps overscrupulous pains to see that his own research could never be used to harm, only to heal. After all, he had studied medicine to save his mother, not to slay her.

Throughout his thirties, Jacob Hyde experienced the struggle shared by many basic scientists — how to devote more of themselves to people and less to test tubes. His solution in his forties was to leave Edgewood Arsenal and to return to a university setting. Here he tried to use his sophistication in pharmacology to consult to the World Health Organization, to brainstorm cures for schizophrenia, and to try to supply a human element to discussions of disarmament. Nevertheless, because of his intimate knowledge of nerve gases, he also continued as a consultant to the United States Army.

Like many another altruist, when asked at forty-six with whom he discussed his personal problems, Hyde replied "I find I usually assume the position of recipient in such discussions from other people." When his father died, Hyde raced to his mother's side. In order to comfort her he put his own very real grief aside. The lesson of this experience for him was to teach him "the value of having someone else to care for, to occupy one's own thoughts and to keep from brooding."

In the course of an altruistic life, Jake Hyde had achieved much of the power that he had sought. He was an expert in the effects of the deadliest poisons known to man, and yet he had used his knowledge only in the service of men. In contrast to Dr. Tarrytown, Dr. Hyde never became immobilized by the fear of his own aggression. He did not need to relegate it to the safer world of fantasy. Nevertheless, as is the case with martyrs and saints — the specialists at altruism — Hyde remained passionate in only one area of his life: religion. As an adolescent, he was described as "unswervingly religious"; and as a very controlled forty-five-year-old he confessed "My religious feelings are still rather intense." Since altruism is fueled with just as intense an energy as artistic creation, saints and martyrs barely avoid falling into the devil's lair. Surely, Hyde had beaten swords into plowshares, but for a peacemaker, he had kept dangerous company.

The defense of anticipation involves premature but mitigating emotional awareness of future inner discomfort. For half a century psychoanalysts failed to label this process an unconscious adaptive mechanism. However, in the 1950s, as psychiatrists began the deliberate study of healthy adaptation, they discovered that moderate amounts of anxiety before future events promoted adaptation. David Hamburg and his colleagues at the National Institute of Mental Health studied the psychologically healthy parents of children with leukemia and healthy college students away from home for the first time.[1] Irving Janis studied psychologically healthy patients awaiting surgery.[2] Psychiatrists responsible for preparing Peace Corps volunteers for overseas assignments studied the facets of training programs that most contributed to subsequent adaptation.[3] All learned to appreciate the value of anticipatory anxiety and of anticipatory grief. In fact, future success among Peace Corps volunteers was predicted more on their capacity to map out future anxieties than on their apparent emotional stability on psychological tests.

As the Study subjects matured, so did their use of intellectualization; anticipation became a means by which involuntary worrying and passionless rumination over future danger could be used to advantage. Of the nineteen men who most used anticipation, all enjoyed their jobs greatly; none ever visited a psychiatrist; only one took as much as five days of sick leave a year; and all but four had happy marriages. More than anything, anticipation reflects the capacity to perceive future danger clearly and by this means to draw its teeth.

More than anyone in the Study, William Forsythe had this special capacity for emotional foresight. Bill was a troubleshooter for the state department, and his specialty was Southeast Asia. I first met him at a time when the crises with which he grappled were making daily headlines. Handsome, charming, sure of himself, Forsythe reminded me of no one so much as Rex Harrison. He was relaxed, energetic, and his ungraying sideburns rendered him young for his age. Yet at the time of the interview, no man in the Study danced on a hotter vocational griddle.

Most of the men whose jobs required that they take an Olympian view of life became inured to many needs of the individual, but what impressed me most about Forsythe was his articulate capacity to describe the people in his life. I marveled that a man so enmeshed in major social issues could himself appear so terribly human.

Forsythe's alert awareness dated back at least to his first Grant Study interview. At this time, the psychiatrist described him as being "like a greyhound before a race"; he observed that "Forsythe has a great sense of humor . . . inspires confidence . . . appears stable and dependable . . . and has drive, energy, and forcefulness." But because Forsythe used prevention (anticipation) rather than cure, it is not possible to illustrate the conflicts in his life as dramatically as those in other lives. In college, he had mastered his exams by making a careful outline of what should be studied in advance. The psychiatrist remarked, "Bill has given a great deal of thought of how one should meet life . . . his thoughts are well-organized and presented." Two years later, Forsythe dealt characteristically with World War II; he became an infantry line officer. His superiors described him as "an impressive officer who systematically analyzes each problem, employs clear thinking, and insists upon nothing but an excellent job." In battle, only unexpected danger gave Forsythe the shakes. When asked what opportunities he was sacrificing through his military service, he wrote back "I am sacrificing no opportunities; if anything, I am creating them."

After the war, Forsythe did not rest; instead he wrote, "I have a pressing desire as well as an urgent need to discover the special field where I shall be able to do my best work." Eighteen months later his career was settled, and he never worried about it again. At thirty-seven, "feeling a need for a broader spiritual and philosophical context in which to order one's life," Forsythe started going to church. From then on his religious commitment steadily grew. The anxieties of middle life were mastered before they began.

At forty-seven, Forsythe was systematically identifying and planning response to the agonizing problems that confronted the United States in Southeast Asia. He worked from a vantage point that provided him with an overview not available to those on the firing line in Saigon, but he had not completely isolated himself from the passions of the real world. Whereas presidents like Johnson and Nixon, who could not easily acknowledge their own anxieties, found student demonstrations threatening, in 1968 Forsythe wrote that hippies and student protesters were "symptomatic of a society in rapid transition . . . the important thing is how society responds to these symptoms." Although he was no stranger to the White House, Forsythe did not advocate our military escalation in Vietnam.

Anticipation is undoubtedly a mechanism that is enhanced by psychoanalysis and long-term psychotherapy; and, to a limited extent, anticipation means the capacity consciously to tolerate feelings that other ego mechanisms would keep from view. Through state department inservice training, Forsythe had had to learn about group psychodynamics. He consciously applied what he had learned at work about group dynamics to mastering emotional conflicts as they arose within his own family. Although he never visited a psychiatrist, Forsythe was able to use the fruits of psychological insight more effectively than many men who had sought therapy.

Humor is one of the truly elegant defenses in the human repertoire. Few would deny that the capacity for humor, like hope, is one of mankind's most potent antidotes for the woes of Pandora's box. As Freud suggested, "humor can be regarded as the highest of these defensive processes. It scorns to withdraw the ideational content bearing the distressing affect from conscious attention as repression does, and thus surmounts the automatism of defense."[4] Like anticipation and suppression, humor allows both the idea and the affect to coexist in consciousness.

However, it is difficult to study humor; and so much of humor is lost in the retelling. Unlike conflicts masked by repression or reaction formation, conflicts mastered by humor do not lie dormant waiting to reemerge. Over time the stoicism of Marcus Aurelius, the projection of Hitler, or the sublimation of Da Vinci or Beethoven becomes highly visible. But humor is short-lived. Like a rainbow, even when reliably perceived, it forever evades our grasp.

The data of the Grant Study were collected under circumstances that made it difficult to document humor as a major defense, but in the adaptive style of several men humor could be discerned as a leitmotiv. I suspect it was more than coincidence that the four Grant Study members who had been editors of the college humor magazine had all in childhood lost a parent through death. By way of explaining a summer spent with his alcoholic mother, one former humor magazine editor wrote to the Study, "My mother got on after a fashion, after an old-fashioned." Unhappy at home and very shy with girls, his idea of entertaining a member of the Study staff ten years older than himself was to take her to the circus. Four years later, during the Battle of the Bulge, this man found himself in a farmhouse surrounded on three sides by the Germans. He turned to a companion and asked, "Isn't this just like a Grade-B western!" Cut off by the Germans' winter offensive, it was not easy for the Americans in the Ardennes to bathe. But he found time to write home to the Grant Study, "God, if my grandmother only knew she'd turn over in her grave. Her grandson with fleas!"

In wit, clowning, and caricature, emotional affect is displaced or concealed. True humor conceals nothing, but as Freud suggested, "Humor is a means of obtaining pleasure in spite of the distressing affects that interfere with it."[5] Such a process could be seen in one man's mastery of his father's sudden death. "I remember even before the funeral appreciating the humor of my father's situation. He enjoyed life and became involved in each aspect of life with enthusiasm. I keep a snapshot of him taken a few hours before his death, photographed with a fish that he had caught that afternoon — the largest he had ever caught — and he was very happy. . . . Since that time my sense of bereavement has gradually disappeared, and a feeling of companionship remains, much as it was in the last ten years or so of his life. I don't think about him very often, but sometimes he seems very near."

A third man used humor in his effort to master his lifelong hatred of authoritarian behavior. Although during the war he was perfectly miserable with military discipline, he wrote hysterically funny letters home about his dilemma; *and* he received excellent efficiency ratings. His response to the Grant Study question "What would you most like your children to have that you didn't?" was to write, "Someone to look after their children." When asked to describe "the chief hobbies that you have developed," he replied, "I have developed considerably less spare time." In response to my inopportune demand for two hours of precious time during his twenty-fifth class reunion, he replied as follows:

> Dear Dr. Vaillant:
>
> Upon receiving your earnest plea I repaired once more to the well-thumbed instruction book for the 25th Reunion — I might also say the Bible of '42. The result of my exhausting endeavors was simply one more frustration. . . . While it is quite true that if anyone participates in all the activities from Sunday through Thursday he will probably be in need of a psychiatrist; on the other hand, if two hours can be found during that time, this old mind and body will be looking for a nap.
>
> In all seriousness, the program is so varied and so interesting that there appear to be very few spans of two hours which do not overlap more than one activity, or cut into eating or dressing time. I finally found one period, which is Tuesday afternoon, June 13th, between 2:00 and 5:00. I assume that this same period has been noted by everyone else in the study.
>
> In any event, this should partially answer the question you have raised in your closing paragraph —

almost everything continues to interest me, and I overcome difficulties by succumbing to them.

The letter acknowledged the fact that I was inconveniencing him
and that he felt irritated, but at the same time his frank response
left me charmed. A conflict between conscience, instinct, reality,
and another person was engagingly resolved.

In my subsequent interview with him, he spontaneously
brought up the subject of humor. "I use humor to get by in
difficult situations. I use humor to meet and get close to people,
but you have to keep it from being buffoonery . . . what I can't
stand is an issue where I can't laugh." There was no evidence in
the record that his efforts at humor ever demeaned himself. Instead, for thirty years he managed to work productively with a
tyrannical father; and he enjoyed one of the most successful outcomes of the study.

Suppression, with its stoic stiff upper lip and Spartan postponement of gratification, is not as elegant as sublimation; it has
none of the humanity of altruism or humor; unlike anticipation,
suppression is regarded by psychiatrists as a vice, not a virtue.
Suppression is the clumsy DC-3, the dun workhorse, the mundane
Volkswagen of the defenses. Suppression gets you through, but it
always sacrifices beauty for truth. Nevertheless, of all the coping
mechanisms in this book, suppression alters the world the least
and best accepts the terms life offers. When used effectively, suppression is analogous to a well-trimmed sail. Every restriction is
precisely calculated to exploit, not hide, the ultimate effects of
the wind's passions.

Consider the example of Richard Lucky, a man who had enjoyed the most halcyon childhood in the Study. He rarely felt or
admitted subjectively unpleasant moods. His normal life tempo
was to work a sixty-hour week as chief executive officer of two
corporations and then run for six miles on Sunday to relax. However, during World War II, he described a navy diving accident in
the following manner. He was forty feet underwater; his air valve
was jammed; his radio did not work; and he knew that there was
only eight minutes of air left in his diving helmet. He immediately recognized that there was nothing that he could do for

himself. "I thought my end had come . . . struggling would not have helped and used maybe three times as much air. I didn't pray. I merely sat, very much like an old cow, and waited for help — very unhappy." He knew his feelings; he knew they would not help, and so he kept them inside until he was rescued.

Since suppression was the defensive style most closely associated with successful adaptation, it merits detailed discussion. America's poets, among them Robert Frost, Emily Dickinson, and Edwin Arlington Robinson, have sung of the bittersweet benefits of postponed gratification. The perennial fear, however, is that the individual will die or the chance pass before the passion is ever expressed. For of all mature defenses, suppression is most susceptible to overuse. Consider the example of an old-fashioned Yankee in the Study who said, "I am happy with my life and have no complaints. . . . Others most admire me for the fact that I find it easier to laugh than cry." When asked how he handled his stormy marriage, he said, "I bite my lip and let it not be an issue." In actual fact, he had tasted briefly the joys of a great love affair and also too much of the grape. Without discrimination, he had pushed both excesses from him. It was not that he ever doubted the honesty or the intensity of his passion; he did not employ Jake Hyde's reaction formation. He could still vividly recall the pleasure of alcoholic oblivion and he remembered, all too well, that he had once been truly in love. Probably both his family and the close-knit Maine community in which he lived were much the better for his forbearance. But what about him? Well, over rough spots, he said he comforted himself with Thoreau's bitter motto, "The mass of men lead lives of quiet desperation."

Since the ancient Greeks, the wisdom of the Stoic has been suspect. Mr. Goodhart defined suppression well when he wrote, "I'm stoical; it takes a lot to bowl me over. . . . It's not a question of inability to accept and deal with feelings myself but rather it is a tendency to deal with them privately rather than working them through with other people . . . it causes me no discomfort, and in many ways it serves me well, but intellectually I realize its limiting effects."

Shortly before he discovered that he had inoperable cancer, a proper Philadelphian member of the Study had asked his proper

Bostonian cousin, "My God, sometimes I wonder what is the price of keeping it all in?" The price is straightforward. Those who can bite the bullet do not need other anesthesia. Those who used suppression most had the least need for the other defenses in this book; but their lives hurt.

Psychiatrists stress that an intrinsic part of mental health is the frank expression of feelings. Thus, the reader may ask, will not suppression, if practiced too long, have grave consequences on the mental health of the user? Because of its longitudinal nature, the Grant Study provided a means of assessing whether the price of suppression comes too high. Of the ninety-five men in the Study, twenty clearly used suppression as their most prominent defense. These were the Stoics. Then, there were also sixteen men who, in dealing with the stresses of life, appeared unwilling or unable to use suppression at all. These were the Lotus-eaters.

Their comparison is instructive. Among the twenty Stoics, five seemed rather colorless; but among the sixteen Lotus-eaters, there were eight who could be called either schizoid (virtually incapable of intimacy) or chronically depressed. For example, Tarrytown was a lotus-eater; Jefferson, Lion, and Clovis were Stoics.

Not surprisingly, the employment histories of the Stoics were dramatically better than those of the Lotus-eaters; that observation can be dismissed as part of the pathology of the Protestant work ethic. But what about the marriages? In song and legend, life is sweeter for Lotus-eaters. Hoboes and happy hookers have more fun than tight-lipped certified public accountants. Thus, one Stoic described his marriage as "held together by decision, not desire." Another revealed that fifteen years before he had accepted the fact that his marriage was going to be bad forever. "It is clear," he added, "that our principal output is children . . . our sexual life is fairly awful; but once the first year has gone by without any sexual relations, you've made it." To him, his marriage was "like a man with a sick mother . . . you could take care of her or put her in an old age home." He chose to stick it out; and he closed his questionnaire as only a Stoic could: "Incidentally, I'm half to blame."

However, when the marriages of the two groups are systematically compared, suppression seemed more a blessing than a curse. Among the twenty Stoics, only two had been divorced, and only two (cited above) had to survive their marriages with gritted teeth. Eight of the Stoics' but only three of the Lotus-eaters' marriages were judged excellent. The sixteen so-called Lotus-eaters had accounted for ten divorces; and nine Lotus-eaters had sexual adjustments that were "not as good as wished" or even nonexistent.

In myth, stoicism leads to emotional sterility. But this generalization has proved specious in the face of systematic comparison. In college one Stoic had been described by the dean as "not a good mixer" and the "hardest person I ever interviewed." The psychiatrist had said, "He had an inscrutable manner, which makes it difficult to feel into his affective reaction . . . there is a dead quality to his affect." However, if the relationships of the Stoics with their parents, their spouses, and their friends are compared with those of the Lotus-eaters, then there was only *one* Stoic whose human relationships (as assessed by his score on the social adjustment scale — see Appendix C) were as bad as those of *eleven* of the Lotus-eaters. Suppression, like Robert Frost's fences, makes good neighbors.

At twenty-nine, one Stoic was given the Thematic Appperception Test in which he was asked to tell a story about an ambiguous picture. He began with, "Well, this is someone who has probably cried himself to sleep"; then, he tried to change the subject. When the examiner pressed him to continue the story, he began hesitantly, "I just can't think of a story. . . . I just can't do it. . . . I don't know why . . . well, maybe he was turned down on something which was pretty important." Reluctantly, he then told of a long period of separation from his parents in childhood. At forty-seven, when I asked this man about periods of homesickness and separation in his childhood, he minimized them and said that his philosophy of life was, "Get over rough spots or through them, and keep as calm as possible." For him, successful suppression had exacted a heavy price. At nineteen he had been called "a whippet . . . highly trained, extremely sensitive . . . a great deal of sensitivity . . . prefers to deal with things that have to do with feelings." At forty-seven, I was appalled to discover that this erstwhile poet, who once had "the manner of an English prep school boy," could now only show life's calluses. He sported a T-shirt, a tough creased face, and the crude manner and language of Archie Bunker. This artistic college student had evolved into an anxious middle-aged man with the emotional carapace of a New York cabdriver.

Deliberately, I cite the exceptions. In general, the Stoics showed no more emotional constriction than the Lotus-eaters. Only one Stoic, but eight Lotus-eaters, could have been called mentally ill. The latter were five times as likely to have manifested the traits of dependence, passivity, fear of sex, self-doubt, and pessimism. As would follow from the data, but not from our expectations, it was the Lotus-eaters, not the Stoics, who had experienced barren childhoods. The gratified child can postpone gratification, and adults only act "spoiled" if they have received too little love — not too much.

Instead of denying their troubles like Pollyannas, the Stoics actually used less dissociation (neurotic denial) than the Lotus-eaters. Many students of psychosomatic illness predict that to hold in feelings is to risk disease. Certainly, there were men among the Stoics with high blood pressure, ulcers, headaches, and, inevitably, hemorrhoids. But these illnesses occurred with similar frequency among Lotus-eaters. In fact, on most parameters of physical health, the Stoics fared better than the others. For example, under emotional stress, Stoics were significantly less likely than Lotus-eaters to experience — or perhaps to admit to — headaches, constipation, abdominal pain, and insomnia. It was the men from barren childhoods, not the Stoics, who developed hypertension.

The life of Eben Frost brings the mechanism of suppression to life. Eben Frost had grown up in a family that scratched an annual income of $1,000 from a Vermont hillside. Eben would work all summer on his parents' dairy farm, and in the winter would walk three miles to a two-room schoolhouse. He perceived that he was lonely and that someday he wanted a job where he could talk to people. By age ten, in silent rebellion against his farm chores, Eben secretly decided to leave the farm forever. He would go to college and then on to Harvard Law School. And that was exactly what he did.

When I first met him, Frost presented himself as a charming, warm, happy, outgoing man who was terribly interested in people. Despite his calm, Eben Frost was a very different man from Horace Lamb. The way he spoke was unambiguous and incisive, and there was an ease about him that was contagious. He was a good-looking man who conveyed a rich sense of humor, and at forty-five he looked far more like a museum or hospital trustee, more like an old grad at an Ivy League tailgate party, than an impecunious farm boy grown up. In direct contrast to Lamb, all Frost's activities were described in terms of other people. Only when, after an hour, I tried to push Frost to talk freely about emotionally conflicted areas, did there appear to be constricting boundaries to his happiness. Like a balky horse, his manner became less cooperative and more abrupt until I returned the interview to less conflicted material. (In contrast, the implicit permission of the psychiatric interview led men who characteristically used little suppression — especially physicians — to rush on and discuss the painful areas of their lives with candor that was sometimes cathartic and sometimes confessional.)

In the Frost family, there had been little outward warmth; feelings were never discussed; and yet without exactly saying so, the family cared for each other. Although Eben suggested that "the family bonds have been almost entirely lacking insofar as the tie of intimacy is concerned," he may have been too harsh. The father was called "unruffled" and "a great man of character and old world morality." The mother "never let things prey on her mind" and she told the Study little about Eben except that he was "nice to live with. When we had a job around the house to be done with neatness, we called in Eben." Indeed, until he left the farm behind him to go to college, Eben was an extremely helpful child. Unlike Lamb or Tarrytown, Frost learned early to value intimacy. Although in high school he had "run the school" and had been valedictorian, his greatest accomplishment, Eben said, was "the ability to make friends." At college, he preferred team sports; and through all his working life what he enjoyed most about the law was "direct client contact."

When Eben Frost first entered the Grant Study, he was observed to be "well-poised, extremely friendly, very active, forceful, and energetic." At that time, one observer commented, "He still impresses me as being supernormal." The next thirty years did not produce much change.

Even at eighteen, Frost perceived that he paid a price for his self-sufficiency. "Although I hate nobody," he said, "I'm sometimes afraid I can love nobody." He admired "Latin marriages," where he believed couples became completely absorbed in each other. Later he said, "I'm so self-sufficient, or something, that I actually don't have any rough spots. This does not mean that things are perfect, it's just that nothing really bothers me — and I'm well aware that this is not necessarily an ideal constitution — I've been this way all my life." At twenty-five, Frost said, "I'm a very easygoing character." And twenty years later he said, "I'm the most reasonable of men." Nevertheless, he clearly appreciated how his sweet reasonableness could be infuriating to others.

For Frost, suppression was a way of life. At age twenty-one, when he found his military service interfering with his career, he wrote that it "disrupted my plans to a slight extent . . . but war changes the plans of all of us. Besides, it is my contribution to the war effort." Despite many questions about engagement and marriage, his questionnaire answers always left the Grant Study in the dark until one day he wrote, in the laconic mode of Calvin Coolidge, "Married on furlough" — nothing more. In fact, Frost's marriage had been planned for many months.

To the Study's repeated queries about marital problems, Frost wrote, "Only the stupid or the liars will say 'none,' but that is my answer." Twenty years of further follow-up suggests that he was neither dumb nor dishonest. At age thirty he had written that his wife was the person in his life whom he most admired, and at forty-seven he regarded his marriage as stable. His only concern was for the problems that his emotional self-sufficiency made for his wife, but he believed that her personality produced no problems for him.

When his father died, Frost, unlike Tarrytown, went back to the funeral. However, Frost wrote, "Some people pretend that death doesn't exist and use deliberate self-delusion. Going back to the funeral was something that had to be done . . . but there was no point in carrying on. I disagreed violently — not violently, just 100 percent — with their having a wake. . . . I never looked at him when I went there."

But if he kept things inside of him, Frost's health did not suffer.

At eighteen, the internist had noted that he was "in extraordinarily good health." At forty-seven, Frost had still *never* spent a day in the hospital, *never* missed a day from work due to illness, and for over thirty years had always described his overall health as "excellent." But Frost was no Christian Scientist. He had no problem seeking the truth and going for regular physical examinations. As his recent and thorough physical exam documented, his only physical defect was hemorrhoids.

In adaptation to life, Frost certainly fell among the top third in the Study. As a successful New York corporation lawyer, he was almost alone in managing to work only a forty- to fifty-hour week. "My practice doesn't have pressure; I chose a career without tensions. . . . I am the most unpressured person that exists." Difficulties with his colleagues were nonexistent, and he was president of his suburban PTA. Five years previously, discussing his law career, Frost had candidly admitted, "I'm not satisfied, so I am doomed to frustration." During this midlife reassessment, he wished he could have been a creative artist. He comforted himself by designing his own house; and six years later, Frost had so altered his law career that he had gained more of the personal, caring contact that he craved. He was responsible for training the young associates and could say to me enthusiastically, "My job turns me on."

In summary, the findings from all the subjects in the Study showed that suppression and anticipation were the mechanisms most often associated with positive mental health, warm human relationships, and successful careers. These defenses seemed to play only a minor role in the lives of the poorly adapted. In contrast, sublimation and altruism were seen as often among the poorly adapted as among the more successful. But these latter defenses often saved the day and provided (as illustrated by the careers of Bright, Goodhart, and Hyde) safe paths out of the maelstrom of conflict. What differentiates sublimation and altruism from the neurotic defenses (illustrated in the next chapter) is the elegance of the former mechanisms, their flexibility, and their capacity to mitigate future as well as present suffering.

Chapter 8

The Neurotic Defenses

> The earth for us is a place to live in, where we must put up with sights, with sounds, with smells, too, by Jove! — breathe dead hippo, so to speak, and not be contaminated. And there, don't you see? Your strength comes in, the faith in your ability for the digging of unostentatious holes to bury the stuff in — your power of devotion, not to yourself, but to an obscure, backbreaking business.
>
> — Joseph Conrad, *Heart of Darkness*

Perhaps Freud's most original contribution was not his realization that feelings, not ideas, underlay mental illness. Perhaps it was not his discovery that dreams could reflect our lives and that unconscious feelings could govern them: poets had known all this for centuries, if not millenia. Rather, Freud transformed nineteenth-century psychology when he showed us that unusual human behavior could be compensatory and adaptive rather than immoral or deranged. In his 1894 essay "The Neuro-Psychoses of Defense," Freud suggested that feelings could be ingeniously separated from their ideas, their owners, and their objects.[1] The result of such defensive manipulation of feeling was the development of neuroses. In previous chapters, we have seen how mature adaptive mechanisms *modified* feeling, idea, subject, and object without ever totally sacrificing one in favor of the others. Sublimation and altruism channeled feelings; they did not dam them. In this chapter, however, we will see how Freud's neuropsychoses of defense provide "unostentatious holes" in which to bury feelings, ideas, loved ones, and at times even one's self.

I have suggested that five defenses (intellectualization [isolation], repression, displacement, dissociation, and reaction formation) encompass the fundamental mechanisms of psychoneurosis. Isolation underlies obsessions; displacement can lead to phobias and hysterical paralyses; and the two mechanisms together explain compulsions. Dissociation is the mechanism behind fugues and dual personalities, and repression and dissociation together result in hysteria. Finally, reaction formation begets hair shirts and asceticism. What psychiatrists and psychologists too often lose sight of is that neurosis — obscure, back-breaking business that it is — can be used for adaptation as well as for self-defeat. Every subject in the Study used these defenses often, and sometimes to great advantage. In fact, the two men in the Study who displayed virtually no neurotic mechanisms were plagued by continuous conflict. Both diagnosed themselves as "chronically depressed."

Repression is the prototype of all the adaptive mechanisms — if you cannot bear it, forget it. In fact, throughout much of his career Freud used the terms *defense* and *repression* synonymously. "Repression," he wrote, "is the cornerstone on which the whole structure of psychoanalysis rests";[2] and there are still many psychoanalysts who would take issue with my suggestion that repression is merely one defense among many.

Outwardly, repression is characterized by a curious forgetfulness. The amnesia that results from repression is curious because the affect surrounding the idea remains in consciousness and because the repressed idea has an uncanny way of returning — albeit in disguised form. Often, the user of repression can associate to what has been forgotten. At nineteen, one subject said that he could remember nothing of his life before age seven, but simultaneously remarked that poetry "sometimes seems to arrive full blown from my unconscious mind." Years later poetry served as a catharsis for painful, repressed war experiences.

The psychiatrist had remarked of another nineteen-year-old member of the Grant Study, "His memory is very poor for early events." The Study internist remarked, "I was amazed at his lack of memory and utter vagueness about dates." At thirty-two, however, the same member was able to say, "Yes, I recollect the troubles in the family very clearly," and went on to describe, for the first time, terrible parental fights that had plagued his childhood. At forty-seven, he himself developed temper outbursts. He could not divine what caused them; but each time that he mentioned them, his associations led to muted criticism of his wife. At our interview, he amazed me because he could not remember the date of his mother's death, yet she had died only the year before. He said, "It's a funny thing I can't remember," and then started to look through a desk drawer for a clipping, which in turn reminded him of the date. Of course, this associative rummaging through mental drawers is an important facet of psychotherapy and its recovery of repressed memories.

For most of his life, Richard Lucky was a master of healthy repression; perhaps that was why he appeared so fortunate to others. Lucky once wrote, "Fear is our biggest enemy. When I discover myself thinking in a vicious circle of worry, I try to break it by forgetting the whole situation . . . basically I found it most healthy to accentuate the positive and eliminate the negative." Once he returned a questionnaire to the Study with the following remark, "I found this report packed with my papers. It was sealed and ready to be mailed, but somehow it had been misplaced." The facts were that Lucky had received the questionnaire two years before, at a time when his career seemed lost in a blind alley; he did not "remember" to mail it until he had once more redirected his career into a more gratifying area. Once the danger of career stagnation was averted, the repressed could return, and he could share with the Study the account of his previous job dissatisfaction.

At forty-five, Lucky enjoyed one of the best marriages in the Study, but probably not as perfect as he implied when he wrote, "You may not believe me when I say we've never had a disagreement, large or small." During our interview, Lucky had told me that he had also been so fortunate as to have never been hospitalized. His seventeen-year-old son was in the room at the time and reminded his father that he had been hospitalized after breaking his leg ten years before. What is most important, however, was the fact that Lucky's forgetting never got in the way of living.

The life of Richard Stover helps to underscore the fact that repression need not result in neurosis. Dick Stover was a happy, healthy man. When I arrived for an interview, he was in his yard playing catch with his two sons. Putting away his glove, he motioned me into his house. We sat down together in his rustic, comfortable living room, he in a plaid lumber shirt, I in a stuffy business suit. He was a big man, with big hands and the reassuring naiveté that Eben Frost might have kept had he never left Vermont. Stover spoke in a slow, laconic, relaxed way, and radiated an inner peace. His commonsensical, studied calm was reassuring rather than irritating, and it came not from the denial of a Pollyanna but from a man who derived peace of mind by living a simple life free of embellishments. Somehow he had resisted the occupational and social doors opened for him by his college experience. Like Mayor Jefferson, he had chosen to survive as a very well trained frog in a small pond.

Until he graduated from college, Dick Stover was the model of a boy scout, and a virtuoso of repression. He asserted that before he was sixteen he had never had sexual thoughts or feelings. He denied having been sexually curious in high school; and instead, he was shocked and disillusioned to think that his parents had ever had sexual relations. When the Study psychiatrist first asked him about masturbation, Stover said that he could not hear the question. When it was repeated, he replied that he was uncertain what masturbation meant (a unique response). Finally, he dismissed the question by saying that he had never engaged in masturbation except when he was half asleep and lacked the willpower to prevent it. (The Grant Study investigation confirmed the old schoolboy adage; in college ninety percent of the men acknowledged having masturbated, and by age forty-five, most of the remaining ten percent acknowledged having lied.)

In college, Stover's identification was thoroughly masculine; nothing was effeminate about Stover physiologically or in life-style. As the center on his college basketball team, he starred. Since he had never had a girl friend, his incredulous teammates all vied as to who would be the first to fix him up with a date; but throughout college, Stover ingeniously outmaneuvered them. Even during World War II, while stationed in Italy, he managed to meet no girls. No wonder Freud first thought repression was too astonishing to be unconscious.

Soon after returning from Italy, Stover married. He made an excellent and active sexual adjustment, and had no trouble fathering two sons and three daughters. At forty-nine, when I asked him about his early shyness with girls, he had lost all recollection of it. In a way, he resembled many girl-crazy sixteen-year-olds, who have no memory of hating girls in grammar school.

In real life, Stover saw crying as a sign of weakness, but in the movies, tears came easily. He knew that to others he seemed outwardly calm, but confessed, "People don't know what's going on inside." I asked him what did go on, and he said he did not know. He could not even remember his daydreams and said that under stress, "My mind tightens up."

A major thesis of this book is that with time defenses evolve into more mature styles. Thus, as Stover grew older, he became more able to substitute suppression, a relatively flexible and adaptive mechanism, to master his difficulties. Admittedly, the boundary between repression and suppression is no more distinct than the spectral border between yellow and green; one merges imperceptibly with the other. (Freud once said, "I have omitted to state whether I attribute different meanings to the words 'suppressed' and 'repressed'. It should have been clear, however, that the latter lays more stress than the former on the fact of attachment to the unconscious."[3]) Suppression implies an element of choice and a conscious awareness of the affective significance of the idea, and repression does not. At forty-six, Stover's philosophy over rough spots had become: "This too shall pass. Things work out OK as long as one works hard enough to make them come out that way." Often, Stover had to free-associate to discover the source of his emotions. "People insult me," he said, "but don't irritate me. . . . Someone else might punch them." When I asked him how, after being insulted, he felt inside, he admitted, "I don't feel right — then I think, 'Why don't I feel right? It's not physical,' so I figure out the reason and then I try to solve it." He had never seen a psychiatrist, but to master his repression he had learned how to practice a crude sort of self-analysis.

One of the first defenses identified by Freud was isolation. He first described the mechanism in 1894, then buried it in his own memory, then in 1926 wrote that the defense "which we are setting out to describe for the first time, that of isolation, is peculiar to obsessional neurosis."[4] He then defined isolation for the second time. If repression banished the *idea* from consciousness while preserving the *affect*, Freud showed that isolation spared the *idea* and banished the *feeling*. In Freud's words, "The ego succeeds in turning this powerful idea into a weak one, in robbing it of the affect — the excitation with which it is loaded, . . . the idea, now weakened, is left in consciousness, separated from all association."[5] Such is the nature of obsessions. They go around and around in our mind, but they seem so unimportant.

Of all the defense mechanisms, intellectualization (under which I have included the psychoanalytic terms *isolation, undoing,* and *rationalization*) was most clearly associated with a specific character type — the obsessive-compulsive personality.

Histrionic personalities are often expert at repression, and although oblivious to the *idea* of sex, they may radiate animal magnetism. In contrast, a very obsessional subject wrote at twenty-seven, "I'm still trying to determine why I have not yet engaged in sexual relations, for I have no objection to it." Unlike Stover, this subject could keep the *idea* of sex in mind, but the staff perceived him as "one of the most unattractive, unresponsive boys seen in the entire Study . . . flavorless, colorless; he could not even feel the emotion of hunger."

Men who used intellectualization extensively were twice as likely as other men to exhibit traits like perseverance, orderliness, obstinance, parsimony, overscrupulousness, rigidity, and emotional constriction. Compared to the rest of the men in the Study, intellectualizers were far *less* likely to have extramarital affairs and far more likely to have "very satisfying" sexual adjustments with their wives. They were more likely to be without friends and less likely to be without jobs.

Dean Henry Clay Penny was a rational man who saw both sides of every question. Characteristically, he was exactly on time for our appointment. His uniform was a tweed jacket, chamois sleeve patches, a pipe, a bald head, and a no-nonsense aura. His serious demeanor was mitigated by a cheerful twinkle in his eye, and by the fact that he spoke openly and remarkably frankly. The college psychiatrist had rated him high on empathy, and Penny still made a great effort to see my point of view. Thirty years before, he had made an exceptionally good impression on the staff, and I agreed with their descriptive adjectives — "warm, optimistic, sympathetic, frank, charming, and cheerful." But throughout his life there were other character traits that had distinguished Mr. Penny — orderliness, perseverance, rigidity, and thrift. Indeed, it is hard to separate the metaphor of money from the factual lives of such men. Careful cost accounting and money management is done best by people who can totally separate fact from feeling, but they make less amusing dinner companions. At twenty-eight, with a family of four, Penny saved $400 of his $3,600 salary. In midlife, this former scholarship student had accumulated a nest egg of $100,000 — despite having always been generous to charities and never leaving the academic world.

Penny always filled his life with unemotional detail. When his father died, Mr. Penny told the Study it was regrettable because his father had been on the verge of an important raise in salary. Years later, in describing his very real sense of loss over his father's death, he perseverated upon how poor he had been as a graduate student. The idea of poverty replaced the public affect of grief. Privately, Penny wept for his father. Whereas Mr. Stover could not even remember the date of his mother's death, Mr. Penny had written the Study two pages on the events surrounding his mother's illness and death — but never once did he mention his own sadness.

In high school, Mr. Penny had contracted polio. His first response was to "know" that he would get better. He began to pray regularly, not because he was particularly devout, but because prayer was a way of intellectually willing things to happen. Since he could no longer play baseball, he became the team manager with an encyclopedic grasp of baseball statistics. In college, this once-athletic boy was still slower than almost everyone else in his class. He gave up tennis singles to become a ranking squash player. His game was built on tactical planning, stamina, and perseverance.

Unlike Stover, Penny could not extrude ideas from his mind; he had to see both sides of a question; and so, his life was filled with doubts and self-criticism. That made it hard to make decisions. In the era of Joseph McCarthy, this defense became an asset. When emotional political polarization clouded the minds of many, Penny, with his Ph.D. in modern history, could argue the capitalist and communist positions with equal clarity. Later, he used the same skills in the 1960s to conciliate students and faculty. His academic career was brilliant, but in graduate school Henry Penny regretted that his intellectual work increasingly isolated him from his friends.

Since the beginning of history, ritual has been a device to separate ideas from terrifying feelings; and, like many otherwise rational men, Penny showed reliance on ritual. At twenty-five, he had severe attacks of asthma. He found that he could avert them by using a specific brand of inhaler. Later, he discovered that simply carrying the inhaler with him at all times was amulet enough to keep the asthma at bay. Penny said of his wife, "We have found that we can't maintain a disagreement when we say our prayers together at the end of the day. This is one ritual we promised each other to maintain." His marriage has prospered for thirty years. Just after Penny completed the 1951 questionnaire, his father died. Because of this chance connection, a year later Penny was reluctant to complete the 1952 questionnaire. "The more I think about it," he explained, "the more I believe in accidents and fate." And so, at forty-six, in telling me that his health was very good, Penny knocked on wood.

Unlike more exhibitionistic men who seek fame, repress dangers, and cannot wait to see their names in lights, intellectualizers often fear that to be too prominent in other men's eyes will arouse dangerous feelings. Mr. Penny was an excellent and loyal lieutenant, and much of his scholarship was published under the names of others. Like many intellectualizers, his capacity for hard work was highly valued. He never took direct part in the actions and passions of his time; instead, his whole career had been devoted first to the academic study of politics and then to the mediation of academic politics. Like Mr. Goodhart, Dean Penny became an expert in human relations.

As Dean Penny ended our interview, he described a serious argument he had had with his university president. I asked him how the matter had been resolved, and he replied, "Why, I hope I left the disagreement back there in his office." Henry Penny could shed feelings in the same way that Peter Pan could part from his shadow, yet inwardly he was sensitive and emotionally aware.

Samuel Lovelace was another man who used intellectualization as a dominant defense. Unlike Penny, he *could* be called neurotic. Penny was lonely only in graduate school; Lovelace was lonely much of his life. In high school, Lovelace did not repress his sexual curiosity but read extensively on masturbation. He could think about and discuss intellectually the ideas that Stover could not remember or bring to consciousness, but Stover's affective expression of those ideas surpassed that of Lovelace.

In college Lovelace habitually crammed before exams. He knew that he did not learn anything that way, but the ritual gave him "reassurance." In the army, he did not befriend his mates but instead engaged in a "sociological study of my fellow soldier." Over rough spots, he maintained "an almost religious belief in logical thinking, scientific purpose, and control of emotions," and he found lonely comfort in coin collecting. After getting married, Lovelace intellectualized: "Abstractly, I feel the same fascination I did before marriage; biologically, lack of sexual tension is the problem." The idea was present; the affect was missing. Progressively, his marriage became more painful. Lovelace complained, "Living with her is exasperating and frustrating," and in self-defense, he said that he became "rather clinical and unemotional." Lovelace never could build up a sufficient head of anger to leave his wife; instead, "through my wife's illness, I learned what a complicated thing the human personality can be." Finally, in describing his own unsettling capacity for seeing all sides of his tortured marriage, Lovelace blurted out, "You can even rationalize Adolf Hitler." In our long and painful interview, this was the closest to real passion that he showed.

It is clear that in adults, mature defenses are generally adaptive and immature defenses are generally maladaptive; but to understand why the same neurotic defense, isolation, should have served Penny so well and Lovelace so poorly requires a small digression. In studying adaptation to life in two small Canadian communities, Alexander Leighton,[6] Dorothea Leighton,[7] and Morton Beiser[8] and their colleagues have studied the degree to which mental health depends upon the external environment. These social psychiatrists focused especially on the ways that mental health was maintained by adaptive structures in the environment rather than within the individual. They observed that certain psychiatric symptoms (which in this book would largely be termed "neurotic defenses") were often an integral part of an individual's personality structure, but that the social and psychological disability resulting from such symptoms could fluctuate markedly from *none* to *severe*. For example, they observed that some very vulnerable individuals could survive beautifully in a benign and structured social setting; they called this the "hermit crab" position. They have also pointed out the kinds of sociocultural conditions that tend to foster symptoms of psychiatric disability. These conditions are those that deprive the individual of self-esteem, love, mentors, self-determination, and a stable place within the social system. To confirm these observations, the Leightons and their colleagues have shown that experimental integration of uncohesive communities significantly improves the mental health of the residents.[9]

Consistent with these findings, all the Grant Study subjects used some neurotic defenses and showed some neurotic symptoms. However, there was a group who, like Penny, could use them to advantage. These men had had stable and cohesive childhoods; they had multiple social supports (stable marriage, church affiliation, athletic outlets for aggression, and political identification with the status quo). In contrast, men who had unhappy childhoods and lacked social supports were far more likely to use neurotic defenses maladaptively and to seek psychotherapy.

In other words, the chief differences between Penny and Lovelace were not so much the dangers against which they had to defend as the outside help upon which they could rely. Penny, despite his polio, was blessed with a childhood that fell among the top quarter of the group. As an adult, he enjoyed the support of formal religious affiliation, a happy marriage, and competitive sports with good friends, and was in 1968 a Nixon Republican who saw hippies and student activists as not his cup of tea. He never felt the need to take his emotions to a psychiatrist. Protected as he was by social supports, Penny's use of intellectualization never raised more problems than it solved.

On the other hand, Mr. Lovelace had had one of the worst childhoods in the Study. In adult life he had few supports to fall back on. He was supported neither by his marriage nor by church membership. He enjoyed no comradely activities with his friends, and he not only saw the world as requiring massive change, but he believed that student activists and hippies should lead the way — a comforting belief at eighteen but an unsettling one at forty-five. For years, Mr. Lovelace had sought psychiatric help to remedy his intellectualization and excessive indecision. (Indeed, the lack of social supports turned out to be as powerful a predictor of which men sought psychotherapy as their actual psychopathology.)[10] To summarize: like Hamlet, Lovelace was destroyed by his inability to make up his mind; and by avoiding firm decisions, Penny won praise as a mediator.

Finally, a proper Bostonian in the Study, Russell Lowell, illustrates once more how men can grow out of neurotic defenses and replace them with suppression. At nineteen, if Lowell won a debate, he would wear the same tie and clothes for the next one. His headmaster had called Lowell "a natural leader with all this implies in the best ways"; but unlike Penny and Goodhart, Lowell did not become a leader; he worked as a lawyer for a major Boston bank, clarifying the details and tangles that the captains of industry left behind. All his life, Lowell believed that abstract thought was the best way to deal with feelings. When I asked him how he coped with personal problems, he replied, "Basically, I dislike talking about personal problems until I've thought them out, and then talk is unnecessary." As with other adaptive intellectualizers, Lowell's magical thinking was tempered by strict attention to detail. Dick Stover, master of repression, could never remember the names of his medicines; Lowell knew the names, dosages, and side effects. Prior to back surgery, he spent his time "being careful to understand everything." Like Penny, when Lowell told me that his health was good, instinctively he knocked on wood.

Despite his wish for intellectual control, however, over time Russell Lowell learned to bow stoically to the inevitable. When I asked Lowell, who hated dependency, how he dealt with having to return to the hospital for a second back operation, he replied, "I got a portable radio, some slippers, and sacked out; I can't operate on my own back." When Lowell was asked what he had learned from grief, he replied, "Life has to go on, but I learned that at nine, when my mother died." When asked to describe the most illegal thing that he had ever done, he replied, "I've never tried to be a goody-goody, but my cumulative impression, gained in a lifetime, is that nearly everything that is illegal does not make much sense as a thing to do." With regard to smoking, he gave up cigarettes when his consumption passed a pack a day; "It seemed to me silly to keep on doing something that did not give me any great pleasure." He made it sound so simple!

It was in his approach to sexuality that Lowell best illustrated the way in which suppression tempered intellectualization and mediated between the demands of his culture, his own biology, and his need for other people. At age thirty, Mr. Lowell had been asked to describe his sexual adaptation prior to his marriage. Good lawyer that he was, Mr. Lowell gave an unusually full reply: "Since the age of fourteen, I have enjoyed spending time with and doing things with and taking out girls of my own social standing. . . . Sometimes I'd ask them to dinner at my home or occasionally to spend a weekend. Some of them I held hands with and kissed — with one, on the night I went overseas in the army, I went further . . . but I limited my physical or sexual conduct with these girls to what I have described above and never went any further — and never wanted to except in the sense of wishful thinking — because I felt it would just make for trouble and unpleasantness subsequently. I did not want — or think it right — to get involved in that way with girls whom I was going to live among socially for the rest of my life. . . . In college I got to know my best girls better as people and as real friends. One whom I never even kissed is today as good a real friend of mine as many of my male acquaintances. The same is true of my best girl when I was in the army."

He went on to discuss his liaisons while in the army with girls not of his social standing. These provided "an outlet for sexual desires as well as a relief from loneliness. . . . How do I feel about these? I admit they were immoral by publicly accepted standards of thought, but I have no remorse or regret. They served a practical need, and I know that I have been able to do my army work better and was more contented after having these occasional experiences." He went on to describe them with tenderness.

At the time of this writing, Lowell is happily married and has been for twenty-five years. However, when asked on a multiple-choice question what degree of satisfaction he derived from his marital sexual adjustment, he managed to magnify the distance that obsessive science puts between cold idea and warm affect. Lowell put his checkmark halfway between "satisfying" and "very satisfying," and then he wrote, "*sufficient* is a better word." The reader winces. Lowell had never known the exciting love affairs of Bright, Lion, and Byron. But Lowell's world fits in well with that of the Stoics. In an imperfect world, to achieve "sufficient" sexual satisfaction is perhaps not too little to ask. Besides, unlike Penny, Lowell could talk of feelings as well as dollars and cents; unlike Lovelace, he could fall at least a little in love with his mistress.

Displacement provides a third neurotic solution to intra-psychic conflict. In 1894, Freud observed that affect could not only be *dislocated* or *transposed* from disturbing ideas via repression and isolation, but that it could also be *reattached* to other ideas via displacement. Freud wrote, "The obsessional idea, which, though having little intensity in itself, is now supplied with an incomprehensibly strong affect. . . . The separation of the sexual idea from its affect and the attachment of the latter to another, suitable but not incompatible idea — these are processes which occur without consciousness."[11] For an everyday illustration, marital conflict arising from sexual disputes is often displaced to obsessive wrangling over money.

The defensive task of displacement, then, is to shift emotional attention from mountains to molehills. One subject was about to make the conscious discovery that divorce was inevitable. Affectively, he was on the verge of murder or suicide. Nevertheless, he wrote the Study that his only marital complaint was "My wife talks on the phone too damn long!"

Displacement is the major mechanism underlying a wide variety of human behavior. Phobias and hysterical conversion symptoms, wit, caricature, and parody, games and hobbies all reflect affect displaced from one object to another. Unlike the other neurotic defenses, displacement permits instinctual discharge. In this way it resembles the mature defenses that channel conflictual impulses which most neurotic defenses block. Granted, the border between displacement and sublimation or that between wit and humor is difficult to mark with any kind of precision. One distinguishing point, however, is that once the conflict is removed, the use of displacement disappears; but the continued enjoyment of activities once used for sublimation can continue for a lifetime.

For example, one Study member with a beautiful but frigid wife developed a passionate interest in gold coins. Significantly, this was a collection that he shared with nobody but his wife. In one questionnaire, he sadly described his wife's apathy toward his gold coins: "I do all this work — I've got all this stuff, and who looks at it?" Three years later, after divorcing his wife, this once ardent numismatist was actively involved in the courtship of his new wife-to-be. I asked him about his coin collection, and he had literally "forgotten" that he had ever been interested in coins. In contrast, Professor Clovis still derives as much pleasure from French drama as he did twenty years ago.

If displacement is a mechanism behind several so-called neurotic behavior patterns, it also is important for healthy adaptation. Konrad Lorenz has pointed out the importance of displacement in mitigating aggression between animals of the same species.[12] Through ritualized deflection of attack behaviors, carnivorous predators challenge each other without bloodshed; bucks fight over does, and business rivals do friendly battle on the tennis courts. Through such games, dominance can be achieved, and yet combatants escape with only minor scratches.

Richard Fearing was a man who mastered life through displacement, and he serves as an object lesson that phobic children do not all grow up to be phobic adults. As vice-president of a huge computer firm, Fearing's career was outwardly a success, and inwardly his job gave him pleasure. His marriage was solid; he was close to his children; his friendships were warm; and my interview with him convinced me of his mental health. Ignoring pomp of office, Fearing left the executive suite and came downstairs in his striped shirt sleeves to meet me. He introduced himself by his first name and warmly shook my hand. Although the very model of an establishment executive, he radiated energy and vital affect. If his office was filled with evidence of his hard work, it was also filled with people who walked in and out without knocking. If his office reflected self-discipline, it also contained sofas, not hard-backed chairs, for its occupants to relax in. His self-control never interfered with his talking openly and confidently to me about human things.

When Fearing was a young man, it had been far less certain that his energy would see the light of day. Until he was eight, Richard Fearing had had terrible tantrums, but as a college sophomore he remembered himself as having been always unaggressive. Instead, he told the Study of his childhood terror over thunderstorms and his nightmares of being chased by gangsters. His earliest memory was a phobia of wolves — wolves who, if he were bad, were going to bite off his fingers. He was strictly toilet trained, and even in college, if Fearing did not move his bowels twice a day, he had to take laxatives. Then, as if to add insult to injury, his mother complained that her overdisciplined son was "chronically ill, constipated, and restricted from athletics." As she explained to the Study, "Dick wasn't strong enough to have physical outlets, so it was all mental outlets." In his own mind, Fearing's Victorian parents were blameless for his inhibitions and phobias. Active revenge never crossed his mind. Instead, when he was separated from them, he was terrified that some horrible fate — a disaster that *he* imagined — might befall them.

The Grant Study staff agreed with Fearing's mother when she revealed, "I don't think Dick will ever be anything outstanding." The internist remarked upon his "flabby muscles." The psychiatrist described him as a "lackadaisical, lazy individual with no strong interests or drives . . . this boy has no spunk, no energy." However, once in college, Fearing's concerns over his rage — formerly expressed as a helpless fear of angry storms and fierce animals — now miraculously were replaced by an interest in subjugating storms. Like Jacob Hyde, he reveled in cloudbursts; he played an active role in rescue work during the devastating hurricane of 1938; and like four other men with unusually strict internal prohibitions about premarital sexual relations, Fearing learned to fly.

As an adult, Fearing did not just *transpose* his conflicts into gratifying external behavior, but he also *converted* them into physical complaints. At nineteen, for example, he had told the psychiatrist that he could not understand why people ever became emotionally upset. Fearing could say this because under stress his own emotions were expressed only as physical symptoms; they never reached consciousness as feelings. In childhood, headaches had often interfered with his ability to take trips away from home. As a young adult, shortly before his marriage, Fearing was one of several inhibited young men in the Study who came in with a complaint first of constipation, then of impotence. Yet with a little reassurance his impotence vanished, never to return. As an overachieving adult who never felt conscious stress from his work, Fearing suffered from fatigue and regularly took Vitamin B12 for his imagined "pernicious anemia." At a critical point in his work, he was hospitalized for a week for low back pain — but no cause was ever found. However, unlike the hypochondriacs in the next chapter, Fearing exhibited an unexpected *belle indifférence* over his medical complaints. He took none of the interest in his medicines that one might have expected from such a well-organized and symptom-beleaguered man. At the time of his hospitalization, he casually wrote to the Study, "Despite my wife's theory to the contrary, the back condition seems to have no relation to overwork."

Twenty years later Fearing was able to acknowledge that his back trouble had occurred at a time when he had been seriously depressed over his vocational progress. Like his impotence, his low back pain was very brief. It served its purpose of providing him a time-out to catch his breath and to communicate his anxiety to others who might help him. Then he was able to master the very tasks he feared — the success that his mother unwittingly suggested was improper.

As time passed, Fearing's displaced conflict over aggression left his body. It became more cerebral and philosophical. For example, as he got older, he described that although he had no conflicts with his job or with his wife, "I have a feeling of insecurity that is at times overwhelming. . . . I'm afraid that the world we live in is one of violence, and I'm not equipped to make my way in that kind of world." This, from a computer magnate! But remember he also used to fear that his Cleveland suburb was full of wolves.

Finally, ten years after his back pain and his "pernicious anemia" had been forgotten, Fearing finally made it clear to the Study just how ambitious he was. "Do I consider myself a success?" he wrote, "Yes! Is that important? Yes, very important! . . .

I wish I were not driven to prove quite so much to myself. I wish it were not so important to be a vice-president of my company. I wish we could all relax a little bit more about ourselves." He also wrote, "In 1970, I experienced quite regular headaches, stomach cramps, and diarrhea. Doctors decided they were all tension-related. Symptoms have largely subsided."

Displacement not only rescued Mr. Fearing from his drives but also from his conscience. Richard Fearing liked to joke and liked to play. He could sometimes relax, and then his use of displacement merged into sublimation. Although conservative in his business dealings, Fearing allowed himself to be shamelessly exhibitionistic and aggressive in the arena of public speaking. If he had been flabby as an adolescent, he had now become active in tennis, golf, sailing, squash, and skiing. He was as physically fit as any man in the Study. In his interview with me, his favorite social ploy was to bridge formality and humanity with a funny story. Although he answered my most searching questions, at one point he burst out laughing and exclaimed, "This is the damnedest set of questions I ever heard." Wit transforms irritation into a form that permits its guiltless discharge.

Without a complete record of these men's lives, it is hard to be sure why displacement worked so much better for Mr. Fearing than for some of the other men in the Study. One clue can be found in the fact that there was a mitigating gentle wisdom in Fearing's overdiscipline. The family worker described the elder Fearings as "liberal-progressive parents . . . there is a spirit of youth and fun in this closely knit family." Fearing's mother was described as having great charm, and the social investigator called her "one of the most intuitive people I have ever met." She wrongly believed her son's masturbation harmful, but at least she taught him how to sail. If Fearing still worked a sixty-hour corporate week, he also took long and imaginative vacations. Although he saw his greatest fault as sarcasm, neither tantrums nor passivity poisoned his relationship with others. In short, Fearing was a man who could organize his life so that his feelings remained warm and in focus. He had learned to wring pleasure out of his chronic need to earn the respect of others.

How are we to know when passionate concern reflects displacement and when it reflects a primary interest? Is not the assertion of transposed passion just one more evidence of the superstitious and unscientific nature of psychoanalytic thinking? As with all defensive behavior, if it is not to be just the psychiatrist's word against the patient's, detective work is necessary to prove displacement.

Consider the following sequence — a sequence that illustrates the benefits of longitudinal study in unmasking would-be unidentifiable defenses. As a child, one of the Grant Study subjects had been, in his mother's words, "spanked forever and anon. It made him fear his father." In high school he had been among the one or two percent of the subjects who ran away from home. In the army, he was among the one or two percent of the subjects who were threatened with court martial. In young adulthood, his rebellious nature was brought to heel. Then, at thirty-five, he wrote to us that he had developed "an acute fear of thunderstorms. Though it [the phobia] had been building up for a year or so, in September and October, the fear became almost incapacitating." The phobia lasted for two years, then disappeared. In retrospect, this man associated his phobia with anxiety over completing his Ph.D. thesis. This pressure had begun during the year that the phobia had built up and vanished on completing the thesis. As he wrote, "I don't think I really connected the things until later." In other words, when his anxiety was reattached to the thesis, his fear of thunderstorms dissipated. However, just as in grown men phobias of thunderstorms are rare and suggest displacement, so too, Ph.D. theses are sometimes difficult to complete because of transposed fears. But for ten years, careful reading of this exphobic's questionnaires gave no further clues.

Then, at forty-six, he casually informed the Study staff of a fact he had not bothered to tell them previously. In May of the year he developed his phobias, his father had had a severe stroke; over the summer it had become clear that his father's mental incapacity was permanent. If, when a young man is trying hard to succeed, his harsh and once-feared father is stricken down, the young man may feel guilty and fearful of success. Because to fear retaliation from his stricken father was illogical, he reattached his fears onto thunderstorms; yet it took eleven years of patient waiting for the Study to uncover a dying, once-cruel father invisibly buried in the "unostentatious hole" of a phobia.

Reaction formation reflects an inflexible attitude, affect, or behavior that exactly opposes an unacceptable impulse. In healthy adult development, it is a way station — the child of delinquency and the parent of altruism. Of all the neurotic defenses, use of reaction formation declined most sharply as the men matured.

As an adaptive mechanism, reaction formation is most useful when it effectively controls genuinely dangerous behavior. For example, Alcoholics Anonymous is effective in part because it makes a virtue of total abstinence. Similarly, stopping smoking is easier if suddenly cigarettes evoke disgust and not longing. But reaction formation, precisely because it leaves no options open, *can* lead to dangerous rigidity and to pointless loss of pleasure. Excessive cleanliness is valuable in an operating room, but it takes all the fun out of fingerpainting. We may be glad that a particularly mean state policeman is combating rather than abetting the Mafia, but we mourn his lack of tolerance for human foibles.

Reaction formation is usually deployed against too free an expression of anger, sexuality, or dependency. For example, as a child, one man had had several prolonged, crippling illnesses; as a result, even when he was an adolescent, his mother continued to wash his back. As an adult, he turned into a rigidly self-reliant man who condemned dependency in subordinates. Another man at nineteen was singled out by his classmates as being the least likely to lose his virginity; and he himself was seriously considering the priesthood. At forty-nine, although he had long since given up his monastic aspirations, the same man now worried that he was *oversexed*. (He was not.) Still another member confessed at midlife that for years he had been unsuccessfully trying to give up smoking, which had been a compulsion with him ever since he gave up drinking, which had been a compulsion with him ever since he became afraid of becoming "addicted" to women ("After all," he had mused, "you just can't go around loving people all the time").

Sometimes proof of a subject's reaction formation was not found until his children reached adolescence. For example, none of the promiscuous Grant Study subjects had children with similar behavior, but three Study members who at nineteen or twenty were most outspoken in condemning sexual promiscuity and who in youth scrupulously curtailed their own sexual activity had daughters who were unusually promiscuous. In his heart of hearts, the staunchest member of Alcoholics Anonymous may still long for a drink.

In the case of Mayor Jefferson and Dr. Jacob Hyde, reaction formation was only a phase in healthy adult development, and the price was not too high. Men, however, who continued to use reaction formation throughout their adult years tended not only to suffer but to appear neurotically ill to the outside observer. In general, there were two patterns. One group of men used reaction formation against assertiveness and creativity. They tended at age fifty to retain an adolescent insecurity, to be failures in their careers, and to engage in behavior that almost inevitably led toward failure. A second group of men used reaction formation against sexuality. Often, in their twenties, they were extroverted, sexually experimenting, hard-drinking romantics; in their thirties they had brought their impulses to curb and by forty had become ascetic guardians of the establishment. Scared of burning their candle at both ends, they became old men before their time; and as if poisoned by holding all their feelings in, they experienced significantly worse physical health. In both groups, virtually all who did not abandon reaction formation had unhappy marriages.

Judge Conrad Spratt was perhaps the outstanding example of reaction formation; he was positively allergic to pleasure. Yet Spratt was not bland — rather, like Dr. Hyde, he, too, rumbled with volcanic, if subterranean, energy. Few men in the Study had so much to hate and few were so dependent, yet no man so firmly forbade himself these traits. As a young child, Spratt's mother had perceived him as messy and subject to "violent temper tantrums"; unlike most of the other men in the Grant Study, Spratt had sucked his thumb until age twelve. Then, in adolescence, the very traits that distinguished him from his fellows in the Grant Study were reversed. If he was the only twelve-year-old thumbsucker in the Study, he was the only nineteen-year-old who was earning his entire way through college, and also sending money home. If as a child he had been messy, as an adult he was compulsively neat. In college D. H. Lawrence, Byron, and Goethe were his idols; but during much of his adult life he subjected himself to monkish abstinence. He spent his entire life among angry people, and yet he was forever turning the other cheek. In the end he came very close to killing himself.

I met Judge Spratt soon after his near-suicide. My initial impression was of a somber, academic man. He met me in his chambers with great kindness. He was a small, energetic man with curly hair and bright eyes. Surprisingly, there was nothing contagious in his smile. In its presence, I felt somber, even a little sorry for him. Every now and then his saintliness jarred me. Perhaps it was a hint of the old arrogance, first noted in his original Grant Study interviews. The aggressive Lion was easily loved; but the gentle Judge Spratt had few friends. Unwittingly, people who use reaction formation convey an abrasive superiority.

Nevertheless, as Spratt talked to me, there was also a curious process of self-renewal. Listening to Spratt talk was like listening to the prime minister of an underdeveloped country talking about "Operation Bootstrap." At the end, Spratt said good-bye with a very warm smile, and I left feeling that Judge Spratt was the Grant Study's tragic hero. So anxious was he to avoid doing harm to any living thing, he could not adequately serve himself. As in other men who have crucified themselves with reaction formation, there was a pervading sweetness to his personality. If the world mistreats its martyrs, eventually it learns to love them.

As we have seen before with other neurotic mechanisms, it was external circumstances that made Conrad Spratt's reaction formation so rigidly maladaptive. He grew up in Manchuria as the child of a pious Methodist missionary. Spratt's earliest memory was of being beaten by his father, and at forty-five, he still could look back on the "terrible violence that my father represented." Spratt's mother was also a very strict woman, who neglected her son's needs for those of the mission children. To compensate, Spratt won considerable praise for being protective of his younger sister, and he organized a singing group to put on entertainments in Chinese orphanages. Rather than marvel at her son's adaptation, his mother told the Study that at times her son could be "a conceited ass."

After the Japanese invaded Manchuria, Spratt's father insisted on remaining with his family behind the Japanese lines. At four-teen, to protect him from Japanese reprisals, Conrad was sent to the United States to live with strangers. In 1940, his father did not leave until the last moment. When his parents returned to America, Spratt, having spent his adolescent years without fam-ily, was at college, shackled by a thirty-hour-a-week job. Instead of admiring his son, his father spitefully demanded that his son send money home.

By the time Spratt came to college, however, he was also pro-viding his own chains. For example, although he was afraid that the Grant Study would "bludgeon information" out of him, he willingly agreed to participate. Although earning all of his college expenses, Spratt threw himself into the most difficult courses in the college and graduated with an A– average. Spratt asserted, and lived by the assertion, that he did not need to depend on anyone for financial support because "the less obligation in-curred, the greater freedom I will have." Nor did he need love; rather, Spratt asserted, "I only needed someone who could de-pend on me for love, who had need to be loved by me."

Spratt's response to World War II was equally extreme. Before his family had been forced to leave China, they had been re-peatedly threatened by the Japanese. Spratt knew that the Japanese had killed and imprisoned many of their Chinese friends. Nonetheless, as late as December 19, 1941, after Pearl Harbor, Spratt stated that he wished to serve as a noncombatant ambulance driver on the *Western* Front! Implicit in Spratt's credo "I am a pacifist" was another self-revelation that clarified the basis of his reaction formation: "My father has a temper which I am happy not to have."

Eventually, Spratt fought the Japanese in New Guinea and later in the Philippines. He wrote, "My feelings of pacifism are gone. I am glad I learned to handle a machine gun." But Spratt was by no means free. During the war he took greatest pride in his capacity to rescue friends when his stamina had held out beyond theirs. Spratt was assigned to intelligence, but to prove to himself that he was not afraid, he insisted on learning parachut-ing. During a parachute jump, Spratt broke his leg. As a result, he developed osteomyelitis, a chronic bone infection, in his thigh and hip bones, which returned to cripple him in later life. The shackles of reaction formation are not cheap.

After the war, Spratt returned to Japan with a missionary group to "atone for having spent three years trying to destroy Japan." This self-sacrifice was more than even Spratt's reaction formation could accommodate. The Japanese had been his enemies for too long, and after repeated altercations with the Japanese, he was sent home by his missionary group. Unless reaction formation can evolve into altruism, it is not flexible enough to bury the sort of hostilities that boiled within Judge Spratt.

Only in his ideals, where he imagined himself a Tolstoy or a Schweitzer, did Spratt let himself run free. In real life, he continued to forbid gratification. On his return from Japan, he married, more out of a false sense of self-sacrifice than from love; he described his wife as "a very constrictive person." At twenty-six, Spratt went to Harvard Law School. Characteristically, he supported himself *and* his wife *and* his wife's child by another marriage, *and* still made the Law Review. He also became a vegetarian. After graduation, hard work and dedication to children won Spratt a rapid appointment to the Chicago bench. He spent the next fifteen years presiding over juvenile and family relations courts. Highly motivated to help neglected children, Spratt became an outspoken advocate for the battered child. He also continued to write for law reviews, assumed an unusually active role in raising his own children, and never allowed himself a vacation.

During this period, Spratt took a Thematic Apperception Test. Later, this projective test was interpreted by Grant Study Director Dr. Charles McArthur, who knew nothing of Spratt's life after 1950. McArthur wrote, "One wonders if he went through an important part of his life crying for rescue from his bitterly staked-out claim to independence, and by that very defense, prevented himself from being rescued . . . the TAT was a real distress signal. This inhuman man wanted help." In predicting Spratt's future, Dr. McArthur's comments illustrate one of the most dangerous aspects of reaction formation. By its very reversal of the subject's needs, the defense can stand in the way of subsequent rescue. Reaction formation proved Judge Spratt's undoing.

As we have already seen, before middle life Spratt's wishes for dependency lay well concealed. He had always rated his physical health "excellent," and he never missed any time from work. Then, at thirty-three, he was hospitalized with viral pneumonia.

This hospitalization occurred shortly after the "plea for help" was expressed in his Thematic Apperception Test. Two years later Spratt developed a worsening of symptoms at the site of his old leg fracture. For the next six years he suffered intermittent and at times incapacitating pain; a hypochondriacal trend seemed clear.

In his early forties, Spratt's defense of pacifism was again breached; for the first time he openly fought with his father, but only because his father had mistreated his sister. Once his anger was exposed, Spratt became increasingly depressed; for if reaction formation against anger is given up too quickly, the anger is often directed against the self. After verbally castigating his father, Spratt became so disabled from chronic pain that he required three weeks of hospitalization and opiates. The final straw was that Spratt's wife became increasingly resentful and critical toward her invalid husband. She felt that his prolonged work days brought on his leg pain; and despite his growing entitlement she showed him scant sympathy. (In contrast to Fearing's conversion hysteria, note that Spratt's hypochondriasis failed to get him what he needed — thus its chronic nature.)

Judge Spratt entered psychotherapy, but at first he did not pursue it intensively. If gratification was conscious, it had to be forbidden; and Spratt disparaged his psychotherapy as merely an indulgent excuse to get the attention he was not getting from his marriage. At this point, he began seriously to contemplate suicide. Fortunately, his psychiatrist successfully confronted him with the question, "Judge Spratt, what would you recommend if a defendant came before you with such a story?" Spratt admitted he would recommend more intense psychiatric intervention. But remember, a defense cannot be breached by prescription; rather, relief came when Spratt was finally able to ask another person to help him bear his burdens. The frequency of psychotherapy was increased, and for the first time in his life, the "inhuman" Judge Spratt overtly admitted that he needed help for himself.

There was tangible benefit from abandoning reaction formation. For the first time in years, the chronic pain from the site of his bone infection was alleviated. He took his first vacation in a decade, and jubilantly told me, "I am no longer ashamed to admit pleasure for pleasure's sake." He obtained a divorce from his first wife. Shortly after our interview, Spratt remarried. A year later, he could write, "As our friends put it, we have both been granted a renaissance!"

Of all the ego mechanisms, dissociation is the most dramatic. In order to escape emotional stress, an individual can employ the mechanism of dissociation to modify his character or his personal identity. An obvious and adaptive example of the replacement of one affective state with another is found in successful theater — especially Stanislavski method acting. In less flexible forms, dissociation mediates the equally dramatic fugue states and double personality. For example, consider the extraordinary transformation of character in *Dr. Jekyll and Mr. Hyde*, in *Sybil*, and in *The Three Faces of Eve*. Just as Pollyanna was always smiling through her tears and finding joy in ignominy, just as hypnosis and religious ecstasy let pleasant feelings emerge in the most appalling situations, just so dissociation permits the beleaguered persona to alter itself. In one respect, dissociation is different from all the other mechanisms of defense: It is the only defense that can be invoked voluntarily. Alcohol and drug intoxication, trance states, and meditation all permit profound alteration of consciousness, and each may be deliberately produced.

Because of its capacity to alter both idea and affect, many psychiatrists call the process of dissociation "denial." While this is semantically legitimate, I think it is important to qualify such denial as *neurotic* denial, in order to differentiate it from *psychotic* denial, where external reality, not just the inner emotional reality, is adaptively distorted. The world of the theater is ruled by illusion and not by hallucination and delusion. If the men who used dissociation were likely to rush in where angels fear to tread, they did so not as fools or lunatics. Byron, Bright, and Lion used dissociation to conquer life — not to be destroyed by it.

The point at which repression ends and dissociation begins also needs clarification; for in hysterics, the two mechanisms are usually joined in concert. A physician in the Study provided a nice distinction between the two defenses. He said that he put any kind of sexual relationship with his wife simply out of his mind, and as a result he perceived his marriage as excellent; "I suppose," he said, "you would call that repression." In actual fact, it was not *repression*, for he was conceptually aware of his conflict. What was extraordinary was that due to his use of drugs and meditation he was *dissociated* from any emotional tension that might arise from his chastity.

Again, the difference between the Pollyanna and the Stoic can be a subtle one. Psychiatrists can argue for hours over whether looking for silver linings reflects a denial or an acceptance of reality. In human adjustment, it seems important to experience anxiety in optimal amounts — too little inhibits growth and too much precludes functioning. What is important is that suppression mitigates anxiety, but dissociation abolishes it. In studying preoperative patients, Irving Janis has observed that those who had the best postoperative course were those who experienced a modest amount of preoperative anxiety.[13] Those who minimized the realistic problems of their operation (suppression) fared better than those who perceived their upcoming operation as providing a "vacation" (dissociation) or those who were overwhelmed by anxiety (no defense).

It is also instructive to contrast the men who relied on dissociation with those who used intellectualization. Indeed, the two mechanisms seemed quite incompatible. The men in the Grant Study who used dissociation as a dominant defense tended to be high on so-called hysterical traits like sexual provocativeness, emotionalism, exhibitionism, and egocentricity; traits like rigidity, orderliness, and strict conscience seemed absent from their makeup. Dramatic personalities utterly ignore external details lest they interfere with a contrived but comfortable inner state. As a result they often seem marvelously spontaneous. Contrary to psychiatric prejudice, although dissociaters in the Study were able to express emotion freely, they experienced more mental illness and unhappiness than the more emotionally constricted intellectualizers. The price that the former paid for being such charming dinner companions was that they often remained uncertain of their own identities.

Despite being chosen from a group of male professional men, the life-styles of dissociaters resembled those of theater people the world over. All but two of the eleven men who used the greatest amount of dissociation seriously considered divorcing their wives, and as a group these eleven men accounted for twelve divorces — more than all of the other eighty-four men in the Study put together. Eight of the eleven men who employed the most dissociation were at some point in their lives excessively heavy drinkers; and they were three times as likely as other men to be two-pack-a-day smokers.

In contrast, a rather obsessional Grant Study member boasted to the Study that he had not changed in thirty years; his case record supported him. Obsessive-compulsives shun dissociation. They try hard to adjust their inner state to the exact details of the world about them. They have strict consciences, and appear uptight; they often employ isolation and rationalization.

Of the twelve men who used the most intellectualization, only one used alcohol heavily and only two were heavy smokers. Although several intellectualizers had had unhappy marriages, none had gotten divorced; only two had seriously considered it. They were not, however, the world's most entertaining dinner partners.

An example of dissociation was provided by the lawyer in the introduction to this book. He had responded to his wife's infidelity and failure to cook supper with a total absence of anger. Unlike Spratt, he did not protest his pacifism too much, nor did he suppress it. Instead, he altered his own self through naïve, joyous participation in producing humorous plays. He literally extracted himself from his predicament. There had been other times in his life when he had been able mentally to remove himself from danger. During the anxious year of the Berlin blockade, he was unique among the subjects in suggesting that "Russia's suspiciousness is a passing phase," and recommended that we should be "magnanimous." He closed one questionnaire by saying, "I believe I'm an optimist, undismayed in the face of all cynicism." There was a delightful, touching charm to this man. His innocence was engaging, but it interfered with his capacity to adapt. At several times during his life, to alter his internal reality, he had resorted to alcohol and amphetamines. Once, because of depression, he finally entered psychotherapy. He told me, however, that he found professional help of little avail, for "I tried to engage my psychiatrist as a human being, and get him to laugh." The reader may nod in sympathy and think that this is what wrong with psychiatrists — they have no sense of humor. But the lawyer suffered by not keeping his mind on the facts at hand. Such escape artists are not, as might be expected from their jovial exteriors, happier than other people.

A physician had used dissociation to far better advantage. At nineteen, the staff psychiatrist had described this man as "grateful, controlled, warm, mature, contented, pleasant, wholesome, healthy, happy, and sound." The family worker had described his family as "thoroughly nice people. . . . I can't remember receiving a more genuinely warm and enthusiastic reception." Over the years I had been suspicious that this all sounded too pat. Clearly, he tended to gloss over life and see things in positive terms. Nevertheless, this doctor's tendency to dissociate himself from pain had not interfered with his capacity to see the situation clearly. He told me that while his mother died slowly of cancer he had flown to her bedside every weekend for four months. As he told me this, he began frantically searching for his cigarettes and finally left the room to find another package. He found one, lit a cigarette, and then, inhaling deeply, he explained that although he had seen people dying in wartime, "this was my first experience with death . . . my mother and I had a very peculiar relationship. I would just kid the devil out of her. I purposely guided the conversation not to be morbid. Yes, we would just kid the heck out of each other." (His humor was not for displacement so much as for escape.) At the time of his mother's death, he had also begun taking three drinks before dinner. However, he became consciously concerned about his drinking, and for him alcohol never became a problem.

George Byron and Dr. Carlton Tarrytown both used dissociation, but with very different effects. Mr. Byron had always known that he had "a grasshopper mind." At age twenty, he went on a two-day bender, "just to see what it was like." Throughout his life, he engaged in other exotic activities to titillate himself with altered consciousness. He dealt with dissatisfaction in the navy by brief benders; at other times of stress, he drugged himself with ten hours of sleep a night. Unlike many of the active, performance-minded men in the Study, when Byron became stressed at work, he would retire to bed with a minor cold and a good book. At thirty-four, there was a profound crisis in Byron's family. He left home for several weeks to go to a foreign country and lose himself in the excitement of a love affair. Again, in middle life, at a point when he was close to punching out his boss — a member of Kennedy's cabinet — he again went abroad. There he spent the first week in bed and the next five weeks absent without leave. During the same period, later described as the unhappiest of his life, he was able to write the Study, "Life is quite meaningless, and delightful as I find it." But Mr. Byron truly escaped. Like an actor coming home from the theater, he was able to return to America and find his world essentially as he had left it.

In contrast, Dr. Tarrytown always paid the piper. We have already had many examples of Tarrytown's dissociation. In his mother's words, "He was the worst little liar there ever was, in terms of telling them and getting away with them." He remembered his college years as the happiest of his life because "permanent intoxication was in part successful." His mother marveled that he could "stop his emotions from acting and can be the most dispassionate person." However estranged he felt from those close to him, Tarrytown never lost the capacity to have love affairs with strangers. When the intellectualizers got into deep trouble in their marriages and in their lives, they usually stopped returning questionnaires until their lives were once again under control. But Dr. Tarrytown never failed to keep the Grant Study fully informed. His right hand remained oblivious of his left.

In comparing Byron and Tarrytown it becomes clear that they, too, differed in the social supports that they could fall back on. However much Byron may have wanted to run away from his feelings, his mother had accepted and admired them. With his faculty for turning dissociation into sublimation, Byron's devotion to escape led him to genuinely exotic places, where he was able to live, support himself, and raise a family. In college, Byron had found comfort in philosophy, not alcohol; and this interest was useful to him in later life. Contrast this with Tarrytown's wistful remark at forty-seven: "In college I would like to have learned more about Eastern philosophies"; but instead, Tarrytown's efforts at escape led him only to the lonely burial of his own emotions and the "obscure backbreaking business" of self-intoxication. Nothing in Tarrytown's life had ever given him the sense that he was entitled to be concerned about or to focus upon his own pain. Rather, his mother's depressions and her own dissociative escapes had always usurped priority. (In fact, there is considerable evidence from those experts at dissociation, heroin addicts, that their parents often denied them the opportunity to experience even small amounts of anxiety.)

To summarize this chapter, isolation leaves the idea in consciousness, stripped of all affect. ("I think of killing him, but I feel no anger.") In contrast, repression leaves the affect in consciousness, but so stripped of conscious ideation that even the object remains obscure. ("I feel angry today, but I cannot think at whom.") Displacement allows the subject's conflict-inducing idea and affect to remain linked but directed toward a less dangerous object. ("Today, after lunch with him, I got very angry at my dog.") Reaction formation allows the subject to keep in consciousness an idea and affect that are quite opposite to those in his unconscious. ("It's my Christian duty to love him.") Dissociation permits the ego to so alter the subject's internal state that the pain of conflict becomes irrelevant. ("Every time I see him, we get drunk and laugh over old times.")

With all neurotic defenses, what is important is that they alter the interior of the user. Outsiders are spared involvement in the user's backbreaking task. Unless specifically told, outsiders may never learn of the user's painful phobias and obsessions. Unlike mature and immature mechanisms, which often become entwined with moral or social judgment, neurotic mechanisms are regarded as individualistic quirks. Nevertheless, patients do not go to physicians or shamans because they are paranoid or altruistic. Rather, it is largely the neurotic mechanisms that allow the user to present himself to others in the sick role. Perhaps this social response has been facilitated by mankind's discovery that in the setting of the consulting room, "healers" may interpret neurotic defenses and provide helpful insight.

Half of all the defensive maneuvers used by the ninety-five "healthy" men in this Study were neurotic defenses. Thus, it seems to follow that although neurotics seek help from physicians, the users of neurotic defenses are not sick. They are everyone. The immature defenses are not so easily given up. Perhaps this explains why psychoanalysis may relieve the "neuropsychoses of defense" but has not banished mental illness from the world; for as we shall see in the next chapter, it is the immature defenses that underlie real human suffering. Not only are the immature mechanisms less amenable to interpretation, they often actually rupture the healer/patient alliance. The user of neurotic defenses is a self-diagnosed sinner who gratefully confesses and thereby wins absolution. In marked contrast, the user of immature defenses either rushes from priests to throw stones at the cathedral door, or he views himself as the only righteous man in the world, a seer unjustly persecuted by fools.

Chapter 9

The Immature Defenses

At beauty I am not a star;
There are others lovelier by far;
But my face, I don't mind it;
You see I'm behind it;
It's the people out front that I jar.

— Attributed to Woodrow Wilson

The modes of adaptation that underlie the neuroses are as distressing to the owner and as insignificant to the observer as a run in a stocking or a stone in a shoe. In contrast, the immature defenses seem as harmless to the owner and as unbearably gross to the observer as a passion for strong cigars or garlic cooking. The immature defenses include fantasy, projection, masochism (passive aggression), hypochondriasis, and acting out. Psychiatrists often assign the pejorative label of *character disorder* to the users of these mechanisms. They regard such individuals as unmotivated for treatment and impervious to recovery. In fact, the reason that individuals with character disorders remain poorly understood is precisely because nobody likes them. Psychiatrists beg tolerance for the psychotic, the bad-tempered melancholic, and the shy introvert, but not for the users of immature defenses. Perhaps this is why it is so hard to present a sympathetic picture of the eccentric Lamb, the prejudiced Tarrytown, or the passive-aggressive Smythe. One has the fear that they are incurable.

Only a longitudinal view can mitigate such pessimism. After participating for thirty years, the Grant Study members demonstrated beyond a doubt that immature mechanisms of defense can be dynamic modes of adaptation and not simply a rigid armor that deforms the personality. But patience is needed. Consider, for example, that hopeless disorder — adolescence.

Characteristically, adolescents use mood-altering drugs without moderation and see others, not themselves, as out of step. Their physical complaints are often imaginary; so are many of their most passionate loves. Adolescents are positive geniuses at being hoist by their own petards. Indeed, it is for these reasons that I have chosen to call the adaptive mechanisms that underlie drug addiction, paranoia, hypochondriasis, eccentricity, and maso-chism "immature defenses." Adolescence, however, is a self-limiting disease. True, we are unable to cajole, psychoanalyze, or beat anybody out of adolescence. They need to grow out of it slowly — with a little help from their friends. But like today's neurotics, yesterday's intractable adolescents were us.

Two disparaging words that psychiatrists use to dismiss the so-called character disorders are "narcissism" and "passive de-pendence." Adolescents, too, are extraordinarily self-centered, and although they are reluctant to support themselves, adoles-cents complain that their parents interfere with their right to act independently. In similar fashion, the Grant Study subjects who used immature defenses tended to be the most self-centered; and the traits of passivity and dependency were significantly corre-lated with each of the immature adaptive styles discussed in this chapter.

Although we build walls (concrete or social) to protect our-selves from character disorders, our efforts to save ourselves are in vain. We punish drug addicts, and they multiply like rabbits. The alcoholic and his long-suffering spouse become inextricably entwined. The more we push the masochist from the door and the hypochondriac from the consulting room, the more persistently do they return. Like adolescents, character disorders never learn, and yet the more mature members of society cannot resist trying to reform them.

All the above facets of character pathology are maddening and defy logic. But, wait! Can you imagine a hypochondriac, an exhibitionist, or a paranoid existing alone on a desert island? Of course not. These seemingly immutable character traits exist only in the presence of other people. In brief, immature defenses are not always the incurable bad habits that they appear on the surface. Sometimes they are a means of making a painful truce with people whom we can neither live with nor without; for if neurotic defenses are often the modes by which we cope with unbearable instincts, immature defenses are often the ways we cope with unbearable people.

In Chapter 5, it was shown that immature defenses interfered with overall adaptation; each mechanism was associated with impaired psychological function. One reason that immature defenses are so maladaptive is that they perpetuate in adult life a subtle process that we usually recognize as occurring only between mother and infant and perhaps between lovers. Immature defenses effect a merging of personal boundaries. They induce a breakdown of clear knowledge of what is mine and what is thine. Poets and songwriters have long understood that we cannot free ourselves from invasion by character disorders; so, unfortunately, have the demagogues and the villains of history.

Immature defenses allow their users, like ghosts and devils, to pass through human flesh, to leave facets of themselves behind or to take on the character of another. A cherished or a loathed person may suddenly cause pain within a hypochondriac's body. In prejudice the obnoxious trait of a parent, inadvertently absorbed in childhood, may be projected out onto some hapless minority group. The promiscuous daydreams of a minister become mysteriously acted out by his delinquent daughter. In *The Glass Menagerie*, Laura's fragile glass animals come suddenly to life — inside her head.

Put another way, throughout our lives we populate our inner world with people. If, thanks to a benign childhood, our inner worlds come to include constant people, toward whom we have relatively unambivalent feelings, then in real life our relationships will remain relatively assured, loving, autonomous, and well-demarcated. No group was better loved as children than the Stoics. No group as adults were more sure of their own identities and more likely to remain stably married. No group was less passive and dependent or *less* likely to regress to immature defenses. Conversely, the interpersonal relationships of the men who depended upon immature defenses remained perpetually murky and entangled. In an unconscious effort to preserve an illusion of interpersonal constancy, immature defenses can permit unsatisfactory mental representations of other people to be altered. Such internalized people can be conveniently divided into good and bad parts; they can be projected or combined with other representations. Just as neurotic mechanisms achieve legerdemain with feelings and ideas, immature mechanisms magically maneuver feelings *and* their objects. Con men, demagogues, and the great seducers of legend and fact all deploy immature defenses to their short-term advantage.

But how can a fetish, a prejudice, or an imaginary headache achieve this? How can misbehavior ever hold on to people? That was what Br'er Rabbit asked when he slapped the Tar Baby for discourtesy and found his paw stuck fast; he kicked the Tar Baby for this new affront and found himself still more entangled. To Br'er Rabbit's amazement, each irate blow brought him ever closer to the object of his disapproval. We are no different, for we, too, take immature defenses so personally. Perhaps that is why we often label these mechanisms as perverse or taboo. We fear that perversions like tar, once touched, will attract us forever. In the presence of a drug addict, liberals become prejudiced; the masochist brings out our latent sadism, and the malingerer our passive aggression. When baited by their adolescent children, even the most reasonable and staid parents become hopelessly involved and utterly unreasonable. Yet, the process by which this all happens is obscure; and even if noticed, it seems quite mysterious to an outsider. Consider the characters in Eugene O'Neill's autobiographical *Long Day's Journey into Night.* Collectively, they displayed all the mechanisms in this chapter, and for decades they remained bound to each other. Yet they never could stop torturing and being tortured; they never could forget; nor, tragically, could they ever openly admit how much they genuinely loved each other.

Granted, this all sounds a trifle abstract. But consider real case histories from the Grant Study.

Next to repression, projection is probably the best-known mechanism of defense. Projection allows us to refuse responsibility for our own feelings and to assign responsibility to someone else. In organic brain disease, drug intoxication, and deafness, projection is the mechanism most often invoked to bring external order out of internal confusion. It is easier for a senile woman to decide that her nurse has maliciously hidden her glasses than to accept the fact that due to her failing mind she has mislaid them. But like other mechanisms in this chapter, projection is essentially a social defense. Many of life's most "obnoxious" character types — the prejudiced, the injustice collector, the pathologically jealous spouse, and the professional rebel — use projection. No one is harder to reason with than the person who projects blame; and no one is more reluctant to accept love or more eager to dispense hate than the paranoid. No wonder we do not like him.

Two startling facts about paranoia: first, the persecutor will often bear a striking similarity to the persecuted; and second, the paranoid often fears love as much as hate. For example, one subject in the Study was active in a right-wing political group that was trying to defend the United States against a "conspiracy" run by "malicious people." However, Democrats, socialists, not to mention communists, escaped his full venom. Instead, as the most dangerous enemies he singled out two *Republican* politicians, two politicians who bore striking ethnic, social, and facial resemblance to himself and to his family. Although this man was financially secure, no member of the Study had endured greater emotional neglect. Nevertheless, what he feared most was a government that would care too much about its citizens.

Men who used projection were terrified of intimacy. Just as they too readily assigned their feelings to others, they also were frightened of what feelings others might offer them. At ten, one paranoid wrote, "The better I get to know people, the more I prefer animals"; he never really changed. Another such man wrote, "People have an instinctive tendency to avoid contact with one another." As a result, the paranoid character finds himself without the social supports that often mitigate the use of neurotic defenses. None of the men who were close to their fathers when young were paranoid in adult life; and conversely, few of the paranoid members of the Study retained gratifying contact with anyone in their original families.

There is something curious, almost eerie, about projection. Paranoia, jealousy, severe prejudice, and demonic possession all result in obsessive overinvolvement with the enemy. If projection produces a fear that those close to you may harm you, it also promises a special kind of intimacy with strangers. For example, to be singled out by the world for undeserved criticism suggests more concern than does being utterly disregarded. It is gratifying to be on *somebody's* "Most Wanted" list; and if loved by no one else, neglected spinsters are desired by the imaginary lechers who lurk beneath their beds. In short, projection is neither a defect nor a definite sign of insanity; it is merely one of the more extraordinary ways in which humans comfort themselves.

The careers of the paranoid men were the most unsuccessful in the Study; and not one of the men whose adult adjustment or whose human relationships were above average made significant use of projection. Perhaps this is because projection, like dissociation (neurotic denial), makes it impossible for the individual to see the truth, and if we distort our outer worlds too much, we become difficult to love. A commanding officer said of one of the most paranoid members of the Study: "He is modest and intensely loyal. He has a keen mind and is very creative, but his failing is the [in]ability to judge correctly and fairly." Earlier, the staff psychiatrist had noted that what was "outstanding" about the same man "is his lack of interest, energy, or drive." The subject, however, maintained that the staff psychiatrist had given him the "inhibitory ideas" that kept coming up whenever he tried to do things. When the subject had walked into an exam well prepared and then walked out without writing down a single word, he did not turn to the Grant Study for help. Instead, he viewed the Study as the college organization that quite possibly was to blame for his failure.

There are other paradoxical facts about projection. We think of the paranoid as aggressive; but in fact, no defense is so highly correlated with the traits of self-doubt, pessimism, and passivity. As the contrast between Lamb and Lion suggests, consistent assertiveness requires the capacity to love and to trust. The life of John Kennedy displayed far more aggression than the life of the injustice-collecting assassin Lee Harvey Oswald.

Although we think of the paranoid as exceedingly selfish, the kinship between projection and altruism is fascinating. Both empathy and projection result in a merging of individual boundaries. But to empathize is to perceive clearly and to put yourself in the other person's shoes, not him in yours. The paranoid character comforts himself, but enrages others, by incorrectly treating them as if they owned his feelings. In contrast, the altruist, using empathy, also feels his way into other people; but he accurately perceives his own feelings within them, and tries to help them. The proof is that he wins their gratitude and not their enmity. In public life empathy and projection merge. How many great leaders of history have been seen as saviors by some and by others as selfish, suspicious despots?

Reaction formation appears to be an intermediate step between projection and altruism. The life of Dr. Hyde has already shown how reaction formation merged imperceptibly with altruism, but in other men projection evolved into reaction formation.

The life of Grant Study subject Harry Hughes illustrates this evolution of projection. He was an adolescent dominated by pessimism and self-doubt. In boarding school, Hughes was frightened of sexuality and felt that masturbation led to mental illness; but he externalized the blame. To all, he tried to demonstrate that it was the school authorities, not himself, who were afraid of sex. Indeed, he created a campus controversy around himself by asking that the prize he won in an essay competition be an unexpurgated copy of Henry Miller's *Tropic of Cancer*.

In college, although the Study staff felt that Hughes "seems and looks unhappy," the only discomfort that he admitted was embarrassment that people noticed his blushing. Hughes resented being dependent on people and remained on guard. He found criticism difficult to tolerate, and instead of admitting inner distress, he was vitally concerned with air and water pollution. He wondered if he could blame his failure to become a successful creative artist on the political unrest in the prewar world. For him, it was easier to focus on unclean air and war-torn Europe than to appreciate the adolescent gloom and war within himself. Nevertheless, in anticipating the need for reform in antipornography and antipollution laws, Harry Hughes was many years ahead of his time. Paranoids often provide the cutting edge for social progress.

In college, Hughes profoundly doubted the honesty of other people, and the psychiatrist's opinion was that "Harry projects his distrust and cynicism onto others." Two years later, Hughes himself was able to admit that he had felt "paranoid" toward the Study. Nevertheless, just as in 1940 Hughes had been right to fear air pollution, his hypervigilance uncovered a covert truth; several of the Grant Study staff *had*, in fact, "disparaged" him behind his back. Their notes called him "a real psychoneurotic" and "a sick fellow." If he picked up such judgments in their manner toward him, no wonder he felt misused.

Like many men who use projection, Hughes had special difficulty in recognizing where persecution stopped and intimacy began. In his twenties he had stated flatly that he had "no intention of getting married." At twenty-nine, when he fell in love, he saw himself as pursued by his wife. Years later, in describing his internal grief over his mother's death, he semantically put responsibility outside himself. "My mother's death," he wrote, "introduced a period of stress which I am just getting over." Finally, although most men saw their continued scrutiny by the Study as some kind of acceptance, Hughes protested that he had not known that he would "be pursued so long" by the Grant Study.

As Hughes matured, he increasingly substituted reaction formation for projection. Instead of becoming a revolutionary, he became a hardworking, obsessive book editor with a very strict conscience. The change came slowly, and at first the boundary between his reaction formation and projection was difficult to draw. As an eighteen-year-old, he declared to the Grant Study that dancing was unhealthy and that "band music stirs up people's emotions and is to be condemned for that reason." At twenty-six, he no longer was quite so fearful that sexuality would harm him. Instead, he decided to remain celibate for religious reasons. As he said, "My religious concerns excluded me from most areas where trouble was likely to arise."

At nineteen, both physiologically and metaphorically, Hughes tried to put inner anger outside himself. To feel angry literally made him want to vomit. Then, as he had done with his sexuality, he began to use reaction formation, not projection, against hostility, and at twenty-four, Hughes was not only celibate but had become a conscientious objector as well. If his daydreams were entirely of fame, in real life Hughes noticed that "I do have a need to run myself down." At forty-six he could still insist, "I fear competition from the fear of doing harm." Yet simultaneously he admitted that he had very deep competitive feelings. Finally, at fifty, he was able to confess that he liked winning for its own sake, and he could now seek refuge in altruism. He regarded his success as a trade publisher as "positive activity on the side of the angels." He raised his children with the "belief that service is the way to happiness." In maturity Hughes even proved to be a loyal participant in the Study that he once felt had persecuted him, and the one-time loner was now sought after at parties. Hughes still continues to suffer inner anguish, but free of projection, he now acknowledges it and outwardly has brought pleasure and competence to the world.

Unlike Harry Hughes, Francis Oswald was a man whose reaction formation gave way to projection. His record as a father and employee was as bad as that of any man in the Study. He changed from a charming nineteen-year-old to a middle-aged man who was so isolated that just being in his presence made me feel lonely. The cause of his defensive shift may well have been that obscure — possibly genetic — biological defect that underlies some psychotic depressions.

Like Lieutenant Keats and Harry Hughes, Frank Oswald had been strictly brought up. Not only was he bowel and bladder trained at one, but he was cured of thumbsucking by having his fingers painted with Tabasco. For irregularities in his bowel habits, he was treated with Ex-Lax and enemas, and later he found himself antagonistic toward his father for always "expecting things out of me."

At first, when the going got tough, Oswald got tougher. He took great pride in his ability to master the difficult. In single sculls, he rowed in all kinds of weather, and like Judge Spratt prided himself on his endurance. In college he suddenly became excessively kind to a sister whom previously he had always resented; as his parents said, "All of a sudden, Francis goes completely into reverse." During the war, Oswald was a much-decorated marine platoon leader who always volunteered for the most difficult assignments. Nevertheless, the Grant Study described him as "very gentle in speech and manner," and Captain Oswald must have been one of the very few marines to emerge from the South Pacific a virgin who had never been drunk. He was the very model of reaction formation.

However, Tabasco and reaction formation were not enough. In his midtwenties, the very feelings that Oswald condemned came back to haunt him. While still celibate he was conscious that unwanted sexual thoughts intruded into his mind and interfered with his work. When Oswald went out with women, he found himself "automatically reading motives into the picture that do not exist." He assured the Grant Study that he was "not at all interested in making money," but as the Grant Study interviewer remarked, "throughout Oswald's conversation the question of money creeps in." For years, the killing in which he had engaged in World War II came back to persecute him in his nightmares.

The year Oswald turned thirty, both his parents died. Although he had relaxed his inner prohibitions enough to marry, he now found himself fighting with his wife over the children's discipline. Identifying with his parents' strictness, Oswald was in favor of strict toilet training, and he wrote, "A young child does not know enough to be upset by the process. A child is just a bundle of habits, and the sooner you start establishing good ones, the better off the child will be." He projected; he did not empathize.

By age thirty-one, the evolution of Oswald's reaction formation into projection was complete. At this time, Oswald deeply resented the fact that his boss was trying to "pressure" him to work in areas that he did not want to go. The next year, at a time when Oswald, in fact, was openly coveting a former boss's job, he suggested that his present boss was persecuting him. As time passed, feeling increasingly persecuted by his employers, he moved from job to job. He engaged in an extramarital affair, and then complained that his mistress was "a neighbor who tried very hard to interest me in breaking up my marriage."

By forty Oswald felt increasingly that the children whom he had brought up so rigidly were persecuting him. At times he dimly perceived that he treated his sons too severely, but usually he was oblivious to his own role. On the one hand, he would say, "You can't be permissive unless you don't care whether your kids are knifed or not." On the other hand, he wrote that his daughter, in her promiscuity, was "trying to knife my wife and me." But the truth was that Oswald had recently taken his daughter sailing in weather that had come very close to killing both of them. The next year, Oswald considered suicide, developed florid delusions of persecution, and was hospitalized. As his use of projection increased, his capacity to engage the real world deteriorated. After release from the hospital, Oswald spent much of his time unemployed. Like many another revolutionary who creatively transfers the dangers within to the world outside, he played out the role of a twentieth-century Don Quixote, gallantly fighting to save the Florida Everglades. At fifty, he became touchingly dependent on the Grant Study and turned to us for help, but this was at a time of the life cycle when most of the men were independently helping others, and the Study staff were too far from his home in Florida to be of real help.

Two years later, he drove his car into a bridge abutment and was killed instantly. The state police found no evidence that he had tried to use his brakes. Suicide, alcohol, or both were thought to be the culprits. Oswald's demons persecuted him to the end.

Cranks and adolescents are experts not only at projection but also at fantasy. Fantasy provides all of us a means of making events all right in our heads — even if in reality they are unbearable. The disavowed reality may include our external world, our consciences, our bodies, or even our feelings. Fantasy provides young children the omnipotence of kings and queens, ten-year-olds exquisite revenge against the schoolyard bully, and adolescents a chance to rehearse fearless mastery over sexual intimacy. After they fall asleep or while they dream at traffic lights, fantasy provides wish fulfillment for adults. Unfortunately, in real life fantasy does not work, except as a means of rehearsing future action. Fantasy almost always provides comfort, but it is a poor substitute for action, friendship, or games. As a friend of mine put it, "Head jollies are bad stuff."

Nine of the ninety-five men that I studied used fantasy often. None of them engaged in games with others, none had close friends, and only four stayed in touch with their parents or siblings. Both anticipation and intellectualization are mechanisms by which men in the Study achieved independence by using their heads; but with fantasy this was not the case. Intellectualization allows us to play with ideas and to practice behavior with real people; fantasy brings imagined people to life within the mind and so excludes succor from the real person without. In fact, fantasy was more highly associated with dependency than any other defense mechanism except projection and masochism.[1] Other dominant traits among the men who tended to use fantasy were egocentricity, pessimism, stubbornness, and emotional constriction. Thus, a paradox exists. In the omnipotence of daydreams, we seem to need no one; but in fact, it is only the lonely and the needy who must content themselves with imaginary friends.

The hermit and the eccentric mean no harm, but the outsider is outraged. In part he is outraged at being excluded. Looking back over the college interviews of men who habitually used fantasy, I discovered the following pejorative comments: "He literally stood out in a crowd for being gloomy, sad-faced, frozen, and humorless." "Looked like the devil, unkempt, and unshaved." "Headed for trouble . . . smells." "He looks like a janitor . . . slops around in an old acid-eaten T-shirt."

We also wax suspicious of dreamers because daydreams allow true originality. To be truly original means to appear independent of others, and to be independent of others is to be branded odd. All great artistic endeavor springs from idiosyncratic fantasy; and the artist, almost by definition, never asks for help in his creations. For example, one of the great fantasizers in the Grant Study prided himself on building a barn. He boasted that he did it without asking anyone else for help. He installed the wiring and the plumbing without consulting any books. He was delighted at the thoroughly original, if eccentric, solutions he achieved; but perhaps the barn's next owner was less pleased.

Real creativity transmits one's private dream to others in a moving way. Thus, as epitomized by Professor Clovis, there is a definite maturational sequence in human development that leads from fantasy through intellectualization and ends in sublimation.

Let me give examples. The mother of one Grant Study fantasizer had a nervous breakdown when her son was about three, and her son became depressed. His parents would often punish him by not speaking to him for twenty-four hours at a time, but his mother projected responsibility for the result by explaining to the Study, "By age five, his nurse took all the gumption out of him." To adapt, the boy learned to travel mentally. He became utterly engrossed in his foreign coin collection; and in his mind he visited all the countries that they represented. In high school he was a recluse. "I thought he was getting to be a hermit," his mother complained; but instead, he wrote endless letters to coin collectors all over the world. He dreamed of becoming a railroad man and traveling; but in reality he was not yet ready to put fantasy into action. At college he entertained himself by sitting alone in the lobby of a local hotel, "to study people and to be near life." He went on to graduate school, "just for the feeling that I am learning about new parts of the world." At this time he was still not dating, but he went on long solitary automobile trips. When one of the Study staff wondered if he would enjoy traveling even more if he took girls with him, he said, "No, . . . their mothers would object."

By age twenty-eight, he had begun to work for International Telephone and Telegraph. At first, stationed in New York, he still collected coins, but found they now provided less pleasure. By the time he was thirty-five, he was happily married and had begun a promising new career in the World Health Organization. By forty-five, his job had taken him to many parts of the world, and he was being seriously groomed for upper-level administrative responsibilities in the United Nations. The fantasies of his childhood had evolved into a sublimated interest in travel that was tangibly useful to others. No longer was he dismissed, as he had been at eighteen, as an "unusual boy."

Unlike projection, masochism, and delinquency, fantasy did not interfere with the men's work. Nor did fantasy preclude their subjective happiness; for if fantasy interfered with friendship, it was the only defense that made having no friends tolerable. Professor Harvey Newton was a subject who illustrated how fantasy could be used to advantage; in his work, his psychological adjustment, and his medical health, there were few problems. As he told me, "If you have work that you enjoy doing, nothing else can throw you very much . . . and besides, I don't have problems that need help." Only the loneliness of his life gave mute testimony to the price that he paid.

Like most men who used fantasy, Harvey Newton took almost

no vacation and never played games. Instead, his chief source of relaxation was to split wood on his Vermont farm. His closest friend was a man whom he had not seen in years. But Newton was philosophical about his lack of friends: "I don't care much about people, or I wouldn't be in this field." He was one of the leading physicists in the country.

Unless one appreciated his inner fears, Professor Newton, like Dr. Tarrytown, seemed an infuriating companion. In 1940 a staff psychiatrist had complained, "This boy is more difficult to interview than any encountered in the group." Thirty years later, I agreed. However, on a questionnaire, Newton finally revealed that he believed "My getting close to people could be harmful or destructive . . . if I get too involved with people I'm afraid I may overwhelm them."

More than any other adaptive style, fantasy correlated with bleak childhoods. Newton, like Tarrytown, and a majority of the fantasizers, had had a mother who was mentally ill. For five weeks at a time, Mrs. Newton would withdraw to her bed with vague hypochondriacal illnesses. I met her, and she treated me like a stone. She was the only parent I met who did not warmly recall Lewise Gregory Davies, the family interviewer. Not surprisingly, at age fifty Professor Newton marked the following statement in the affirmative, "Experience has taught me to expect little from people."

In adolescence, Harvey Newton, an otherwise literal boy, was fascinated with mythology. Although he had no verbal interests or emotional outlets, fairy tales became terribly vivid and seemed to "represent a higher plane of being." He put himself to sleep thinking of them. As a young man, Newton married a woman because of the similarity of their intellectual interests. He had known her for only two weeks, and it was, in his words, "a cold, cerebral affair." A few years later, he divorced her because he "could not enjoy the difference in the speed of functioning of their brains."

Later his efforts to imagine relationships with people led to adaptive intellectualization. He became deeply engrossed in the study of nuclear physics and described himself as "very happy." Pure science, he said, "is the most direct way to find out about the physical world and to adjust to it." Newton went to MIT to "build a structure to solve the problems I want to solve. . . . I don't want any administrative job, I simply want to be left alone with a few people to play at physics of the armchair kind." Nevertheless, at MIT he was able to transmute his fantastic notion of a "structure" that would answer the riddles of the universe into an effective team of physicists. At fifty he could boast, as any artist might, "We have just founded a new laboratory in an image I've been working on for ten years. . . . What I do is exciting as hell to me!"

In theory, people who live within their minds should be the freest spirits and most able to play. This is true for artists; but their fantasy, through some mysterious mental alchemy, is transformed into sublimation that allows their private dreams to be embraced by others. It is true that in our dreams, the perfect vacation is a desert island, but in reality vacations require real people.

The life story of William Mitty, Ph.D., illustrates how a man who could not love or play discovered how to invent comforting people in his own mind. At eighteen, the psychiatrist had said of William Mitty, "One wonders if he does not make more work so he does not have time to play." And at forty-seven, Mitty confessed to me, "I would really like to take a vacation, but I don't know how to do it." Later, Mitty tried to describe to me his marriage of thirty years' duration. "There ought to be some way we could share more, but I don't know how . . . somehow I just feel it ought to have been a lot more fun."

I first met Dr. Mitty in a railroad station. A friend was trying to offer him a ride home. Three times Mitty was offered a ride by the friend, and each time he would not accept. Yet, Mitty needed the ride; and he seemed quite unable to convince his friend he did not want it. As in a Pinter play, a gift from one human to another remained suspended in awkward limbo.

For Mitty, people had always been distant. As a child, William Mitty's mother had generalized, "I don't think Willy cares a great deal for people. He works pretty much alone with his telescopes and his fossils." But she had not helped. When for the first time William Mitty left home for college, a thousand miles away, she and her son shook hands.

Physically uncoordinated, Mitty avoided athletics. Instead, he built himself a beautiful telescope and became president of the high school astronomy club. Although fascinated by photography, Mitty preferred photographs of things to people. By design, he learned to write so that no one could understand him. Like a surprising number of other Grant Study subjects, in lieu of dating Mitty obtained a flying license. But unlike Lieutenant Keats, Mitty had no male friends either. Indeed, even in his nightmares, he found himself floating in space, out of touch with anyone.

To anchor himself, Mitty created an interpersonal world within his own head. In high school, when the boys talked about sexual topics, he ran away, but on his own he read a great deal about sex. He regularly masturbated with heterosexual fantasies; yet he was puzzled that he could not get sexually excited in the tangible presence of pretty girls. In college, Mitty's only friend seemed to be the Grant Study. "On several occasions," a physician observed, "William has had the tendency to come into the Grant Study and sit as long as we made him welcome." After graduating he wrote the Study to ask them to find him a roommate, a ride home, and a fellowship. If the Grant Study had made Mitty a guinea pig, it at least had tried to understand what was going on inside his head; and unlike most friends, the Study never asked that Mitty understand what was going on inside the minds of the staff. Indeed, psychiatrists are sometimes the best friends that schizoid characters (chronic users of fantasy) ever find.

In spite of his dependence, however, the staff found it hard to warm to Mitty. Outsiders resent the lonely fortress of the dreamer. The Study psychiatrist had summed up Mitty with the comment "His empathy is low, there is something lacking." Finally, at fifty, through the impersonality of a true-false questionnaire, Mitty, like Newton, was able to hint what the problem was. (I have italicized his ad-libbed comments.) "My day dreams enable me to need other people less — *presumably*. . . . I avoid closeness and familiarity with other people — *but I really don't know why*. . . . I have sometimes thought that the depth of my feelings might become destructive. . . . Sometimes I feel I will devour or consume those I need the most." He was so hungry for people that he was afraid to be left alone with them.

In his twenties religion momentarily permitted Mitty to replace fantasy with the riskier, if more gratifying, defense of sublimation (or dissociation?). He was at the California Institute of Technology, two thousand miles away from his family and light-years away from the stars that he studied. Mitty had been profoundly homesick and wrote to the Study that "the alarming deterioration of the American home is as dangerous to our freedom as all the atomic bombs that might be used against us." (In other words, like many fantasizers, Mitty equated the pain of his inner mind with world disaster.) Then, at the age when Erikson suggests that individuals must achieve intimacy or suffer a life of isolation, a small miracle happened. Mitty welcomed God into his life. Through his closest acquaintance, his mathematics professor, he became passionately involved with the Oxford movement. Six months later he could write, "It's wonderful to be happy." He called his interest in the Oxford movement "fanatical" and his newfound happiness "beyond description." "Prayer is man's greatest source of strength," Mitty wrote. "It's surprising how much He wants to help us if we could only ask Him properly."

Perhaps as the cause of his conversion, or perhaps as a consequence, Mitty fell in love. Characteristically, Mitty had first known the woman only through correspondence. But in his own mind, his pencil-and-paper love became real. His girl friend was also in the Oxford movement; and as he said, there was an "enjoyment in relating a belief in God to everything we did . . . it was a childhood dream come true." Years later, when Mitty reminisced to me about his earlier involvement with religion, he allowed a warm smile to brighten his whole face. Almost joyfully, he confided that the Oxford movement was "something that for years I'd been searching for . . . it fitted in with what the inside of me needed." (Two other lonely Study members had enjoyed similar religious experiences in their twenties — for one it was the Catholic Church in the Midwest, for another a commune in New Mexico.)

For most of his adult life, however, Mitty's loves lived most vividly in his imagination. In our interview, I asked Mitty how he had dealt with his father's recent death. He replied that he had tried to recollect all the good times that he and his father had had together. But Mitty had not seen his father in over a decade! When I asked if he could tell me about his closest friend, he said that several people whom he rarely saw came to mind. As an example, he then cited a friend that he had not seen for eleven years; he assured me that "when we get together there are no holds barred." Like the stars in space, Mitty's relationships that to me seemed so distant attained immediacy in his own mind.

Dr. Mitty did not see himself as odd. He did not appreciate that he rubbed others the wrong way. Besides, what was inside of his head was valuable. If at times his history seems too agonizing to bear, remember that he survived. With only average intellectual abilities, Mitty had won a full college scholarship on the basis of real achievement. His professor of astrophysics at the California Institute of Technology described him as "extremely capable as a researcher" and credited him with "unusual originality." With a Ph.D. in astrophysics, he now works outside of Boston as a respected designer of radio-telescopes and as a consultant to the Smithsonian Observatory. He has married and raised three sons. If he is not the best friend in the world, he is a devoted father and husband.

Originally, the term *acting out* was used by psychotherapists to describe a patient's conflictual wishes as they were transferred from consulting room fantasy into outside action. In this book I have broadened the term to embrace the dynamic underpinnings of what is pejoratively labeled criminal behavior. First, acting out involves giving in to impulses in order to avoid the conscious tension that might result with any postponement of expression. Second, acting out translates impulse into action so fast that the user escapes *feeling* or thinking about what he does. Third, acting out permits the user to express an unconscious impulse directly while ignoring internalized taboos that forbid the act.

For example, from the Texas University bell tower, Charles Whitman, having mindlessly killed his mother and his wife, shot to death several strangers. At the time, he was probably quite unconcerned with social prohibitions of murder, quite unaware of the actual dimensions of his own rage, and ignorant of the identity of the person (possibly his father) at whom his explosive rage was aimed.

In criminal justice, there has always been a riddle: Where does paranoid insanity end and incorrigible delinquency begin? Certainly, we all forgive the lunatic more easily than the psychopath. Even to the relatively tolerant psychiatrist, delinquency — mindless delinquency — is the least forgivable mode of adaptation. It is a rare psychiatrist who spends much time inside prisons, and responsible textbooks of psychiatry still describe the psychopath as a troglodyte — incapable of human guilt, depression, or anxiety. In short, the psychopath is made up of the very antimatter of humanity. Without elaborate journalistic research (for example, Truman Capote's *In Cold Blood* or J. Anthony Lukas's research on Linda Fitzpatrick in *Don't Shoot, We Are Your Children*), the pain of the public psychopath remains invisible. Yet the men in the Study who most used acting out were unhappier, more anxious about sex, and more pessimistic than any other group in the Study.

The mechanism of acting out can be conceived as underlying a wide variety of misbehaviors, from chronic use of drugs and self-inflicted injuries to repetitive criminal behavior and self-defeating perversions. As with any complex human behavior, however, no single hypothetical defense mechanism will totally explain misbehavior. For example, a "simple" perversion can be an elaborate symphony of reaction formation, sublimation, fantasy, projection, and acting out.

Ultimately, the results of acting out are disastrous. With protracted drinking, the drunkard becomes more, not less, anxious; the embezzler and the prostitute rarely allow themselves to enjoy their riches; and temper tantrums often leave the user feeling sullen and angry at himself. Nor, in spite of popular myth, does the psychopath evade retribution from his own conscience. The criminal who has escaped from jail twice — and has been imprisoned thrice — has often facilitated his recapture. He may even have had the slogan "Born to lose" painfully tattooed into his flesh before the cycle began; yet people say he has no conscience.

Acting out is common in youth. It is then that, relative to the ego's capacity to quench them, the instincts burn most brightly. Overwhelmed by unfamiliar passions and incapable of maintaining them in consciousness, teenagers act first and try to rationalize their behavior afterward. Of all the mechanisms in this Study, acting out was the one most clearly confined to the adolescent years.

One adaptive facet of acting out is that it diffuses the impulse rather than focusing it on any one individual. The man with the most bizarre sexual perversions may be quite unclear about the kind of person or even what part of a person he is really looking for. Thus, a Grant Study member who set compulsive fires in childhood was, in adolescence, still unable to focus his attention on what bothered him. At forty-five, when he finally became the master of his inner life, he was able to say matter-of-factly, "I always thought that my fire-setting was out-and-out hostility toward my parents." In fact, although in college he was unable to admit it, his childhood had been as grim as any in the Study.

Not only is there a link between projection and acting out in dangerous criminals, but in more adaptive form these two defenses are also fused within the revolutionary. In the 1960s it was never clear to our state department whether Fidel Castro was a political visionary or an outlaw with a chip on his shoulder. Like the humblest delinquent from the ghetto, the revolutionary has often been victimized as a child. Violence begets violence, and perhaps the only creative use of violence is in revolution.

Robert Hood was a Grant Study member who illustrated the less-adaptive aspects of acting out. Since the Grant Study's somewhat Victorian selection process was designed to exclude rebels, Hood's presence in the Study never ceased to amaze the staff. Although he came from an upper-class home, he behaved like a street urchin. He started smoking by twelve and was addicted by fifteen. In boarding school he was in chronic danger of expulsion. By his freshman year in college, he was an extremely heavy drinker who boasted of driving 120 miles an hour. To avoid studying for an exam, he would get violently drunk for a week and then when the exam came would play hooky. In the service, Hood was a severe disciplinary problem; and he was one of two Grant Study subjects to be broken in rank. While married, Hood was grossly promiscuous; and he came perilously close to becoming a child batterer. On the surface, Mr. Hood was a bad seed. The Study staff called him "psychopathic" — without sadness, remorse, or anxiety.

If we look at his whole life, however, Hood's delinquency seems less mindless. He had been the delinquent child in Chapter 5, who found the giants and witches in fairy tales so real that he believed that they actually would chase him. (Remember, the paranoid and the delinquent are close cousins.) These fears occurred during a time that Mr. Hood, unlike any other Study subject, was repeatedly separated from his mother. (At regular intervals, she enjoyed — or needed — three-month vacations away from her preschool children.) In adolescence, during the time that Hood was violating school rules and engaging in reckless, almost suicidal driving, his mother was being openly courted by her next husband and was suing Hood's father — who was suicidally depressed and in hospital — for divorce.

After a fashion, Hood's defensive pattern worked. As with many delinquents and drug users, the striking aspect of Hood's first thirty years was that his depression and unhappiness were never mentioned. The very fact that he was chosen for the Grant Study showed how well his inner pain and family turmoil were masked. At the time that Hood was chosen, the Study internist wrote, "Robert doesn't see any concrete problem to ask anyone about and sees himself as happy." Impulsive *acting* protected him from *feeling*. Hood's military demotion for disorderly conduct, his extreme promiscuity and possible child battery occurred during the period that he himself was in the throes of divorce. Once the divorce went through, his severe drinking and promiscuity waned, and his military career became successful.

But what excuse could Robert Hood have had for wanting to beat up a one-year-old child? The cause, I believe, was that his child threatened to render him conscious of the pain of his own childhood. Always, he had kept that pain from awareness . . . at five, through delusional projection, and in college by projection and acting out. So, as a young adult, Hood flew into rages against his hapless child, because, as he said, "The prospect of vicariously reliving the years of my boyhood is quite intolerable." After his divorce, he never saw his child again.

At thirty-two, Hood finally admitted to the Study, "From age eighteen, I had the belief that my life would necessarily be terminated by suicide." And had he not escaped through alcohol and acting out, Hood might well have been as dangerously depressed as his father. Consider how little help others offer those driven to acting out, for although society tries to respond to overt depression with solicitousness, in many states suicide, the ultimate acting out, is kept on the statutes as a felony. Twenty years later Hood's son, utterly rejected by his father, was expelled from Yale for "insubordination." Perhaps college deans are no more perspicacious about the management of unhappiness than they were in Hood's day. Or perhaps acting out so skillfully conceals misery that nobody, however well trained, cares to notice.

With time, the careless *cool* of "lower-class" delinquents (and many adolescents) becomes replaced by the *angst* of "middle-class" neurotics (and many middle-aged parents). When in middle life some addicts and delinquents "recover," their subsequent lives may appear restricted through reaction formation. When in middle life some criminals "burn out," they replace their seemingly mindless delinquent acts with intellectualization and dissociation and become jailhouse lawyers or anxious alcoholics.

So it was that by age thirty-five Hood's earlier Grant Study diagnosis of *psychopathic personality* was no longer applicable. For the next fifteen years, Hood could certainly have been called *psychoneurotic*. First, instead of acting on his feelings, Hood substituted intellectualization. In his early thirties, when Hood was still struggling with his alcoholism, he worked as a psychologist in a cancer center; he *studied* the pharmacological relief of human pain. In middle life, when asked what his philosophy was over rough spots, Hood replied, "I always have had a great deal of faith in the integrity and excellence of my own mind." Instead of openly indulging his reactionary views, he subscribed to racist tracts.

Second, rather than altering his mind with alcohol and sleeping pills, Hood discovered he could use transcendental meditation to dissociate himself from anxiety. His current plan is to give up working entirely, and live with his wife off a recent inheritance, while meditating in the Virgin Islands.

Third, at forty-five, Robert Hood became a master of reaction formation. He had achieved sobriety, a stable if asexual marriage, and a job; he had given up friends, children, alcohol, and sexual intercourse. The price he paid illustrated Freud's quip that a young whore makes an old nun. At fifty, the age that most Grant

Study men are experiencing what it means to be truly generative, Robert Hood is an unemployed upper-class welfare case. But he is alive, still married, and in good health, and that is more than he expected at thirty-two.

In everyday life, hypochondriasis is a common mode of adaptation. Sometimes hypochondriasis can be a means of obtaining much-needed care. For example, one independent and well-adjusted subject told me that whenever he needed human attention he would get sore throats. More often it is used as a profoundly irritating means of containing hostility. One subject admitted that when he became uncontrollably angry he would become sick. Rather than reproach others who in the past have failed to care for him, the hypochondriac berates his doctor. In lieu of openly complaining that others have ignored his wishes (often unexpressed) to be dependent, the hypochondriac may prefer to belabor others with his own pain or discomfort. For this reason, the hypochondriac who has transformed covert rage into complaints of pain is incapable of being comforted. The thirteen men in the Study who most frequently used hypochondriasis were far more likely than other men to take medicines, see psychiatrists, seek out medical attention, and get admitted to hospitals for emotional reasons. Even when in perfect health, they rarely described their health as excellent.

Unlike many of the neurotic defenses, the defense of hypochondriasis can never be breached by suggesting "It's all in your mind." In response, hypochondriacs will only amplify their pain. Hypochondriasis is a plea that attention must be paid. Like the Ancient Mariner, the hypochondriac seems driven to let others know the most excruciating details of his agony. He is relieved only when the observer acknowledges that the hypochondriac's pain is the worst since the world began; and so like other immature defenses, hypochondriasis binds others to the user. Often this is achieved by evoking guilt in the caretaker, and always someone else ends up taking responsibility for the hypochondriac's anger. We get so angry at his complaints that we become oblivious to his covert rage; we believe it to be our own.

As we have seen with other defenses, hypochondriasis is part of a developmental sequence of adaptive strategies. For example, a recovering schizophrenic, when he gives up delusional projection and psychotic denial, may use hypochondriacal complaints to initiate his first tentative relationship with his psychiatrist. Then, there is the dramatic example of Mary Baker Eddy. After years of incapacitating hypochondriacal complaints, she founded the Christian Science Church, which states that all physical complaints are imaginary and reflect "mortal error" — a reaction formation against physical complaints if there ever was one. Conversely, Judge Spratt provided an example of a man who under severe stress replaced reaction formation with hypochondriasis.

In severe depressions, hypochondriacal concerns can easily regress into frank persecutory delusions — a "Level I" or psychotic mechanism. But in delusional projection a person usually conceives of the tormentor as outside himself, while with delusional hypochondriasis, he perceives the tormentor within.

Ignoring human boundaries, the hypochondriac often takes some facet of a lost love inside. For example, the father of one man died of a ruptured appendix. Immediately, the latter, then age ten, developed retching and vomiting attacks. No physical cause was ever found. Unlike healthy identification with beloved caretakers, an internalization that permits the user to grow and develop, hypochondriacal introjection produces dysphoria and a sense of affliction. The people or human traits internalized by the hypochondriac seem like invaders who attack rather than sustain.

While it is easy to conceptualize projection as a simple process, understanding hypochondriasis, like understanding acting out, necessitates considering a variety of subprocesses. First, in hypochondriasis, interpersonal conflict or feelings are displaced onto some part of the body. Second, hypochondriasis covertly accuses and punishes others. Third, hypochondriasis, by containing a reproach toward others within one's own body — by eating one's own heart out, as it were — appeases the hypochondriac's conscience. Fourth, unlike most defenses, hypochondriasis exaggerates affect; it is the one defense that was negatively correlated with repression. Thus, unlike Vice President Fearing's conversion symptoms that reflected neurotic displacement, hypochondriasis is accompanied by affects that are the very opposite of *la belle indifférence*.

Not only can hypochondriasis modulate distress arising from anger, unmet dependency needs, and guilt, the mechanism can also be used to manage sexual conflict. At twenty-five, a studious Boston lawyer became fanatically preoccupied that his teeth needed to be straightened. If he did not straighten them, he believed that he would lose his teeth and develop "dyspepsia" like his timid father. In the seven years the Grant Study had followed him, this was the first time that this man identified himself in any way with his father or became concerned over his teeth. But he had a hidden agenda. Belatedly, the subject had become interested in women and was frightened lest, at twenty-five, he was maturing too fast. He abandoned the first serious efforts that he had made at a courtship, gave up a romantic trip to Italy, and devoted his attention to shackling his wayward teeth. As he later confessed to the Study, "I already looked and acted young, and here I was making myself look twelve years old." In retrospect, he told me that his teeth-straightening was a parallel to his subsequent psychoanalysis. "It was a repairing of my bungled self, the first thing I did to help myself . . . it was also a regression." He entered psychotherapy and became able to deal with his concerns about sexuality on a more conscious basis. He could abandon his fear of internalizing his father's indigestion. He could give up his own braces. Twenty-five years later, his teeth are intact; he does not have dyspepsia; and he does have a wife, three daughters, and a satisfying sexual adjustment.

In some ways, the distinction between hypochondriasis and displacement is semantic, for both mechanisms provide symbolic ways of expressing abstract feelings.

Angry feelings give us a pain in the neck. Sexual feelings make us hot and bothered. Anxiety makes us choke up. Grief puts a lump in our throat and a pain in our heart. We tremble and grow cold with fear. In displacement, however, the symptom serves as a synonym, a means of communication, a *conversion* of affect into its somatic equivalent. Fear does reduce blood flow to our skin, and anxiety does result in a sense of breathlessness. In hypochondriasis, however, the physical complaint is exaggerated and takes on a life of its own. The hypochondriac forms a relationship with his symptom, and his symptoms are rarely accompanied by physiological signs.

The most outstanding example of symbolic pain in the Study occurred in John Hart, a man who could read blueprints before he could read primers and was always better with numbers and symbols than he was with words. What made Mr. Hart's hypochondriacal concern over his cardiac status qualitatively different from Mr. Fearing's conversion symptoms was that in some ways Hart's pain represented his father.

John Hart's father had been a distant man, practical but with no sense of humor. He felt remote from his son and told the Study that he rarely knew what his son was thinking. However, John Hart was good at doing things for himself. He became one of the most brilliant mathematicians that his university had ever seen. While at college, he enjoyed excellent health, and, unlike some subjects, had exhibited no particular concerns about his heart.

In September 1944, John Hart's father, who had had angina for many years, died of a coronary thrombosis. That year, Hart first noted the onset of his own chest pain. Two years later, after a friend had a heart attack, the chest pains became more severe. Finally, in 1952, he read an article in the popular scientific press on "imaginary" heart disease. Later that year he wrote the following letter to his college internist:

> I have been having some difficulties over the past few years in which I thought you might be interested. *You may remember my father died of heart trouble in 1944* [italics mine]. During the next year or so I felt occasional pains in my chest and suffered several dizzy spells which became more frequent, until finally — I think in 1947 — I had a physical examination and was assured by the doctor that there was nothing wrong with my heart. He asked me whether the pains were comparable to someone crushing my chest; I said no. I had no more attacks for about six months. Then, they began again, this time accompanied by a crushing feeling, like a muscle cramp in the chest. I tried to tell myself it was all imaginary, but that didn't seem to help; finally, after a very severe attack in which my heart rate rose so fast I could not count it, I became really frightened. I went to

see another doctor again, and I described my symptoms.
He said it certainly was not heart trouble — probably a
spasm of the stomach valve — and asked if I had pains
in my arms, which I did not. I also had an electrocardiogram taken. After all of this, I was fairly convinced
that my difficulties were psychosomatic.

I had no trouble again for six months or a year. Then
in the early spring of 1950, when I donated blood to the
Red Cross, I reacted so strongly with high pulse rate
(even before giving the blood) that they were going to let
me go. I was somewhat ashamed, but also pleased to
note that here was a clear case of psychologically in-
duced symptoms very similar to my previous attacks.
About a month later, I began having the same sort of
attacks again, for no apparent reason. This time they
lasted all night, *with pains in arms* and legs. [My italics.]
I returned to the doctor and had another electrocardiogram and chest X-ray, both negative. I was particularly
disturbed to discover that even after being convinced
that the symptoms were psychosomatic, I still could not
make them disappear permanently.

In the fall of 1950, I mentioned my attacks to another
doctor; he called them "anxiety states" and gave me
some sleeping pills, which I still have but have not tak-
en. For the last two years, I have managed to control my
problem, to the extent that I no longer have any dizzi-
ness, but still have occasional pains — sometimes dull
aches, sometimes sharp ones — across the chest and
arms.

Fifteen years later Hart told me that in 1951 a doctor had indicated that a sign of real cardiac trouble would be edema (swelling
in the ankles), and that shortly afterward he had developed ankle
edema for the first and only time in his life.

Hart closed his letter as follows: "The pains do not frighten me
now, except that I am irritated at not being able to exert any
mental control over them, and I wonder whether this sort of thing
may not eventually bring on some real heart trouble."

That was in 1952. From then until the present, Hart has been
a loyal member of the Study. He never again has had any
symptoms or pain related to his heart. Despite his previous con-

cern about the possible physical aftereffects of his hypochondriacal symptoms, he described his biggest health problem at
forty-seven as "dandruff and boils." (Under stress, he says, his
stomach muscles now get a little tense.)

When Hart was interviewed in 1967, I asked him about his
cardiac symptoms. He acted surprised and *did not remember* his
long confessional letter to the internist. Even more surprising,
this brilliant scientist *could not remember* the year or the season
of the year when his father died. Hart did remember, however,
that at his father's funeral "I had wondered what was expected of
me emotionally"; and then admitted that he had felt somewhat
inadequate and "inclined not to show grief." He related that until
he had read the paper on "imaginary heart disease" he had made
no conscious connection between his father's death and the onset
of his cardiac symptoms.

We can only speculate why his cardiac symptoms vanished.
But certainly, in 1952, two things happened to this man that had
not happened before. This brilliant logician did what none of his
physicians had done. First, he consciously *connected* the death of
his father with the beginning of his symptoms. Second, he then
wrote, in great detail, the entire story to another person in whom
he had trust, a trust that was justified because the physician to
whom he told the story listened and did not minimize Hart's
distress. Instead, the Study internist wrote back that in such
cases he was convinced the cardiac pain was real — not imaginary. In oversimplified terms, once Hart admitted to a sympathetic physician, "My father has died, and it hurts," he no longer
suffered from the psychic reality that his father's diseased heart
lived on within his chest. Having at last acknowledged his
father's death, Hart could bury him.

Like hypochondriasis, passive-aggressive behavior is surprisingly provocative; for in turning anger against the self, one
by no means spares other people. Since it outwardly disavows her
anger, the martyrdom of the inwardly enraged housewife makes
her family miserable; there is no way for them to combat the rage
that she denies. Privates drive their sergeants crazy through pet-
ty, self-defeating infractions of the regulations. Suicide can be the

cruelest revenge of all. The psychoanalyst calls the process masochism; the military psychiatrist calls it passive-aggressive personality, but they only view the same phenomenon from different vantage points. Indeed, it always makes a profound social difference how retroflexed anger is viewed. For example, the relationships between sainthood and martyrdom and between martyrdom and misbehavior can be extremely subtle. Gandhi will go down as one of the great heroes of world history, but for decades he was regarded by the British Foreign Office as a troublemaker and a criminal. He certainly got under their skin.

The dangers of masochism do not just lie in the eyes of the beholder. Even in retrospect, Gandhi was a poor husband and a worse father.[2] How could this be? Probably because sadism and masochism are irrevocably intertwined. For example, the long-suffering child, to punish his parents, may run away from home with inadequate clothing. The rejected lover may cut her wrists because her boy friend cannot stand the sight of blood. Conversely, men confined in high security prisons for violent crimes toward others consistently engage in a wide variety of self-destructive, self-mutilating, and masochistic behaviors.

No defense is more social than turning anger against the self, and none poses greater problems for society. If society is wrong to call suicide a felony and to imprison prostitutes, neither "crime" is truly without victims. Ultimately, a major purpose of turning anger against the self is to protect important relationships. For example, most adolescents need to establish their own autonomy but are not yet ready to leave parental care. They procrastinate and rebel; they provoke their parents and defeat themselves. They engage in whole sequences of behaviors which simultaneously challenge, yet preserve, the parent-child relationship. It does no good to punish a teenage son for failing to wear his rubbers; the pain of punishment is never enough to cancel the rewarding assurance that his mother still cares. Martin Luther King's use of passive resistance was a carefully planned and fully conscious strategy and so cannot be called a "defense mechanism"; but his conscious behavior illustrates the less-visible ingenuity of unconscious martyrdom. Through passive aggression, Martin Luther King preserved the social fabric of a nation and yet won freedom for his followers.

Some people have divided humanity up into the "guilties" and the "paranoids," into those who blame themselves and those who project blame. Common sense and cynicism might lead us to suspect that the "guilties" get the short end of the stick. At least in the Grant Study, that suspicion was unfounded. The paranoid lost everything. The guilty masochist, if equally dependent and unhappy, at least held on to friends. By that I mean that although passive-aggressive behavior was negatively correlated with good overall adult adjustment, it did not interfere with good social adjustment (see Chapter 14).

With maturation, passive aggression is often given up in favor of displacement, reaction formation, and altruism. But the converse can also be true. When altruists became severely stressed in middle life and when their reaction formation failed, regression to less mature mechanisms was not uncommon. As suggested in Chapter 6, Lieutenant Keats was such a man. At thirty-one, in the last questionnaire that he ever returned to the Study, Keats wrote, "The most important element that has emerged in my own psychic picture is a fuller realization of my own hostilities; I used to pride myself on not having any." Thus it was that Lieutenant Keats who, as a young man, was a model of sublimation and altruism, in middle life reverted to a pattern of behavior that he had first demonstrated in early adolescence. For at thirteen, Keats had earned a reputation as a class clown, and after age thirty-one, his professional colleagues once more found it difficult to take him seriously. Despite repeated promises and despite a life ostensibly dedicated to the service of others, after 1952 he never returned a Grant Study questionnaire. (But once he "generously" gave his questionnaire away to an interested professor.) In response to the Study's phone calls and letters, Keats never directly expressed hostility or reluctance to continue his participation. Instead, he would write in November thanking us for "your good letter last May." But it was not just toward the Grant Study that he procrastinated. From forty to forty-seven, Keats remained a perpetual graduate student, unable to complete his thesis and unable to return to full-time social work. Although he lived apart from his wife for several years, Keats could never admit his dissatisfaction to the point of seeking a divorce.

One reason for the shift in Keats's defensive style is that circumstances change, as well as men. Once the unique situation of World War II ended, Keats seemed unable to sublimate his aggression. The very different realities of the Vietnam war led Keats to employ a very different adaptive style — passive resistance.

But even when they are used for the benefit of mankind, society puts sanctions on immature mechanisms. Thus it was that the former hero Lieutenant Keats, the winner of three air medals, was arrested when he took an active role in the Vietnam war. He committed the "crime" of leading a sit-in at his local draft board. In contrast, Lion's openly aggressive journalism against the Vietnam war led to promotions and national recognition.

Passive-aggressive behavior is closely linked to an adaptive process which Anna Freud called *identification with the aggressor*.[3] Through such identification, an individual, who hitherto has felt safe only by prostrating himself before a potential aggressor, now achieves mastery by incorporating or identifying with the very traits in the aggressor that he used to fear.

In the Grant Study, the life of Thomas Sawyer best exemplified passive aggression and its evolution into displacement and identification with the aggressor. On the one hand, Sawyer's masochistic mode of adaptation was a source of pain to himself and irritation to others. On the other hand, the college psychiatrist had to admit, "A force in this boy has enabled him to shake off unpleasant memories and experiences and allowed him to go ahead with some degree of freedom." Eventually, he triumphed.

The outstanding aspect of Sawyer's childhood was that he was forced to do things. He grew up with the big lie that "Mother is not dominating"; but as Tom acknowledged, "One of the facts of my family life was covering things up." At four and a half, he was taught to read by his mother. When he did not clean up his room, he was locked in it until it was picked up. At age eight, despite years of lock-ups, the battle over a clean room continued. Tom went on strike and refused to touch the mess at all. His mother persisted in jailing him; surreptitiously, Sawyer retaliated by hiding more and more mess under his bed. Finally, the battle with his mother over discipline became so severe and the lock-ups so repetitive, that Tom — like many a famous passive resister before him — won. His mother, defeated, withdrew from the battleground and turned the room project over to her gentler husband.

Throughout his youth, Sawyer had dealt with his unacknowledged domination through either passive rebellion or masochism. But Tom never could understand why the other children in his quiet university community should single him out for continued hazing and victimization — "No matter how much I turned the other cheek."

As Tom grew older, his mother told the Study, "I was inclined to make moral issues out of everything," and Tom's father, a Professor of Moral Philosophy at William and Mary, was not much better. The staff psychiatrist observed, "The parents have controlled their child not so much by corporeal or other punishment as by the use of their own feelings." Tom confirmed this: "I suppose it is just as much a form of punishment when a parent uses her hurt feelings to make one feel badly. . . . We would never lie or cheat because we knew how much it would hurt them."

When Tom first arrived at the Study, he exhibited such a mixture of virtue and naïveté that he seemed hardly old enough to be in college. Five different observers labeled him "immature." Others called him "youthful, extroverted, and charming; idealistic, unsystematic, altruistic, and humanistic." He smiled readily and "would like to take everything as a rather funny game." The psychiatrist had noticed that Tom had "a fear of his own aggression." Nevertheless, his fingernails were chewed to the quick.

In college, Mr. Sawyer had tried to police himself; outwardly, he did not admit rebellion. Although his intellectual aptitude test scores were lower than those of the majority of his classmates, he made Phi Beta Kappa. To his mother's delight, he became president of the most prestigious political organization on campus. In the army, he worked his way up through the ranks from private to first lieutenant, *and* wrote to his parents several times a week. At twenty, he told the Study, "my mother is like my father, just as close to an ideal parent as one could want." (This must be contrasted with the fact that the usually charitable family worker labeled Tom's mother "vindictive," and with the fact that at forty-five Tom himself was to describe his mother as "an angry person . . . who wore the pants. . . . I felt she robbed me of all the triumphs that I ever had.")

In his own way, Tom fought back. His toilet training lasted

longer than almost anyone's in the Study. In college, despite his professed idealism and altruism, he missed more than the average number of Grant Study appointments; he was chronically late to those that he kept. When this future Phi Beta Kappa lost his scholarship through low grades, the Dean commented, "chaotic freshman year . . . the result of determination not to follow the rigid mold of an academic family." In college, Tom's mother still told him to wash behind his ears; nevertheless, the Study internist noted that Tom's neck and ears were dirty and then, gratuitously, the physician added, "and his feet are powerful." The anthropologist noted that even at thirty, both Tom's face and hands were dirty.

In his marriage, Tom went from the frying pan into the fire. At twenty-five, he said of his wife, "It won't be her fault if we fail . . . she is a fine mother and a fine wife . . . things could not be better by any stretch of the imagination . . . she is amazingly thoughtful — most of the time."

On a multiple-choice marital questionnaire, Sawyer made the uncomplaining revelation that he washed all the clothes and all the dishes, put all the children to bath and to bed, and worked full time. (His wife had no job.) The next year the questionnaires probed the men's marriages in greater detail, and Sawyer did not return the questionnaire. Instead of complaining about his marriage, Sawyer developed abdominal pain that was so severe that he consulted a gastrointestinal specialist. After three appointments the internist wrote that Sawyer had "gastritis and hyperacidity with suggestive signs of early ulceration." When as a child he had been tied to trees, Tom had never struck back. Now, despite specific questioning, the psychologically minded internist could elicit no evidence of domestic strife; instead Tom's anger gnawed only at his own vitals. Ten years later, Tom revealed that he had lied to the internist. He described to the Grant Study the myriad indignities and infidelities to which his alcoholic wife had subjected him. "One of the annoying things was that I was shoved into the cultural role of babysitter and feminine roles. My wife was a very destructive person, a very tormented person." I asked him how he had mastered this at the time. Without a pause, Sawyer replied, "Letting the waves wash over me and taking satisfaction in letting it happen. It infuriated my wife when I did not fight back."

With time, Sawyer's defenses changed, and so he escaped the domination of his wife and of his mother. His passive aggression evolved into reaction formation and displacement. (As soon as that happened his stomach pains vanished — never to return.) Two factors seemed to contribute to the evolution of his defensive style. First, in 1965, Sawyer joined Nelson Rockefeller's staff. As an accepted member of the Rockefeller team, he was able to identify with and to internalize some of his leader's aggressiveness. In his own family, both his mother and wife had been aggressive, but always covertly. In the hurly-burly of the 1968 primary battles, Sawyer was able to see people use aggression openly, joyfully, and creatively.

At forty-six, Sawyer divorced his wife and at forty-eight he was *consciously* aware of provoking his mother: "For example, I tell her, in an uninterested fashion, 'Gee, I'll try to do better.' " Then, identifying with his earliest adversary, he added, "A lot of my mother's hostility I have observed in myself; I can use her aggression to get things done." He was right. Once Sawyer was able to identify with his mother's aggressiveness rather than to be a passive victim of it, his life changed.

The second factor was that, finally, his own passive aggression was successfully confronted. His alcoholic wife blatantly demonstrated her inability to care for his children as well as for him. His extraordinary acquiescence to humiliations from his wife became simply too obvious. In other words, once jarred by his own face in the mirror, Sawyer was able to change.

Sawyer became able to use the more flexible mechanism of displacement to master aggression in his relationships. He ceased to be victimized by his family; instead, he relished political brawls. Perhaps the most common example of displaced aggression is its translation into verbal metaphors with excretory overtones. Thus, Mr. Sawyer was able to say quite frankly of his first wife, "She was always bugging me that I wasn't dynamic enough. I should have said, 'shove it up your ass,' or just laughed at it." Of his mother he said, "When she gets impossibly bitchy now, I just laugh at her." In his happy second marriage, he genuinely loved his wife; but when he got angry at her, "Instead of withdrawing, I just get pissed off."

By age fifty Thomas Sawyer had finally become a formidable man. As he talked to me, he was immaculately and fashionably dressed. His face and hands were clean. He was genuinely charming, genuinely dedicated to serving others, and he no longer mouthed platitudes of how important it was to "be a real Christian." As the president of a small sectarian college in the Midwest, he was openly aggressive in his work, but like Harry Hughes, he now fought on the side of the angels. He was furthering his mother's evangelism and his father's scholarship. In contrast to our interview five years previously, I was now a little in awe of the man. Nevertheless, Mr. Sawyer still managed to be "accidentally" late. By chance, the same man whose feet had been "powerful" thirty years earlier had left the bottom button of his expensive shirt undone. His hairy stomach peeked out at me as if to sneer secretly at his mother's injunction, "Tommy, tuck in your shirt." The ego is mysterious, ingenious, and unconscious.

The purpose of this book is to depict adaptation to life, and at times adaptation involves maturational arrest or regression. This chapter is to underscore that such defensive immaturity occurs even in socioculturally favored men specially selected for health. Both this chapter and the next two indicate that such regression is dynamic and reversible.

Nevertheless, in writing this chapter, I wonder if I have betrayed these men. They joined the Study to serve as models of healthy development; but this chapter has examined only their warts. By following the single thread of a maladaptive defense over time, I have ignored the more complex warp and woof of their generally successful lives. If I have hurt anyone, I apologize, for that was not my intent. (The reader may well ask, "How can you be sure; against what conflicts of yours may not this chapter defend?" "Bravo," I reply — a bit defensively. "You are learning!") In any case, members of the Study who imagine that they see themselves in this chapter can be comforted in knowing that it was a painful chapter for me to write.

For two months, while I wrote their histories, I was continually confronted by a mirror that reflected my own jarring behaviors. Since confrontation is the only way to breach the immature defenses, pots call kettles black at the risk of noticing their own soot.

Part III

Developmental Consequences of Adaptation

Chapter 10

The Adult Life Cycle — In One Culture

> One man in his time plays many parts,
> His acts being seven ages . . .
>   . . . and then the lover
> Sighing like furnace, with a woeful ballad
> Made to his mistress eyebrow. Then a
>   soldier . . .
> Seeking the bauble Reputation
> E'en in the cannon's mouth. And then the
>   justice . . .
> With eyes severe and beard of formal cut,
> Full of wise saws and modern instances . . .
>   — William Shakespeare, *As You Like It*,
>   II, vii

> At 20 to 30, I think I learned how to get along
> with my wife. From 30 to 40, I learned how
> to be a success in my job. And at 40 to 50, I
> worried less about myself and more about
> the children.
> — excerpt from a Grant Study questionnaire

Caterpillars and Butterflies

The first point to be made about the adult life cycle is that, as in childhood, the metamorphosis of aging alters belief systems, instinctual expression, memory, even the brain; indeed, the passage of time renders truth itself relative.

One Grant Study man had said of America's growing hostility toward Germany, "I feel extremely disheartened. The war in Europe is none of our business." The date was October 1941. Nevertheless, in the winter of 1966–67, he subscribed fully to Lyndon Johnson's military policies, and condemned his sons for publicly demonstrating against American involvement in Vietnam. He could only recollect his active, patriotic participation in World War II. Another man, who debated dropping out of college, had said in May 1940 that he would rather live under Hitler than be dead. He could never fight for something about which he was uncertain. In middle life, however, he had trouble understanding either his dropout sons or war protesters generally.

At nineteen, yet a third man, Mr. Robert Jordan, had assured the Grant Study staff that there was no truth in Freud's sexual theories. At fifty, he had changed his tune. Why? The change was not cognitive. He had taken no course in psychology. It was not due to a chance event; he had not met an influential psychiatrist. Instead, the change seemed due to an evolution of his personality.

Certainly, there was no adolescent in the study who better illustrated Freud's ideas about repressed sexuality than Robert Jordan. At nineteen, he had boasted to the Study psychiatrists that he would drop a friend who engaged in premarital sexual intercourse. However, the psychiatrist noted that "while disapproving of sexual relations, Bob is frankly very much interested in it as a topic of thought." Mr. Jordan related a dream to the psychiatrist that he had experienced perhaps forty times. The dream involved two trees growing together; at the top the trunks met to form a chest which contained two drawers side by side. He would wake from this dream filled with anxiety. His earliest memories were two recollections of himself at age four or five. In one he was setting fire to newspapers in his mother's kitchen, and in another he was in her kitchen breaking "a dozen expensive eggs, one by one." In both his recollections, he recalled his great fear that his mother would discover him. However much the adolescent Mr. Jordan disavowed Freud, both his dreams and his memories exhibited symbolism that to a psychoanalyst would suggest sexual conflicts that are common to five-year-olds and adolescents.

In college Mr. Jordan not only disavowed Freud; he was terribly prejudiced against "sneaky liberals." He tore up "propaganda" from the college Liberal Union, and he attended Catholic mass four times a week. He also made a confession to the Study that "I have a drive — a terrible one; I've always had goals and ambitions that were beyond anything practical."

At age thirty, Mr. Jordan had matured. Like many a late adolescent, he suddenly had perceived that his earlier intellectual goals were derived from a parent; "All my life I have had Mother's dominance to battle against." Like many a man in his late thirties, he then added, "A major change in my philosophy is relevant to my goals in life. They are no longer to be great at science, but to enjoy working with people and to be able to answer 'yes' to the question I ask myself each day, 'Have you enjoyed life today?' . . . In fact I like myself and everyone else much more."

By age fifty, Mr. Jordan thoroughly approved of Freud's theories. As he had matured, as his own sexually adventurous children had reached adulthood, just so his prohibitions against premarital sexuality were reluctantly abandoned. Now, at fifty, he no longer feared the "sneaky liberals"; instead, he believed that the world's poor were the responsibility of the world's rich. He saw "law and order as a repressive concept," and this boy who had once gone to mass four times a week proclaimed "God is dead, and man is very much alive and has a wonderful future."

What had happened? As Mr. Jordan learned to tolerate the reality of his own sexuality, he had become free from the anxiety disguised in his dreams. Thus, Mr. Jordan's life illustrated a normal process Freud had not recognized. During adulthood, Mr. Jordan had recapitulated the developmental process that leads the grammar school child into the tumult of adolescence. He had struggled free of parental domination; he had achieved a less-repressive morality; he had attained less-repressive sexual beliefs; and most important, as he achieved this growth, he moved toward a greater willingness to be responsible for others. Of course, changes in his culture played a part — but only a part.

There was one problem: at fifty, Mr. Jordan could no longer correctly remember what had happened at age nineteen. When I interviewed Mr. Jordan he maintained that as soon as he arrived in college he had doubted the validity of religion and given up church altogether. He said he could only recall one recurrent childhood dream, and that was of urinating secretly behind the garage. A dream repeated forty times and churchgoing repeated four times a week had been forgotten. How then may we obtain truth about the adult life cycle? Clearly, it must be studied prospectively. It is all too common for caterpillars to become butterflies and then to maintain that in their youth they had been little butterflies. Maturation makes liars of us all.

As a concrete example, let me cite the men's shifting perspectives of their own sex education. The records of one man's psychiatric interviews at age eighteen read as follows: "It was not until he was fifteen years old that masturbation and nocturnal emissions began; apparently, there was no guilt or shame centering around these two things. . . . At the present time, the boy continues to masturbate; there is no guilt or shame connected with it." At twenty-five, the same subject flew halfway across the country to seek a New York psychiatrist's advice about his masturbation, only to find out that the psychiatrist "told me that masturbation didn't seem all that serious to him." At forty-six the subject wrote, "Since the age of fourteen and a half I've been a masturbator. I worried about this in college, and I think I discussed it with the Grant Study psychiatrist at the time." At forty-six, he still saw masturbation as a sin and a major problem in his life. He could not believe that he had ever concealed such concerns.

Another man told the Study psychiatrist that all of his sexual information had come from his companions and that he had never had any information from his parents except "vague admonitions." Simultaneously his parents had told the Study, "Problems of sex were discussed freely and openly when the boys were young, all questions being answered truthfully." Still another man's mother had told the Study "I answered any question about sex that I was asked perfectly openly and clearly." At forty-nine, the subject remembered: "My family never did anything, as far as sex education went, with any of their children." Another mother told the Study that she had considered masturbation "disgusting" and that her son's masturbation was "excessive"; she claimed that she convinced her husband to tell her son that it caused "nervous debilitation." At nineteen, the same subject told the Study that sex had never been discussed with him by his parents, and that one of the things that he most wished counsel on was masturbation.

Unconscious gratifications of wishes also distort the past. A simple example was the man who originally reported to the Study a military school class standing of third out of 150. By the time he was fifty, he had become second out of 900. One Grant Study subject did not approve of his adolescent children's use of marijuana; yet in 1940 he had praised the potlike effects of alcohol. "I get gentler, sweeter, less sarcastic, and enjoy dancing more," he wrote. "My mind is usually quite bright, I feel closer to music than ever, more open to people. Alcohol is always a pleasant experience." In worrying over his adolescent children he had also almost forgotten that in adolescence, he, too, had been a long-haired university dropout who wandered across Europe.

The purpose of relating these inconsistencies of memory is to show that the same kinds of forgetfulness and distortion can occur between adolescence and middle life as are well known to occur in childhood. Remarkable discrepancies occur between what parents think they have told adolescent children about affectively important issues and what those children subsequently remember.

In understanding the adult life cycle, then, as in understanding modern physics, we must be guided by concepts of relativity and complementarity; for as soon as time is included in an equation, the old Newtonian verities are lost. Psychological novelists have always known that the world looks different to the same person at different ages. Artists have always recognized man's inability to capture the whole truth about his life. The Grant Study offers hope that social scientists, too, may make sense from apparent ambiguities.

There *are* patterns and rhythms to the life cycle. The secret of discovering these rhythms lies in our capacity to circumvent the distorting effect of time upon our vision. This is not easy. There is no way that we can study the continuity of a symphony except by listening to it in its entirety; for we, the audience, are caught up in time. If at my twentieth reunion I try to discern the changes in my college classmates, I fail; for I, myself, have changed too much.

But consider trees. There is nothing confusing or ambiguous about the fact that our concept of trees constantly changes from one season to the next. What is a tree? A bouquet of pink blossoms, a dark green umbrella, a torch of autumnal orange flame, a stark black latticework softened by a silver glaze? A tree is all of these things; and if we regard such change as predictable, it is only because our own life cycle is so much longer. After we have seen the seasons repeat themselves in orderly fashion two or three times, dispelling all hint of ambiguity, we are only two or three years older. We remember, and we understand. By studying the cross-section of a redwood tree, we can discern a millenium of forest history — in minutes. In our view of a thousand concentric rings we stand outside time. Just as a time-lapse photographer can show us in two minutes the opening of a flower that in truth takes two days, so as I read the folders of Grant Study members, I viewed behavioral incidents spread over three decades unfold in two hours. Unlike the situation of my own twentieth re-union, time passed for the observed but not for the observer.

It is only in the last half century that physicians and parents have learned to anticipate orderly shifts in the personality of children. In the nineteenth century many physicians still consid-ered children adults in miniature. As a specialist, the pediatrician is a creation of the twentieth century. Parents' recollections of the milestones of child development are notoriously poor. Only through the invention of the photograph, the baby book, the fam-ily doctor's case files, and finally through prospective studies of growth and development, were scientists able fully to circumvent the distortions that time produces. Now we know that the roman-tic swain at five will at seven regard the opposite sex with loath-ing, only to become a romantic swain once more at age sixteen. But a hundred years ago, the works of Benjamin Spock were not available; the phases of childhood were regarded as relatively unpredictable. Today we watch children develop as our savage ancestors learned to watch the orderly waxing and waning of the moon. As our children shift from phase to phase, we pray; we cross our fingers; we worry or are grateful; but we are not totally surprised.

However, adult development is still a mystery. Humans are not mature at Freud's five or Saint Loyola's seven, or even the law's eighteen or twenty-one. Ronald Reagan's ultraliberal college politics must seem utterly foreign to him now; for one price of growing up is to lose touch with one's past. As an adolescent, one Grant Study man loved modern jazz. At fifty, having grown to appreciate the classical composers, he had only contempt for his children's passion for rock and roll. He thought musical tastes had deteriorated while he had remained constant.

At one a child cannot walk, at four he cannot ride a bicycle, at six he is unable to imagine a room from the perspective of another, and at ten he still cannot examine concepts in abstract terms. At eighteen he can do all those things — not because he has been taught, but because both he and his central nervous system have evolved. Could not a shift in one's politics be for the same reason? When Mr. Jordan, now a liberal butterfly, flies past a John Birch caterpillar, they may exchange glances, but both must fail to recognize their kinship. By the time the young communist has grown into an old reactionary, the changes within have been so imperceptible, if so profound, that he believes that he still sees with the same eyes and feels with the same heart. He believes that only the times have changed. Until thirty-five or forty, Jung warns us, "Many — far too many — aspects of life which should also have been experienced lie in the lumber-room among dusty memories; but sometimes, too, they are glowing coals under grey ashes."[1] Watching such coals burst into flame has made pursuit of the Grant Study infinitely exciting.

Unlike the seasons, the individual life cycle occurs only once for each person. In 1950, Erik Erikson, who cut his teeth on the first great longitudinal studies of human development at Berkeley, argued convincingly that adults, like children, evolve and mature.[2] He was among the first social scientists to appreciate fully that adults do not march on from life event to life event, from graduation to marriage to "empty nest" to retirement. Instead, he demonstrated that adults change dynamically in the process. Certainly, Shakespeare had said it all before; but most textbooks of human development associate changes in adult personality with external events.

The evidence from the Grant Study confirms the adult life patterns outlined by Erik Erikson in *Childhood and Society*. Erikson suggested that in a variety of cultures the grammar school child, having already passed through stages of *Basic Trust*, *Autonomy*, and *Initiative*, develops *Industry* while keeping his adventurous passions under control. Then, in adolescence, as his suppressed passions return, the child strives for an *Identity* — an effort to differentiate himself and his beliefs from his parents. Next, as a young adult, he seeks genuine *Intimacy* with people his own age, and then, finally, somewhere around forty according to Erikson, if he is healthy he achieves *Generativity*, a rich, ripe stage of human existence already hinted at in prior chapters.

Generativity is not just a stage for making little things grow. The world is filled with irresponsible mothers who are marvelous at bearing and loving children up to the age of two and then despair of taking the process further. Generativity, in the sense that it describes a stage in the life cycle, implies responsibility for the growth, leadership, and well-being of one's fellow creatures, not just raising crops or young children.

Between the decade of the twenties and the forties, Erikson left an uncharted period of development. In their early thirties, men seemed to be too busy becoming, too busy mastering crafts; too busy ascending prescribed career ladders to reflect upon their own vicissitudes of living. Equally important, they were too colorless, too conforming, to attract the attention of other observers at other ages. At thirty-five the men of the Grant Study could not wait to step into the driver's seat. At fifty they were far more concerned about those who worked for them and with them. In short, between Erikson's stage of Intimacy and his stage of Generativity appeared an intermediate stage of Career Consolidation — a time when they, like Shakespeare's soldier, sought "the bauble Reputation." This maturational pattern of identity to intimacy to career consolidation to generativity has been confirmed for both men and women by the major American studies of adult development.[3]

However, the full life cycle can unfold only when humans are provided both the freedom and opportunity to mature. John Clausen, a Berkeley sociologist at the Institute of Human Development, has identified four major variables affecting an individual's life cycle that help to put the Grant Study into a broader context. These variables are (1) "The opportunities available to him or the obstacles he encounters as these are influenced by his social class, ethnic membership, age, sex . . . as well as the effects of war, depression and major social changes"; (2) "Investments of effort that the individual makes on his own behalf"; (3) "The sources of support and guidance that help to orient him to his world and assist him to cope with it"; and (4) "The personal resources that the individuals can command."[4]

Due to the homogeneous selection of the Grant Study subjects, the first two of Clausen's factors — cultural opportunity and achievement motivation — were held constant. First, the Grant Study men had an equal chance in life: white, male, American, well educated, they each had entrée into their culture's power elite. Each shared the same period in world history. Clearly, had they been malnourished throughout childhood, locked into an assembly line, or born into a caste that was not respected; had they lacked the educational permission to develop their talents or had they been denied by a fluke of history or health the chance to grow, they could not serve as models for a healthy life cycle.

Second, as Clausen points out, human development involves free choice, and not everybody wants the responsibility that comes with Generativity. The Grant Study men, however, were all hard workers and achievers; they were all chosen for their adolescent willingness to invest in their own growth and development.

It was Clausen's third and fourth variables that appeared most important in differentiating the life trajectories of the Grant Study men and in determining their eventual positions (at age fifty) within the life cycle. In Chapter 13 I shall discuss the effects of Clausen's third factor. Certainly, the available sources of support and guidance made a big difference to the men. Without love it is hard to grow.

If interpreted as differential choice of adaptive styles, the effects of Clausen's fourth factor, "the personal resources that the individual can command," made a big difference, too. If the physical health and intelligence of the Grant Study men were roughly similar, their choice of defenses differed greatly. Of the twenty-five men with the least mature defenses, only four achieved Generativity; almost all (four-fifths) of the men with the most mature defenses did so. This finding will be discussed at length in Chapter 15.

The life of Dr. Adam Carson provides a frame on which to display the Study's statistical findings on the life cycle. The biography of Dr. Carson illustrates his halting passage from identity to intimacy, through career consolidation, and, finally, into the capacity to *care* in its fullest sense. When he entered the Study, Adam Carson's parents had described him as a model child.

"From the minute Adam was born," his mother boasted, "he has been completely perfect as to conduct, ambition, and everything." His lawyer father perceived him as an "almost perfect little youngster." In short, Carson's adolescent struggle for autonomy with his parents never got fully under way. It is true that his father admitted to the Grant Study that from sixteen to eighteen his son had become "a bit of a hell-raiser." It is true that unbeknownst to his father, young Carson had acquired a motorcycle, an appetite for sexual conquest, and a love for ballroom dancing such that he considered abandoning his future medical career to dance professionally. But at twenty, Dr. Carson put these interests aside. His father was too perfect, too broadminded; there was not enough to rebel against, and so Carson's brief adolescent respite from his father's tight control became too short-lived for smooth adult development.

By twenty, in all aspects of his life Adam Carson justified his father's boast that his son was "leading a planned existence; Adam has his emotions beautifully under control." Young Carson attended Harvard Medical School; he interned at the Massachusetts General; he did postgraduate work at the Rockefeller Institute, and then he returned to Harvard Medical School, alleging that he loved research and disliked private practice. Had not his father explained to him that research was the road to becoming a truly great physician? But there was a price that Dr. Carson paid for choosing an identity that his father, not he, had selected. When Carson was nineteen, the Grant Study psychiatrist had seen him "giving an impression of considerable mental energy ... his affect is vital, rich, happy, and colorful"; but the same observer called the twenty-eight-year-old Carson "not a very broad-dimensioned person in my mind." Carson's Thematic Apperception Test revealed him to have become, in the mind of one psychologist, "a superficial guy, with a passive kind of dependence on circumstance; unsure about his own fate, and passively awaiting it. There is a constant rejection of women and their sexual charms. ... [He is] seeking out the socially acceptable in order to avoid private emotion." Looking at the same tests, another psychologist wrote, "There is a complete avoidance of aggression and depression; a rigid, inhibited, neurotic, utterly nonintrospective response." "Adam," the Study anthropologist chimed in, "is gangly and awkward, young, and adolescent . . . dependent on his family . . . unsure and terribly concerned that he is following the established pattern."

The anthropologist was right. In young adulthood Adam Carson followed the dictates of his culture. He not only won initiation into a respected career, but he became a husband and father. At twenty-six, he wrote, "I treasure my marriage above everything else in the world; I get tremendous happiness from it." But when he looked back on that same marriage at forty-seven he could write, "I felt that she was a rattlesnake, who would do something mean and awful." It was not that he did not know his own mind at each age. A third grade boy is honest when he tells us that he hates girls and that his mom is perfect. The conventional Dr. Carson had married an ascetic wife, suitable for him as an immature twenty-six-year-old caterpillar, one who had damped his adolescent passions before they had hardly been kindled. Originally his wife provided him with a conventional, sisterly intimacy, but as he matured, Dr. Carson's passionless marriage degenerated into a series of angry, repetitive conflicts.

Although Dr. Carson's research productivity was modest, he wrote, "I have given up practice completely . . . work consists almost entirely of research . . . my work fills me with constant ever-increasing pleasure, which private practice never did." After a decade of winning merit badge after merit badge, Dr. Carson obtained academic tenure. He became an Associate Professor of Medicine at Harvard Medical School. Once obtained, however, this badge of academic acceptance, his title-on-the-door, brought little satisfaction. Instead, Dr. Carson became so depressed over his marriage and career that he considered suicide. Consciously, he experienced such "depression" not as an affect, but as "a sense of fatigue." Why? He had always told the Study that he was happy.

Ten years later, I met Adam Carson. He had gone through divorce, remarriage, and a shift from research to private practice. His personal metamorphosis had continued. The mousy researcher had become a charming clinician. Dr. Carson's dramatic office looked out over the Charles River; in his long white coat with the ivory-tipped stethoscope peeking out one pocket, he appeared suave, untroubled, kindly, and in control. Eagerly, he shared the pleasure he got from private practice in a way that was exciting rather than tedious. The vibrant energy that had characterized his adolescence had returned. In describing his general mood, Dr. Carson confided, "I'm chronically depressed, I think." But now his depression was clearly an *affect;* and he was anything but fatigued. In the next breath he confessed, "I'm very highly sexed, and that's a problem, too." He then provided me with an exciting narrative as he told me not only of recent romantic entanglements, but also of his warm, fatherly concern for patients.

A ten-year-old pays attention to what his parents say; a sixteen-year-old pays more attention to what they do. Like an adolescent, Dr. Carson now perceived his father in a very different light. At twenty-eight, Dr. Carson had said of his father, "I resemble him, but he betters me in every respect." At that time Dr. Carson was hard at work at the research that his father had recommended. This advice was in spite of the fact that Dr. Carson's father took great pleasure from an active, glamorous law practice that involved working closely with individual clients. While urging Adam Carson, M.D., to make a lasting academic contribution to humankind, Mr. Carson, Esq., enjoyed the present. At forty-five, instead of perceiving his father's admonitions as a hindrance, Dr. Carson, now like his father in private practice, could find his father a valued example. Despite different professions, their careers had suddenly converged.

The life of Dr. Carson was chosen because it caricatures the process described so simply by the Grant Study subject whose quote begins this chapter. ("At 20 to 30, I think I learned how to get along with my wife. From 30 to 40, I learned how to be a success in my job. And at 40 to 50, I worried less about myself and more about the children.") After reading Carson's history (in its present disguised form), another Grant Study man wrote back, "I think I see in myself most of the generalities you discussed — pretty strong self-centeredness at an earlier age, preoccupied with establishing a career, etc. Your frequent reference to Erikson encourages me to read some of his material. Heretofore, he's been just a name. His idea of achieving generativity is intriguing — I feel I have achieved it to a substantial degree over the last few years — almost in spite of myself. Guiding teenagers through adolescence and maintaining a happy stable marriage at the same time almost requires it!"

Adolescence — The First Time Around

In general, the prospectively studied lives of the Grant Study men supported Erikson's hypothesis that the stages of the life cycle must be passed through in sequence. Although one stage of life is not superior to another, a given stage of development could rarely be achieved until the previous one was mastered. Men did not usually achieve real responsibility for other adults without having first consolidated their careers and having learned to love their wives.

The entrance to the adult life cycle is through the portal of adolescence. According to Erikson, and his mentor Anna Freud, adolescence is a time for painful self-differentiation.[5] Family shibboleths are cast aside, and an identity is forged that is the individual's alone. Identity formation in adolescence is fostered by a curious fact of human nature; as we lose or separate ourselves from people that we love, we internalize them. Thus, as adolescents turn to communes, to a college-on-the-opposite-coast, as adolescents consciously focus on all that is bad about their parents in order to extricate themselves from the backwards pull, they escape and take their parents with them. This proves important for two reasons. First, the Dr. Tarrytowns and the Casper Smythes, who had never really had parents to internalize, remained forever lonely. Second, other men who continued to be dominated by external parents — like Horace Lamb and Dr. Adam Carson — were delayed in achieving maturity.

Not only is adolescence — at least in our culture — a prerequisite to entering the modal adult life cycle, a stormy adolescence per se is no obstacle to normal adult maturation. In fact, it often bodes well. Two psychologists, Harvey Peskin and Norman Livson, of the Institute of Human Development at Berkeley, suggest that an individual's chances for subsequent mental health are improved if control over one's emotional life is achieved during preadolescence and if this very control is weakened or abandoned during adolescence. Shifts from a placid to a tense and edgy temperament, from rare to frequent whining, from strict impulse control to explosive outbursts of temper, and from independence to dependence all predict subsequent mental health at age thirty.[6] Peskin and Livson summarize their findings by observing, "The adolescent contribution to adult character often reverses rather than maintains the effect of pre-adolescent behavior." This helps explain why, too, strict emotional control gained during the early years of adolescence can lead to emotional instability at thirty or forty. As in the case of Dr. Carson, to shut off adolescence prematurely is to run the risk of an unusually stormy middle life.

There were in the Grant Study seven men who at age forty-seven had never really completed adolescence. Instead, they lived out their adult lives like grammar school children — or Perpetual Boys. Like earnest boy scouts, they worked hard at their jobs and required little in the way of psychiatric care; but they never traversed the sequential stages of adult maturation — Intimacy, Career Consolidation, and Generativity. In middle life, all but one of these Perpetual Boys, an orphan, remained inextricably bound to their mothers. Only two of the seven men spent even half of their adult lives married, and each of these men assumed a feminine role in a rather distant marriage. Children were either never conceived or avoided. Friends were virtually nonexistent. At fifty they stood on life's sidelines, often downwardly socially mobile and filled with self-doubt.

The failure of the Perpetual Boys to commit themselves to careers had begun right after college. During World War II, none of them saw a shot fired in combat, and most never put on a uniform. After the war they remained journeymen; they never themselves became master craftsmen or mentors for younger men. Although all of the Perpetual Boys were responsible to their employers, none became really responsible for the next generation or to those who worked for him. As a result, their career success was the worst in the Study.

At forty-seven, one of the Perpetual Boys described the time from one to thirteen as the happiest years of his life and maintained that his had been an "idyllically innocent and serene childhood." Adolescence had frightened him, and the years from thirteen to twenty were his most unhappy. Although neither homosexual in identification nor physiologically a eunuch, at thirty-three he still retained his prepubertal plumpness, and he lived at home helping his mother arrange floral centerpieces.

At thirty, the anthropologist had described him as "interesting on an impersonal, intellectual level"; and at fifty he was still more interested in details than he was in the big picture. Eventually he achieved a stable marriage, but he and his wife never wished to have children. He took little interest in and assumed no responsibility for the small New England college where he worked; and, unlike the Study's most creative and productive academicians, he was more interested in his own scanty publications on early colonial history than he was in his students. Like many another well-adapted sixth-grader, intellectualization remained his chief mode of adaptation.

When another such man came to see me I was struck by the curious contrast between his workingman's hands, his cheap shoes with low socks, and his Brooks Brothers tweed jacket, patched at the elbows. Despite a socially proper mother, a private boarding school education, and a college degree, he worked for a heating and plumbing firm, ate alone in blue-collar diners, and felt overwhelmed by bills.

The Study had seen this man at nineteen as psychologically stable, if a little bland, and ironically, in college his mother had described him as "a grown man when he was two years old." Without the usual problems of adolescents he had been unusually creative in building ship models, tree houses, and an automobile from old junk. He wanted to become an automotive engineer. But the anthropologist had noticed that at twenty-nine he was still "closely tied to his mother, unwilling to make new associations," and at forty-nine he was still unmarried, living a few blocks from where his parents had lived. His life revolved around his pets; "Catering to six cats," he assured me, "can be a big affair."

Curiously unable or unwilling to distort his universe through effective defense mechanisms that might have brought him mental illness or glory, he remained in the latency child's haven of underperformance. Despite above-average intelligence, in twenty-four years this man never rose beyond a $10,000-a-year position in his heating and plumbing firm, and his occupational responsibility had not changed. Nevertheless, he took pleasure from his job because, as in childhood, he could build things. He told me in detail and with real enthusiasm about furnaces; but he had no responsibility for other people. For a brief two years in his late thirties he had been married to a kindergarten teacher, but most of his life he had had only his cats to care for.

He felt perpetually out of control of his life. At twenty-nine he had written, "The brevity of my answers leads me to believe that my life must have been pretty substandard. It still may be." And at forty-six, when far less socially privileged classmates like Goodhart were firmly established in the upper middle class he wrote, "I feel deeply inadequate. . . . I have always felt that I could never sell myself." Yet he had a Yankee dignity and a curious quality of self-respect that I could not help admiring. A ten-year-old is often better integrated than his adolescent counterpart. One stage of life is not "better" or "healthier" than another.

It was hard to tell what stunted the growth of this man. My guess — and it is no more than a guess — is that we stop growing when our human losses are no longer replaced. In adolescence, both of his parents had let him down; five years apart both had had nervous breakdowns. Guilty and ambivalent, he was unable to take leave of his parents; yet he still felt diminished by their loss. At eleven, when his father was hospitalized for the first time, he had stopped believing in God. At forty-five, he told me that whenever a friend died, he lost a piece of himself. (Another somewhat similar Grant Study member expressed this same dilemma when he told me that his philosophy over rough spots was "Do not ask for whom the bell tolls; it tolls for thee" — a credo more suited to age seventy than forty-five.) The seeds of love must be eternally resown.

The other eighty-eight men in the Study all negotiated adolescence and achieved an identity distinct from their parents. However, born too soon, the original Grant Study investigators had not read Anna Freud, Erik Erikson, or George Goethals. They mistakenly believed that several normal facets of adolescent development were really ominous signs of future instability, and their predictions of mental health in college were often proved wrong.

In college each man had been rated on a checklist of twenty-five personality traits. A Study psychiatrist then examined which traits were associated with the Staff's prediction of future psychological soundness or unsoundness.[7] Three traits — vital affect, friendliness, and humanism — were powerfully associated with a favorable staff prediction of successful adult adaptation. However, follow-up demonstrated that these traits in adolescence showed little correlation to midlife outcome. In many men, such "virtues" seemed to have been more associated with a transient phase of development than with enduring character. By their nature, adolescents are spontaneous, gregarious, and idealistic.

Similarly, the Study staff observed that the traits "shyness," "ideation," "introspection," "inhibition," and "lack of purpose and values" were seen most often in adolescents whose future emotional stability was thought to be in doubt. Once more, follow-up revealed that these latter traits were merely symptoms of that self-limiting mental malady, adolescence; they did not predict the men with worst outcomes. Indeed, it was three traits that are rather uncharacteristic of late adolescence that were most often diagnostic of future mental health. It was the adolescents who were seen as "well-integrated" and "practical and organized" who were best adapted at age fifty, and the adolescents who were "asocial" who were least likely to be called "Best Outcomes."

The adaptive function of adolescent "disorganization" can be illustrated by two vignettes. As a child, one man had been rigidly overconcerned about the welfare of his younger siblings. During his early adolescence he worked to help support them; then, in college, he rebelled. He became sloppy, lazy, and careless, and he saw himself as "very selfish." He had little idea who he was. On the one hand, he became preoccupied with philosophy — Dostoevski and all-embracing theories. On the other hand, his ambition was to become a self-serving international banker and a Morgan partner, with a fat abdomen, "in order to make myself more imposing." The Study staff was disturbed by his apparent selfishness and turmoil.

By age twenty-three, brought to his senses by the realities of World War II, he reintegrated his personality. He put aside his idea of becoming an international banker in favor of helping alleviate starvation in postwar Europe. He wanted to become a "high-minded old idealist," and gave this ambition shape by joining the foreign service. With less rigidity and appropriate concern he could again devote himself to the economic problems of America's younger "siblings." Reaction formation became altruism. At forty-seven, without the need of a pot belly, he knew exactly who he was — a trustworthy, unselfish, meticulous career diplomat. Of course, he no longer remembered his adolescence. He criticized his underlings for their sloppy English and condemned his son for his incomprehensible selfishness.

Another man who had been stable and well controlled during childhood remembered his adolescence as the unhappiest period of his life. During those years he experienced a disturbing loss of control that in fact proved the harbinger of inner dynamism that was to serve him well in adult life. He recalled that his powerful father would tease him about his lack of sexual prowess, and the result was explosive. Unable to tolerate his adolescent hatred of his father, he defended himself with projection and acting out. He was involved in deliberate damage to school property; he repeatedly smashed up his car, and he flunked out of his first college. He was one of the few Grant Study men to go to jail. Finally he graduated with one of the lowest grade averages in the Study; but by 1942 he had learned to focus his rebellious energies into the varsity lacrosse and wrestling teams.

In 1936, although he lived in Omaha, Nebraska, this Grant Study subject had been preoccupied with the persecution of Jews in a Hitler-run world. Like most adolescent idealism and much paranoia, his was a perfectly legitimate concern; but, significantly, no other Jewish member of the Study, even those whose families had been in real danger from the Nazis, had fears of the same intensity. In 1940, when such concerns were still more appropriate, his concern over the fate of European Jews had subsided. By then he was in control of his own instincts and openly acknowledging his struggle with his Hitler-like father. With only average eagerness to serve, he completed ROTC and entered the army in May 1943. With adolescence behind him, he took more pride in making the division football team than he did in fighting Germans.

As an adult, he learned to use his aggression as gracefully as

Lion. He enjoyed his marriage and his children; his business prospered. When he ultimately triumphed over his father, the two men remained friends. In middle life, although nobody could have called this staunch Republican an idealist, he worked hard in redeveloping twenty-five acres of downtown Omaha in order to facilitate racial integration. This ex-delinquent and jailbird put many an adolescent's dreams into action.

If adolescent instability is not malignant, however, recent research does not support the ubiquity of the fabled Adolescent Identity Crisis. Instead, review of the Grant Study data confirms findings from other studies of unselected normal adolescent populations;[8] dramatic identity crises are relatively rare and are associated not with psychological health but with vulnerability. During their actual adolescences, the Grant Study men perceived their lives as far less stormy than they did looking back on them in middle life. In part, this shift in viewpoint was due to the fact that at fifty the men could admit conflict and struggle with parents far more easily than they could at eighteen. In part, it was because the stages of the life cycle are often invisible to the participant until after the fact. In part, as it is in character disorder, much of the turmoil in adolescence is invisible to the protagonist for purely defensive reasons.

Of the ninety-five Grant Study men, five experienced prolonged confusion over their identity; of these, four at midlife continue to remain uncertain of who they are and where they are going. Their prolonged quest for identity has made such men appealing to young people; their search has kept them strongly identified with their family of origin and refreshingly open to new ideas. Yet, they have regarded their own lives as painful and their careers as unsatisfying; and as they are still bound to their past, their marriages have sometimes been in disarray.

At forty-eight, Harry Hughes, the editor who was described in Chapter 9 as having outgrown projection, expressed the dilemma bluntly. "I'm in the midst of an identity crisis," he told me. "I don't feel that it's desirable to plaster this over." Then, he confessed, "I would not admit to many people how inadequate I feel in my job." Yet the truth was that however unsure he was of himself, he did his job uncommonly well.

In adolescence Harry had projected the turmoil within. In a world headed toward violence and social change, how, he asked, could he ever become the artist that he wished to be? The fact was that although he wanted to become a painter, he could not decide what he wanted to paint. Like many adolescents, he "maintained a skeptical attitude toward the integrity of other people and their social behavior," but that only reflected his view of himself. He vacillated between joining idealistic religious communes and assuming the "dishonest" life of an advertising man. His compromise was to become a journalist and editor. Not until he was fifty did he really master what he wanted to paint. Today, his paintings hang in public galleries.

At forty-eight, in contrast to most subjects "over thirty," Harry Hughes still maintained that ideals and faith were more important to him than action. He still looked wistfully at the communes of the 1960s. Unlike most of his colleagues in the Study, he did not condemn "hippies." "If I could embrace their views," he wrote longingly, "I would not have a worry in the world." What others admired and found endearing about him was his capacity to give advice, his capacity to "affirm the larger meaning of pain." (It is well to remember that artists often never leave adolescence behind — hard on the artist, but a blessing for humankind.)

The writers who have best described the turmoil of adolescence — Goethe, Hesse, Twain, Anna Freud, Thomas Wolfe, Erik Erikson, even Salinger — had each experienced an unusually unsettled adolescence themselves. Indeed, there is a definite parallel between the life of Harry Hughes and that of Erik Erikson, who articulated our concept of the prolonged identity crisis.[9] As an adolescent Erikson had wished to be completely different from his pediatrician stepfather (who had raised him since he was three) and he wandered Europe trying to find himself as an artist. Just so, Hughes had vowed that he would be completely different from his newspaperman father and had tried to paint. Then, in young adulthood, Erikson found Anna Freud, a well-camouflaged child doctor, as his mentor, and in midlife, Erikson, like her, became a therapist to children. In similar fashion, Harry Hughes found an ex-newspaperman turned painter and religious leader to be his mentor; and at midlife, as an editor, he had become a well-camouflaged version of his father. On occasion Erik Erikson has been called "the man who invented himself." When I asked Hughes who his role models had been, he stoutly maintained, "I may have had dependent relationships, but I don't know that I've ever emulated anyone."

Intimacy and Career Consolidation

Having disengaged itself from the past, the newly hatched butterfly must reestablish viable links between itself and the outside world. Thus, psychiatrists who work exclusively with young adult (especially graduate student) populations discover that regardless of diagnosis, difficulties surrounding intimacy are the dominant motifs of their patients' complaints. The emotional disorders that selectively afflict young adults — schizophrenia, mania, impulsive delinquency, and suicidal inclinations — all reflect anguish about or protest against failures at intimacy.

So it was with the Grant Study men from age twenty to thirty. Wives were wooed and won, and friendships that were to endure into adulthood deepened. As soon as the men could win real autonomy from their parents and a sense of their own independent identities, they sought once more to entrust themselves to others. Many adolescent friendships vanished; for the group loyalties of adolescence are different from the requisites of adult intimacy. Often adolescents choose friends who remind them of themselves or of what they want to become. Sometimes they choose friends who by sheer numbers will provide the support and comfort that they need to enter the larger world. But in young adulthood such relationships are replaced by ones that respect individual differences. At least in our culture, if the commune prevents loneliness before thirty, it perpetuates it afterwards.

To fail at intimacy, however, was to forfeit mastery in the next stages of the adult life cycle. Of the thirty men who, at forty-seven, had received the highest scores in overall Adult Adjustment, the Best Outcomes, all but two had achieved stable marriage before thirty and had remained married until fifty. Of the thirty Worst Outcomes, twenty-three men had either married *after* thirty or separated from their wives *before* fifty. Proportionately, fifty-nine percent of the best marriages and only half as many of the worst marriages were contracted between the ages of twenty-three and twenty-nine. In other words, to marry too young, before a capacity for intimacy was developed, boded as poorly for successful marriage as to exhibit a delayed capacity for intimacy.

Obviously, marriage is not the be-all and end-all of intimacy; it is merely a tangible marker that flags that invisible, ineffable human process called love. In other cultures and at other points in history, alternative markers of intimacy would have to be used. The church, the teaching professions, and perhaps the armed forces contain highly generative individuals with clear Career Consolidation who have never married. In their twenties, many such men and women have experienced real difficulty with intimacy, yet over the years they have managed to give richly of themselves to the next generation and to grow in the process. I suspect it is not coincidence that such individuals all achieve strong group allegiance, as if the security of group membership provides them the security and strength that most adults find in one-to-one intimacy.

Once human relationships had been recemented, outside of their family of origin, the Grant Study men were free to devote themselves to the next stage. From age twenty-five to thirty-five they tended to work hard, to consolidate their careers, and to devote themselves to the nuclear family. Poor at self-reflection, they were not unlike their grammar school children; they were good at tasks, careful to follow the rules, anxious for promotion, and willing to accept all aspects of the system. (In describing a group of infants followed until maturity, Jerome Kagan identified many facets of young adult personality that appeared to correlate more highly with that person at six to ten than they did with that person in puberty or midadolescence.[10])

Once serious apprenticeship is begun, the refreshing openness of a Harry Hughes is lost; adolescent idealism is sacrificed to "making the grade" — be it tenure, partnership, or a vice-presidency. In working hard to become specialists at their careers, the Grant Study men tended to sacrifice play. Rather than question whether they had married the right woman, rather than dream of other careers, they changed their babies' diapers and looked over their shoulders at their competition. Self-deception about the adequacy of both marital and career choices was common. The relative dullness of the Grant Study men at thirty was reflected in the anthropologist's notes on her 1950–1952 interviews. The excitement and potential excellence of the college sample became lost in conformity. Men who at nineteen had radiated charm now seemed colorless, hardworking, bland young men in "gray flannel suits."

Of course, a major difference between the ten-year-old child and his thirty-year-old counterpart fighting to be a success in his job is that the latter is trying to differentiate himself from his peers. Cub scouts enjoy membership in the pack, but a bright medical student is terrified lest he remain an undistinguishable pebble on a beach full of bright medical students. Having achieved intimacy with a few fellow humans, he then tries to run faster and in a slightly different direction from all of his classmates. (Even prior to 1960 available comparative studies suggest that the shift from the search for intimacy to the quest for Career Consolidation during the fourth decade is as real for women as for men.[11])

But success brings problems. In the thirties there is a precarious balance between growing roots in order to settle down and simultaneously striving for the room-at-the-top, which is often somewhere else. Women, concerned with their nuclear family on the one hand, withdraw from their less-conventional unmarried friends and put their children's needs and household security first. At the same time, they strive to give exciting parties, resume postponed careers, and inadvertently push their husbands toward the very promotions that would disrupt their own roots. For men and women, dissatisfaction with earned income probably peaks between the ages of thirty-five and forty,[12] and progression up the career ladder means sacrificing much more than geographic roots.

Just as the most common psychiatric complaints of the twenties reflect yearnings toward and retreat from intimacy, the emotional complaints of the thirties reflect conflicts about success. The alcoholism, the sadomasochistic marriages, the depression, and the psychosomatic ailments accompanying both occupational overachievement and passive-aggressive self-defeat reflect the young adult's difficulty in obtaining or accepting success. If I become sergeant, will I lose my friends? If I finish my thesis, what will I do for the rest of my life? Now that New York has opened my eyes, how can I bear to go home? I've worked so hard becoming a doctor, now won't someone take care of me? If I emulate Ibsen's Nora and slam the door, can I bear to be an independent woman? These are the unconscious, unanswerable questions that plague the young adult in his or her thirties.

A consequence of the materialistic concerns during Career Consolidation has been that inner development during this decade remains a mystery. Erikson ignores the thirties totally, and available prospective studies of development from twenty-five to forty have focused almost exclusively on career choice and its evolution.[13] Thus, the saga of the thirties not only makes dull reading for all but vocational guidance counselors, but for a time the apparent lack of dynamic change led students of personality development to wonder if the major longitudinal growth studies at Yellow Springs, Ohio, and Berkeley had anything to teach them.

However, during the period of Career Consolidation, one important inner change is the acquisition, assimilation, and finally the casting aside of nonparental role models or mentors. Daniel Levinson, a Yale sociologist and a perceptive student of career development, has extensively investigated this process.[14] Just as nonfamilial models once served to assist the process of freeing the adolescent from his parents and establishing an independent identity, so the new role model of the late twenties and early thirties seemed associated with the acquisition of solid career identification. At forty-seven, when the Grant Study men were asked to review their lives, the role models or "ego ideals" that they had acknowledged important at nineteen had been forgotten or denied. The place of the adolescent's hero had been taken by the mentor acquired in young adulthood, the "master craftsmen," as it were, to whom they had apprenticed themselves. However, while acknowledging that their mentors were often "father figures," the men took care to differentiate these mentors of adulthood from their real fathers. In more than ninety-five percent of cases, fathers were either cited as negative examples or were mentioned as people who were *not* influences. Then, after forty, mentors ceased to be important. One man closed his description of his mentor with an epitaph: "I was the featured speaker at his retirement." Other men assured me that the models of their young adulthood now had feet of clay. Even more illustrative of the relativity, the unremitting change, of maturation was the fact that by the time I interviewed them, many of these men now served as mentors for young men apprenticed to them. Grant Study men with relatively unsuccessful careers either had not discovered mentors until their early forties, or had mentors who served only during adolescence. One man in this group sadly acknowledged his lack of such career guides. "I have not had them, not enough, not nearly enough." Made uncomfortable by the question, another man grumbled, "I've never had one, or I've repressed him." (The absence of available role models for women in many careers now open to them may contribute to the developmental crisis that afflicts some thirty-year-old women and impedes their Career Consolidation.)

Eventually, most Grant Study men outgrew the crassness and the narrowness of Career Consolidation. At thirty-one, a humorless Study member had written, "I've reached the point where I would appreciate material gain and improvement in status. I'm striving toward that goal; this makes me enthusiastic about my work and career." At forty-seven, having achieved modest success, he was able to say with laughter, "I should have become company president. I must have screwed up somewhere." He then related, much more seriously, what was at that time his greatest occupational satisfaction: "You have to get through a lot of people." Now, he most enjoyed seeing *others* become more fruitful in their jobs; he strove to improve his company's performance and to win the affection of the shop steward. He had moved on into Erikson's stage of Generativity.

Perhaps the modern generation will be less obsessed with issues of Career Consolidation, less materialistic at thirty-five than their parents, but I doubt it. The journeyman goldsmith or wheelwright of the Middle Ages, I suspect, had much in common with modern surgical residents and junior executives. Each stage of development has a place in the life cycle.

Generativity — A Second Adolescence

Then, the fifth decade arrives, bringing with it once again the *sturm und drang* of adolescence. As adolescence is a period for acknowledging parental flaws and discovering the truth about childhood, so the forties are a time for reassessing and reordering the truth about adolescence and young adulthood.

At age forty — give or take as much as a decade — men leave the compulsive, unreflective busywork of their occupational apprenticeships, and once more become explorers of the world within. In their midthirties Frederick Lion and Adam Carson broke out of their "gray flannel" straitjackets and began to reorder their lives. Dr. Tarrytown waited longer; he was forty-eight before he admitted to the Study the long-obvious fact that he had hated his father. Not until fifty did another man reveal his mother's suicide when he was fourteen; for years the Study had known, but the subject had disavowed the fact. It was only at forty-seven that Dr. Hyde, at last having torn himself free, could describe his mother as "pathetic, hypochondriacal, hateful, and threatening." In adolescence, despite exhaustive projective testing, skilled psychologists could detect only "reverential attachment."

Perhaps the most succinct definition of this period of life was offered by a forty-five-year-old Grant Study member. In response to my question, "What did your psychoanalysis do for you?" he replied, "I don't bite my nails anymore. . . . And I am more like I was at four than at seven." The same was true for many forty-five-year-olds who had not undergone psychoanalysis. From four to five we are all romantics; we are all embryonic royalty, budding ballerinas, or intrepid astronauts; we are all fearless, open, affectionate, and beautiful. We have not yet learned that "nobody likes a show-off." Then, the serious, practical, asexual years of grammar school quench our instinctual fires — until adolescence kindles them once more. The turmoil of middle life exerts a similar effect on the conformity of the thirties.

It is said that a dying maple or oak tree will, as a last gasp, produce more seeds, but impending death does not account for the fresh vigor of human midlife. Rather, the pain of the forties is preparatory to entering a new stage of man. The increased instinctual strivings of the so-called midlife crisis are no more a reflection of the "male menopause" than these same strivings were at fifteen. Elliott Jacques, a psychoanalyst much quoted on the "midlife crisis," is, I believe, wrong when he suggests that the *angst* of the forties is from a fear of death.[15] Jacques is nearer the truth when he directs us to Dante Alighieri, who wrote, "In the middle of the journey of our life, I came to myself within a dark wood, where the straight way was lost. Ah, how hard a thing it is to tell of that wood, savage and harsh and dense, the thought of which renews my fear; so bitter is it that death is hardly more." It is true that in midlife concern with dying increases, but it also does in adolescence. It is true that the suicide rate goes up — but suicide reflects a fear of living, not of dying. "Fear of death," like "orality," is a metaphor; death connotes change as well as literal mortality.

To be sure, at age forty funerals begin to become as important a sacrament as marriages were in the twenties. "My father died in September," one man wrote, "after several months of steadily increasing weakness. I had not realized before that I would feel a period of grief for some weeks thereafter, since I generally think of myself as a reasonably well-controlled individual. The first death of a parent, and especially the father, really shakes one up and alters one's views of so many things — one feels so much more vulnerable." But it is also true, according to Kinsey, that at forty extramarital affairs reach their peak.

If fully half of the Grant Study men who were observed to show especially vital affect in adolescence had become bland and colorless around age thirty, then fully half of the men who as adolescents were seen as unusually bland and colorless became vibrant and interesting around age forty-five. The sort of rebirth experienced by Judge Spratt and Dr. Carson around age forty was not uncommon. At forty-seven, Mr. Robert Jordan wrote triumphantly, "I am onto a whole new life, a personal renaissance, which has got me excited most of the time. If I can make it pay adequate to my family responsibility, I will 'really be livin', man.'"

In his early forties one man took up underwater archaeology and deep sea diving in the Mediterranean. Another man built a dramatic, shamelessly exhibitionistic house. A third man, who from his projective tests at twenty-four was seen to possess an inner life like "some Brazilian jungle spilling out onto a North Dakota plain," was at fifty finally able to let that Brazilian jungle emerge into his conscious life; yet he was the last man that the

Study had ever expected to have an exciting love affair. A fourth man whose life had been as dry and inhibited as any in the Study wrote at forty-five, "Today, scientists are the jet set and get the best things; whereas in the 1930s [in other words, during his adolescence], people had to sacrifice to go into science." In part he was talking about the real world, but he also was describing his own instinctual experience of changing from a frightened, mother-dominated adolescent into a famous scientist, the chairman of national committees, and the beneficiary of tremendous personal prestige and autonomy.

Thus, if men in their forties are depressed, it is because they are confronted by instinctual reawakening and because they are more honestly able to acknowledge their own pain. It is not because they fear death. If they are no longer satisfied with their careers, it may be because they wish to be of more service to those around them. If their marriages are sometimes in disarray and their groping toward love seems adolescent, it may be because they are less inhibited than they were in their thirties. The reader need only think of any mature artist or political leader and compare him with the same man at thirty to understand what I mean. It was not just the cultural changes in America in the 1960s that accounted for these shifts.

In other words, the cub scout, having mastered puberty, puts aside his coin collections and his contempt for the opposite sex and enters the exciting and self-searching despair of adolescence. Similarly, the Grant Study men at forty put aside the preconceptions and the narrow establishment aims of their thirties and began once again to feel gangly and uncertain about themselves. But always, such transitional periods in life provide a means of seizing one more chance and finding a new solution to old instinctual or interpersonal needs.

Just as pop psychologists have reveled in the not-so-common high drama of adolescent turmoil, just so the popular press, sensing good copy, has made all too much of the midlife crisis. The term *midlife crisis* brings to mind some variation of the renegade minister who leaves behind four children and the congregation that loved him in order to drive off in a magenta Porsche with a twenty-five-year-old striptease artiste. Like all tabloid fables, there is much to be learned from such stories, but such aberrations are rare, albeit memorable, caricatures of more mundane issues of development. As with adolescent turmoil, midlife crises are much rarer in *community* samples than in *clinical* samples. The high drama in Gail Sheehy's bestselling *Passages* was rarely observed in the lives of the Grant Study men.

Contrast the runaway minister with a less colorful Grant Study man. In his youth the latter had been a very careful and meticulous man whose secret dream was foreign travel. At fifty, he admitted that his travel fantasies would never become reality. Nevertheless, at age forty he had become senior editor of a large-circulation travel magazine. For the next ten years he spent his energies surrounding himself and his readers with color photographs from exciting foreign lands that only the most intrepid tourist visits. In his thirties another man had told the Study of constant dissatisfaction with his asexual marriage. Throughout this period, like a good boy scout, he remained virtually celibate. Then, in his forties, he had engaged in a series of discreet but enjoyable affairs, while at the same time his marriage had modestly improved. Today, at fifty-five, both he and his wife see their marriage as stable.

Certainly there is nothing magical about a given year; Elliott Jacques's thirty-seven, Gail Sheehy's "Catch 30," Daniel Levinson's forty-to-forty-two definitions of middle life crisis are as arbitrary as suggesting that adolescent crises occur at sixteen. Certainly, there were many men in the Study who between thirty-five and fifty got divorced, changed jobs, and became depressed. However, divorce, job disenchantment, and depression occur with roughly equal frequency throughout the adult life cycle. If such events occur during the dangerous, exciting ripening of the forties, we can pause and say, "Ah-ha! The midlife crisis, the dirty forties, menopausal depression!" But that is to miss the point. Progression in the life cycle necessitates growth and change; but crisis is the exception, not the rule.

Bernice Neugarten, a University of Chicago sociologist, has provided us with the best empirical studies of late middle life.[16] She points out that throughout the life cycle events that occur at the appropriate time are rarely crises. "The events are anticipated and rehearsed," she tells us; "the grief work completed, the reconciliation accomplished without shattering this sense of continuity of the life cycle."[17] Life events that are too sudden, too late, or too early are the most traumatic. Recent research suggests that the menopause is no more traumatic than its anticipation,[18] psychotic depression is not more common during the menopause,[19] and statistically, the first two years after retirement are happier than the preceding two years.[20]

I do not mean to convey that the decade of the forties is without problems. When rebirth is sudden, old value patterns are cast aside and ill-fitting identities, no longer faithful to their owner, must be discarded. And so middle-aged men, like adolescents, often do experience pervading depression.

In his fortieth year, one man had boasted, "Prior to the last questionnaire, I believe I indicated the feeling of being trapped by filial duty, the son of the president, victim of the system" (a typical complaint for a man of thirty-seven). He then went on, "During the past three years, I've changed this attitude to a great degree. Through the growth of our little company [which, due to his father's death, he had inherited] from 12 to 80 employees, I've gained confidence and a sense of freedom of decision, for which I am grateful." But this man's second coming of age as company president was not smooth. As he assumed the task of filling his father's shoes, he became depressed, his marriage trembled, he developed a serious drinking problem. In a developmental sense he had finally *gotten even* with his father; but the ambiguity of that phrase "to get even," whether in the jealous fantasies of the Oedipal child or the innocent reality of men and women in the prime of life, evokes tremendous guilt and awe. Not until eight years later could this man confidently point to a year's sobriety, a rescued marriage, and a company that "I think Dad would have been proud of." Over and over throughout the Study the lesson was repeated. Childhood does not end at twenty-one, and the battle to wean oneself from and to pull even with one's parents continues into middle life.

Adolescent children were another bittersweet source of midlife growth. The adolescence of children and the second adolescence of their parents do not usually harmonize. Thirty-year-old men have fun in bringing up their grade-school-age children; latency children of any age recognize and enjoy each other. But at age forty fathers often acted as if there was no kinship to their adolescent children at all or explained the differences between themselves and their sons by "the times, they are achanging." They were unaware that the heightened sexuality that so frightened them in their daughters was often a projection of their own forbidden wishes toward their suddenly attractive children. As one man reminiscing over his relationship with two teenage daughters confessed, "In retrospect, none of us enjoyed it."

On the other hand, the importance of the interaction between teenage and middle-aged adolescents cannot be overemphasized. A colleague of mine suggested that most men cannot become truly effective administrators until they have come to terms with their own adolescent children. Perhaps this explains why in their early thirties some unmarried schoolteachers, having grown expert in caring for adolescents, become generative ahead of their time. In his discovery of his adolescent children, the adult remembers, rediscovers, and often defensively reworks parts of himself. Like the character disorder and the infant, the adolescent has the capacity to get under our skin, rekindle old flames, and to stimulate parents in parts of their innermost selves that they had forgotten existed. These fresh identifications act as catalysts for changes within adult personalities and allow for further growth.

It was possible to contrast the twelve members of the Study who had experienced the widest "generation gap" between themselves and their children with seventeen men whose children, throughout adolescence, had remained closely aligned with their parents. Surprisingly, vigorous parental condemnation of marijuana, of long hair, of interracial dating, and of war protests did not create a generation gap; nor did approval of such behavior bring fathers close to children.

The critical factor in creating a generation gap turned out to be not parental conservatism but parental dishonesty. The fathers most alienated from their children were specialists in the defense mechanism of reaction formation and did the opposite of what they really wanted to do. Such fathers were also three times as likely to be prisoners of their consciences, to be rigid and emotionally constricted. They were more likely to see their children's rebellion as an affront to themselves rather than as part of the natural process of growing up. In the most extreme cases, these fathers were liars. They were the fathers who concealed from their sons their own adolescent peccadillos, who lied to the government about their taxes, who "took the fifth" when asked by the Grant Study about their illegal acts. Paradoxically, the generation gap was often greatest for fathers with excellent marriages, but marriages of the sort that excluded the children.

I first began to interview the Grant Study men at their twenty-fifth reunion. I was thirty-three; they were forty-six. The reunion was brief, and I compressed several intense two-hour interviews into the space of three days. Afterward I was alarmed by what I learned about the next decade of life, and I rushed to discuss my experiences with my fifty-four-year-old department chairman. Like a grammar school boy, having just perceived the Weltschmerz of a teenage sibling, I exclaimed to my chief, "I don't want to grow up; these men are all so . . . so depressed." A few months later, when I first began to report on the adult development of these men, a forty-five-year-old psychoanalyst, hearing me speak, commented, "All these men you talk about seem to be leading lives of quiet desperation."

As I was to learn, the men were by no means despairing; but like any child first discovering the facts of life, I had subtly distorted what I had seen. In part, the Grant Study men had grown up enough to acknowledge real pain that the caterpillar in me still denied. The grammar school child sees sexuality as disgusting, the late adolescent regards it as the source of all the poetry and beauty in the world. The pain and danger are still there, but instinctual power, once harnessed, is no longer chaotic. Despite their inner turmoil, the Best Outcomes regarded the period from thirty-five to forty-nine as the happiest in their lives and the seemingly calmer period from twenty-one to thirty-five as the unhappiest. It was the men who in midlife seemed least well adapted who longed for the relative calm of their young adulthood and regarded the storms of later life as too painful.

As I continued to interview these men, I became less disillusioned and frightened by Dr. Carson's frank and honest recognition of his depression. It became clear to me that the great vintage wine laid down by the Grant Study staff thirty years before had come of age.

The consequence of this ripening of human personality was illustrated in the careers of the forty-four Grant Study men who had gone into business. But why do I choose businessmen and not altruistic doctors or teachers to illustrate the concept of Generativity? Perhaps the reason is that a surgeon can save lives by cutting and sewing an immobile, silent mass of flesh; a professor like Newton can succeed by merely recording lonely observations on neutrinos; but a businessman who fails to meet a payroll or who does not enhance the growth of his underlings is rarely able to survive. (I write here not of eccentric tycoons or of conforming Babbitts, but of ordinary leaders who lead ordinary people to ordinary success in the marketplace.)

Seven of the forty-four businessmen in the Study never reached middle management. Of these, none achieved Intimacy as reflected by the indices of stable marriage and lasting friendships. Seventeen of the forty-four men were still lieutenants and vice-presidents into their fifties. Of these seventeen, nine were either unusually bland and colorless or remained, at fifty, as status conscious and anxious to please as Dr. Carson had been at thirty; they still wrestled with Career Consolidation. The other eight fifty-year-old "lieutenants" carved themselves special niches within their company where they could create and be their own men.

By age fifty, however, nineteen of the forty-four men who entered the business world had become their own bosses. Almost always, full leadership involved a shift in career focus. Instead of delving progressively deeper into their specialized careers and acquiring progressively more competence, in middle life the men's career patterns suddenly diverged and broadened; they assumed tasks that they had not been trained for. Being truly responsible for others is no job for a specialist. Yet contrary to common mythology, it was the very men who enjoyed the best marriages and the richest friendship patterns who became the company presidents. (Admittedly, many such men were clear enough about who they were and what they wanted so that they would prefer to run a small boatyard than to grow rich as a vice-president of someone else's large one.)

Of course, this move toward Generativity was by no means confined to the businessman. In her paper on the midlife changes in activities that take place in scientists, Ann Roe cites this illustrative self-report: "If you go into administration, you must believe that this is a creative activity in itself and that your purpose is something more than keeping your desk clean. You are a moderator and arbiter, and you try to deal equitably with a lot of different people, but you've also got to have ideas, and you've got to persuade people that your ideas are important and to see them into reality . . . this is part of the excitement of it. In both research and administration, the excitement and the elation is in the creative power. It's bringing things to pass. Now, I think [administration] is more exciting than research."[21]

Erikson has suggested that the major causes for failure to reach Generativity may be found in "faulty identifications with parents, in excessive self-love based on a too strenuously self-made personality, and in the lack of some faith, some 'belief in the species' which would make a child appear to be a welcome trust."[22] Thus, some men in the Study, the majority of them lawyers and business vice-presidents, ignored the rising sap of the forties; they never outgrew Career Consolidation. Such men often served as guardians of the establishment and made large incomes; but still striving for the top, they never reached the point where they "worried less about myself and more about the children." Their subsequent lives followed Erikson's script; to fail at Generativity is to risk *stagnation*.

"My major ambivalence is my attitude towards business and career," wrote one vice-president, at forty-five. "One part of me wants power, prestige, recognition, success; the other part feels all of this is nonsense and 'chasing the wind.' I like my privacy and my own life-style, I like my free time to be free time, and not filled with corporate obligations. And yet as I look at my contemporaries who are now board chairmen and presidents of major companies, I find myself envying them (sometimes) and at other times feeling that I wouldn't want that life at all. This is a troublesome thing for me . . . no plans have gelled for a second career, mainly because I find I need a substantial income to support the seemingly endless education of my kids. I have thought about teaching or helping to run a small school, but I simply can't afford it at this time."

When compared with their classmates, these men seemed prematurely old, yet paradoxically, in their twenties some of these men had been the most venturesome. At thirty, one New Orleans lawyer had had one of the most dramatic love affairs in the Study. At that age, he was aggressive, exhibitionistic and extroverted, and had been a candidate for governor of Louisiana. However, he failed to win statewide support, and his convivial drinking evolved into alcoholism. Quickly, resolutely, he gave up alcohol and politics forever. He entered his forties as a man whose life was all work and no play. As the best trust officer in the city, this model of sobriety is now the patriarch of a solid family and runs two important community activities. However, he is responsible for things, not people, and wonders what will happen "when I can't carry this superhuman work load . . . the thought of old age or helplessness horrifies me."

Only time will tell if without attaining fresh growth in their forties such men can weather the fifties and sixties. Oliver Kane could not. At fifty, the childless, perpetually striving Oliver Kane wrote, shortly before his self-inflicted death, "I am less sure, less hopeful and I think narrower in view than I have been at any previous time in my life. Ironically, as I have acquired more external success and the apparent confidence and recognition that go with it, I have more and more doubts that I have chosen a way of life that really means anything — and very little doubt that I shall have lived a very busy and peripatetic life without having made any lasting contribution." An absolutely brilliant corporate consultant, Oliver Kane had never really accepted a caring responsibility for a family or for the administrative and personnel needs of his company. For most such men, however, midlife stagnation did not lead to death, but only to a sense of muted dissatisfaction.

A much more concerted study is needed of the problems that beset this period of life and of the determinants of Generativity. What should a thoughtful dean, personnel manager, or president do for the employee who stops growing in his thirties? At fifty-five, a man can do only sixty percent of the physical work that he could at forty; intellectual capacity has begun its inevitable decline. But who at fifty-five is willing to accept a forty percent cut in pay? Deadwood stifles young growth in business and bureaucracy as surely as it does in gardens, and there always will be too few slots at the top. The military habit of pensioning off the twenty-year man is cruel and wasteful. Perhaps Bismarck was right; instead of receiving pensions, soldiers who failed to grow were given not a pension but a sinecure in the bureaucracy. In the vastness of a federal agency, failure to grow becomes a blessing, not a liability.

The Keepers of the Meanings

Where are the Grant Study men heading? What is the next stage of the life cycle? At this point, I have no statistics to illustrate the vicissitudes of the fifties. However, after fifty the Grant Study men themselves have been unusually articulate, and I can let them speak for themselves. They described a period of life that seems to come after their struggle between Generativity and stagnation and before Erikson's final stage — Dignity versus Despair. It is possible to summarize this intermediate period in terms of a tension between *Keeping the Meaning* and *Rigidity*.

After fifty, the best adapted Grant Study men prepared themselves to see that the old culture be carried on rather than replaced. Having weathered their children's and their own second coming of age, the Grant Study men have attained a certain tranquillity, but a tranquillity suffused with an undercurrent of mild regret.

The men are unanimous in reporting that the fifties are a quieter time of life than the forties. Candles burn dimmer; martial drums are muffled; and pain is not so keenly felt. One man summed up his sixth decade by saying, "Prior to 50, a scramble to get there; now I am there, I hope I am more relaxed." A fifty-five-year-old man writes, "My wife and I have reached a modus vivendi. . . . My work has changed little in 12 years; it continues to be satisfying. For good or evil, I find myself with few hopes or ambitions for the future — but contented rather than in any way despairing." Only ten years before this same man had been in turmoil over his adolescent children's delinquencies and complained bitterly that he and his wife had *not* found a modus vivendi. At forty-five, also, he had been at the top of his profession and reaching higher; at fifty-five he was content with what he had achieved. A third man sums up his secret to late midlife dignity succinctly, "You discover that your experiences and whatever sense you have gathered in the course of your life are *needed.*"

By the time the men reach their fifties a new generation is taking over. As this happens, rigidity interferes with Generativity. A once clearly Generative man described his increasing sense of alienation from the world and his lessening sense of personal control. "I get discouraged by a good deal that I see and read. Individual morality, taste, and self-restraint have declined. The degree of theft in schools and in colleges appalls me. The degree of filth and wretched conduct in the movies disgusts me — and I am not a prude. . . . In general, I think life has become more crowded and less civilized than a generation ago. I think the vote for 18-year-olds is a mistake — it adds a volatile, unduly idealistic, and arrogant element to the electorate." Another man reports, "I am distressed at the weakening of our nearly ideal form of democracy by liberals, the disappearance of authority, the loss of religion, the weakening of family, immorality, and the disregard for the dignity of age." Of course, both men are partly right, but they would have been equally right in Shakespeare's day or in the Age of Pericles. Besides, they have changed as much as have the times. To their sorrow, both men have forgotten that it is through the adolescent that the race matures.

A more positive aspect of this rigidity is that the men have crystallized into a final identity — or so they think. One man writes, "I am more likely to take a definite stand on an issue." Another says, "The move to my new life was tough, long in being made, and the strongest thing I've ever done." A third admits, "I am becoming more of a loner, more outspoken, and more set in my ways." A fourth simply trumpets, "It's still the same game and I am still the coach." In the fifties, the very "establishment" that in adolescence and the late thirties had seemed a prison becomes transformed into a haven. The church, the country club, the old neighborhood and the Grand Old Party are no longer stultifying, but contain old and irreplaceable friends.

It appears that the men with prolonged adolescent identity crises, those who in adult life have never found a niche for themselves, are those who most successfully remain in touch with modern mores and are not distressed with where the world is going. One such man reveals, "I have returned to a concern for the bigger issues that preoccupied me from age 21 to 26 — the meaning of life, death, suffering. How can I serve and contribute."

Rigidity brings compensations. Jung writes, "In primitive tribes we observe that the old people are almost always the guardians of the mysteries and the laws."[23] Granted, increasing rigidity means that the adolescent, who once with willing wonder reveled in Europe's newness, now with crabbed intolerance complains of unpredictable drivers and lukewarm martinis. But after age fifty a more positive aspect of rigidity allowed the Grant Study men to become, in Charles McArthur's words, "keepers of the meanings." Since their fifties is not a time of life in which Grant Study men can easily change careers, teaching what they have already learned appears to be the only fresh track open to them — a means of institutionalizing their care of others. One man writes, "I don't plan on leaving any big footsteps behind, but I am becoming more insistent in my attempts to move the town to build a new hospital, support schools, and teach kids to sing."

At fifty-five, asked for his most important concern, another Study member replies, " 'Passing on the Torch' and exposure of civilized values to children has always been of importance to me but it has increased with each ensuing year." A third man, with a brilliant career in the state department, answers the same question, "The concerns that I have are now much less self-centered. From 30 to 40 they had to do with too many demands on too little money; whether I could make it in my profession; whether I was doing the best for my family, education for the children; etc. Post age 45 my concerns are more philosophical, more long term, less personal, and with a less intense feeling that all problems must be solved at once in my time. I *am* concerned about the state of human relations, and especially of our society. I am concerned to teach others as much as I can of what I have learned."

A fourth, equally successful man — and perhaps it is no accident that these four men were all Best Outcomes — writes, "I am at a questioning period in life — what to do to get the most out of the acceleratingly decreasing number of years left. My routine work of managing our firm is no longer challenging — hence the professionally related writing, course development, speech and seminar giving. I am looking . . . to use some of the knowledge and skills I have picked up in the area of small business management. This is not a pipe dream, as the speeches, seminars, and my book all give me a rechanneling of interests and energies. Meanwhile, I have become more ruthless in the use of time."

A final example of this quest to perpetuate the capacity to care is a man who reports, "I look forward to a somewhat calmer period ahead — hopefully — and perhaps a little more time to read books, go to plays and museums, to travel for pleasure. I think my wife and I really enjoy each other's company, although not in a cloying manner. . . . My wife says that for a man the fifties are the peak of one's career. Professionally, these are for me the most exciting and interesting times yet. I consult for some of the top companies in the United States — sit on national advisory committees, and secretly enjoy that form of immortality, which I believe Sinclair Lewis referred to: seeing one's name in footnotes and in indices, quoted here and there — my name."

If the steps from infancy to childhood to adolescence lead in sequentially mastering our body, our reality, and our emotions, then from forty to senescence the steps lead in the reverse direction. Thus, if the forty-year-old struggles with feelings, the fifty-five-year-old struggles once more with reality. If bitterness is to be avoided, the promises and dreams of the thirties must be reviewed as nostalgia. Reality must replace the ideal, and we must accept that life's seesaw has tipped; that there are now more yesterdays than tomorrows.

One man writes, "One concentrates on the birds in the hand in contradistinction to those in the bush." A professional man expressed the same realization more fully: "There is a change with the fifties in pulse and in rewards of living. Some pretend to remain thirty; others start off on a fresh tack, at least they seem to; and there are those who are squeezed dry by now. . . . My professional work still means much, but does not dominate as it used to. Our farm, our children's lives and ideas capture my mind more than the mechanics of medicine. Working with admissions to medical school gives a special reward. I'm not old and tired; just more selective."

The old person, like the infant, struggles with his body. At fifty-five, some men were slowly entering the last stage of the life cycle, where the task is to replace the indignities of physical decay with a sense of unshakable self-worth. Worry over their own death is still of little significance; but for some, worry over or even rehearsal for the death of one's spouse has emerged as a major concern. (Neugarten confirms this observation.[24])

As the most important life issues of the fifties, those men cited "flagging sexual powers and complaining joints"; "Will I become too deaf to make it to retirement age"; "I may be unable to qualify for a retirement fund"; "I can no longer obtain an erection"; "I feel under attack by ambitious young people"; "I accepted a new assignment at a reduction in grade and salary. It was a particularly severe life issue." Deterioration, not death, is the enemy.

Parenthetically, with advancing age, sexual differentiation becomes less sharp. As they grow older, women grow facial hair, and men's beards grow more slowly. Women become flat-chested; their voices deepen; their facial features sharpen, and the estrogens that may inhibit dominance decrease. The breasts of old men grow, their faces soften, and the androgenic hormones facilitating dominance decrease.[25] Perhaps older women may frighten younger men precisely because they have grown more comfortable with assertive impulses. Perhaps older men may appeal to younger women precisely because they can let themselves become more gentle and nurturant. In any case, in old age, we all become more like Tiresias; and as Carl Jung suggests, it is in the fifties that this slow transformation first becomes manifest. The young reader is horrified, but a wise grandparent will nod and recall that all life is a journey.

Bernice Neugarten suggests, and the Grant Study confirms, what she calls "body monitoring" or protective strategies for maintaining performance and for combating a new sense of physical vulnerability.[26] "I now keep a pocket notebook," writes one man. "It's much harder to learn new concepts," he continues; "from being a board certified internist — the smartest in the city — I became a G.P." "It bothers me," another man admits, "that I do not have the natural sexual powers that I took for granted before. I've tried to persuade myself that at my age it is to be expected, but it is difficult." Another man, in assessing his fifties, writes simply, "We all slow down, but we expect that."

The life of one man vividly illustrates this adaptive use of anticipation. When he was eighteen, he was interested in understanding young people's reactions and in "boy's work — counseling at camp." At twenty-two, after graduating from college, he wrote that he was trying to raise the standards of his school where he enjoyed working with adolescents: "The teaching staff here is excellent, but the administration and organization under the dictatorship of a 75-year-old dreamer is almost non-existent."

At fifty-four, his life has taken a very different turn. He now writes, "I am doing graduate work on aging, successful or otherwise, I suddenly find myself not only aging, but heavily involved in understanding the process. I gradually found a great need to work with the elderly and to train others to work with them . . . we offer an evening course in the psychodynamics of aging. I have offered, and will again, pre-retirement courses. All this is very exciting, and I plan to apply for a grant in adult education for the elderly. . . . I want to be sure there are some damned exciting projects around for the elderly when I get there!"

Bernice Neugarten has written that forty-year-olds "see the environment as one that rewards boldness and risk-taking, and see themselves possessing energy, congruent with opportunities presented in the outer world. Sixty-year-olds seem to see the environment as complex and dangerous, no longer to be reformed in line with one's own wishes, and to see the self as conforming and accommodating to outer world demands."[27]

The Grant Study data support this observation. At forty-one, the Grant Study men were asked to rank a wide variety of values as very high or very low. At the top, the men put being physically active and fit, being able to maintain good public relations, a personal philosophy of life, and a professional code of ethics. At fifty-five, there was little change in their answers to the same questions, except in two areas. They were much less concerned with maintaining good public relations and a wide range of acquaintances and they were much less concerned with establishing new contacts or acquiring new information relevant to their professions.

My view of the men during this period is distorted in a way that my view of their lives before forty-five was not. If I watched the men grow from eighteen to forty-five in a few hours of record review, I have watched them grow from forty-five to fifty-five over the span of a decade. I, too, have altered. Now, when I try to compare the men with themselves at forty-five, I discover that I have also changed, and in ways I cannot understand. I begin to see the life cycle from a new perspective; its trajectory alters . . . but, then, this whole chapter is but a tentative beginning, the very antithesis of the last word. The harvesting of the major longitudinal studies of human development is still in the earliest stages.

How universal are the findings in this chapter? Are not the men of the Grant Study as arcane, as irrelevant to the average reader as Samoans, Zuni Indians, and other protagonists of anthropological treatises? Certainly, if the seasonal cycle of a mature tree repeats itself from year to year, such cycles differ from species to species and from climate to climate. Trees grow differently in dry soil and in damp. Flowering, fruiting, and leaf-shedding occur at different times on windswept mountainsides than in sheltered, semitropical valleys.

In like fashion, the sociocultural narrowness of the Grant Study sample severely limits the conclusions of this chapter. I am uncertain if the life cycle that I depict here occurred in these men's medieval ancestors or even if it will occur in their granddaughters. Perhaps what we call adolescence is but an artifact of the prolongation of childhood that resulted from the Industrial Revolution. Perhaps these men's adult maturation was further delayed by the peculiar demands of our modern technocracy.

Certainly, in any society, as with any individual, the age at which the stages of the life cycle occur will vary tremendously. I would agree that Cleopatra, Thomas Jefferson, John Keats, Alexander the Great, Joan of Arc, and Jesus of Nazareth were all at the peak of their powers far earlier than the men in this chapter. Nevertheless, I suspect that not all of the findings in this chapter are culture-bound. Most of the great men in history did not mature at thirty, and the prolonged biological maturation of the human nervous system, a maturation that continues into adulthood, has been true for all humans for thousands of years.

In the future it behooves us to study the unfolding of adulthood as carefully as in the past we have studied the unfolding of childhood. "For now we see through a glass, darkly; but then face to face: now I know in part, but then shall I know even as also I am known."

Chapter 11

Paths into Health

> And when he had come out of the boat, there met him out of the tombs a man with an unclean spirit . . . night and day among the tombs and on the mountains he was always crying out and bruising himself with stones. And when he saw Jesus from afar, he ran and worshipped him. . . . And the unclean spirits came out, and entered the swine; and the herd, numbering about two thousand, rushed down a steep bank into the sea. . . . And people came to see what it was that had happened. And they came to Jesus, and saw the demoniac sitting there, clothed and in his right mind, the man who had had the legion; and they were afraid.
>
> — Mark 5:2, 5–6, 13–15

Without hesitation or judgment, we can accept the spontaneous recovery of children from measles, but we regard an adult's recovery from mental illness in quite a different fashion. Sometimes mental illness is seen as a sign of moral weakness; other times it becomes an insidious malady that only proper treatment can cure. In the former case, we prescribe punishment or the exercise of conscious willpower; in the latter case, we prescribe psychiatrists, shamans, or tranquilizers. If these two courses are impractical, we often regard mental illness as reflecting some indelible defect in character, from which remissions are as miraculous as spontaneous recovery from cancer.

More recently, a third solution has become fashionable — a solution that suggests that there is no such thing as mental illness. If definitions are carefully chosen, it is quite possible in lecture halls or at cocktail parties to defend this position. But to ignore mental illness, it seems to me, only begs the question. What would Thomas Szasz or Irving Goffman or R. D. Laing do if one of their friends began "crying out and bruising himself with stones," or if their airline pilot developed delusions that the control tower was giving false information?

This book supports a fourth solution. In the case of measles, the child's symptoms display not malfunction, but adaptation; the body deploys a rash, a fever, and a cough to cope with and to master an invading virus. In virtually every case of measles, the body recovers — without antibiotics, without moral resolutions, and without pretending measles does not exist. Let us entertain the possibility that mental illness, like the symptoms of measles, reflects our efforts to adapt to pathologic conflict (be it viral, demonic, or emotional). Let us suppose that mental illness, like measles, is not a deficit state, that it is neither immoral nor imaginary, but instead that the symptoms of mental illness reflect an unconscious effort at mastery through an aggregate of defense mechanisms. The counterargument is that the body masters measles in several days, while mental illness, like Wagnerian opera, goes on and on. But as we shall see, mental illness does not always go on indefinitely.

In 1883 Sigmund Freud's Viennese colleague Joseph Breuer made psychiatric history in an only partially successful effort to cure the multiple neurotic symptoms of his patient, Anna O. Following the death of her father, Anna O. had been beset with phobias, paralysis, and hypochondriacal complaints. As a method of treatment, Dr. Breuer employed catharsis by free association. Anna O. called the method "chimney sweeping," and it was later rechristened psychoanalysis.[1] But the long-term follow-up of this famous effort to *treat* mental illness makes a fascinating study.[2] Toward the end of her psychotherapy, Anna O. imagined herself pregnant by Breuer. As no one had yet discovered the mechanism of displacement, by which feelings can mysteriously leap from the mind to the body and by which both conversion symptoms and transference can be understood, her startled and respectable doctor fled her overheated imagination, thereby abandoning Anna O. to her uncured neuroses.

His patient (in real life, one Bertha Pappenheimer) relapsed into her former invalidism and shortly afterward was institutionalized as a morphine addict. From there her "spontaneous" recovery began. She returned from fantasy, addiction, and the helpless invalidism precipitated by her father's death. She began composing fairy tales, not to comfort herself as she had in childhood but to comfort other, younger, orphans. Step by step over the next two decades she assumed leadership in the orphanage. Then she founded a home for unwed mothers. Finally, dedicated to saving girls with "moral insanity," she became a world authority on white slavery. Although she publicly disparaged the psychoanalysis that three decades earlier she had helped to discover, perhaps because of (or perhaps in spite of) its catalytic effect, Bertha Pappenheimer cured herself. Intractable hypochondriasis was replaced by altruism and relative health. In old age, afflicted with real somatic illness, she was an uncomplaining patient. After her death, she was much mourned. Martin Buber wrote, "I loved her and will love her until the day I die," and in 1954, the German government printed a commemorative stamp in her honor.[3]

In examining the recovery of the Grant Study men from seemingly intractable character disorder, we shall see that recovery from mental illness is analogous to passing from adolescence to adulthood. The person is the same — no "lesson" has been learned; no tumor has been excised — but different defenses have been deployed. Often, no sweet, oblivious antidote can cure "that perilous stuff which weighs upon the heart," but rather, as Lady Macbeth's physician suggested, "Therein the patient must minister to himself." In short, shifts in adaptive mechanisms allow patients to cure themselves.

For example, through the evolution of his defenses, one Grant Study man, Robert Brooke, vividly illustrated the onset and recovery from anxiety neurosis, an emotional disorder often arising from maladaptive repression. Robert Brooke was brought up by a very anxious mother. She herself had been afraid of many things and had discouraged her son from aggressive activities. Her son adapted with repression. Powerful feelings often flooded his mind, but he never could think of the people or situations with whom these feelings were associated. Unexplained, his feelings led to unease and anxiety. Before the war, the Grant Study impression of Robert Brooke was that he was on the verge of frank neurosis. During the war, as a B-17 bombardier in the Pacific, he became horrified at the damage that he was doing. Since the social realities of World War II did not permit him to follow the dictates of his conscience, defense was necessary. At first, he tried to dissociate himself from the war and became extremely religious. Rather than think about his bombing missions, he became preoccupied with a gigantic image of Christianity — a cross superimposed upon the world. "The symbol of the cross," Brooke wrote, "struck me as so enormous and so complete." Twenty-five years later, I asked him what a Norden bombsight looked like; and he replied that it worked by "flying the plane via the bombsight so that finally the two crosshairs of the bombsight intersected each other over the target." At this point the gentle Robert Brooke, exposed in the Plexiglas nose of his bomber for all the world to see, would release thousands of pounds of TNT onto largely civilian populations.

As the war progressed, Robert Brooke was transferred to a yet more powerful bomber, the B-29 Superfortress; at last the repression and dissociation that allowed his countrymen to ignore Dresden, Hamburg, and Tokyo failed him. He became overwhelmed with persistent fears, restlessness, and vague physical symptoms. He had no idea what was wrong, but he was sent back to the United States as a psychiatric casualty. Brooke received little in the way of formal psychotherapy, but ingeniously he used his unexpected leisure time to write poems about the war and the dreadfulness of bombing civilian targets. At forty-five, when I asked him about his mental breakdown, he had forgotten all about it. Instead, he described a poem from that period that lingered in his memory. It was called "Remember, We Must." He added, "I still have a very large guilt about our bombing. This has come out in my war poems."

Off and on during his life, Brooke spoke of the role in his life of poetry. "Poetry sometimes seems to have emerged full blown from my unconscious mind." Then he said, "People write poetry only when distressed. . . . My poems weren't lies — they tell more than I can tell you. . . . Only reliving with a psychiatrist would ever dig these things out." But he never needed to. Nor did he need tranquilizers. Through the evolution of dissociation and repression into sublimation, he had ministered to "a mind diseas'd" and managed to "raze out the written troubles of the brain." Lady Macbeth's physician might have been impressed.

Usually, mental illness manifests itself through a defensive regression — the retreat from adaptive mechanisms at one level to those at a less mature level. Many psychiatrists regard *regression* per se as a defense mechanism. But the user of regression has to regress to some other state — to some other mode of adaptation. In Chapter 9 regression was depicted as the process by which in adult life immature adaptive mechanisms (e.g., projection, schizoid fantasy, and hypochondriasis) reappeared and resulted in "mental illness." However, since the Grant Study men were followed up for thirty-five years, it could also be observed how such "mentally ill" men recovered and how so-called character disorders *matured* from maladaptive defensive postures to more successful adaptation.

The lives of four men were especially illustrative. The first case history illustrates how, once his brain was no longer chemically intoxicated, James O'Neill, Ph.D., replaced "psychopathy" and "schizophrenia" with altruism and sublimation. The story of Francis DeMille highlights a pattern where a young man, as part of biologic maturation, evolved from a youth afflicted with a neurotic fear of women and homosexual preoccupation into a mature father and husband. The life of Herman Crabbe, Ph.D., showed how a man escaped from dangerous envelopment by a needy mother into the more benign embrace of his motherly wife. (As his life became safer, Crabbe abandoned schizoid eccentricity.) Last, Dr. Godfrey Minot Camille, through prolonged care by doctors, evolved from an emotionally crippled hypochondriac into an effective internist.

In his recovery from alcoholism, a Grant Study economist, James O'Neill, illustrated the developmental linkages between the three ego mechanisms, acting out, reaction formation, and altruism.

James O'Neill had been strictly brought up by warm but abstemious parents. Although O'Neill once went so far as to label his upbringing "Prussian," in 1972 a child psychiatrist — blind to the eighteen-year-old O'Neill's future — considered his childhood environment and his psychological soundness in college as above average. (Indeed, the prospectively gathered evidence of the Grant Study has demonstrated that sanguine childhoods and good college adjustment provided little insurance against the subsequent development of alcoholism.[4]) Ten years after O'Neill's graduation from college, the director of his college health services summarized all the data that the Grant Study had gathered up to that time as follows: "A sufficiently straightforward, decent, honest fellow . . . should be a good bet in any community." Before that time, O'Neill's adaptive style had been most consistently characterized by the neurotic, albeit normal, mechanisms of reaction formation and intellectualization. "I deal with ideas," he said; "I love ideas." And so, O'Neill had helped pioneer the statistical and actuarial techniques now used in the economic management of large corporations.

By age thirty, however, James O'Neill had lost control of his ability to drink socially; and yet, still drawing upon his excellent intelligence, he wrote a creditable Ph.D. thesis, obtained lucrative industrial employment, and evaded diagnosis as an alcoholic. Nevertheless, much of his day from morning to night involved secretly drinking in bars. His chronic intoxication led to maladaptive regression, and his intellectualization and reaction formation were replaced by acting out and anger turned against the self. This once straitlaced man was repeatedly and senselessly unfaithful to his wife. This shrewd mathematician compulsively borrowed funds so that he could reinvest them at parimutuel windows across the country. This honest and conscientious man was caught stealing equipment from the Bell Telephone Laboratories to finance his drinking bouts. Not only did O'Neill always lose, but also he did nothing to hide his identity either during his hotel trysts or during his gambling sprees.

In 1958, he was hospitalized and labeled an "inadequate character" by his physician and a "psychopath" by himself. Eight years later, after hundreds of hours of psychotherapy, O'Neill was again hospitalized. This time the functioning of his brain had been further disrupted by the acute withdrawal of alcohol. Due to his resulting mental disorganization and wild hallucinations he exhibited the most primitive defense mechanisms — distortion and delusional projection — and he was relabeled on discharge both alcoholic and schizophrenic. (Delirium tremens would have been a more accurate label.) He received no further psychiatric treatment, but a physician introduced him to Alcoholics Anonymous.

When I met Dr. O'Neill, he had been sober for three years. Intellectualization was once more a dominant defense, and his former reaction formation facilitated his passionate espousal of sobriety. Characteristically, he had only one quibble with Alcoholics Anonymous. That organization and many knowledgeable physicians regard alcoholism as a disease; but O'Neill, now the antithesis of a conscienceless psychopath, still felt that his uncontrolled alcoholism had been a moral problem.

In three years of sobriety, sobriety spent within the socially supportive network of Alcoholics Anonymous, O'Neill had developed two additional adaptive styles: sublimation and altruism. These mechanisms introduced some pleasure into the life of this recovered thief, philanderer, and officially diagnosed "inadequate personality." His old passion for gambling was now sublimated into a considerably more remunerative task of consulting to the Massachusetts State Lottery Commission. He was proud that his current job no longer used his analytic talents to help Bell Laboratories and the military establishment plan global warfare; instead, he now performed actuarial analysis for a major foundation concerned with population control. Modestly religious in adolescence, utterly nonreligious during his two decades of alcoholism, he now took an active role in his church. Within Alcoholics Anonymous, he was positively addicted to helping other people.

His meaningless affairs stopped with his last drink, and he was struggling with the arduous task of rebuilding his tortured marriage. "My wife and I," O'Neill assured me, "have put the marriage back together where it is more wonderful now than the first five years." Such a statement may have been too optimistic, but his marriage was in better shape than it had been for twenty years.

In 1940, Francis DeMille had immediately impressed the Grant Study staff with his charm. With his fresh complexion, he looked hardly old enough to be in college, and despite his erect carriage, he struck several observers as rather effeminate. His manner was open, winning, and direct, and he discussed his interest in the theater with a cultivated animation.

To a degree that almost exceeded belief, as a college student

Francis DeMille "forgot" to think about sexual fantasy, aggressive impulses, or independence from his mother. At nineteen, the psychiatrist marveled that "DeMille has not yet begun to think of sexual experience." The staff noticed that his dreams were not well remembered and that he reported that "distressing emotional reactions fade quickly." Throughout college, he never dated, totally denied sexual tension, and blandly observed, "I am anything but aggressive."

Although in retrospect it seems hard to understand how DeMille was included in a study of normal development, the truth was that his excellent dramatic skills pulled him through. If the staff wondered at his repression, they still perceived him as "colorful, dynamic, amiable, and adjusted." If Francis remained quite unaware that it was his mother who was pushing him into the theater, he still took an active and enjoyable part in college dramatics. Like many people who use repression as a major defense, Francis reported that he preferred "emotional thinking to rational thought," and on one occasion he told the Study, "I worked up a beautiful case of hysteria."

Like many hysterics and actors, DeMille was a master of dissociation. For example, he found it "revitalizing to free myself from inhibitions by venting my emotions on someone else in a play." Christian Science greatly appealed to him, and despite the fact that the staff worried about his inner unhappiness, during psychiatric interviews he seemed "constantly imbued with a cheerful affect."

Francis DeMille had grown up in suburban Hartford. He had never known his father, a businessman who left home before his birth and died shortly thereafter. His father's relatives played no part in his upbringing, and the DeMille household consisted only of his mother and two maiden aunts. From the age of one to ten, Francis grew up in an utterly female ménage. He was encouraged to play by himself in a well-equipped playroom, and his mother proudly reported to the Study that he "never played with other boys." During his adolescence, she boasted, "Francis would take me to a nightclub as a man does a woman," and even during World War II, Lieutenant Francis DeMille managed to remain emotionally and geographically at his mother's side. The navy never took him farther from Hartford than Groton, Connecticut;

and the Study internist feared that he would become a lifelong neurotic, fixated on his mother.

It was in the navy, however, that with continued maturation DeMille's repression began to fail. DeMille became conscious of his lack of sexual interest and he became fearful of possible homosexuality. Discussing this problem with the Study, he made, as do many people who use repression, a revealing slip of the pen. "I don't know whether homosexuality is psychiological [*sic*] or psychological in origin." As it turned out, DeMille's unconscious was right; there was nothing *physiologically* wrong with his masculinity.

In manageable doses, however, anxiety promotes maturation, and it was in the navy that Francis began to replace dissociation with sublimation. Francis wrote to the Study that he was always "rebelling" against the navy, always standing up for his own individuality and for that of his men. Had we not had access to his military efficiency records, his own report of his behavior might have been labeled "passive-aggressive." Objective evaluation of his behavior, however, revealed that he had received his highest officer efficiency rating in "moral courage" *and* "cooperation." In short, this timid man had made his military rebellion well appreciated, a veritable work of art.

By twenty-seven, DeMille's worried letters about possible homosexuality were replaced by his joyful announcement, "I enjoy working with girls!" He had found a job teaching dramatics at Vassar. By managing the move from Hartford to Poughkeepsie, he had also gratified the "great necessity I feel for breaking away from home." Three years later, he shattered maternal domination still further by marrying an actress whom *he* had formerly directed. Today, his marriage, if not the best in the Study, is stable and has survived a quarter of a century.

After marriage, DeMille's repression became still further transformed. In reply to a questionnaire that asked him about his marital adjustment, he wrote, "I must have a mental block on the questionnaire. My reluctance to return it seems to be much more than ordinary procrastination." He was in conflict over his sexual adjustment, and he knew it. With insight, however, comes resistance, and that was the last the Study heard of DeMille for seven years. During this time, he never saw a psychiatrist. Instead, in keeping with his fresh capacity for sublimation, he wrote a successful comedy called *Help Me, Carl Jung, I Am Drowning.*

DeMille returned to the Study, and in middle life revealed to me the ingenious way in which his ego had sublimated his enormous reluctance to present himself as an aggressively masculine businessman. Fifteen years earlier, in the same questionnaire that confessed his procrastination over discussing his marital adjustment, Francis wrote, "I didn't tackle the career problem properly, unless all the while I subconsciously had decided to work for money — which I always figured I wasn't doing."

In fact, DeMille was more mercenary than he had thought, but his solution was artistic. Although he had vowed that he would never associate himself with the "spectre of American business," he became a very special corporate success story. Despite his theatrical interests, he succeeded as an executive in Hartford, where insurance was king; and in an industry not known for its opportunities for individual expression, DeMille crafted a niche in the advertising department where he had autonomy, conventional occupational status, and a chance to exercise his artistic flair. He took pains, however, to assure me that his success in the marketplace threatened no one and that he was not "overly aggressive." As he put it, "The ability to stay alive in a large corporation took all the craftiness I have." Only in his community theater group could he unashamedly enjoy playing aggressive roles.

Without psychotherapy, DeMille's earlier repression of important masculine figures in his life had given way at age forty-six to his vivid recollection of a hypermasculine uncle who, during his adolescence, had been an important, if previously unmentioned, figure. Five years after our interview, DeMille further elaborated on his uncle, "The only consistent male influence — very dominant — a male figure that earlier I had rejected." But not entirely, for behind his pipe, tweed jacket, and leather study furniture, the middle-aged DeMille now rather resembled this uncle. The charming emotional outpourings of his adolescence were gone, and he now hid emotions behind lists, orderliness, and a gruff, bulldog, over-forty exterior. "In college," he mused, "I was in a Bohemian fringe; but I've changed since twenty-five years ago. Maybe some clockwork ticked inside me and made me go down this route." Perhaps that explained why a few years before he had given up his mother's religion and was "suddenly smitten" with his father's Baptist tenets. Certainly, he hoped that his sons would not discover that their father had once worn long hair; for in 1970 DeMille thoroughly disapproved of unshorn locks.

A final example of how DeMille had turned the "illness" of being an effete mother's boy into relative mental health was the way in which he successfully extricated himself from dependence on his mother. Although he lived only four blocks from the West Hartford house where he had grown up, his mother was now realistically dependent on him. He lived his life independent of her and reduced her to one of his children. The dependency needs he still experienced were age-appropriate. Because he had accumulated so many fringe benefits from his paternalistic insurance company, he now felt unable to change jobs.

The life of Herman Crabbe, Ph.D., illustrates that decreased danger and sustaining relationships also contribute to adaptive maturation. Originally, the life of Herman Crabbe was marked for disaster. At nineteen, Herman was almost bizarre. The Study staff called him "solitary, stammery, unkempt, and ill-bred." "He looked no one in the eye, but wore a chip on his shoulder," the Study notes say; "he makes a poor impression socially."

Herman had grown up in a small mining town in West Virginia; and the Crabbe yearly income rarely exceeded a thousand dollars. In high school, his towering achievement had been his marvelous collection of moths — a collection that, if it did not bring him friends, won him statewide recognition and a full scholarship to college. Other classmates may have been more natively gifted, but due to Crabbe's single-minded devotion to biology and the fact that good grades gave him pleasure while people gave him pain, he graduated *summa cum laude*.

Herman Crabbe suffered perhaps the most pathological mother in the entire Study. Mrs. Crabbe was a paranoid woman who, on the one hand, accused her crippled husband of going out with other women and disparaged him to his son, and on the other hand, capitalized on her husband's old back injury in order to keep him unemployed and an invalid. During Herman's childhood she had shopped around until she had found a doctor who could hear her son's "heart murmur" and helped her to exclude him from any kind of athletic or independent social activity. (The college physician found Herman to be in excellent health.) Mrs. Crabbe was terrified lest college take Herman away from her or make him into a "goat." Later, accepting that Herman had indeed escaped, she confided to the social investigator, "I'll have to cling to Sammy [Herman's younger brother] if I'm going to lose Herman." In those early years, one of the few honest statements that Herman made to the Study was that his mother was "not cheerful. . . . She nags me and ties me to her apron strings." After visiting Herman's mother, the social investigator agreed and wrote, "It was the most pathetic interview I've ever had."

Until age thirty, isolation, fantasy, and projection were Herman's dominant modes of survival. As a child, Herman had been as adept at intellectualization and fantasy as DeMille had been at dissociation. In contrast to DeMille, Crabbe *knew* that his mother was clinging to him, but he could not muster the appropriate emotion. Instead, he withdrew into the safety of his own head, and spent his time with moths, not people. Both the psychologist and the anthropologist diagnosed him as schizoid. At college, he summed up his philosophy, "Everyone is out to get as much as he can. . . . It doesn't pay to pay much attention to the other fellow." He lied to his parents, had no friends, and was one of the few subjects who was never in military uniform.

In high school Herman had identified with his paranoid mother and believed that the other children were out to get him. After college, because he dared to marry the one close friend he had had in high school, he believed that it was his wife's mother, not his own, who wished to stand in the way. Crabbe also imagined that his university would persecute him for getting married at twenty-three without telling them. His fears of retaliation reflected a projection of his real guilt about escaping from his mother's embrace.

At thirty, Herman Crabbe still resembled a village eccentric or a very young child. He asked two members of the Grant Study to propose him for the local skating club, and then failed to join. He avoided people and worked in his laboratory until 9 P.M. The social anthropologist commented that Herman was preoccupied with his own inferiority. "He seems to lack basic courtesy; he does not see people as they are psychologically but rather in terms of whether or not they provide support, whether they make demands or leave you."

At last Herman's mother died, and instead of devastation, both Herman and his father enjoyed a sudden burst of health. His father arose from his sickbed to get his first job in twenty years and to rejoin his old friends at the American Legion. Herman renewed his relationship with his rejuvenated father, cut back on his compulsive research, and for the first time began to move toward people. The Study internist commented that Crabbe "appears more confident and happier than I have ever seen him." Herman bought a boxer dog and wrote the Study, "I enjoy dealing with people to an extent I did not anticipate." His marriage prospered.

The year after his mother died, as part of the Study Herman received psychological testing, and at this time he no longer seemed schizoid. A clinical psychologist who was provided no information other than ten stories which Crabbe had told in response to the ambiguous pictures of the Thematic Apperception Test wrote: "His mother is seen parasitically wanting her son for herself because of her own frustration in marriage. . . . In his fantasy world, ignorant armies clash by night . . . some eccentricities may be present due to occasional intrusion of fantasy into a well-wrought obsessive-compulsive surface. Unlikely that this would reach schizoid proportions." The psychologist summed up his interpretation of Crabbe's test, "Slightly off kilter, but outwardly normal enough."

At fifty, the change in Crabbe had gone further. The two men used to illustrate fantasy, Harvey Newton and William Mitty, both gave questionnaire answers at fifty that underscored the persistence of their fear of intimacy. In contrast, at fifty Crabbe's answers to the same test put him a little on the extroverted side. He now seemed comfortable with his feelings. He no longer used daydreams for comfort, or "avoided closeness and familiarity with other people." Instead, he wrote, "I react to events with a good deal of feeling."

In my own interview with him, although Crabbe's jokes were still a little adolescent, he maintained eye contact throughout. As our time together passed, there was a progressive thawing of his demeanor. He was now the director of a research team of twelve Ph.D.'s at General Foods. He was repeatedly cited for superior achievement and, like DeMille, was an individualist surviving in the American corporate jungle. At nineteen he had stated flatly that he preferred things to humans, but at fifty he now told me, "I don't think I'm worth much working with things. I would prefer to work through other people." He still worked a sixty-hour week, but it was not for his own sake. As he told the Study, "I am not a great scientist, but I'm good at guiding others."

What were the steps that accounted for Crabbe's change? What allowed him to outgrow fantasy and projection?

First, a danger had passed; he was at last free from his mother's psychopathology. Second, at thirty-five, Herman experienced several hours of group psychotherapy. Third, in his early thirties he made friends with his father and for the first time acquired a second parent. Most important, he was blessed with a marriage that was one of the most fulfilling in the Study. He had married young, and there is no question that in part he married to obtain the competent mother whom he had never had. It worked. His wife did far more than college to free him from his family. After twenty-five years of marriage, he could write to the Study, "I have the same wife, and am getting more attached to her all the time."

In middle life, perhaps as a catalytic result of these events, this once lonely biologist was like a hermit crab who had finally found his shell in a safer world. Fantasy could be replaced by its logical successor, intellectualization. He lived his life on strict schedule. Each event of the day was ritualized, and all his social relationships were either at work or with his wife. Although he was reserved, I was impressed as we talked by the extraordinary candor with which he discussed his own psychological workings. He described sexual problems graphically but without emotion. Perhaps as a legacy from living so long within his own mind, he understood how he felt. Intellectualization has advantages as well as drawbacks.

Crabbe's projection gave way to its first cousin, displacement. When his mother died of breast cancer, he suddenly noticed pains in his own chest and wondered if he had finally developed the heart trouble that his mother had always feared. Later, as he increasingly accepted jobs that allowed him to work with people more and test tubes less, he became less preoccupied with the paranoid sense of his own inferiority; but the previously indefatigable scientist found that this new sort of work "exhausted him." He took a vacation for his "health." But after the vacation, he did not seek medical attention for "fatigue." Instead, he sought psychiatric help for "depression" (i.e., for his conflict over moving from test tubes toward people). In brief psychotherapy, Crabbe came to grips with his dependency — the curse of the projector's and the fantasizer's life — for the first time. He discovered "I was very skillful at manipulating my wife to keep me dependent. My dependence became clear to me. I had been blaming others."

Instead of projecting, he displaced his reluctance to join the conviviality of his college reunion onto the effort that it took to drive four hundred miles and onto the danger of a possible flu epidemic. But he came! In each case, his ego evaded full responsibility for his fears. But whereas his earlier style had led the Study staff to perceive him as mentally ill, at age fifty-two, by any criteria that the Study used to assess its members, Herman Crabbe was healthy. In his own words, he wrote, "It's a hell of a note to graduate *summa cum laude* at 22 and grow up and feel secure and confident in your own ability only after 50. . . . At 52 I have more ambition, more confidence, and more good ideas for work than ever before. . . ."

The final example of the ego's capacity to cast the demons of mental illness into swine is that of a Baltimore internist, Godfrey Minot Camille, M.D. What appeared to help his ego mature was a sustained relationship with loving people. In 1938 Camille had presented himself to the Study as enthusiastic and socially poised. He was a tall redheaded boy with pink cheeks and a charming manner, who said that he was headed for the ministry or medicine. Only gradually did self-consciousness and low self-esteem appear beneath his pleasant social manner. In college, he became an intractable hypochondriac, and eventually, by staff consensus, he was given an "E" for personality stability and declared by one insensitive observer "not fitted to the practice of medicine." Yet with the passage of decades, Godfrey Camille's psychogenic invalidism was replaced, first with displacement and then, as he became an effective physician, with altruism.

Only Dr. Earl Bond, one of the giants of American psychiatry and an inspirational force behind the Grant Study, had intuitively anticipated the future. After interviewing Godfrey at eighteen, he had written, "attractive, clean, forceful, modest, sense of humor, direct, easy, open — an 'A'." The other psychiatrist saw him as "distant, suspicious, floundering, stubborn," and a "C."

As a child, Godfrey Minot Camille had grown up in Brookline, Massachusetts, with very disturbed, if proper Bostonian, parents. Both parents were socially isolated and pathologically suspicious. Although overprotective, they seemed incapable of giving warmth to their children or allowing them to be aggressive in any way. At nineteen, Camille succinctly expressed the problem: "Mother hasn't exactly made up for Dad's shortcomings." At forty-six, he sadly affirmed his earlier statement: "I neither liked nor respected my parents."

As part of a hypochondriacal life-style, Godfrey may have exaggerated his parents' shortcomings, but other observers confirmed his general impression. The social investigator called the mother "fragile, nervous, lonely, pathetic, a master at self-deception . . . one of the most nervous people I have ever met." Godfrey's participation in the Study was almost blocked by his parents' convictions that the Grant Study physicians were going to give him dangerous experimental injections. His parents repeatedly wrote to the Study to discourage Camille's proposed summer trip to Nova Scotia. On one occasion, they said that they feared he would fall prey to grizzly bears; on another occasion, their excuse for withholding permission was that Germans might invade Nova Scotia by U-boat. Godfrey told the Study, "A friend of mine, when she met my parents, was just dumbfounded at the way they behaved."

Godfrey had been cared for in all the wrong ways. Throughout his childhood, a maid had accompanied him to school, and he had often been forbidden to play with neighborhood children. From thirteen on, Godfrey was conscious of an urgent need to escape this parental stranglehold, but he was so unused to independence that the task was not easy. Finally, he convinced his parents to send him to boarding school, "where I was put on my own to make my own way and to depend on myself." On one occasion at college, when he confessed to the Study social investigator that he was depressed, she had advised him, "When you come to the end of your rope, tie a knot and hold on." He responded forlornly, "But the knot was tied so long ago, and I have been hanging on tight for such a long time." On his Grant Study Rorschach, in response to an ambiguous ink blot, Camille expressed his dilemma over dependency as follows: He imagined a butterfly fighting to get out of a cocoon, but the butterfly died because a boy, not the butterfly, had opened the cocoon. Godfrey explained that the butterfly had needed the struggle to escape, and the premature release had been fatal.

Still unloved and dependent, Camille's unconscious strategy for survival was to frequent the school, then the college, infirmary. After having his finger pricked for a Study blood test, he demanded a bandage and sugar water "to keep from fainting." On five occasions during college, Godfrey was hospitalized; he made over twenty visits to the outpatient department. In almost every instance there was no evidence of tangible illness. In Camille's junior year, a usually sympathetic college physician reached the end of *his* rope and dismissed Godfrey's "imaginary" complaints with the disgusted comment, "This boy is turning into a regular psychoneurotic."

Camille's behavior was in contrast to his perceptions, for hypochondriacs rarely connect their dis-ease to emotions. Consciously, Godfrey thought of his health as "excellent," and the only physical effect of emotional stress that he would acknowledge was moderate insomnia.

In medical school, Godfrey began to shift defenses. As with DeMille, one adaptive style merged with another. With tentative insight, his hypochondriasis changed focus. If his physical complaints decreased, he became frightened about every textbook psychiatric malady that he encountered. First, he feared that he was schizophrenic, then homosexual. He wrote, "I worry about my health, but it seems very good." Finally, on graduation from medical school, Dr. Camille made a suicide attempt. He was hospitalized with a diagnosis of "depression and hypochondriacal trends." An important consequence of this was that he was able to postpone the internship he feared. In spite of the fact that his medical school dean described him as "handling patients exceptionally well," this frightened man was not ready to care for the needs of others. Like his butterfly, he still needed a cocoon.

For the first time, Dr. Camille did something honest for himself. Instead of plaguing doctors with ills they could not relieve and trying to relieve the needs of others before his own house was in order, he made several visits to a psychiatrist. After a few sessions, he wrote to the Study, "My hypochondriasis has been mainly dissipated. It was an apology, a self-inflicted punishment for aggressive impulses . . . a week of depression was the price of a little normal aggressiveness." (If children are reared in such a way that basic trust and autonomy are both denied, then they often view their own quest for healthy independence as unforgivably mean.)

On his Thematic Apperception Test, Camille excavated the underlying dynamics of his hypochondriasis still further. A psychologist, ignorant of any information about Dr. Camille's life except his response to the ambiguous pictures, wrote, "His mother is represented as a self-absorbed woman who forces herself not to believe that her son is suffering and miserable, no matter to what lengths he goes in desperation to gain her attention . . . the more the mother forces herself not to recognize his suffering, the more he suffers and agonizes."

Once Herman Crabbe acknowledged his projection, and Dr. Camille his hypochondriasis, these defenses could be abandoned. In lieu of hypochondriasis, Dr. Camille used its close relative, displacement. He shifted attention from the emotionally charged to the neutral. He developed a phobic aversion to any words that sounded like schizophrenia. When his sister died, Dr. Camille sent the Study the medical report; but his feelings, or even the facts of the death, were not mentioned. He simply wrote, "Enclosed is a copy of an autopsy protocol which I expect is also an item of news. As for me, I'm in excellent shape." After a moratorium of months, he was able to acknowledge to the Study his deep sense of personal loss. Similarly, he could not tell the Study about his mother's death, but as a way of avoiding feelings he cryptically informed the Study that "I received an inheritance from my mother."

Camille also developed conversion reactions; in other words, his feelings were displaced, transformed, into physical symptoms. When we lose someone whom we love, it is never our mind that is broken, only our heart, and feelings can mysteriously leap from the mind to the body. Thus, when a relative was dying of lung cancer, instead of feeling grief, Dr. Camille got an X-ray of his own chest. At twenty-seven, after breaking up with his fiancée, Dr. Camille did not burst into tears; he became overwhelmed with a sudden fear that he would become an hysterical cripple — "I lapsed into a semi-rigid state for an hour with paresthesias [tingling] up and down my arms." This was followed shortly afterward by insight into the etiology of his symptoms, and immediate "recovery"; for unlike hypochondriasis, conversion symptoms can be relieved by understanding interpretation. Dr. Camille no longer used his physical complaints to convey outrage or to make someone else responsible; instead, after psychotherapy Camille's physical symptoms became for him a clue to his own emotions.

As a hypochondriacal adolescent, Dr. Camille had been quite unconscious that his feelings affected his body. Under stress, he believed that he was without physical symptoms. As a thirty-two-year-old, however, emotional stress now led Camille to complain of indigestion, abdominal pains, cold hands, and gastric distress. In other words, he no longer saw the manifestations of psychological stress as tangible disease but correctly viewed them as physiologic evidence of emotion.

During this period in Camille's life, reaction formation was used in concert with displacement. He told the staff that he had developed several substitutes for being an aggressive male. For example, he compulsively sought out and befriended his friends' mothers — not their sisters. "A more mature adjustment was fantastically dangerous to something in my own unconscious." At thirty-two, Dr. Camille made an abortive attempt to get married, and later said, "I look back on this near marriage as an effort to help someone with whom I fell in love." Still too frightened fully to admit his own dependence, he spent much of his courtship efforts trying to give his fiancée the insight and comfort that he desired for himself.

Then, at thirty-five, a real illness provided Dr. Camille the emotional security that his hypochondriacal symptoms and wistful reaction formation could not. Secondary to a skiing accident, Camille developed a chronic bone infection, osteomyelitis. He was hospitalized for fourteen months. He recalled his initial attitude: "It's neat; I can go to bed for a year, do what I want, and get away with it." Later, he confessed, "I was glad to be sick." He realized that for him his illness had been akin to religious rebirth. "Someone with a capital 'S' cared about me," he wrote. "It made me feel that I was nutty for awhile, but in the Catholic church it's known as Grace. Nothing has been so tough since that year in the sack."

As his bone infection improved, he went into psychoanalysis. In part, he rationalized therapy as a means of freeing himself from dependency on hospitalization, but in part intensive psycho-therapy also provided him with a continuation of the real care that so long had been denied him. First, Godfrey had un-ashamedly accepted care during his physical illness. Then, through psychoanalysis he discovered inner strength that had hitherto been lacking. Just as previously his hypochondriasis had evolved into reaction formation, displacement, and the capacity to accept real care for real illness, now these neurotic defenses were replaced by altruism and the capacity to function as a giv-ing adult. Now, whenever he feels overwhelmed by patients, Dr. Camille takes a handful of vitamins, a Communion-like acknowl-edgment that the power to master conflict now lies inside him-self, where once that strength lay outside.

As an adolescent Godfrey Camille had entertained altruistic fantasies of becoming a minister and a physician; but in real life he had experienced great difficulty in translating these fantasies into practice. Throughout early adulthood, Dr. Camille remained unable to assert himself aggressively or sexually. His medical internship had taken several years to complete, and in the early years of medical practice, he worked exclusively in the protective environments of private sanatoria and in the military dispensary at Camp Meade, Maryland. Finally, at age forty, wish became behavior. As an internist, Dr. Camille had obtained additional psychiatric training, and he now specialized in patients with psychosomatic allergies. He started and directed a large Balti-more clinic for allergic disorders — the first time he had ever been in charge of anything. He wrote papers about the psycholog-ical needs of asthmatic patients with deprived childhoods; but these papers were useful to others as well as to himself. Whereas he once had felt overwhelmed by the dependency needs of the military wives that he cared for, he now became gratefully responsible for his private practice. He admits that what he likes most about his job is that "I had problems and went to others, and now I enjoy people coming to me."

In treating allergies, he often employs psychotherapy. "In psychotherapy," he revealed, "there is a kind of distant closeness that I like. It means a lot to me, and psychotherapy lets you get paid for it"; that is the difference between altruism and reaction formation. At age forty, too, Camille finally achieved a successful marriage — one in which he served his wife as "some sort of analyst/mother" . . . but at least both enjoyed it.

Dr. Camille's more mature defensive style also permitted him to engage in games. He played much more squash and tennis than in his younger days, and he flirted with the wives of his friends instead of their mothers. But at some level, creativity still frightened him; unconsciously he equated it with dangerous aggression. After building his own house, he reflected, "It does something to someone's image to live in a new house; it was stretching some notion of myself." To bear his anxiety, he took antidepressants, although I suspect that he knew in pharmacological fact that under the particular circumstances they could have served only as placebo. The cause of his fear was perhaps revealed by an unconscious turn of phrase. He told me that "I built the house from ground zero" — a metaphor more suited for the Alamogordo or Bikini atomic test sites than for a building plot.

In 1957, Dr. Camille had written to the staff, "I must be the most screwed-up Grant Study lad." But, of course, by the time he was able to write that he no longer was. More recently, Dr. Camille has summed himself up: "I am tedious and stuffy, but I can be fun; I can be fairly warm, and I can be really quite helpful."

As I finish this chapter, I find I start to anticipate responses from critical readers. "This book is not about health. The Grant Study studied a bunch of nuts." Or perhaps, "There must be something terribly wrong in families that propel their sons to top-flight universities." But I want to remind the reader that I am looking at defenses, at psychological white corpuscles, scavenging and mastering potential sources of pain and incapacity. Even astronauts and saints suffer boils. If we wish to study mastery of psychological pain, we must focus upon what is usually conceived of as disease. In everyday life, if the reader met Newton or Smythe, Camille or DeMille, he would perceive them as quite normal. What is more, their childhoods were probably no more distorted or damaging than those of the majority of humanity. Since the beginning of time, psychological war, drought, demons, and pestilence have ravaged mankind; I have selectively drawn attention to their depredations to demonstrate how the human organism has fought back.

Chapter 12

Successful Adjustment

Occasionally I would start thinking how such dull people could make money. I should have known that money-making has more to do with emotional stability than with intellect.

— J. P. Marquand, *Women and Thomas Harrow*

At sixteen, I remember almost walking out of the film version of Tennessee Williams's *A Streetcar Named Desire*. Marlon Brando and Vivien Leigh played the leads, and I was appalled by Brando's Stanley Kowalski. His emotional insensitivity, simian crudity, and unconscious brutality seemed unbearable. Blanche DuBois, as played by Vivien Leigh, seemed to me a frail, vulnerable heroine, a sensitive victim of Kowalski's impulses. Decades later, I reread the play for a course I was giving in psychopathology. I paid attention to the text and not to my emotional response. I was astonished that the very criteria I had used to gauge successful adult adjustment in the Grant Study now identified Stanley Kowalski as a model of mental health.

How can this be? On the surface, Stanley stands for all that is crass, mean, and destructive of beauty; his energy suggests the very "aggression" that Sigmund Freud suggested was equivalent with Thanatos, the death instinct. Exuding self-love, chauvinism, and cruelty, he growls to Blanche, "Well, it's a red letter night for us both. You having an oil millionaire and me having a baby."

However, the fundamental difference between Blanche and Stanley is that her millionaire is delusional, and Stanley's baby is quite real. To survive, humanity needs real babies more than it does imaginary oil millionaires. Stanley is regularly employed and is tenderly in love with his wife. He looks forward to the new responsibility of a child; and, at least by the next day, he is al-

ways willing to accept full responsibility for past temper outbursts. His life is filled with friendships that have endured for
years, men with whom he plays games and with whom he drinks
in moderation. If chauvinistic, he has pride in himself. He is a
man in whom "animal joy in his being is implicit in all his
movements and attitudes . . . the power and cry of a richly feath-
ered male bird among hens."

In the play, Blanche calls Stanley insane, and in adolescence, I
wanted to agree; but it is the gentle and sensitive Blanche who is
insane. It is Blanche, the hapless victim, who is unemployed,
childless, in love with nobody, and whose friendships are ambivalent, of short duration, and with "strangers." Stanley is guilty of
one violent rape (seduction?). But what hostilities were reflected
in Blanche's repeated seduction (rapes?) of young men? "I must
keep my hands off children," she vows. While Stanley brought his
wife only joy, did not Blanche contribute to her husband's
suicide? Stanley deals directly with sex and hunger; outside the
bathroom door, he can unambiguously growl, "It's my kidneys
I'm worried about." In contrast, Blanche DuBois washes her
grapes, renders sex dirty, and makes elimination an inconvenience for everyone. Blanche can accept neither criticism nor
responsibility for past misdeeds, and she is utterly unable to re-
pair what she breaks. It is Blanche, not Stanley, who misuses
alcohol; and, of course, it is Blanche who, beneath her veneer, is
condemned to hate herself and is removed to an insane asylum.

In expounding Kowalski's mental health, I do not wish to res-
urrect the ghosts of Nietzsche's Superman or G. B. Shaw's An-
drew Undershaft. But I do ask that the reader come with me onto
the dangerous ground of comparative "mental health" — and
dangerous ground it is. A friend of mine listened to me compare
the "Best" and the "Worst" outcomes in the Grant Study. He
heard me suggest that — statistically — a financially rewarding
career reflects mental health and not mere wanton pursuit of the
Bitch Goddess Success. My friend looked astonished and then
asked me, gently, "What are you, George, some kind of fascist?"
In responding to his thoroughly legitimate question, I should like
to make three points: First, if carefully done, the study of psychological health is just as benign as the study of physical health in a
well-baby clinic; second, creative aggression is not the same as
mayhem; and third, psychological health is not dull.

In order to separate successful adjustment from platitude and value judgment, I employed several strategies. Since behavior over time offers a better index of mental health than pencil-and-paper tests or assessment at a single interview, the items that comprised my Adult Adjustment Scale were longitudinal in nature.

Another strategy was to keep raters who judged the thirty-two items that made up the Adult Adjustment Scale ignorant of the men's defensive styles, childhoods, and objective physical health. In that way, a "halo" effect from one set of judgments would not affect others. The final strategy was to avoid ideal definitions of mental health and to substitute a battery of thirty-two less humanistic but more objective behaviors. Whether any one of the thirty-two given behaviors was in fact relevant to mental health could then be verified post hoc; did that item correlate with other items in the Adult Adjustment Scale, and did it correlate with independent measures of mental health? In that way, the validity of objective but value-laden items like divorce and income could be tested.

The thirty-two items used to describe health are defined in Appendix C, and already the comparison of Mr. Goodhart and Dr. Tarrytown has offered an overview of the general scheme. In brief, adjustment in each of four areas — work, social, psychological, and medical — was assessed by separate eight-item scales. Work was assessed by items like income, success relative to father, and consistency of promotion. Social adjustment was assessed by operationally defined items reflecting stable marriage, friendship patterns, and relations with parents and siblings. Psychological adjustment was measured by length of vacations, job enjoyment, psychiatric visits, and use of mood-altering drugs. Items reflecting medical adjustment included days of sick leave, number of hospitalizations, and subjective assessment of health. (Obviously, if the scale were to be valid in less-privileged samples, the parameters of the objective behaviors [e.g., income] would have to be adjusted.)

Items in the scale are disparate, but in assessing adjustment, it is important to realize that mental health is multifaceted. An analogous abstraction is human intelligence. No single criterion reliably indicates intelligence, but in designing the widely used tests that bear their names, both Alfred Binet and Israel Wechsler

found that a *battery* of tests provided a reasonably reliable definition of intelligence — provided, of course, that major cultural
variables were held constant. But what is meant by reliable? An
intelligence test is considered reliable to the extent that it correlates positively with all other measures of intelligence. Using this
model, most of the items in the Adult Adjustment Scale proved
their worth. For example, men who took enjoyable vacations
were more likely to enjoy their jobs and to engage in community
service. Men who enjoyed their family of origin were statistically
far less likely to see psychiatrists and more likely to stay with
their wives. In short, almost every item in the Adult Adjustment
Scale was positively associated with every other item.

There were thirty men who succeeded at all but two to six
items; they are called Best Outcomes. Like Goodhart, Lion, and
Byron, they experienced good career adjustment *and* social adjustment *and* psychological adjustment. Put differently — within
the Grant Study, for at least thirty of the men, great success in
career had not been won at the price of poor marriages and neglected children; nor had freedom from psychological complaint
been achieved through the substitution of physical distress.
Thirty men failed twelve to twenty-eight of the thirty-two items;
they are called Worst Outcomes. Among these men were only two
who fell in the top fifth of social *or* occupational *or* psychological
adjustment.

However, to call any of the men in the Grant Study mentally
unhealthy is only a relative judgment. By the standards of
epidemiological studies like the one of midtown Manhattan (by
Leo Srole and his associates),[1] roughly ninety-five percent of the
Grant Study sample would have fallen into the healthiest twenty
percent. By the criteria of Lester Luborsky's 100-point health/
sickness rating scale, the average Grant Study man would score
about 90; and only two — except temporarily — would have fall-
en below 65, the level Luborsky used to identify the mentally ill.[2]
Indeed, the average Grant Study "Worst Outcome" had
graduated from college, often with honors, had won a commission and good officer fitness reports from the army, had married
and raised children who also completed college, was steadily
employed as a professional or upper-echelon businessman, enjoyed an average income of over $25,000 (in 1967), surpassed his

father's occupational success, and at forty-five was still in good physical health.

Two life histories serve to illustrate the kinds of distinctions that the Adult Adjustment Scale illuminated. The man whom I shall call Steven Kowalski failed only four items on the Adult Adjustment Scale; he was clearly a Best Outcome. Leslie Angst failed fourteen items and so fell among the Worst Outcomes. The real differences in their life adjustments went far deeper.

I first met Leslie Angst at his twenty-fifth reunion. He was a worried, frightened man. His ears stuck out through his dirty, curly hair. His unsmiling eyes looked too large behind thick, metal-rimmed glasses, and they avoided mine whenever possible. Every now and then he would wring his hands. He looked far more the harassed, small-town bookkeeper than the upper-middle-class member of the establishment, who was returning in smug privilege to his college reunion.

There was a quality of mental disorganization that pervaded Angst's participation in the interview. When I began the interview by asking him to describe his job, he replied forlornly, "I don't know what I'm doing." When he returned to my office after lunch, he said he had had difficulty remembering where it was. When I asked him to describe his dominant mood, he replied, "I don't know how to describe moods. . . . I feel I'm always optimistic. . . . But I wasn't exactly joyous. There was . . . uhh . . . a lot of anxiety." I interviewed no man who was less in touch with his feelings.

Dostoevski writes more engrossing novels than John Marquand; the characters in great drama often border on insanity; and I am sure that Chapter 9 on the immature defenses makes bettter reading than Chapter 7 on suppression and altruism. Nevertheless, anyone who worries that in real life normality is dull or believes that the modestly deranged are intrinsically more interesting than the stable should have met Leslie Angst. In 1940 when he entered the Study and thirty years later when I interviewed him, Angst was one of the most emotionally tortured men in the Study, and one of the dullest. Thirty years before, the usually tolerant social investigator had grumbled, "Leslie is one of the most unattractive, unresponsive, strangest boys I have seen in the entire Study"; then added the unkindest cut of all: "Flavorless!" I felt the same way.

Leslie Angst's lack of social polish at forty-seven did not come from the absence of opportunity or privilege. He was born of German and English Protestant stock. For generations, everyone in the Angst family had gone to college. His father was a bank president in Larchmont, New York; his maternal grandfather had also been a bank president; and his mother had grown up amid privilege and had graduated from Smith.

As a child, Leslie had been a very good boy, almost plastic in his mother's hands. "He was always ready to do anything I asked him," she told the Study. She had given him a violin and for ten years had made him play it. Then at seventeen he finally revealed to her that at seven he had desperately wanted to have a bicycle, not a violin. But he had never told her; for as she assured the Study, "Leslie has never been the kind of person to get into scrapes." His father described the dilemma of Leslie's passivity rather differently. "I was so anxious to teach him the proper way to use tools that he, being amenable, lost his own initiative." Leslie himself provided the Study with a third view. "I was always scared from the beginning. I don't know why."

Except for one great-uncle who had been alcoholic, there had been no mental illness in the Angst family. Leslie had gone to Scarsdale High School and then entered college with a comfortable allowance. But once there, he made no friends, joined no clubs, and dated rarely. He went to no parties or dances; and his financial resources merely served to endow his two hobbies, "to waste time and to drive a car around aimlessly." Unlike Herman Crabbe, Leslie Angst feared to become too interested in science. He believed if he did so he would be unable to use words. As he told the Study, "You can get lost in a laboratory." Unfortunately, he had no choice but science; for "novels," he explained, "don't seem to be a part of life." After college, work in a munitions laboratory had the advantage of helping him avoid the draft, but he still felt trapped. In his thirties, he fled DuPont and returned to the family bank in Larchmont.

Here, he continued to be trapped, always too busy but never successful. He was a fine "company man," but that only added to his dullness. Eben Frost was a smashing success as a corporation lawyer who got by with a forty-hour week; other men *enjoyed* working long hours; but Angst was merely busy — neither happy nor successful.

How did Leslie Angst fare on the Adult Adjustment Scale used to measure mental health? On the eight-point career scale, he received credit for slowly moving up the ladder in his family business. He passed two more items because he both earned $20,000 a year and served as treasurer of the Larchmont Congregational Church and the boy scouts. "If I take a living out of the community," Angst believed, "I have to put something back in."

But he also failed five items. Rather than being more successful than his father, he was decidedly less successful; for at Leslie's age, his father had been bank president. He was making $28,000 a year, hardly a failure, but by their twenty-fifth reunion, most of the men in the Study who had gone into business were making more. He was not in *Who's Who in America*, and lastly, he himself felt that he was a failure at his job. For the last six years, his mortgage section of the bank lost money. Sometimes he believed his main problems came from incompetent employees, "who have their little cliques"; and so he endlessly fired the people that he hired. But his section went on losing money, and Angst went on losing self-esteem.

Leslie Angst passed four items on the social adjustment scale. He married; he never actually got divorced; he fathered two children; and in adult life he enjoyed his parents. However, although he got credit for the items on marital adjustment, his marriage was not happy. His sexual life was "not as good as wished," and his wife was difficult to live with. "She reserves the right to criticize me," he complained, "but she gets in a tizzy if I criticize her." He then temporized, "But still, I love the girl. I wouldn't give her up." She, on the other hand, wrote that she was in despair about him.

Angst also failed four items on the social adjustment part of the scale. Despite social privilege and old family ties, he never belonged to a social club. As he put it to me, "I never felt I've had a real friend; I only had acquaintances." There was no objective evidence to contradict his subjective view. Finally, his own children were also unhappy; although in their late teens, neither had close friends or had ever had a date.

Angst passed only three of the eight items on the psychological part of the scale. He never had been hospitalized for psychiatric illness; he, certainly, could not be accused of being too calm and unruffled; and the blind rater could not find three places where this inarticulate man had actually expressed dislike of his job. However, there were many other ways in which his psychological adjustment seemed objectively poor. First, he never had expressed enjoyment over his work. Second, although he worked for a family firm, he never took more than two weeks of vacation a year, and he spent the time he took in unhappy visits to a hypochondriacal, dominating father-in-law. Third, he drank half a bottle of whiskey every evening; as he put it, "I come home mighty tense, and it relaxes me." He also regularly took tranquilizers. Fourth, he had made fifteen visits to a psychiatrist. Finally, during the course of his life, Angst had repeatedly described himself as depressed, and after my own interview with him, I saw no reason to change his self-assessment.

It was only in terms of subjective physical health that Angst showed excellent adjustment. At forty-seven, he assured us that since college he had never been hospitalized and that he missed less than two days a year for illness; indeed, over the years he had always perceived his physical health as excellent, and he claimed to suffer from no chronic illnesses. He failed only one of the eight medical health items; he regularly took prescription medicines.

Unfortunately, Angst was as out of touch with his body as he was with his feelings. By his physician's more objective assessment, he had high blood pressure and emphysema. Within four years of our interview, Leslie Angst died from the complications of these disorders. Undoubtedly, his three packs a day of cigarettes and his heavy drinking had not helped.

Although he also employed fantasy and projection, Leslie Angst was a subject who dramatized the many different ways in which displacement can be deployed. He exhibited phobias, defensive wit, obsessions, and conversion symptoms.

Foremost were his obsessions. He was an expert at splitting his feelings from disturbing ideas and reattaching them to trivial concerns. As a child, his nightmares were not about the usual lions and tigers which already for most children represent displacements. Instead, Leslie Angst dreamed of terrifying geometric shapes and dots. Angst could not express overt emotions about business worries. "When you are trying to handle a business problem," he told me, "you leave your emotions at home." Nevertheless, if he had not had enough to drink, he woke up at night powerless to stop the *ideas* of business problems from racing through his head.

For years, Angst avoided facing his chief business worry — that he worked in the same bank as his aging father. Years before, when he was still working for DuPont, Angst had hesitated to work for his father's bank because "I had seen too many people swallowed up by their fathers." Much later, during the four years prior to our interview, his father had become progressively more senile. In explaining his current business difficulties, Angst confided, "I feel it's the old men who created most of my problems." Nevertheless, although Angst fought with everyone else in the bank, his relations with his father remained harmonious. "He is a great friend as well as a father," Angst insisted. Later, when Leslie was forty-eight, in order to master his father's death, he became frantically busy with concrete things — "So you don't have time to dwell on feelings," he explained.

Under stress, Angst often displaced his worries onto a multitude of distressing physical symptoms. When he was bullied by his wife into seeing a psychiatrist, he did not talk of his anger toward her but instead, "All I did with the psychiatrist was tell jokes. . . . I talked over business problems with him." Angst also illustrated how isolation and displacement create not only obsessions but also phobias. At twenty-six, he intellectualized, "I'm still trying to determine why I have not engaged in sexual intercourse, when I have no objection to it." As a displacement for sex, Leslie took up pilot training, but he had to give up flying, too; he developed a fear of heights.

Since, aside from his "humorous" encounter, Angst never went near a psychiatrist, the evidence that his fears were phobias rests on longitudinal follow-up. (More usually, the discovery of the source of a phobia is learned during psychotherapy.) When Leslie Angst was eighteen, his beloved grandfather — "If there was anyone I patterned a life upon, it was after him" — died unexpectedly. Angst experienced no feeling of grief, but through anorexia and inexplicable vomiting lost twenty pounds. At the time, he attributed his nausea and loss of appetite to stage fright. During the same period he had been embarrassed by vomiting during a school play. Thirty years later, when I asked Angst why he had lost so much weight during his senior year in high school, he rationalized that it had been due to a touch of the flu. I asked him point blank if he thought that his symptoms had had anything to do with the death of his grandfather. Suddenly, he became fascinated, his face became animated with uncharacteristic feeling. "Gosh," he exclaimed, "I wish someone had asked me that before."

In 1916 Sigmund Freud wrote, "The difference between nervous health and nervous illness (neurosis) is narrowed down . . . to a practical distinction, and is determined by the practical result — how far the person concerned remains capable of a sufficient degree of capacity for enjoyment and active achievement in life. The difference can probably be traced back to the proportion of energy which has remained free relative to that of the energy which has been bound by repression, i.e., it is a quantitative and not a qualitative difference."[3] What Steven Kowalski possessed and Leslie Angst did not was unbound energy. As an infant, Steven was described as "an extremely active and alert baby." In 1940, when he first visited the Grant Study, the psychiatrist noted, "Steve appeared as an energetic, active boy, who bounced into my office." At forty-five, the social investigator observed that he was "still wound up and alive."

When I first met him, Steven Kowalski was a much bigger man than I had expected. His vivacity, good looks, and engaging smile were the first things that struck me. Then, under a brush of gray hair, his bright eyes fixed on me, and despite the fact that his telephone often interrupted the interview, I continued to feel I had his entire attention. Kowalski took care that he was always talking to me rather than about himself. He had a special way of apologizing for interruptions that did not demean him but instead left me feeling that he had put himself in my shoes. He spoke not the way a star does to a newspaper reporter, but as a good teacher does to a student. I was struck by his magnetism, and — rightly or wrongly — I believed that it came from warmth and interest, not facile charm. He was excited by chance-taking, not for the sake of a gambler's gain, but for the opportunity of creation. He closed his interview with me by saying, "I'm satisfied. It's been a very lucky life. I can't say that it's been hard." But for Kowalski, gratitude was an habitual posture. "The Grant Study," he enthused, "was the most wonderful thing. Everyone in it got a good deal out of it. They were wonderful people . . . they were careful not to intrude, careful to prevent you from making an ass of yourself."

But always, Kowalski's responsiveness had been balanced with self-control. The physiologist's note that Kowalski was "quick to blush" was balanced by the psychiatrist's writing that "Steve maintains an excellent impression of outward calm." At forty-seven, Kowalski remarked, "I just love to work and never knew it until my job with Harris Upham. It keeps my energy channeled, which is useful."

Kowalski's childhood environment was rated as being as happy as that of any other member of the Study; and the social investigator commented, "The family are closely united and devoted to each other." Undoubtedly, Kowalski's unfettered initiative had been fostered by his mother's tolerance of his aggression. If Mrs. Kowalski called her son "an awfully satisfactory, easy child," she also noted that originally her son "did not curb his impatience." But she did not curb it for him, nor did she bully him into ten years of violin lessons. Rather, she allowed her children to talk back to her and to outwit her; but she nevertheless managed to maintain their respect. Mrs. Kowalski related to the Grant Study staff a favorite story. She had asked her son if he had dropped a toy on the floor, and at two and a half, little Steven replied, "Where do you think I dropped it, on the ceiling?"

In his turn, her son acknowledged that his mother had "a good sense of humor" and was "a leader in almost everything she does." Then, unable to resist adolescent riposte, he added, "Like my father, she is keen and inquiring, too, but does not always remember what she is keenly inquiring into." The fact that contrary to orthodox psychoanalytic expectation, Kowalski's rebellious spirit was undaunted by testicular surgery at six supported a dominant conclusion from the Grant Study: It is sustained relationships with people, not traumatic events, that mold character.

A full professor at thirty-two, Kowalski's father was an authority on international banking and had enjoyed a distinguished career as a public servant. Yet he also took an active part in the family's activities together, canoeing and sailing. Mrs. Kowalski described her husband as possessed of "great gentleness and understanding, and a delightful sense of humor." Kowalski described his father as "on the brilliant side and very modest."

Like Angst's, Kowalski's mental health could be expressed in numerical terms. Two of the four Adult Adjustment items he failed were that he did not excel his brilliant father and, unlike his father, by age forty-five he was not in *Who's Who in America*. However, in most respects, Kowalski matched his father's brilliant career; and he certainly enjoyed himself. "One's career," Kowalski said, "is one's dominant motivating force." He had started his own business from scratch, and it had prospered. Then, three years before our interview, conditions had changed; he saw them coming, and so he had had to shift into an entirely new financial field. He did so, and became even more of a success. I asked him whether he had been scared. "No," he told me, "that's what I like best; I like to organize and get the deals." Somehow, danger for Kowalski seemed to vanish in the heady mists of creation.

Steven Kowalski, man of action, preferred Wall Street's soot-stained towers of mammon to his father's ivory towers of academe. He managed hundreds of millions of dollars, from a stark Wall Street office that was without a single frill; instinctively, he reserved his energy and sense of the dramatic for people, not things. Like Angst, he managed other people's money, but he did so for the good of others. By pioneering innovative management of the endowments of small universities, he made three times Angst's salary. Kowalski explained that over other people's wishes, "I aggressively pushed through a plan to provide mortgage funds to small towns and minority groups."

He loved his work, and he knew that he was a success; yet he failed one item in career adjustment that Angst had not. Kowalski preferred to spend his weekends skiing with his wife and daughter in Stratton, Vermont, rather than engage in public service.

Kowalski easily received credit for all of the sixteen items used to reflect manifest social and psychological health. Happily married for twenty-five years, he remarked to me, "It still gets better all the time." Although he clearly fell among the Stoics, he and his wife talked over their problems, "such as they are." To Kowalski, his daughter was a source of great pleasure and little worry. "She is interesting," he told me, "genuinely nice, and not as aggressive as I am." Kowalski took pleasure in his parents, saw them five times a year, and enjoyed sharing business interests with his father. He enjoyed skiing and tennis with both friends and his wife, and there was both objective and subjective evidence that he had friends. (In college, the usually anti-Semitic fraternities overcame their prejudice to welcome Kowalski as a member; the WASP Leslie Angst was not asked.)

To elicit their friendship patterns, my standard question was to ask the men whom they would feel most free to inconvenience. Initially, that stopped Kowalski cold. "Boy," he exclaimed, "I'd be careful not to do that! I have this feeling I don't need anyone to help me . . . I don't notice problems." Nevertheless, he told me that his closest friends were now the people with whom he went skiing, because that sport "lets you spend a lot of time just talking." He treasured the communication that took place in the long drive up from Long Island to Vermont. He thoroughly enjoyed his vacations and spent twenty days a year with his friends and family at Aspen or Stratton. He certainly was not too calm, and except for a single year of discontent, which led to a prompt change in his job, Kowalski over and over again expressed pleasure in his work. He had two cocktails before dinner, but in 1963 had successfully given up his habit of smoking a pack and a half of cigarettes a day. With adaptive reaction formation, he declared, "I've never done anything I was more pleased about! . . . Smoking is so disgusting!"

Two vignettes sum up how far Kowalski was from psychiatric diagnosis, hospitalization, or therapy. At nineteen, the psychiatrist had written, "Perhaps Steven's energy, activity, good sense, and intelligence stand out the most." At forty-seven, I had asked him what his dominant moods had been in the past six months. He replied, "Wild, buoyant enthusiasm!" I believed him.

Medically, Kowalski lost one point because he had been in the hospital twice since college — once in the navy for flu and once when he had fractured his ankle while skiing. Asked his own opinion of his health, Kowalski replied, "It's just great." He rarely visited doctors; and when he did, he forgot about it. When I asked how he dealt with colds, he replied, "I pretend I don't have them." In thirteen years, he had missed only three days of work, but he admitted, "Sometimes I go to work feeling pretty crummy." In response to stress, he did not develop physical symptoms; instead he replied, "I'm getting so I like it . . . under stress I have a tendency to put on a calmer front and start doing things slower and planning new ventures, thinking of alternative options."

Steven Kowalski was unashamedly assertive. In eighth grade, he was one of the first of his group to go around with girls. At fifteen, like the most primitive savage, he would go out on tours of surrounding towns in order to bring back new girls with whom to impress his friends at school dances. In high school, he had organized a political clique that had "ruthlessly run the school." It was also true, however, that at eighteen he had still held on to the friends that he had made in nursery school.

In college, Kowalski began to use reaction formation (and to worry lest he become "obnoxiously aggressive"). Although he especially liked venison, he would not eat it because it had been shot. In 1940, his record notes, "The boy states that he is quite sensitive to someone else being hurt in an argument or criticized, but he usually gets angry at the person who is doing this, so much so that he begins to jump on the boy who has been cruelly tormenting the other person."

In college, Kowalski also displaced his high school aggressiveness into intramural football and varsity lacrosse. He wrote for the college humor magazine, and he helped to organize the American Defense League — a ROTC-like organization that opposed American antiwar sentiment. In order to get into the navy, he cheated on his eye exam, and he went on to serve on small craft in the vanguard of several Pacific invasions. (Yet in 1967, he was in favor of our withdrawal from Vietnam.)

In midlife, Kowalski had transmuted his father's academic world into the hurly-burly struggle of Wall Street. He perceived himself, realistically, to be in a business that was surrounded by "corporate raiders," and whose motto was "Fight, seize, attack, plunder." But Kowalski had always enjoyed competition. Asked to describe how he and his wife solved arguments, Kowalski told me, "I am the aggressor . . . but she gets upset and furious, too; we both have hot tempers." Then he described that anger led to tears and "I feel so contrite that I am the first to apologize." Divorce had never been considered by either one of them, and I rated their marriage as one of the happiest in the Study.

In contrast, Leslie Angst had struck many people as passive. At twenty, he had told the Study that he had had vague daydreams of people feeling sorry for him. During World War II he remained a civilian. As a young man, he had played "casual squash" and bowled, but allowed that if he played squash he was tired all the next day. As he grew older, he gave up athletics altogether. At twenty-eight, he wrote, "I am tired of doing the same work. I hope it's not my permanent career." But for three years he took no action and then returned to his father's bank. At forty-seven, Angst's hobby was watching television. If no one could accuse him of being aggressive, he confessed that sometimes he had "tantrums"; and before his death, his wife had considered divorce very seriously.

Perhaps the differences between Angst and Kowalski were illusory and could be explained by Kowalski's tendency to use repression. Kowalski himself admitted, "I am very poor at self-analysis, which may account for some of my happiness. . . . People who don't worry about themselves seem to get along best." When I asked Kowalski how he mastered "rough spots," he told me, "The personal side of my life has been so pleasant that I haven't bothered to worry." Nevertheless, three times, Kowalski had encountered real crises in his life; and each time he had directly addressed and mastered the crisis. Illustrative of his selective and adaptive use of repression was that he told me he took no medicines. I inquired about the medicine for stomach spasms that he had reported on a prior questionnaire. "Oh," he told me, "I had forgotten all about that." But, in fact, each evening he would take his medicine without thinking; and, indeed, he had had no further trouble with his stomach. In 1975, Steven Kowalski's doctor reported that Kowalski's physical health was still excellent; Leslie Angst had been dead for three years. Once again, I am compelled to posit that mental health is not just a value judgment.

However, cannot individual case histories be selected to prove any wished-for comparison? How can I convince anyone that the "Adult Adjustment Scale" really describes mental health? If I try to define intelligence by choosing a person I consider bright, others may disagree. If I wish to define beauty by pointing out someone that I see as attractive, that beauty may be but in the eye of this beholder. But if platonic concepts are relative when applied to individuals, operational concepts are not so relative when applied to groups. By anyone's standards, the student body at the California Institute of Technology is brighter than the student body at an average trade school; the contestants for Miss America are better-looking than a random selection of high school wallflowers. This is despite the fact that some wallflowers and some trade school students will be incorrectly categorized. In keeping with the principle of group comparisons, the contrast of thirty Best Outcomes on the Adult Adjustment Scale with the thirty Worst Outcomes is illuminating.

The contrast suggests that the Best and Worst Outcomes really defined two very different groups of people. For example, unlike Steven Kowalski, two-thirds of the Best Outcomes took part in community responsibilities outside of their jobs, and unlike Leslie Angst, three-quarters of the Worst Outcomes did not. In 1967, half of the Worst Outcomes but only one of the thirty Best Outcomes made less than $20,000 a year; and in relation to their fathers, almost all of the thirty Best Outcomes but only half of the Worst Outcomes were upwardly socially mobile. Still more differences in career are illustrated by Table 4.

Under normal circumstances, such differences could be explained by external factors, but in the Grant Study, wherever social mobility occurred, it seemed more affected by *inner* ego styles of adaptation than by *external* events. Since all the Grant Study members competed for and then obtained an "establishment" college diploma, important variables like the effects of social prejudice, parental push, and education are minimized. Indeed, in the Grant Study, social class in college exerted no effect at all on midlife outcome. (For a review of *external* factors in longitudinal career success, see Glen Elder's important monograph.[4])

Almost all the Best Outcomes but only a third of the Worst Outcomes enjoyed at least ten years of a stable, allegedly satisfy-

TABLE 4
Dramatic Differences between the Best and Worst Outcomes

	Best Outcomes (30 men)	Worst Outcomes (30 men)
Adult Adjustment Scale Items:		
No steady career progress	10%	57%
Real income less than father's at same age	13%	53%
Less than 20 years of enjoyable marriage	23%	77%
No real evidence of friends	0	30%
Stints vacation	17%	63%
Heavy use of alcohol and/or tranquilizers	17%	52%
Independent Items:		
Ever unemployed for 3 months	3%	47%
10 or more vignettes of passivity, dependence, pessimism, self-doubt, or fear of sex	3%	50%
Dissatisfied with life*	0	40%
Often used immature defenses	0	60%
Clinical evidence of psychopathology	3%	67%
Children have social and emotional problems (1975)	23%	67%
Poor physical health or dead (1975)	3%	50%

*Four or more of the following true: From a man's own point of view, he is unhappy in his marriage, unhappy in his job, unhappy with career progress, unhappy with his health, feels present not the happiest period in life, feels present the unhappiest period in his life.

ing marriage. All of the childless, almost all of the divorced, and all of the friendless fell among the Worst Outcomes.

However, the difficulty of using objective evidence of Freud's *lieben und arbeiten* to support mental health is that critics protest that such items only reflect middle-class morality. To demonstrate that the Adult Adjustment Scale has any real validity, the same items that reflect working and loving must also correlate with alternative definitions of mental health. For example, divorce *can* occur in the lives of the most healthy, but statistically there is a dramatic association of divorce with every kind of mental illness.[5] Similarly, the capacity to work has proved a potent predictor of remission in schizophrenics,[6] drug addicts,[7] and delinquents.[8]

Let me, then, marshal alternative kinds of evidence to show the importance of working and loving in the Grant Study. The Worst Outcomes averaged one hundred and fifty visits to a psychiatrist; the Best averaged three visits. There was an equally clear difference between the two groups in terms of clinically evident psychopathology. By this, I mean that two or more of the following were true for twenty Worst Outcomes and for only one Best Outcome: lifelong problems with anxiety, a clinical psychiatric diagnosis by the staff or me, or hospitalization for emotional reasons. The Worst Outcomes could enjoy neither their jobs nor their vacations, but they were three times more likely to misuse alcohol or to use tranquilizers or sleeping pills regularly. What is more, half of the Worst Outcomes and virtually none of the Best Outcomes felt unhappy. Whether their unhappiness was defined by my observations of redundant examples of pessimism, self-doubt, and dependency, or measured by the men's own expression of their dissatisfactions did not matter.

Still more compelling, however, were the data on physical health. Kowalski and Angst were not isolated examples. During the past twenty-five years, the average Worst Outcome spent thirteen weeks in the hospital; the average Best Outcome spent only two weeks. At age forty, all but one of the sixty men described in Table 4 were still in good health. Fifteen years later, four of the Worst Outcomes were dead, six had chronic illness severe enough to impair their lives, and five others suffered from chronic if not disabling illnesses. Only one of the thirty Best Outcomes was chronically ill, and he was without impairment of function.

Figure 1 illustrates the relationship between "empirical" evidence of adult adjustment and the relative maturity of the egos of the Best and Worst Outcomes. True, half of all the 514 defensive vignettes of the Best Outcomes were labeled neurotic, as were half of the 613 vignettes observed among the Worst Outcomes. But defenses that channel rather than block inner life and affect — namely, suppression, anticipation, altruism, and displacement — were far more common among the Best Outcomes (see Figure 1). Defenses that removed, denied, or dammed inner life — reaction formation, dissociation, and the immature defense mechanisms — were far more common among poor outcomes.

Among the men of the Grant Study there did not appear to be two standards of mental health: one for the inner man and one for society. Internal adaptation correlated with outer adjustment. From the findings in Chapter 5, it can come as no surprise

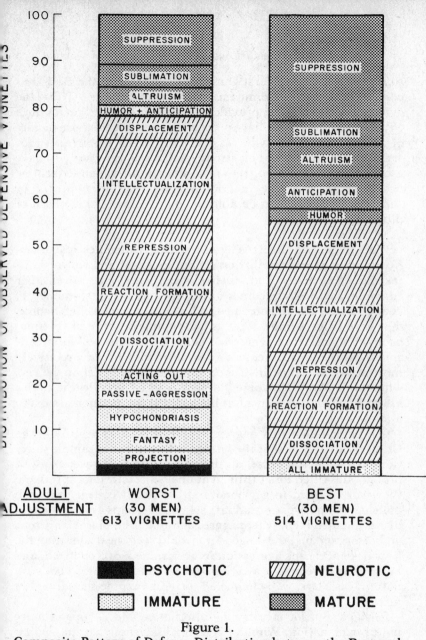

Figure 1.
Composite Pattern of Defense Distribution between the Best and the Worst Outcomes

that eighteen of the Worst Outcomes and none of the Best Outcomes employed predominantly immature defenses. Thus, the evidence of this chapter provides an answer to Heinz Hartmann's 1937 request: "Once we have determined objectively those factors of ability, character, will, etc., which are the empirical — not theoretical — correlates of 'strong' and 'weak' egos, we will have escaped the relativity of the usual definitions which determine ego strength from the individual ego's relation to its id or superego. We will then be able to compare the ego strength of different individuals."[9]

With respect to assertiveness, the Best Outcomes resembled Kowalski. It seems terribly crass, but as Angst and Kowalski illustrate, generosity and assertiveness were interwoven. For example, the Best Outcomes gave six times as much money to charity as the Worst Outcomes and, at any given level of income, they gave twice as much. Yet as a group they exhibited six times as many vignettes of aggressive behavior as did the Worst Outcomes. As the Best Outcomes grew older they became relatively more active in competitive sports than they had been in college, whereas the Worst Outcomes, almost as active in college athletics as the Best Outcomes, in adult life avoided competition almost to a man.

One explanation why aggressiveness seemed so healthy in the Grant Study men is that the finding is an artifact of sample selection. In a Victorian sense, all the men in the Study were *so* well brought up. Often toilet trained at one, valedictorians at sixteen, they worked hard to get honors at a difficult college and then polished themselves at graduate schools. Perhaps among socially disadvantaged men, where aggression might be more dangerous and disorganizing, the do-gooders would seem healthier than the Kowalskis. Perhaps aggression in overtrained, overcivilized, and overcooperative men is a saving grace. If undisciplined floods are natural disasters, well-channeled torrents become the servant of man.

Perhaps. But let me offer an alternative and, I hope, a more useful explanation. Winning and aggressiveness become entangled in our minds with hostility and violence. Among children followed from birth to maturity, Kagan has shown that *aggres-*

siveness in a young child is correlated with *effectiveness* and *competence* as an adult.[10] This is in contrast with the fact that *violent* adults have often themselves been *beaten* as children. Violence and aggression are different. The violent criminal is raised in an environment that has been hostile toward him; the successful adult has been raised in an environment that has tolerated his or her aggression (assertive competence).

Another interesting difference between the Best and Worst outcomes lay in gender identity. Fifteen of the thirty Worst Outcomes and none of the Best Outcomes lacked a fully male identity. Some of the Worst Outcomes had vocational interests that are stereotyped as feminine, had a woman as their ego ideal, went into professions that are usually associated with women, or, like DeMille, were brought up in exclusively female homes. As a child, one of the Worst Outcomes asked, "Do you have to be a woman before you become a man?" Another, as an adolescent, said, "When I grow up, I want to be a big fat mama." (In an era that is trying to do away with false distinctions between the sexes, the meaning of this observation should be clarified. I suggest that there is a difference between identifying with one's own sex and discriminating against another person because of theirs. In our culture the future creativity of many women has been stifled by society's edict that little girls *may* not be as aggressive as little boys.)

Probably related to the above was the fact that at forty-seven twice as many of the Good Outcomes were close to *both* parents and three times as many of the Bad Outcomes saw *both* of their parents as inadequate or even malevolent. Over time, the Good Outcomes had grown closer to and more positive in their assessment of their mothers and still more so toward their fathers. (In their fourteen-year follow-up of healthy men, Grinker and Werble also observed this shift toward more positive assessment of fathers over time.[11]) In contrast, over time the Bad Outcomes became still further estranged from their mothers and fathers (e.g., Dr. Tarrytown).

A major purpose of the men who founded the Grant Study had been to determine college predictors of future mental health. However, this book with its emphasis on unconscious dynamic

adaptation suggests that mental health is not static but evo-
lutionary. Perhaps we should be reassured that little could be
observed about the men at nineteen that would predict mental
health at fifty. For example, if seventeen of the Best Outcomes
had been called "A" in personality soundness while at college,
so had been six of the Worst Outcomes. If ten of the Worst Outcomes had been called "C," so had been two of the Best Outcomes.

But if college was not the time to judge emotional stability, age
thirty was. In 1947, after eight years of follow-up, the men's college careers, their World War II records, and their postwar adjustments were reviewed. "Personality stability ratings" were assigned to sixteen of the thirty men who twenty years later would
be classified as Best Outcomes by a blind judge and for seventeen
of the thirty men later classified as Worst Outcomes. In 1947, all
but one of the sixteen 1967 Best Outcomes had been called "A" or
"B"; all but three of the seventeen Worst Outcomes had been
rated "C," "D," or "E." But even here the lives of Crabbe,
Camille, and DeMille point to the fact that our adaptive capacity
continues to develop well into middle life.

If many facets of life were significantly associated with mental
health, there were many facets that, quite contrary to expectations, proved independent. For example, the men's family history
of mental illness, their body build, their intelligence, their
eyesight, even whether or not they bit their fingernails did not
distinguish the Best Outcomes from the Worst.

Pencil-and-paper measures of mental health did not correlate
particularly well with adult adjustment. For example, comparison of the Thematic Apperception Test that these men completed
at thirty in no way predicted their subsequent mental health at
fifty. The number of physical symptoms and individual experiences under stress (e.g., sweating, headache, heartburn, etc.) was
not significantly associated with poor adult adjustment.

As already mentioned, the men's social class did not influence
outcome. When the men entered the Study, a third came from
families that were clearly upper class or upper-middle class, and
one-third had come from family backgrounds that could be described as lower-middle or blue-collar. Twenty-five years later,
the social position of these men's families, their father's income,

or whether they had experienced public or private education bore no effect on their outcome, or on any of the variables upon which assessment of outcomes was based. These men's earned income, their friendship patterns, their patterns of psychological defense, and their emotional health proved independent of social class. (A recent review of the literature confirmed that, in general, social class is not an important predictor of healthy personality functioning and ego strength.[12])

There were at least seven men who, at fifty, clearly fell in the upper or upper-middle class (e.g., a college president, two senior members of establishment Wall Street law firms, a society surgeon, and a foundation president) whose origins were as humble as Goodhart's. All had been scholarship students; none had had a parent who had graduated from college; and in 1940, their average family income had been $2,000 per year. Yet, by middle life, five of these seven men used predominantly mature adaptive mechanisms, and five virtually never exhibited self-doubt, pessimism, or dependency. All but one fell among the Best Outcomes.

If social class did not affect mental health, mental health had little selective effect upon politics or religious observance. Church attendance proved quite unrelated to mental health. The Best Outcomes were only slightly more likely to have been foes of Joe McCarthy in 1954, advocates of civil rights in 1964, or of Vietnam withdrawal in 1967. Republicans and Democrats, liberals and conservatives were evenly distributed. But then, why should political prejudice have much to do with mental health?

At age thirty, and again at age forty-five, the men were asked to name the public figure that they most admired. Both outcome groups tended to favor Lincoln, Churchill, Jefferson, and Franklin Roosevelt. (Rasputin and Mussolini got one vote each.) Political preference during presidential primaries did not distinguish the two groups; the single exception was that men of action like Nelson Rockefeller and John and Robert Kennedy were preferred by the Best Outcomes, while the Worst Outcomes often favored the more reflective Adlai Stevenson and Barry Goldwater.

To summarize this chapter, the dramatic contrasts between Goodhart and Tarrytown and between Kowalski and Angst are statistically validated. When the men were viewed as a group, mental health appeared to be a recognizable dimension of human existence. The inner man (his defenses, subjective happiness, and physical health) conforms to the outer man (his objective capacity to work, to love, and to play). As illustrated by the tables in this chapter and in Chapter 5, both inner and outer man conform with psychiatric judgment (need for psychotherapy, justification for a psychiatric diagnosis, and use of mood-altering agents).

Previous investigations of "normals" by Roy Grinker and Jules Golden have supported a common prejudice that mental health is achieved "at the price of a more creative and spontaneous type of personality organization."[13] The present findings point in an opposite direction, and emphatically confirm findings from studies of healthy California graduate students[14] and of jet pilots:[15] Mental health is anything but dull. Whether the criteria were enjoyable vacations and sex lives, creativity in academic or business life, or charm and vitality during the interview, the relatively healthy men enjoyed life more and were more appreciated by others. There were dramatic exceptions, of course; but however dull suppression may appear, its use permits more "creativity and spontaneity" than do projection, masochism, and hypochondriasis.

Although this type of study will have to be repeated in many contrasting groups before these conclusions can be considered reliable, the approach offers a means of removing the concept of mental health from the philosophical morass in which it now wallows. Concrete, externally observable items (stable marriage, divorce, relative salary, visits to physicians, long vacations, tranquilizer use, and independent evidence of friends) offer objective correlatives of the more intangible components of psychological health. While the Victorians might say, "I told you so," today such assumptions seem anything but self-evident. Indeed, at the start of this investigation, whether or not value-laden items like divorce and job success would correlate, even modestly, with mental health was very much in doubt.

Thus far, I have elaborated a definition of mental health and a hierarchy of unconscious modes of adaptation. I will now attempt a more penetrating analysis of cause. What is the relation of childhood environment to adaptation? What is the importance of social relationships to health? And finally, what is the association of our position in the adult life cycle to how we adapt to life? In each of the next three chapters tentative answers become possible only because of the longitudinal nature of the Grant Study. The reader may feel free to dismiss all subsequent conclusions with the caveat "This may only apply to one very narrow segment of humanity." It may. Or it may not. In either event, I am convinced that longitudinally studied lives have a great deal to teach us all.

Chapter 13

The Child Is Father to the Man

> Woe to the man whose heart has not learned
> while young to hope, to love, to put its trust
> in life.
>
> — Joseph Conrad, *Victory*

In retrospect, adult outcome can be explained. The crazy aunt, the rejecting mother, the clubfoot, the bad neighborhood — in psychological biography, hindsight permits all the pieces to fall obediently into place. However, clinicians are often blind to the Procrustean maneuvers that they employ to fit past history into their psychiatric formulations. In spite of the fact that we all "know" that childhood affects the well-being of adults, recent scientific reviews reveal that there is little prospective evidence that this is true.[1]

It is only recently that studies of normal development have survived the three or more decades needed in order to follow well-studied children into maturity. Such prospective study has contradicted many cherished assumptions. For example, when the childhoods of Best and Worst outcomes in the Grant Study were compared, there were many surprises. When identified in advance, fingernail-biting, early toilet training, the "tainted family tree," even that old standby — the cold, rejecting mother — failed to predict emotionally ill adults. Birth order, childhood physical health, the distance in age between the subject and the next child, even the death of a parent proved relatively unimportant by the time the men were fifty. Infant/childhood problems of some kind (for example, phobias and marked shyness) were recollected by the parents of virtually all the men who were later judged mentally ill. However, these same problems were also recollected by sixty percent of the parents of men who remained healthy.

Nevertheless, when the lives of twenty-three men whose childhoods were most bleak (the Loveless) were contrasted with the twenty-three men whose childhoods were most sunny (the Lucky), four predictions could be made about the effect of childhood upon midlife adjustment. First, men with unhappy childhoods would be unable to play. Second, they would be dependent and lack trust in the universe. Third, they were more likely to be labeled mentally ill. Fourth, they would be without friends.

Lest hindsight bias the results of environment, the two Grant Study research associates responsible for rating each subject's childhood environment were kept ignorant of the fate of the men after their sophomore year. But since their ratings were actually made in 1970–1974, they were familiar with major theoretical advances in childhood development — especially the work of Erik Erikson — that had taken place since the inception of the Study.

The information available to the research associates was (a) the psychiatrist's *and* the social investigator's notes on each boy's report of his home life, (b) the social investigator's interview with the parents, and (c) the boy's developmental history obtained by the social investigator from the parents. After reviewing all the evidence, eight facets of childhood were rated *superior, average,* or *poor* on a comparative, not an absolute, basis. (See Appendix C for a more detailed version.)

1. Childhood psychological problems (e.g., phobias, social withdrawal, marked feeding problems)
2. Childhood physical health
3. Security and stability of home atmosphere
4. Mother/child ⎫ (How warm, encouraging, and conducive
             ⎬ to autonomy, initiative, and self-esteem
5. Father/child ⎭ were these relationships?)
6. Relationship with siblings
7. High school accomplishment (academic, social, and athletic

8. Global assessment (Would the independent rater
have wanted to grow up in that man's household?)

These eight facets were combined to place the childhoods of the
men in three groups: Lucky, Average, or Loveless. Despite the
ambiguity inherent in each individual judgment, the agreement
among judges' total scores was excellent.

The important statistical correlations between childhood environment and mental health in midlife can be illustrated by contrasting two men who have already been introduced to the
reader. The childhood of Samuel Lovelace was rated as one of the
most uniformly bleak in the Study, and the childhood of Richard
Lucky was the envy of all who read it. (Both these men were first
introduced in Chapter 8.)

When he first came to the Grant Study in 1940, Samuel
Lovelace seemed scared. On the physical exam, even at rest, his
pulse was 107 beats per minute, and the physician wrote, "Sam's
anxiety is far in excess of the average Grant Study man." The
study staff described him as an immature lad who "tires rather
easily," and they were disturbed by his diffidence and his "inability to make friends." After six years, one of the staff summed
Lovelace up as "one of the few men to whom I would assign the
adjective *selfishness*. It was as if he were looking out of a very
small gun barrel." But perhaps in college the Grant Study investigators did not pay enough attention to Lovelace's childhood, or
perhaps they underestimated its influence. If the Grant Study has
taught me just one thing, it is that "selfishness" occurs not in
those who were given too much as children but too little. I doubt
that anyone viewing Lovelace's whole life could possibly regard
him as selfish. Certainly, even in college there were many Grant
Study staff who were touched by Lovelace. They called him a
"nice boy . . . intelligent, warm, open chap . . . with potential
ability that has not yet found an avenue through which he could
direct it." At graduation, the staff regarded Lovelace as neither
more nor less sound than the average member of the Study.

When I met Mr. Lovelace at fifty, he was a distinguished man,
neatly dressed in suit and bow tie. His hair was gray, and, as in
college, he looked older than his years. During the interview, he

smoked incessantly, and gazed out the window. Since I never received his direct gaze or his smile, I felt excluded; but Mr. Lovelace was not anxious anymore, just unhappy. The reasons were not hard to understand.

Sam Lovelace entered life as the result of an accidental pregnancy, and he never received the attention from his parents that he needed. When asked by the social investigator what she would do over again in bringing up Sam and his brother, Sam's mother replied, "I would try to provide better care and feeding during infancy . . . and more companionship. I may have preached at them too much, nagged them to go to church . . . always expected them to be adults." (When asked, at thirty, what he wanted his children to have that his childhood had lacked, Sam replied, "A richer environment in terms of stimuli.")

Sam grew up feeling that he "didn't know either parent very well," and recollected "little demonstration of affection from either of them." They, in turn, dismissed Sam as being "too dependent." His mother believed that "people like him more than he likes them." It was true that as a child Sam spent most of his time with his dog, and "grew apart" from his only brother.

In college, Sam viewed his mother as "very moody, unpredictable, and given to worry. . . . I don't feel too close to her." He also had little respect for his father. At forty-seven, he still saw his mother as "pretty tense and high-strung," and dismissed his father as a "remote," anxious, tired man who believed in vegetarian home remedies.

Throughout his life, Sam Lovelace was a stranger to games. Although he got all A's in high school and was editor of the school paper, Sam was seen by his parents as "not good at sports, and he hates those that he does." (Yet to the Grant Study staff, Sam appeared "graceful and coordinated.") As an adult, Lovelace engaged in neither sports nor games. He took less than two weeks of vacation a year and, like Leslie Angst, spent such time in dutiful visits to relatives. He visited his parents often, not from love as much as because he feared that they would soon die. Often his time with them ended in spirited arguments over politics, which reduced his conservative parents to tears and left the more liberal Sam feeling still more bereft.

In adult life, as in childhood, Sam Lovelace found love as difficult as play. At nineteen, Lovelace had said, "I don't find it very easy to make friends"; at thirty, he had acknowledged it was "difficult to meet new people." By fifty, nothing had changed. He told me that he did not socialize much, and he described himself as "sort of shy." At work, he felt bullied and manipulated by his boss; and when I had asked Mr. Lovelace who his oldest friend was, he told me instead of a man whom he envied tremendously. When asked what friend he would feel most free to inconvenience, he said first he hated to inconvenience anyone. Reluctantly, he identified such a friend, only to qualify the friend with the summary statement, "He's a mess." In the twelve months prior to our interview, he and his wife had not entertained.

But Lovelace's problems were not just internal. As was pointed out in Chapter 8, one of the enduring problems in the adult life of Sam Lovelace was the absence of social supports. Until college, because of his mother's nagging, he had gone regularly to church, but he had not gone since. His difficulty with friendships and reluctance to play games excluded him from social organizations, and his marriage to a chronically ill woman was unhappy. He thoroughly approved of hippies, adding, "Generally, I'm for anything that will shake up the adult world." Finally, the only meaning that Lovelace could find in the status quo was to hope that it would change. At eighteen, such a philosophy is healthy; but at fifty, it is correlated with social isolation and with seeking psychotherapy.[2] Thus, lacking other people, Lovelace's chief source of comfort was a psychiatrist, to whom he had turned for fifteen years.

Psychiatrists tell us that unhappy childhoods lead to "orality" in adult life. But orality is only a metaphor for hearts that have not learned when young to hope and to love. Erikson wisely translates "orality" into the phrase "lack of basic trust"; and it seemed clear that the main legacy that Sam Lovelace's parents had left him was not hunger but a profound mistrust of life. It was perfectly true that Lovelace was a man of many "oral" habits. He often used three sleeping pills to go to sleep, took weight-reducing pills to start the day, inhaled three packs of cigarettes to see him through it, and drank eight ounces of bourbon to soothe its end. It was true that as a child he once bit his fingernails and, occasionally, as he talked with me, he still put his thumb to his mouth. But that is not the point; for a major finding of the Grant Study was that childhood eating problems, fingernail biting, and lack of breast feeding were not associated with mental illness. Nor was adult alcoholism associated with unhappy childhoods. Rather, Lovelace's "oral" symptoms only flagged his self-doubt, dependence, and fear of sex. These traits endured throughout his life, just as they had been lifelong themes for Carlton Tarrytown and Leslie Angst.

As a young man, Lovelace was almost unique in that he encouraged his draft board to classify him 4F. He admitted, "I am selfish enough not to want to get into a dangerous branch of the service." But this was because he viewed himself as "oldwomanish . . . unduly timid and lacking in self-confidence." At forty-five, Lovelace viewed himself as "not very successful," as leading an "undisciplined life," and as being in "poor" health. He was "worried about aging, career, health, and money"; and his only solace over rough spots was the philosophy "Things are bound to change; with luck and hard work they might change for the better." But self-doubt still plagued him.

At thirty-nine, Lovelace had written, "I feel lonely, rootless, and sort of disoriented," and of his painful marriage, he wrote, "No matter how hollow a marriage it may be, it still gives one a home and a place in society. The thing about marriage is it gives me a place . . . despite even some hatred, it's easier to suffer with Janie than to suffer without her." He confessed that he was "afraid of giving up marriage and standing on my own." One reason for his fear was that his maiden aunt might disinherit him if he ever got divorced. Thus, his marriage whetted but never satisfied his need for dependency.

As a young man, Lovelace had consulted a psychiatrist because he was afraid of sex. Later, after he was married, he had intercourse only every four months. His problem was anxiety, not impotence. Indeed, although his potency was fine, at fifty he noted that he would have been just as well off if sex had never existed. He sometimes viewed it as unesthetic and distasteful.

Richard Lucky serves as foil to Samuel Lovelace. At his request, I had interviewed Samuel Lovelace in my office. A few weeks later, Richard Lucky invited me to his home in Concord. He lived in a handsome clapboard farmhouse built at the time of the Revolution. It had been well restored, much of it by Lucky's own hands. There was a roaring fire in the fireplace, and the house reverberated with Beethoven's Third Symphony. Mr. Lucky sat by the fire with his feet on the table, dressed in a white turtleneck sweater and looking ten years younger than his age. (The men from bleak childhoods aged more rapidly than men from sanguine ones.) Every now and then, Lucky would get up to poke the fire or adjust the music. In the background, I could hear the domestic buzz of vacuuming.

In college, Lovelace's resting pulse had been a hectic 107, whereas Lucky's pulse rate was 65. Lovelace was viewed as shy, self-conscious, and lacking purpose; Lucky was seen as a sociable, pragmatic chap who knew where he was going. Although the internist suggested that Lucky had "not much depth," the staff saw him as a "very pleasant and attractive, well-mannered boy, with a nice smile." If the psychologist called Lucky a little too aggressive, the psychiatrist relabeled him as "very attractive, with considerable warmth and vitality." Lucky, like Lovelace, received a "B" in psychological soundness, but everybody agreed he was "normal," and that he knew how to play. Certainly, he knew how to play. During his high school career, Lucky, like Lovelace, had been editor of the school paper; but unlike Lovelace, Lucky was always involved in games. Even in law school, Lucky's dean described him as having "more enthusiasm for sports and outdoor activities than for scholarship."

Until he got himself on academic probation in college, Lucky had had no childhood problems, or at least none that he remembered. The social investigator, too, had described the Lucky home as "particularly free of problems." She noticed that the family "enjoy doing things together" and that everyone exhibited "amazing health and vitality." As a child, Lucky had remained close to his brother and sister; and Mrs. Lucky, unlike Mrs. Lovelace, remarked that if she had the children's upbringing to do over again, she would have done nothing differently. Her philosophy was "eliminate doubts, explain the course of action, and let the child decide." Lucky described his father as a man who "likes people . . . he is not rigid or dogmatic"; and Mrs. Lucky told the social investigator, "Dick adores his father."

In adult life, Lucky's view of his childhood universe did not change. At twenty-seven, he described his father as the single person he most admired and "a well-balanced personality." At forty-eight, his father remained to Lucky "a very remarkable guy, a very generous man." He recalled that his father had provided a regular and happy home life and had seldom spoken in criticism. At forty-five, Lucky remembered his mother as "down to earth, practical, uninterested in keeping up with the Joneses."

Lucky's benign childhood was translated into caring for others. During World War II, his commanding officer described Lucky as having a "pleasing personality. He knows how to get the most out of his men." Later, Lucky led the two companies of which he became president to continued growth. He was also much admired by his uniformly successful adolescent children. During our interview, I noted that he was benevolent, relaxed, and accepting of their good-natured bantering, even when their interruptions verged on rudeness. He told me that he had given his oldest son a skiing trip to Sugarbush for Christmas. "I went along," he added, "as part of the present." Finally, Lucky was the only father of adolescents whom I interviewed who could boast, "All our kids are more mature than other children."

In contrast to Lovelace, Mr. Lucky enjoyed many hobbies. He wrote, painted, and sang in quartets. He was an avid skier and golfer, and still played competitive tennis. Although his disposable *per capita* income was no greater than Lovelace's, Mr. Lucky took five to six weeks' vacation a year and visited exciting places. He was close to his own family of origin, but visiting them was not the way he spent vacations. Instead, he invited them to visit him. His children, his marriage, his business associates, and his family of origin all gave him pleasure. He loved and admired them all.

Because his involvement with his own family and his children was so enjoyable, Lucky felt little need for friends. Yet he had had no difficulty in identifying his oldest friend. This was the same man on whom he would also feel freest to call for help. Although Lucky's self-image was that of a man having fewer friends than others, he described to me an active pattern of entertaining — the church fellowship group for supper, his son's basketball team for a week of skiing, a teachers' meeting at the house, and so on.

In contrast to Lovelace, Lucky found his dependency needs met everywhere he looked, and so was independent. Yes, his wife agreed. If Lovelace had told me how difficult it was for him to care for his chronically depressed wife and her many physical ailments, Lucky positively wallowed in having his wife (whose motto was "For it is in giving that ye receive") take care of him. I asked my standard question to learn what Lucky did when he got a cold, and his son interrupted, "He waits for Mom to tell him to go to bed." Over the years, the following quotes appeared in Lucky's record: "I have been most happy since marrying and settling down to family life." "It's been a wonderfully happy marriage." "Marriage is completely happy and very devoted." He had even married an heiress who did not mind vacuuming!

Lucky had no trouble finding other social supports. As a young man, Lucky expressed "an underlying certainty in the existence of a rational God," but later, Lucky said, he became "increasingly involved in our church." Perhaps this was because after his father's death, Lucky experienced a brief period of depression and became more aware of death. As he grew older, he turned more ardently toward the church and wrote to the Study, "Faith in God is the framework that gives meaning to everything." He also belonged to a number of social clubs and continually played games with others. Politically, Lucky was only too pleased to be part of the conservative status quo, and if hippies were a sign of hope to Lovelace, they were anathema to Lucky.

With Lucky's social supports went an absence of "oral" traits. He always perceived himself as in excellent health; and he described himself as "a good businessman, popular, and a good athlete." Just as Samuel Lovelace had better athletic coordination than existed in his own self-image, Lucky was not half so good an athlete as he imagined. Lucky, when young, had been challenged by his instinctual life, but lacking Lovelace's social anxiety, he had mastered it gracefully — without fear. At twenty-four, Lucky wrote, "Sex is a continuous nuisance. I take it when I can get it, and for the rest I am content. Though not a supporter of free love, I will accommodate almost any enthusiastic amateur." Three years later, he wrote, "Sex gives me less trouble; the fires have somewhat subsided, and my will has gained in strength." Shortly afterward, Lucky married, and for the next twenty-five years both he and his wife consistently described their sexual adjustment as "very satisfying." (The Lovelaces consistently described their adjustment as "poor.")

Lucky's trust in the universe and his acquisition of social supports was accompanied by an unbelievable vigor. He confessed, "Sometimes I envy the cloistered existence of some of my friends who returned to university teaching." Nevertheless, despite his long vacations and being coddled by his wife when he got sick, Lucky worked a sixty-hour, six-day week and was a whirlwind at home on Sunday, his only day of rest. It is true, Sunday afternoon I found him in front of a fire, stretched out listening to Beethoven, but he had run six miles a few hours previously.

As I summed up my interview with Richard Lucky, I felt a little uneasy. A debate began to form in my mind. Lovelace was a sympathetic character, and Lucky's aggressive, ebullient energy grated. When I left his house I had the feeling that I had met the first completely healthy happy man of the Grant Study, but I felt that he had achieved this feat by forgetting what he did not want to remember and by using assertiveness without guilt or discomfort. Physically, Lucky reminded me just a trifle of James Bond's Goldfinger, and he was so content with the status quo that he had little social conscience. He seemed reluctant to inconvenience himself. Indeed, interviewing Lucky was more like interviewing a professional athlete for the sports page than interviewing a highly educated man who for thirty years had participated in a psychological study. He was oblivious to the introspective possibilities that the Grant Study interview permitted. Instead, he drew my attention to his tangible possessions and his children. He kept trying to turn the occasion away from self-report and back into a relaxed family Sunday afternoon. I kept having to assert myself as a scientific investigator in order to bring him back to the point. Lovelace had known what to do during a psychiatric interview, but Lucky was a terrible "patient."

Although he did not use projection, Lucky had seemed reluctant to put himself in other people's shoes. I was disturbed by the fact that he had approved of Joe McCarthy in 1954 and had dismissed Stevenson as an impractical egghead in 1960. I disapproved of his 1964 vote for Goldwater and was shocked by the fact that in 1970 he still wanted to blockade Cuba and bomb North Vietnam. Certainly, he had kept his liquor import company in the black, but two of his chief trading partners were in the right-wing power elite of Greece and Spain. In my disapproval of Lucky, I ignored the conclusions of Chapter 12, namely that it is success at working and loving — not specific choice of politics — that accompanies mental health.

In contrast to Lucky, Mr. Lovelace touched me as he had

touched the original Grant Study investigators. I am sure that Lovelace was respected at work for never competing with anyone. He told me that people found him endearing because he was "kind .and gentle" and because "I am steadfast to my wife." The arbitrary Adult Adjustment Scale gave Lovelace no points for the fact that he had loyally cared for a mentally ill and chronically angry wife. It was true, as he told me with self-depreciation, "What I have really done is to rationalize and institutionalize cowardice," but I was impressed by his sacrifice. I am sure that Lovelace's fidelity had repeatedly saved his tortured wife's life.

Lovelace told me, "I'd like to be different"; but as a fellow citizen, I was glad he was not. The self-doubting, pessimistic Lovelace had opposed the witch-hunting Joe McCarthy; he had supported the gentler Adlai Stevenson; and he had hoped Bobby Kennedy would become president in 1968. Lovelace believed that the solution to Vietnam did not lie in American military involvement, and while Lucky wished to slow racial integration, Lovelace wished to hasten it. The unloved often have a special capacity to identify and to empathize with the pain and suffering in the world.

Then, my internal debate shifts to the other side. Is a man like Kowalski or Lucky really so immoral? Is my reassurance over Lovelace's politics worth his lifelong pain? Did not Dr. Tarrytown's unhappy childhood lead to politics that were just as conservative and far more dangerous than Lucky's? And did not Lion's self-confidence allow him to march at the van of the liberal press?

Furthermore, it is difficult for the chronically depressed to put their generosity on the line. If Lucky's gross income was five times that of Lovelace, he supported five times as many people, and his contributions to charity were a hundred times as great. If Lucky's politics were at variance with mine, he still cared enough to serve as campaign manager for *his* candidate for governor. In contrast, Lovelace confessed, "Although I take a liberal stance at cocktail parties, I can't follow it out onto the streets." Sometimes he did not even vote. Mr. Lovelace drafted a plan for inner-city renewal that the Office of Economic Opportunity never funded. Lucky sponsored and personally subsidized (from profits wrung from Greece and Spain?) tennis courts at a summer camp for

Boston's inner-city blacks. True, Lucky provided a less imaginative solution to the inner city's needs than did Lovelace, but his tennis courts were more than dreams.

The debate ends in a draw. It takes all kinds of people to make up a world; this is a book about psychobiology, not morality. Besides, the emotionally troubled make contributions to society that are profoundly valuable. It may seem too pat, this comparison between Lucky and Lovelace, but my purpose is to illustrate with real lives the statistical findings that emerged from the Study. My point is that human happiness is not determined by breast feeding, leisurely toilet training, or the absence of childhood surgery. As Erikson has written, children need to be patiently taught basic trust, autonomy, initiative — then adult games, friends, vacations, and social supports may follow.

The four ways in which the quality of childhood clearly affected the adult life of the Grant Study men can now be examined in greater detail. First, to be unloved in childhood was to be unable to play in middle life. Compared to the twenty-three men categorized by the term Lucky, the twenty-three Loveless men were five times less likely to play competitive sports. They were five times less likely to play games with friends or to take full and enjoyable vacations.

Second, the mistrust and the dependency of the Loveless in adult life was real. The Grant Study did little for the men with the best childhoods, and yet these men consistently viewed the Study as helpful. For example, one subject with a childhood as warm as Lucky's felt grateful to the Grant Study, which had tried to help him not at all. It was *his* wife who gave me a lemon pie to comfort my wife, who was home in bed with the flu; and he explained, "In human relations, I seem to have prospered in bad bargains — that is, I try to give of myself first and trust the other to respond. I seldom transact a relationship on my own terms." He was a warm and successful entrepreneur. In contrast, the Grant Study made a real effort to help some of the men from barren childhoods. Yet, such efforts were often seen as inadequate and the demands of the Study as overwhelmingly difficult. Their "oral" needs were never met. In short, the traits of pessimism, self-doubt, passivity, and dependence were all seen far more often among the Loveless.

There is a common assumption that alcoholism reflects, on the one hand, impaired capacity for warm human relationships, and on the other hand, the "oral" dependency that develops in the aftermath of an unhappy childhood. In most cases, however, such assumption is based upon retrospective evidence. After the fact, the alcoholic Mr. O'Neill's childhood was described as abominable; but in his prospectively assembled record, there was nothing to support such ex post facto reasoning. Among the Grant Study men, the twenty-three Lucky were afflicted with alcoholism as often as the Loveless, and to cure the alcoholism was often to cure the man.

In contrast, multiple drug abuse usually seemed a *symptom* of emotional dis-ease. Thus, the man had to be healed before such symptomatic drug use disappeared. Halcyon childhoods were often followed by heavy smoking *or* alcohol abuse *or* tranquilizers; unhappy childhoods were often associated with all three. Carlton Tarrytown could not give up one anodyne without turning to another, and Lovelace was a heavy user of many mood-altering agents. Indeed, compared to those classed as Lucky at fifty, the men with the bleakest childhoods took *10 times* as much prescription medicine of all kinds.

The third conclusion, namely that overall childhood environment predicts mental illness in adult life, can surprise no one. Half the men from the best childhoods, but only a tenth from the worst, fell among the thirty Best Adult Adjustments. Only a tenth of the Lucky, but half of the Loveless, were at some time diagnosed as mentally ill. The Loveless were five times as likely to be seen as unusually anxious, to receive psychiatric diagnoses, and to have been hospitalized for an emotional complaint. Just as they took more prescription drugs of all kinds, the Loveless were also twice as likely to seek medical attention for minor physical complaints. They spent *five* times as much time in psychiatric offices.

Their ill health, however, was not just emotional or imagined. Childhood environment genuinely affected the men's physical health. By age fifty-three, more than a third of the twenty-three Loveless suffered chronically from illnesses like hypertension, diabetes, and heart attacks; four had died. Among the twenty-three men with the warmest childhoods, all were living, only two were chronically ill. At fifty-three, twice as many Lucky as Loveless still enjoyed excellent physical health.

Mental illness in adult life was rarely the fault of any one person or event; for in human development, it is the sustained emotional trauma, not the sudden insult, that does the most lasting damage to the human spirit. No single childhood factor accounted for happiness or unhappiness at fifty. For example, as a psychoanalyst, I was tempted to explain Lovelace's fear of sex retrospectively and to blame it on an operation he had had on his groin at ten. But by coincidence, Lucky, too, had required genital surgery at the same age. Unlike Lovelace, Lucky always exhibited "considerable curiosity about sex."

In an epidemiological study of mental health in midtown Manhattan, Langner and Michael wrote, "It was found that sheer numbers of factors reported is the most efficient method of predicting mental health."[3] In the Grant Study, too, it is the number rather than the pattern of negative (childhood) factors that predicts mental health risks. Goodhart and Lion both survived painful relationships with their fathers; because there were strengths as well as weaknesses, they still triumphed.

However, if isolated trauma did not affect adult life, chronically distorted childhoods did affect adult outcome. For example, although the mental health of *relatives* was not related to subsequent psychopathology in the men, the mental health of their *parents* was. The Worst Outcomes were twice as likely as the Best Outcomes to have a mentally ill parent. This effect would seem to be mediated environmentally.

In harvesting the Grant Study data, I tried to assess the effect of heredity. Originally, the social investigator had specifically inquired about mental illness in all the relatives extending back to great-uncles and aunts. During thirty years of follow-up, additional family skeletons had often emerged from their closets. But when all the data were combined, the heredity of the Grant Study men seemed to have little predictive importance. Some men had family trees that revealed no hint of insanity, alcoholism, depression, suicide, eccentricity, or disabling neurosis. Other men had four or five mentally ill relatives. Yet the adult lives of these two groups of men did not differ. (Admittedly, when environment is controlled for, there is good evidence to suggest that *specific* subtypes of mental illness do tend to run in families; but overall judgments of mental health in the Grant Study men were not affected by *global* measures of mental illness in their relatives.)

The fourth and cruelest association of bleak childhoods was its correlation with friendlessness in middle life. All of the twenty-three men with the best childhoods, but only fourteen of those from the twenty-three worst childhoods, showed evidence of close friendships in middle life. Men who had warm relationships with both parents were likely to appear charming, extroverted, and energetic thirty years later. One man, formed in a parental mold as loving as Steven Kowalski's, trumpeted at his twenty-fifth reunion, "My father built me in his own image, that's what the old bastard did! So I know he must have loved me."

Men with poor relations with both parents seemed to age sooner, appeared barren of charm, and demonstrated rather frozen interview behavior. For example, one man's parental home was so inhospitable that even the charming social investigator remarked that upon visiting the house she had felt decidedly unwelcome. At forty-seven, the Grant Study man who had spent the first twenty years of his life in that unwelcoming environment confessed, "I don't know what the word *friend* means."

Men who in college had seen their fathers as the dominant parent tended to have the best marriages at fifty, and men who continued after college to be dominated by their mothers had marriages that almost invariably ended in divorce. Mentally ill mothers were twice, and mentally ill fathers were eight times as frequent among the men who got divorced or had very unhappy marriages.

Fathers or mothers per se, however, were not the be-all and end-all for how men turned out. Thus, one of the most impressive findings of the Study was that the image of the *dominating mother* is more a reflection of a young man's immaturity or of his mother's poor mental health than a reflection of actual strength or dominance in the mother. Men with mentally ill mothers remained in thrall to these women in adult life, whereas the men with the warmest relationships with their mothers — or their fathers — tended to see their fathers as the dominant parent. In other words, dominating mothers were rarely strong women; their power to dominate came more from their or their son's view of reality than from their own too-loving or powerful nature.

As men progressed into adulthood, as if by magic mothers were described as weaker and fathers as progressively more dominant childhood figures. But it still proved a tremendous boon to the men's future when a mother could enjoy her son's assertiveness and dominance. Byron's mother admired him for being a "little Tartar" and a good fighter. Other mothers of successful sons boasted: "John is fearless to the point of being reckless"; "William could fight any kid on the block . . . he was perfectly fearless"; and "Bob is a tyrant in a way I adore."

But this permission for aggression produced a paradox. The more successful the man, the more he feared women — not as individuals but as mythic beings. Many of the most independent men in the Study — corporation presidents, successful politicians — men who were not even remotely under the sway of their mothers, men with marriages better than average, nevertheless feared woman as all-powerful. While achieving their generative, "masculine" success, such men saw women in their innermost fantasies in a manner quite analogous to Saint George viewing his dragon — as their most formidable opponent. These were often the men who had had truly strong mothers, and their forthright struggles with life reflected both earlier conflicts and successful identifications.

This paradox is illuminated by Robert Stoller, a Los Angeles psychiatrist who has devoted his career to understanding the development of gender identity. He writes, "Masculinity, as we observe it in boys and men, does not exist without the component of continuous push away from the mother, both literally in the first years of life and psychologically in the development of character structure that forces the inner mother down and out of awareness."[4] As adults, twelve of the thirty Worst Outcomes but *none* of the thirty Best Outcomes remained bound to their mothers — either in fact or self-image.

The greatest unsolved mystery of the Grant Study is what determines a mature defensive style. In summarizing her lifelong studies of human development, Jean MacFarlane wrote, "Many of the most outstanding mature adults in our entire group, many who are well integrated, highly competent and/or creative . . . are recruited from those who were confronted with very difficult situations and whose characteristic responses during childhood and adolescence seemed to us to compound their problems."[5]

If the Grant Study supported the fatalism of Conrad's Axel Heyst, it was more hopeful than Sophocles. Specifically, it contradicted the *Antigone* chorus that warned, "When a house hath once been shaken from heaven, there the curse falls evermore, passing from life to life of the race. . . ." In the Grant Study, successful careers and satisfying marriages were relatively independent of unhappy childhoods. An unusually close marriage, like Crabbe's, or a dazzling business success often seemed to be a way of compensating for relatively loveless childhoods. More important still, ingenious adaptive mechanisms often intervened to comfort the poorly parented and to foil the "Gods infernal" of Sophocles.

As Goodhart, Camille, and Crabbe have all shown us, ingenious defenses provide a remedy for unhappy universes. Like hope, defense mechanisms often provided anodynes for the woes of Pandora's box. Lovelace's adaptive maneuvers were only slightly less mature than Lucky's. Goodhart, whose childhood fell among those of the Loveless, exhibited defenses which were more mature than Lucky's, and his career was more distinguished.

The life of Oliver Kane summarizes what a good ego could and could not do for men with bleak childhoods. Oliver lost both of his parents before his sixteenth birthday, but he went on to a financially rewarding career and a stable, if chilly, marriage. (After twenty-five years, Kane wrote of his wife to the Study, "I can't think of when she has been less than a very fine person.") On the one hand, Kane's adult adjustment and mental health were judged better than average; on the other, he lived out his life without friends, games, or social supports.

When Oliver was one, his father died, and when he was fifteen, his mother died. He never really had a home. After he married, he and his wife lived in residential hotels, and the address that he gave to the Grant Study was his New York men's club. The closest that he ever came to having a child was in fantasy. Like George and Martha in *Who's Afraid of Virginia Woolf?* Kane and his wife would have spirited arguments about how they would manage an imaginary adolescent child; yet to me he bitterly rationalized his childlessness: "If there's anything that the world does not need from Oliver Kane, it's more children." (The twenty-three Lucky brought eighty-seven children into the world; the twenty-three Loveless sired sixty-one.)

What was outstanding about Kane was his cold, excellent intellect and a quiet, "cool" ego that facilitated his occupational success and enhanced his marriage. When I asked him the structured interview question, "What do people admire you for and find most endearing about you?" his response was, "I am admired for my brains, my intelligence, and high standards. . . . I don't think anyone finds me endearing."

Mr. Kane's mind worked like a well-oiled machine. He was a management consultant, and his job was to make friends with promising executives, then put square pegs in square holes, round pegs in round holes, and then move on to the next problem. At this, he was brilliantly successful, but it made him no lasting friends. Certainly, his $70,000-a-year income could never be translated into fun. He showed little interest in athletics, never took vacations, and his only hobby was the elegant manner in which he dressed.

Yet Kane possessed full insight. He could sum up his life with the bleak realization, "I've not done enough to form close personal relationships." He did not project the blame; he did not deny it. His superb ego allowed him to anticipate the tragedy of his life quite clearly. There simply was no pleasure in it. Like a dog, he had no color vision.

Kane was perhaps the most intelligent man in the Study, and except for fantasy, he used only neurotic and mature defenses. He was a master of suppression. When I asked him if it was hard to ask for help, he wrote, "Yes, I have trouble. That is true of me." On another occasion, when I asked him for his philosophy over rough spots, he wrote, "I do not consider myself well-equipped in this area. I make a personal effort to solve what can be solved and to accept with calm dignity what I cannot." Like many men with bleak childhoods, Kane shielded himself by his wit. At first as we talked, I would frequently laugh at Kane's sharp wit, but he never did. Then, at the end of our interview, as if talking with me in the lounge of Kennedy Airport was not frigid enough, Kane handed me his business card. I was furious, furious that he could so coldly underline the fact that nothing personal had occurred between us.

Kane's life ended, as it began, in disaster. During a period of financial crisis, he flew his light plane into a mountain. It may have been accidental, but Kane had always been a meticulously careful pilot, and he had spent the previous week revising his will and putting all his affairs in order. A year before his death, he wrote his last words to the Study. "Ironically, as I have acquired more external 'success,' I have more and more doubts that I have chosen a way of life that really means anything."

As Joseph Conrad said, we need to be taught when young to hope, to love, to put our trust in life.

Chapter 14

Friends, Wives, and Children

> Love suffereth long and is kind; love
> envieth not; love vaunteth not itself, is
> not puffed up,
> Doth not behave itself unseemly, seeketh
> not her own, is not easily provoked,
> thinketh no evil;
> Rejoiceth not in iniquity, but rejoiceth in
> the truth;
> Love beareth all things, believeth all
> things, hopeth all things, endureth
> all things.
>
> — I Corinthians 13:4–7

Mental health and the capacity to love are linked, but the linkages are elusive. We cannot hold love in our hands, weigh it on a scale, or examine it with a hand lens. Poets have no trouble encompassing love with their special language, but for most of us words rarely suffice. Understandably, scientists despair of describing love. Thank God for that! Fortunately, many of us can enjoy love — wordlessly — when it comes our way.

Nevertheless, the goal of this chapter is to examine linkages between loving and mental health. Once again, to make the invisible visible and the intangible tangible, the method will be to use independent observers and long-term follow-up. Impertinent questions will be asked: If mothers are so important, what effect does a father's love exert upon his children? What is a happy marriage? Is divorce really a sign of poor mental health? Can you fear sex and yet love people? Which styles of adaptation facilitate and which most hinder loving? Do people have to have friends?

To begin, not everyone agrees that loving is the alpha and omega of mental health. Kipling wrote, "He travels fastest who travels alone." Frost told us, "Good fences make good neighbors."

Europeans have criticized the perennially adolescent Americans for being too gregarious. Psychiatrists and social workers are criticized for being obsessed with "object relations." Cultural anthropologists have pointed out dangers in the interpersonal intensity of relationships in industrialized societies.[1] A sociologist, William Kephart, has bluntly declared, "Yes, I'm afraid that sex is overrated. But then, so is love. And so is marriage. And (most of all) so are children. The fact of the matter is that we seem to live in an age when emotional attachments *per se* are overrated."[2]

With ninety-five lifetimes stretched out before me, I felt sure that I could answer the above skeptics. I could compare the men who seemed most skilled at loving with those most inept at the task. After my interviews, after reading through 300 pages of questionnaires from each man, I had no trouble dividing the men into groups. At one end of the continuum were the men who had accepted my visit warmly, invited me into their world by locking their eyes with mine. They were men who gave freely of themselves and trusted me, a total stranger, not to abuse that gift. Mysteriously, the gift that they gave me did not burden me but made me stronger. They told of friends, of happy experiences with people. When they spoke of the people closest to them, they did not need to add qualifiers. Instead, they revealed gratitude, trust, and admiration toward their parents, wives, and children. I left these interviews affirmed, liking both the men and myself.

Other men made me aware that I was an intruder in their lives. As I entered the door, they stared at me uncomfortably, and then made sure our eyes never truly met again — as if human intimacy was unwanted, or perhaps even frightening. They told me of unnecessary pain, as if it were my responsibility to bear it, but rarely honored me with real feelings. They explained to me that they had no friends or told of love so qualified and so ambivalent that I wondered how they bore it. Often, their parents, wives, and children had caused them more strain than joy; and their real gratifications seemed to come from the inanimate. I left these interviews feeling lonely, incompetent, and a little contemptuous both of my heart and of theirs.

What could be a better test of loving than its experience? With arrogance and certainty, I ranked the men (1) for warm, (2) for average, (3) for relatively unloving. The computer, obediently, uncritically, gave back elegant, statistically significant correlations. Love seemed very important indeed, and not at all hard to rate.

But who would believe me? Love, by definition, is so personal. A skilled clinician learns to use his or her own responses to recognize many emotions in others — sadness, anger, fear, pleasure. But the capacity to act lovingly is different. It always takes two to demonstrate. What if the subject finds the clinician unlovable? My private judgment of who was lovable and who was not was perhaps more projection than science.

So I devised a far less satisfactory way to measure love — one in which I, the clinician, could stand aside. It is less real but more believable — a common failing of modern science. Over the years, the men had described their marriages and their use of leisure time every two years. In the interviews, they were asked specifically to describe their oldest friends, the friends they could call on for help, and their patterns of entertaining. On the basis of such information, six objective tasks for loving were set, and a blind judge reviewed the data to see how many tasks each man had carried out. The tasks were (1) getting married without later getting divorced, (2) achieving at least ten years of marriage that neither partner perceived as outright painful, (3) fathering or adopting children, (4) believing that he had one or more close friends, (5) appearing to others as if he had one or more close friends, and (6) enjoying regular recreation with non-family members. (The ratings, made by raters blind to much other data, were admittedly subjective, but in eighty-eight percent of instances, the raters agreed.)

Friends

Twenty-seven men — I will call them Friendly — had carried out all six tasks. Thirteen men, whom I will call Lonely, failed to carry out more than two of the tasks. Some had carried out none. As I compare the blind ratings to my own, I would definitely make a few substitutions; but no one would believe me. However, in all but four of the forty cases, I agreed with the judgment of the less-biased independent rater. Thus, her judgment shall stand.

Of all the ways that I subdivided the ninety-five healthy men of the Grant Study, the dichotomy between the twenty-seven Friendly and the thirteen Lonely proved the most dramatic. At first, this observation seems obvious; but if it were, the study of lifetimes would not be necessary. You see, at points in time each of us is lonely; at other points in time we are loved and loving. We pass from one state to the other, and who is to say if we have more friends than our neighbor, or if we are more caring than our brother? On a cross-sectional basis, judgments about capacity to love are meaningless. But as will become evident, if examined longitudinally, the lifetimes of the Lonely and Friendly were really very different.

The classification of a man as Friendly or Lonely was based principally on whether during his adult life he had achieved a relatively stable marriage and made a few sustaining friendships. These facts alone were usually enough to predict the state of his other relationships at other points in his life (see Table 5).

I believe that the capacity to love is a skill that exists along a continuum. In order to make this point clearer, let me develop an analogy. We may like some foods and dislike others, but we all

TABLE 5
Comparison of the Adjustment of Lonely and Friendly Men

	27 Friendly Men	13 Lonely Men
Adolescent social adjustment poor	4%	62%
Distant from family of origin	15%	39%
Distant from own children	13%	50%*
Childhood environment poor	7%	46%
Mother dominant in adult life	0	54%
Childhood relations with mother poor	30%	31%
Chronically physically ill by age 52	4%	46%
Ever labeled psychiatrically ill	11%	54%
Immature defensive style	11%	85%
Stints vacation	22%	85%
10 or more oral vignettes	4%	62%
Immoderate use of drugs or alcohol	11%	39%

*Of the eight men who had children; five more lacked children from whom to be distant.

have approximately the same capacity to enjoy nourishment. Love is not like that. Rather, the ability to love is more like musical talent or intelligence. Even in a population chosen for health, the capacity to love — or what social scientists call "capacity for object relations" — was distributed very unequally; but for the individual the capacity possessed considerable longitudinal stability. Granted that we all have a basic need to love and be loved, but if loving were like eating, we might suppose that men not close to wives or friends could substitute their siblings or their children. Instead, as befits the hypothesis that the capacity to love lies on a continuum, this was not so.

In middle life, twenty of the ninety-five men in the Study had failed to maintain gratifying relationships with their parents or siblings. Such men were three times as likely to be called Lonely as Friendly. Nor could the Lonely substitute their children. All but three of the twenty-seven men one judge called Friendly were rated by another judge as close to their children. In stark contrast, only eight of the thirteen Lonely men had even had children, and four of these were distant fathers.

Over half of those men called Friendly at age fifty had ratings of high school social adjustment that fell in the top third of all the men; not even one of the Lonely had fared so well. Over half of the thirteen Lonely had high school social adjustments (rated by judges blind to their post–high school lives) that fell in the bottom third; and only one of the twenty-seven Friendly fared so poorly. This association existed despite the fact that the two sets of independent ratings were made on evidence separated by thirty years and that the two sets of ratings were based on very different evidence.

As suggested in the previous chapter, each man's childhood profoundly affected his future ability to love. None of the thirteen Lonely but half of the twenty-seven Friendly had childhood environments that fell among the very best in the Study. Only two Friendly but half of the Lonely had childhoods that fell in the bottom quarter. None of the Friendly but half of the Lonely had a mother who continued both to dominate their adult lives and to serve them as a model for identification. Such continued maternal dominance was probably not the cause of their loneliness; rather it reflected the basic difficulty that these men encountered in replacing their mothers with more appropriate and more enduring intimacies. As children their relations with their mothers had seemed as warm as those of the Friendly.

The capacity to love was also associated with subsequent physical and mental health. Half of the Lonely but only one of the Friendly had developed a chronic physical illness by age fifty-two. At some point in their adult lives, half of the Lonely but only two of the Friendly could have been called mentally ill. Not surprisingly, the Lonely were four times as likely to seek psychiatric help, and also far more likely to seek general medical attention. Physicians are loathe to admit it, but they often serve their patients in the capacity of rent-a-friend. Rather than avoid this role, maybe they would do better to learn how to do it well.

Perhaps the biggest difference between the Friendly and the Lonely was that the Lonely were more frightened. In the stage directions for Tennessee Williams's *Glass Menagerie*, the affect of Laura, as she moves away from her dream world and toward people, is indicated by a stage sign that reads "TERROR," and in psychiatric clinics, the schizoid patients are always the most scared. Why? Man has always known that he feared noxious dangers, be they real tigers and dentists' pliers or the more metaphysical states of penury, grief, and sin. However, it is only recently that we have recognized that pleasure, the warmth of sex, and the exultation of victory could also be feared. Child psychiatrists — Erikson with his concept of basic trust, John Bowlby with his examination of maternal attachment, and several who have investigated the fear of strangers anxiety in infants[3] — have all taught us that human fear is not only directed toward the lifeless unknown but also toward the imagined dangers of human intimacy.

In the Grant Study men, the continuum of fearfulness ran parallel to their inability to love. As college sophomores, the Lonely had been more likely to have exhibited a rapid pulse during the personal encounter of the physical exam; and under stress the Lonely were more likely to say that they felt "nervous." Ten of the thirteen Lonely men expressed fear of sex; this was true of only two of the twenty-seven Friendly.

But the difference in trust extended into many areas less easy to quantify. For example, nine of the thirteen Lonely exhibited ten or more vignettes illustrating the "oral" traits of dependence, passivity, self-doubt, and pessimism (consider the case history of Samuel Lovelace); ten or more such vignettes were observed in the life of only one of the Friendly.

Let me provide more graphic illustrations. It is hard to separate capacity to trust from capacity to play, for play is dangerous until we can trust both ourselves and our opponents to harness rage. In play, we must trust enough and love enough to risk losing without despair, to bear winning without guilt, and to laugh at error without mockery. All but two of the Friendly enjoyed competitive sports; all but one of the Lonely avoided such activity. Horace Lamb illustrated that to fear aggression is to forfeit intimacy, and Frederick Lion showed how aggression well tempered by playfulness became a magic bridge between himself and others.

How strange that in real life the capacity to enjoy the holiday desert islands of our imagination should have been a privilege granted only to the Friendly. Three-fourths of the Friendly took full vacations, but this was true for only two of the thirteen Lonely. Without real vacations, the Lonely sought vacations from themselves, and so three times as many Lonely men were heavy users of alcohol or tranquilizers.

The Lonely also inhabited worlds more profoundly distorted by their adaptive mechanisms. In fact, there was a powerful association between a man's capacity to love and the maturational level at which he defended himself. The maturity of defenses was strongly correlated with good marriages, overall social adjustment, closeness to children, and my (and others') subjective assessment of their capacity for human relationships. In simplified terms, twelve of the twenty-seven Friendly showed predominantly mature defenses (altruism, suppression, humor, anticipation, and sublimation). This was true for *none* of the Lonely. The facile equation between love and virtue was never more clear. Conversely, character flaws and unpopularity go hand in hand. Eleven of the thirteen Lonely men showed predominantly immature defenses. This was true for only three of the twenty-seven Friendly. Indeed, vignettes illustrating projection and fantasy were seen *thirty times more often* among the Lonely than among the Friendly men.

However, if our capacity to love and to adapt to life are interdependent, does heart or head call the tune? Which is cart and which is horse? Throughout this book, only modest evidence has been marshaled to suggest that mature defenses were a blessing seen more often in men well loved as children. Suppression was associated only weakly with warm childhoods; it was far more powerfully correlated with the capacity to love as an adult.

What is cause and what effect? Serious depression — to be suddenly without love — leads to sudden mobilization of immature defenses; but those who characteristically are suspicious, self-destructive, and beset with imaginary pains are also more likely to be without love. Maternal love may be devastated by a child with the disturbing defensive distortions of schizophrenia as often as a child is devastated by an unloving "schizophrenogenic" mother. Finally, if immature defenses are often deployed as a defense against lovelessness, just so they can be most easily breached through loving, trusting relationships. In the fellowship of Al-Anon, the alcoholic's wife can first acknowledge her masochism. In the presence of a truly understanding parole officer, the delinquent can stop acting on his anger impulsively and cease turning it against himself. In the pervasive warmth of an open and loving fiancée, a theoretical astronomer like William Mitty could abandon his vivid fantasies of the stars and reenter his own earth. The tragedy is that immature defenses repel love — the very force needed to breach them. The causal relationship between capacity to love and defensive maturation is not simple.

Let me try to balance the rather one-sided *psychodynamic* arguments that I have offered so far for choice of adaptive styles, with the life of Francis Oswald. He was a man who, like James O'Neill, underscored the importance of biological defects in maladaptation. Already introduced in Chapter 9, Francis Oswald was one of the Lonely. His life illustrated that the capacity to love can be destroyed by the unexplained appearance in adult life of persistent projection. His history makes no sense unless his capacity for adaptation is seen as partly autonomous from the people who surrounded him; his depression made no sense unless one postulates a biological component to misery. Yet his life clearly illustrates the linkages between adaptation and capacity to love.

I recall well my interview with Francis Oswald. For Florida, the weather was unusually cold. I had asked to interview him at his home, but he had insisted that he wanted to show me the Everglades. Although Oswald was a scientist and something of an explorer, he relied upon a thoroughly inadequate road map, and, finally, turned to me, a stranger to Florida, to ask for directions. Perhaps the spot he wished to show me was too far; perhaps he simply could not find the way. I never knew. Instead, we parked on a bluff by the ocean and discussed his life, surrounded by the icy chill of his isolation and the gray February Atlantic.

Oswald had an easy laugh and spoke to me with the impersonal clarity of a polished public speaker, but I remained in the last row of his audience. He tried to show me views of himself, but here, too, he substituted winter ocean for the Everglades. I could not feel that he had really given of himself or that I was richer for having known him. Unlike most Study members, Oswald was utterly uninterested in what we would do with the Grant Study data.

When we parted at the airport, I was about to fly around the world; but Oswald did not seem to care. Instead, as I got out of his car, he drew up his pant leg to show me a year-old surgical scar; then he asked me if I could help him justify his delusional system to his boss. In actual fact, his operation was long-healed, and during the interview he had been anything but insane. I suspect that as I left him he was seeking a way to hold onto me and be warmed. It had been so cold in the car.

Oswald's occasional persecutory delusions were not what made him the clearest case of "mental illness" in the Study; the real tragedy was that he had forgotten how to reach people. By all evidence, the childhood and adolescent development of Francis Oswald had been well within the middle range for this Study. In fact, Francis Oswald had grown up in a "very devoted family"; it seemed far more stable than Goodhart's. The blind judge rated his childhood above average.

Oswald had been a high school athlete and an Eagle Scout. According to his mother, he "was always thoughtful of others and has been called 'the guiding light' of so many young people in the neighborhood." When Oswald joined the Grant Study, the social investigator had called him "intelligent, level-headed, ambitious, attractive, well-poised," and observed that he had "excellent social ability coupled with acquired manners and good sense of humor . . . a great deal of dignity." The physician had called him "a very pleasant, attractive, nice-mannered, solid boy . . . rather immature physically and mentally," but "ambitious, careful of self, and very gentle in speech and manner."

Just as the greatest flaw of Oswald's upbringing was that it was too rigid, so in college his own greatest flaw became that his conscience was too strict. Nevertheless, the college-age Oswald did not predict a man who, in the despair of midlife stagnation, would delusionally project the dictates of that conscience and maintain that his hospital roommate sprayed the walls with marijuana in order to get Oswald arrested by the narcotics squad. Retrospectively, I can isolate clues from his childhood record to "explain" his paranoia and his later depression, but the prospectively gathered evidence weakens my after-the-fact reasoning. In Oswald's case, the longitudinal data of the Grant Study rendered his psychiatric symptoms more, not less, mysterious.

Francis Oswald's childhood was not unhappy and, even in retrospect, his family's concern for him appeared appropriate. In graduate school his thesis adviser had loved him as a son, and Oswald had married a woman who was as devoted a wife as any in the Study. It was the way that Oswald saw the world that held others away. For him, his distorting ego was the horse and his lovelessness became the cart. (Oliver Kane, remember, had had a miserable childhood and mature defenses.)

In adolescence, there were hints of future loneliness. It was probably not coincidence that Oswald's two best friends in college were Grant Study subjects whom the Staff regarded as asocial and isolated, and who, like Oswald, fell among the Lonely. Although he had been a versatile high school athlete, in college Oswald chose only the solitary sport of cross-country running. Throughout his college career, his steady girl friend was a thousand miles away. He imagined that if he rejected her and found a girl nearer to college, his old girl friend would magically become an old maid or wantonly promiscuous. Yet, despite his distant faithfulness, he was frightened by the fact that she urged him to marry her. After the war, Oswald endured a persistent nightmare. He found himself inside a prison, defending it, firing out the slit holes at "marauders" trying to break in.

The Lonely seemed to have more than average difficulty in learning the facts of life. Thus, although Oswald was a biology major who had a physician for a father, masturbation was more disturbing for him than for most subjects; and the Study psychiatrists noted, "Francis has never had any accurate information or advice about the subject." By twenty, the staff observed, "The main problem is that this boy's sensitivity almost borders on the paranoid. He thinks a lot of things said to him have a different meaning from the way they sound." As a result, his College Soundness rating was reduced from an "A" to a "B" — a judgment that was, however, still clearly affirmative of mental health.

At twenty-six, Francis Oswald found himself tense, with sex constantly intruding into his thoughts. Yet he could not get close to women, and he found fault with everyone. His philosophy over rough spots was "I'm pretty much disillusioned in general with personal relationships and certainly over the state of man." At thirty, the physician who previously had thought so highly of him wrote, "Francis is suspicious of people's motives . . . and he has experienced feelings of having to restrain himself from possible violence to others." Then, as reaction formation was fully replaced by projection, Oswald became oblivious to his own growing mistrust. "I still tend to trust people until they have proven they can't be. I've been stung a few times on this last score."

In middle life, Oswald's mistrust of the universe overwhelmed him. First, unfeeling universities seemed to block his promotions. Then, his fellow academics became wary of him. Finally, he said, "My boss began to get suspicious of me" — and believed him to be a Communist spy and a narcotics pusher. Oswald became progressively dependent on alcohol and projected all blame. "The stress regarding the older two children," he wrote, "has increased the amount of beer I drink." He was overweight, accident-prone, and suffering from high blood pressure and chronic back pain.

All this is prelude to Oswald's difficulty loving. Still a virgin at twenty-six, Oswald was devoted to a collie — "My constant companion before and after marriage." He would spend months at a time in the woods alone with his dog. Twenty years later, while he was drinking, he would call up distant friends in the middle of the night; but when I asked him about the friends in his immediate neighborhood, he could describe them only in terms of the number of Christmas cards he received. Trustingly, he turned to the Grant Study 1,500 miles away for help; on vacation, he easily made friends with the fire wardens in their lonely towers; but he never developed friends at work. Rather, he perceived his colleagues either as ambitious "politicians" or as manipulators trying to get him to do their research. The paranoid fear love as desperately as they crave it.

Before his death, Oswald worked as a consultant, usually unpaid, to an organization trying to save the Florida Everglades. I asked him who had served as a role model for his current work, and he told me about a man who had gotten fed up with his work in a small college and had become a social worker. But Oswald had only known *of* him; they were never friends. Oswald told me that he would start to cry if someone said something nice to someone else during a television interview. But when I asked him to describe his oldest friend, he described a war buddy who wrote him "half a sentence at Christmas time" and whom he had not seen for fourteen years. Suddenly, he became flooded with memory. "I just love him," Oswald laughed, "and the damn fool won't write me a letter." Maybe, he said, he would get to see him on his trip West next year. I asked Oswald to tell me about the friend that he would be most willing to inconvenience. He described a friend who worked sixteen hours a day, a friend who "has lunch between eleven-thirty and twelve, which is the only time he talks to you." I observed that such a man sounded like an unlikely person to ask for help. He smiled and said, almost in triumph, "But he's the one."

Francis Oswald's isolation from his family was just as severe. He had not seen his brothers or sister since his mother had died in 1952. In 1962, he had not gone to his brother's funeral. In speaking warmly about his sister, he added, "I've never met her family or kids; but we're all reasonably close, I think." By this time, I was chilled to the bone.

Although in Chapter 9 Oswald served as a prototype for the paranoid character, he was, nevertheless, completely trusting toward the Grant Study. Over the years our staff felt a special affection for him. The older Oswald grew, however, the more projection and fantasy dominated his life. His reaction formation gave way to projection and self-destruction — as insidiously as it does in the deaf or in people with degenerative brain disease. As his defenses regressed, Oswald further lost capacity to love. True, the violence of World War II left indelible scars. True, Oswald lost both parents at thirty. True, his drinking at the end reached alcoholic dimensions. But my best guess was that Oswald suffered from a depression that had its roots in his biology.

Fatherhood

In general, the Grant Study men's mental health was reflected in their relationship to their children. When I asked one of the best and most famous outcomes in the Study what people admired him for, he replied without hesitation, "I'm admired for my wife and family." I saw him as a smashing business success without emotional limitations and with an extraordinary capacity for making friends. But he saw himself in the same light that Cornelia viewed herself in ancient Rome — his *family* were his jewels.

Two independent judges were kept blind to all information about the men except for their descriptions in the biennial questionnaires of their children, who in 1975 were fifteen years or older. The judges rated each subject according to how close the subject seemed to be to his children and for each child's "Overall Outcome." Overall Outcome included the child's social relationships with peers, the child's emotional health, and the child's educational achievement. At the time of rating the average age of the children was twenty-two. For example, a rating of 1 for emotional health indicated "a happy young adult with no noticeable periods of depression, crisis, or delinquency," and a rating of 4 reflected "continuing emotional problems, bad adjustment, delinquency, schizophrenia, and/or psychiatric hospitalization." (See the Appendix for further details of how Overall Outcome was assessed.) Although such judgment of a child's outcome appears impressionistic, over time differences between children became fairly clear; and there was reasonable agreement between raters.

Consider the following examples from one of the relatively good fathers, one of the Friendly men, who wrote us that his sixteen-year-old son, Frederick, was "a worrier, very sensitive to others' feelings. Great gift for concentration. Taciturn . . . natural leader, especially in music and athletics. Has very special talents. . . . According to his teachers, could be professional violinist, but interests are athletics, biology, chemistry — *very* well coordinated. Captain of several teams; has girl friend. . . ."

At seventeen, Frederick was still "an athlete interested in pre-med, but majoring in biology . . . slow and easygoing . . . having a lot of talents . . . well-organized and single-slotted." By nineteen he had become a sophomore at Stanford. "Likes country, dislikes cities. Biology, neurophysiology, music are his interests. He will row in the Olympic trials next week. Good at most things and does not know it. His younger sister loves him."

At twenty-one, Fred shifted his major to neurophysiology. "Accepted at Yale for grad study. Now a conscientious objector . . . almost a marine. Should be a doctor . . . very sensitive." The father's reports about his daughter were equally glowing.

When the children of the thirty Best Outcomes were compared to the children of the thirty Worst Outcomes, the differences were dramatic. Yet, the judge of the children's adjustment was given no information about the father's outcome. No man's adolescent children failed to cause him worry and pain; but once the storms of adolescence had abated, the two groups of children looked almost as different as their fathers. Half of the children of the Best Outcomes went to top-flight colleges. This was true of only a sixth of the children of the Worst Outcomes. These differences in educational achievement could not be explained by either economics or intelligence: the Worst Outcomes were as bright as the Best Outcomes; nor was money the problem. Rather, the children of the Worst Outcomes seemed less able or willing to identify with their fathers' own educational achievements.

The children of the Worst Outcomes were twice as likely to drop out of high school and college. Two-thirds of the children of the Best Outcomes were judged as emotionally and socially successful; this was true for only one-third of the children of the Worst Outcomes. One child in seven from the Good Outcomes but almost half of the children of the Worst Outcomes seemed to be consistently unhappy, dissatisfied, and rejecting of responsibility.

There are many explanations for these findings. First, projection may have played a role. Unsuccessful men may have imagined their children caught up in the gloom of their own lives; Good Outcomes may have bathed their children in the glow of their own success. Biased reporting, however, could not account for the differences in the college choice or the fact that only one of the eighty-eight children of the Good Outcomes and five of the fifty-seven children (those old enough to be rated) of the Worst Outcomes were either seriously delinquent or had required psychiatric hospitalization.

Second, it is tempting to attribute the relationship to associative mating. Loving men had generally good marriages, and their children's superior outcome could be explained by better mothering and more stable homes. Thus, perhaps the relation between well-adjusted children and well-adjusted fathers could be a chance finding. As it turned out, however, the quality of marriage correlated less well with a child's outcome than the men's overall capacity to love. That is not to say mothers were *not* important, only that fathers *were* important.

Third, perhaps the explanation was genetic. While genetic influence cannot be ruled out, all attempts to distinguish genetic from environmental influence suggested the above associations were not primarily hereditary. A family history of mental illness, per se, did not affect the children's outcomes anymore than it had affected the outcome of the men themselves.

Environment was important, and the emotional maturity of the fathers was closely correlated with how well their children turned out. Poor fathers were three times as likely to have received a "C" rating in emotional soundness while in college, and they were eight times more likely to have been called mentally ill when adult. During their adult lives, a tenth of the best fathers, but half of the poorest fathers used predominantly immature defenses. As in the case of Francis Oswald, fantasy and projection were the paternal defenses most closely associated with unhappy children.

Half of the best fathers and only a tenth of the worst fathers enjoyed childhood environments that were relatively happy. The effect of the Grant Study men's mothers could not be statistically seen in the outcome of their grandchildren, but men who had had distant relationships with their own fathers were especially likely to become bad fathers themselves.

Social variables played no role in distinguishing poor fathers from good fathers. Subjects who had grown up in upper-class families buffered from their parents by many servants did not make worse fathers than those who had grown up in the more closely knit middle-class homes; the latter did not make better fathers than the upwardly mobile, socially disadvantaged men who had more of an economic struggle in the early years after college. Many upwardly mobile men are bad fathers, but so are many downwardly mobile men.

Obviously, the Lonely rarely reached the capacity for caring that Erik Erikson tells us identifies middle life maturity. Francis Oswald's own failure to become generative was highlighted by an unfortunate slip of the tongue. I had asked him what his greatest worry was, and he replied "That I will be able to support my family." He had meant to say "will not."

Although Oswald's own childhood had been judged comparatively benign, the blind rater, who focused only on the lives of the men's children, perceived only Dr. Tarrytown as a worse father. Oswald's failure was chronicled through his biennial questionnaires. When his oldest child, William, was eight, Oswald wrote, "We consulted a child psychiatrist in Boston, because of difficulty between the two older children, Bill and Jane, which was then resulting in extreme withdrawal on the part of Jane. Progress with Jane has been wearingly slow, and the cost of money, time, and nervous energy has disturbed both parents." For the next ten years, Jane's adjustment was a source of chronic concern. Later, Oswald wrote, "At 16 Jane continues in psychiatry — 2½ years now! And so far, she has made no progress whatsoever in stopping the use of underachievement to rebel against her parents. . . . I'm quite discouraged about the whole business since she is capable of A's and B's across the board. . . . Jane took a few trifling items without paying in a big store. The security guard phoned us to come down and get her. . . .

"She is extremely bright, but disorganized. She is creative, but would be much more so if not so impetuous. She frequently loses control and destroys things that are of prime use to her . . . or destroys the very things she is creating."

He wrote that Jane, at twenty, was "alternately difficult and very gratifying; she causes the most trouble of all three. Can drag her feet till you would not believe it. But can also be so solicitous that you would not believe it. She's at City College, New York, after dropping out for a semester. Doesn't quite know what direction to take. Fantastic coordination, active in badminton and tennis. . . ."

Oswald wrote that his fifteen-year-old son Bill was "discontented with many things, moderately lazy"; at nineteen, "Bill has moved into an apartment with other fellows. This was brought on by indirect and sometimes not so indirect urging on the part of his psychiatrist. He moved out with even more hostility than he had been showing at home. He is beginning at junior college this semester. I feel I have failed him. His underachievement was directed at the parents, particularly me." A year later, Oswald wrote hopefully that the twenty-year-old William "got married the previous winter and is much more serious, with his feet on the ground." Afterward, he told me, "His wife of less than two years divorced him. She wanted out, he didn't. We had the best talks we ever had when he was home in June." Finally, Oswald wrote hopefully, "Bill's a man now, he's an enlisted man at Fort Bragg. He comes home two out of three weekends, plans to go back to college when he gets out of the army. He's a joy to be around now." Regarding his third child, Oswald wrote, "How you can screw up so with two children and do so well with the next one is beyond me."

A great danger of projection is that the paranoid character is driven to repeat with his children the difficulties he has had with his own parents. As in nightmares and prejudice, small wrongs become frighteningly exaggerated. Having originally projected his own anger onto his parents, the paranoid child imagines himself abused by his own reflected anger. Later, he may unconsciously treat his children as he imagines that he was treated. Thus, Francis Oswald saw his son's "general behavior deliberately calculated to bug me most of the time" and feared that both Jane and Bill were "trying to knife my wife and me." In reality, however, it was Oswald who was overly strict and endangered his children's lives. After getting lost in a storm while sailing with his daughter in Maine, Oswald wrote, "My daughter was too exhausted to continue and sat quietly crying to herself in the cockpit. It reminded me of being lost in the fog as a boy with my father off the coast of Maryland. Circling in a motor boat and coming back upon our own oil slick . . . the passing down of values and attitudes from one generation to the next strikes me."

Remembering this, I became frightened as Francis Oswald drove me about looking for his unfound entrance to the Everglades.

Marriage

A good marriage is as hard to define as good mental health, and the concept is every bit as value-ridden. In our society, the role of marriage is coming into increasing question, so much so that to some the evidence on which this Study is based may seem terribly out of date. Is not marriage merely an outmoded custom, once fashionable among white, middle-class men and women from an old-fashioned chauvinistic era? Possibly, but if one accepts the limits of American middle-class culture at one point in history, the Study casts light on several questions: When is divorce healthier than no divorce? In a stable marriage, how important is sexual adjustment? Is it true that a good marriage is a sign of mental health? Indeed, is there such a thing as a happy marriage?

Let me begin by saying that in the Grant Study, there was probably no single longitudinal variable that predicted mental health as clearly as a man's capacity to remain happily married over time. How a man described his marriage over the years predicted his career success, the relative maturity of his defenses, and his own perception of his happiness as effectively as did the more obvious fact of his having been labeled or not labeled mentally ill.

Before examining this finding, it is necessary both to establish that happy marriages exist and to describe how they were identified. In 1954, 1967, and 1972, the men were asked on a simple multiple-choice questionnaire about the stability of their marriages, the extent to which divorce had been considered, the degree to which their sexual adjustment was satisfactory, and the relative ease with which they solved marital disagreements. In 1967, their wives were asked the same questions.

Of the ninety-five subjects, twenty-six consistently reported (and their wives concurred) that they thought their marriages were "stable," that divorce had "never been considered," and that their sexual adjustment was still either "satisfying" or "very satisfying." These men had all been married for a minimum of ten years — and an average of twenty. Thus, after twenty-five years of adult life, out of ninety-five men there were twenty-six stable, enjoyable marriages. These will be labeled Good Marriages.

How does one recognize men with happy marriages? The cynic may regard such men as liars or Pollyannas. However, the defenses of dissociation and reaction formation (i.e., the adaptive modes that let the user substitute happy myths to deny unpleasant emotional reality) were used far more often by the men who came to view their marriages as unhappy. I do not mean to imply that men in the Study never lied to themselves about their marriages; I only wish to underscore that after decades such self-deception became untenable. Suppression, on the other hand, was powerfully correlated with consistently happy marriages.

A second way to test the validity of these men's opinions of their marriages was to let more time pass. In 1972, the twenty-six Good Marriages that seemed most stable in 1967 were contrasted with those of the eighteen men with Bad Marriages. (By 1967, eighteen men had continued to stay married but viewed their marriages as "unstable," their sexual adjustment as "not as good as wished" or "poor," and had at least "casually" considered divorce.) If the criteria used to dichotomize the marriages were entirely ephemeral or built on lies, one would expect five years later to find several Good Marriages in tatters and several Bad, but more honestly appraised, marriages to have improved. Instead, in 1972, twenty-three of the twenty-six men with allegedly Good Marriages still viewed their marriages as thoroughly satisfactory. After five years, only four of the eighteen men with Bad Marriages now rated their marriages even slightly better. Of the other fourteen men, four had actually obtained divorces and six more believed that their marriages had deteriorated still further — and their wives agreed.

It proved interesting to compare the *second* marriages of the men who got divorced with the *first* marriages of men who remained — albeit unhappily — with their first wives. There is unequivocal evidence that divorce occurs more frequently among people with every kind of mental illness,[4] but there also can be little question that in a chronically unhappy marriage only divorce can allow the possibility of a new and stable marriage. In watching a friend consider divorce, many people carry on their own internal debate. On the one hand, divorce violates our sense of family stability, ruptures religious vows, and rarely makes for happy children. On the other hand, divorce is a breakout from outworn social codes and rigid parental morality; it allows escape from a chronically painful emotional prison, and may actually rescue children from an insecure no-man's-land between embattled parents. Thus, the fate of the Grant Study second marriages was of great interest.

By 1973, fourteen of the seventeen men who had obtained a divorce before 1967 had been remarried for longer than a year. Of these fourteen second marriages, eight had ended in a second divorce, and four more showed weaknesses that kept them out of the category of Good. In other words, only two of the fourteen remarriages — both of short duration at that time — were seen as unambiguously happy.

Another test of the reliability of these men's multiple-choice statements about their marriages is to examine what else the men said about their marriages. One man with a Good Marriage wrote as follows: "I couldn't ask for a better marriage. We just seemed to hit it off from the start. For example, I remember our first date; we still celebrate it after twenty years. Very early in the marriage, when one did something the other didn't like, the offended spoke up." Another man wrote, "Our marriage improves year by year. I do not know how I could have chosen so well or been so lucky." A third told us, "Jill and I are as close as two can be . . . enjoying lots of time together."

Contrast these statements with those of men with Bad Marriages. "In the last two years," one man wrote, "it's been the children, and the lack of a viable alternative for either person, that has kept us together — inertia." Another man wrote, "When she throws the plates, I catch them. I never throw them back. When she hits me, I never hit her back, although I've slapped her to bring her to her senses." This last man had never considered divorce, but we should not be surprised that he called his sexual adjustment "poor" and saw the marriage as having "serious weaknesses."

What evidence do I have that stable marriages are an index of mental health? The answer is clearest in the contrast of the marriages of the thirty Best Outcomes with those of the thirty Worst Outcomes. *All* of the thirty Best Outcomes got married and stayed married for most of their adult lives. By the time these men were forty-seven, only five marriages appeared poor, and two more had ended in divorce. In contrast, among the thirty Worst Outcomes, only nine were stably married. Seven more spent most of their adult life unmarried, and by age forty-seven, the thirty Worst Outcomes had accumulated seventeen divorces.

The following quotes characterize the Best Outcomes, whose marriages had endured satisfactorily for twenty years. "My wife is the kindest and most considerate person I have ever known." "Our marriage is completely challenging, completely exciting." "Tennis doubles with my wife is my greatest enjoyment." "We are very happily adjusted; I am very proud of her." "I love and admire her; she is my best friend." "I am proud of her. If I were not so successful, I would resent her success." "I associate my happiness with my wife." "Life is a lot of fun with her." "She is quite a girl; exactly right for me." "It has worked out more easily than expected. We have spent a great deal of time together." "Our marriage is GREAT. My wife has been the best thing that ever happened to me."

The following ambivalent quotes characterize the nine most successful marriages among the thirty Worst Outcomes. "She is affectionate; an extremely good mother." "She is a dominant person; marriage turned out much better than expected." "Stable marriage, God knows why. Marriage revolves around her interests and friends." "She nags me, but is an emotionally warm person." "A good decision, but she is an uptight, careful perfectionist."

Of the remaining twenty-one Worst Outcomes were twelve men who had either established second marriages or whose first marriages were battered but intact. The comments of these latter twelve men were more clearly ambivalent. For example, "She has an inferiority complex; I am not sexually attracted to her." "I am more affectionate than her" (except for weekends, this couple lived apart). "She likes her beer" (again, this couple lived apart). "Divorce seriously considered. It's easier to suffer with her than without her." "Her attacks are sometimes so savage they reduce me to tears; I think I love my wife." "We sleep in separate rooms. If I had it to do over again, I'd marry another."

Table 6 contrasts the twenty-six men with Good Marriages, the eighteen men with Bad but intact marriages, and the seventeen other men who by 1968 had obtained at least one divorce. Among the Bad Marriages, either children or religion were usually cited

TABLE 6
Comparison of the Adjustment of Men with Good and Bad Marriages

	1967 Marital Adjustment		
	Good (26 men)	Bad (18 men)	Divorce (17 men)
Worst Outcome	8%	50%	59%
Distant from their parents and siblings	12%	22%	41%
Distant from their own children	19%	31%	46%
Children's emotional outcome poor	33%	44%	36%
Own mother dominant in adult life	4%	11%	47%
Much passive behavior	35%	61%	35%
Immature defenses	23%	39%	71%
Few friends	8%	33%	53%
Psychiatric illness	8%	50%	41%
Immoderate use of drugs or alcohol	8%	56%	41%
Ever expressed fear of sex	0	50%	41%

as the reasons for holding the marriage together. Certainly, the unhappily married had far more regular patterns of church attendance than the divorced. As one man wrote, "Divorce is pretty unthinkable, so I grin and bear it . . . our marriage would have ended probably 15 years ago but for religion and the presence of children." Another wrote, "The marriage is stable if you will accept that it is held together as much by decision as by desire." A third wrote, "This marriage will stick if for no other reason than we're a couple of stuffy, latter-day Victorians who just wouldn't face divorce anyway." The men who endured unhappy marriages were more likely to be passive in other aspects of their lives than those who sought divorce.

The men who got divorced were more likely to have had their mothers play an important part in their lives after age twenty-one. They were more likely to have used immature defenses and more likely to fall among the Lonely. Often, they were isolated not only from formal religion but also from their families of origin and from affiliation with other social organizations.

Surprisingly, the children of the Good Marriages enjoyed only slightly better adjustments than children born into Bad Marriages. It was true, however, that men with Bad Marriages were more likely to be distant from their children.

The thirty-five men with either Bad or dissolved marriages were *five* times as likely to have been diagnosed mentally ill as the men with Good Marriages. They were also *five* times as likely to have been in psychotherapy and to have used mood-altering drugs. Clearly such findings are biased by sex and by culture. Longitudinal findings from the Berkeley Institute of Human Development suggest that for middle-class American women marriage is a much less powerful predictor of health.[5] In other cultures and other historical epochs marital success may be quite irrelevant to mental health. The critical issue seems not whether a man actually gets divorced but whether or not he can live enjoyably with another human being for twenty years.

In the previous chapter, childhood was shown to predict both future trust in the universe and future friendship patterns, but not stable marriage. Often marriage, like adaptive mechanisms, seemed to be one means that the men had for repairing poor childhoods. In some cases, for example Herman Crabbe and Francis Oswald, the exogenous reality of a good marriage proved an effective antidote to less-than-adequate modes of defense. Oswald had married an absolutely devoted wife, who, in his words, had "more concern for other people than anyone I have known." For the last six years of Oswald's tortured life, his endogenous modes of adaptation could only be described as psychotic, and his wife was the main reason that he survived.

During the course of the Study, it became clear that if a questionnaire delved too inquisitively into the men's sex lives, there was a high percentage of nonreturns. Over the years, then, the only information about sexual adjustment that was systematically gathered was whether the men perceived it as "very satisfying," "satisfying," "not as good as wished," or "poor." Sexual adjustment, assessed in this manner, was not correlated with whether or not a man had a rich friendship pattern, was good at sports, was sexually provocative, or had a masculine body build. Indeed, in contradiction of Freudian dogma, lack of sexual enjoyment was only weakly correlated with objective evidence of mental illness. The sexual adjustment of subjects who used immature defenses was as good as the rest of the men in the Study, and Francis Oswald's sexual enjoyment was consistently better than Goodhart's. But, then, from the beginning of time, prudes and moralists have bemoaned that "character disorders" had the most fun.

The correlates of continued marital sexual satisfaction came from different areas. Men who throughout life continued to find satisfaction in their marital sexual adjustment were much more likely to enjoy good overall adjustment, to enjoy their jobs, and to be successful in their careers. Curiously, these same men were also more likely to have gotten better grades in college and throughout their adult life to have been seen as persevering and abstemious. Looked at differently, men who consistently perceived their sexual adjustment as poor were likely to be seen as depressed, passive, lacking in job success, and to be heavy users of alcohol and sedatives.

A far more powerful predictor of poor mental health than sexual dissatisfaction in marriage was the overt fear of sex. After all, sexual adjustment depends heavily upon the partner, but *fear* of sex was closely linked with mistrust of the universe. For example, half of the thirty-five men who experienced poor marriages or obtained a divorce gave evidence of being fearful or uncomfortable about sexual relations. Such vignettes were not observed in a single man with a good marriage. Yet there were many good marriages in which, by the time the husband reached age fifty, sexual adjustment was less than ideal.

In conclusion, the conventional Freudian wisdom that maturity and "genitality" are defined by a happy sexual adjustment was only weakly borne out by this Study. Whether a man can love friends, his wife, his parents, and his children proved a far better predictor of his mental health and of his generativity than whether at fifty he found bliss in a marital or extramarital bed.

By the time they reached forty-five, Frederick Lion, David Goodhart, and Steven Kowalski were smashing successes at the game of living, but if they had not established the ability to love wives and friends and to care for those that depended upon them, the next decade would have been for nought.

"Yea, though I speak with the tongues of men and of angels, and have not love, I am but a sounding brass and a tinkling bell."

Part IV

Conclusions

Chapter 15

The Maturing Ego

> He [Roy Campanella] pushed the lever and the wheelchair started off bearing the broken body and leaving me, and perhaps Roxie Campanella as well, to marvel at the vaulting human spirit, imprisoned yet free, in the noble wreckage of the athlete, in the dazzling palace of the man.
>
> — Roger Kahn, *The Boys of Summer*

> The striving to master, to integrate, to make sense of experience is not one ego function among many, but the essence of the ego.[1]
>
> — Jane Loevinger, "Theories of Ego Development"

A central thesis of this book is that if we are to master conflict gracefully and to harness instinctual strivings creatively, our adaptive styles must mature. However, since human beings are not simple animals, maturation of their minds cannot be considered in depth without considering the development of both body and spirit. If such a thesis points to the growth of spirit as well as mind, how can I marshal evidence that is more than mere metaphysical woolgathering? If such a thesis points toward a biological view of mind, how can I marshal evidence that adults continue to grow at the same time that their bodies seem to shrink? How can I give a logical explanation for the growth of Roy Campanella, a great Brooklyn catcher who at thirty-six broke his neck, was paralyzed in all four limbs; yet at fifty the crippled Campanella seemed a greater man to sportswriter Roger Kahn than Campanella the baseball star had seemed at thirty.

The first step is to demonstrate that adaptive styles do mature. In 1937 Anna Freud observed that "the chronology of psychic processes [defenses] is still one of the most obscure fields of analytical theory,"[2] but she had no doubt that such a chronology existed. Over the years, several writers have offered developmental hierarchies for the maturation of defenses of children,[3] but these studies have been hampered by the lack of experimental verification.

To my knowledge, no one, with the exception of Norma Haan at the Institute of Human Development at Berkeley, has systematically examined the maturation of adult ego defenses. Norma Haan and Jack Block compared prospectively studied adolescents to themselves at thirty and forty-five.[4] Because their sample contained both men and women, the fact that their findings confirm those of this study is especially significant. The Berkeley investigators observed that, over time, behaviors reflecting reaction formation and fantasy declined, but that those reflecting altruism and suppression increased. They observed that compared to themselves at thirty, forty-five-year-olds were seen as "more sympathetic, giving, productive, and dependable."[5]

The pooled data from the Grant Study has supported Haan's and Block's observations that with the passage of years mature defenses were used with relatively greater frequency.[6] In other words, the middle years of the adult life cycle revealed not only increasing career commitment and responsibility for others but also a progressive maturation of adaptive modes. Figure 2 shows that as adolescents, the Grant Study men were twice as likely to use immature defenses as mature ones; but as young adults they were twice as likely to use mature mechanisms as immature ones; and, finally, in middle life they were four times as likely to use mature as immature defenses.

In Figure 2 the decline of fantasy and acting out, with maturity, and the concomitant increase in suppression, is no news. However, the facts that dissociation, repression, sublimation, and altruism appeared to increase in middle life, and that projection, hypochondriasis, and masochism were most common among adolescents, are at variance with many popular conceptions of adolescence and middle age. We sometimes think of the young as dreamy artists and the middle-aged as hypochondriacal martyrs.

Figure 2 supports an observation from Chapter 10 on the adult life cycle; namely that the decade from twenty-five to thirty-five was a guilty period. Haan, too, has observed that after the rebelliousness of adolescence had abated, the defenses of repression

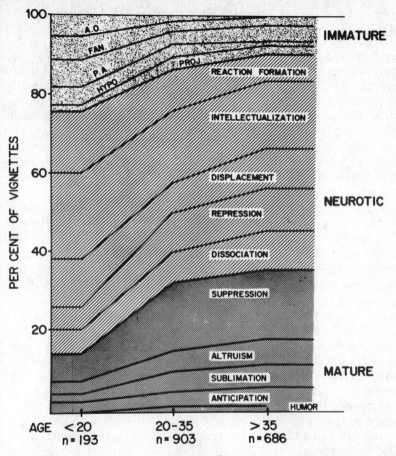

Figure 2.

Shifts in Defensive Styles During the Adult Life Cycle. The figure shows the distribution of defensive vignettes shown by ninety-five subjects at adolescence, young adulthood, and middle age. AO indicates acting out; FAN, fantasy; PA, passive aggression; HYPO, hypochondriasis; PROJ, projection.

The data for Figures 2 through 4 were obtained in the following fashion: Every time an adaptive vignette was observed to occur in a man's record, it was labeled both by age and defense. Thus, each of over 2,000 adaptive vignettes that were observed during the lives of the ninety-five men in the Study could be placed into one of the three age periods: 12–19, 20–35, or 36–50. See Appendix C for further details.

and reaction formation were used with greater frequency.[7] In another study, a Columbia psychologist, Percival Symonds, contrasted the Thematic Apperception Tests of 12 to 18-year-olds with those of young adults aged twenty-five to thirty-one.[8] He noted that themes of criminality went down and themes of guilt and depression went up. It is well known to criminologists that certain intractable criminals mysteriously reform between twenty-five and forty and their disposition to commit crimes of violence disappears. After age twenty-five, murder declines steadily, while suicide and self-recrimination increase.

Figures 3 and 4 illustrate that the presence or absence of a maturational shift in adaptive styles distinguished the Grant Study men who matured psychosocially (advanced through the Eriksonian life cycle) from those who did not. Maturation of adaptive style distinguished those destined to become Generative from those who remained Perpetual Boys. Over time the Perpetual Boys failed to show any significant shift; whereas the adaptive pattern of the Generative men exaggerates the maturational shifts shown in Figure 2 and in midlife their use of immature mechanisms virtually disappeared. (As Roger Gould, a Los Angeles psychoanalyst and an empirical student of adult development, has put it, "To maintain autonomy while sorting out the pressing demands of spouse and children is a task of greater magnitude than previous tasks and requires a more highly developed psychic apparatus."[9])

In examining Figure 3, the reader may ask, why in adolescence did the Perpetual Boys actually exhibit fewer immature defenses than the Best Outcomes? I believe the answer to be that if dramatic adolescent turmoil is not the rule, Anna Freud was probably correct when she wrote, "The upholding of a steady equilibrium during the adolescent process is itself abnormal."[10] Thus, as adolescents, the Perpetual Boys took fewer risks than men who became generative. Perhaps, also, they did not always trust the Grant Study staff sufficiently to tell of behavior that would have identified immature defenses. In any case, during adult life, untempered by adolescent risk-taking, the Perpetual Boys were repeatedly confronted by more complex tasks of living and placed a far greater reliance upon immature defenses than the modal Grant Study men reflected in Figure 2.

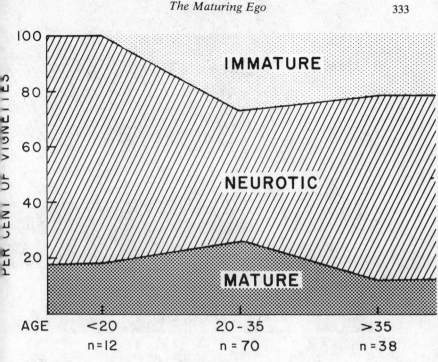

Figure 3.
Shifts in Defensive Styles During the Adult Lives of Perpetual
Boys.

The figure shows the defensive shifts of the seven Study subjects who never really entered the adult life cycle.

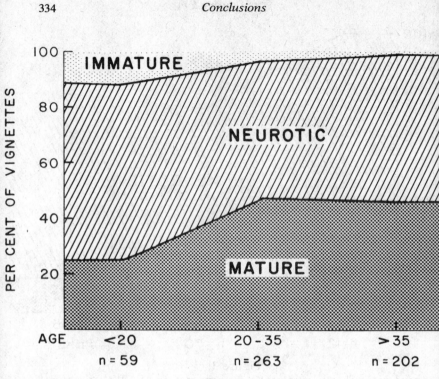

Figure 4.
Shifts in Defensive Styles During the Adult Lives of Generative
Men.
  Defensive shifts of the thirty Best Outcomes.

For the ten years I have worked on the Grant Study I have had difficulty explaining where defenses came from; explanations based on learning and socialization alone did not seem to suffice. I have come to the conclusion that like many athletic or intellectual skills, the maturing patterns of adaptation illustrated in Figures 2 and 4 depend as much upon biological as upon psychosocial factors.

Put differently, I believe that ego development, as illustrated by Francis DeMille, Godfrey Camille, and Herman Crabbe, is distinct from if parallel to psychosocial development as illustrated by Adam Carson. Ego development, while distinct from biological development (physical maturation) and from cognitive or intellectual development (as reflected by I.Q. and age), is also like them, in that ego development is more dependent upon development from within than is psychosocial development, which depends more on the interpersonal environment. Put still differently, psychosocial development reflects the step-by-step negotiation of the neo-Freudian or Eriksonian life cycle. In psychoanalytic jargon this developmental model is often called *psychosexual* and the steps labeled by psychosexual metaphor: oral, anal, phallic, latent, pubertal, and genital. The goal of this model is the achievement of mutual loving relationships with other people. In contrast, models of ego development reflect a more Jungian or Piagetian concept of maturation. They reflect unfolding patterns of mastering and making sense of our own inner experience. For example, a psychosocially less-mature but well-adapted grammar school child may deploy more mature defenses than a psychosocially more mature adolescent.

Let me elaborate this distinction between ego and social development. In the Grant Study men the evolution of mature defenses seemed surprisingly independent of social and genetic good fortune. Men with college-educated parents who sent them to private schools and whose lives had been insulated from the Great Depression ultimately used defenses no more mature than sons of poorly educated parents who had been unable to protect them from harrowing economic privation. The highly intelligent showed no greater maturity of ego operations than did the relatively less gifted. Men without mentally ill relatives did not selectively deploy mature defenses; nor (as long as their parents were spared) did men with family trees "tainted" with insanity, neurosis, and eccentricity prefer immature mechanisms.[11] Still more problematic, maturity of defenses, *unlike psychosocial maturation*, correlated only weakly with warm supportive childhoods. For example, although it is not clear who had had the worse childhood, Goodhart or Tarrytown, the latter clearly employed less-mature defenses. Benign genes and happy childhoods are not our only allies in the struggle for adaptation, and the human ego grows in adversity as well as in prosperity.

The case histories in Chapter II provide clues to the *biological* factors that may have facilitated the evolution of immature mechanisms into those that were more mature.

First, if the brain is injured, a regression to immature or psychotic defenses can reflect healthy adaptation to a biologically impaired nervous system. The life of James O'Neill illustrated how chronic alcoholism could lead to defensive regression, and how recovery from alcoholism could be associated with maturation of adaptive style. As a young man O'Neill manifested obsessional interest in accounting and economics; when chronically inebriated, he escaped into the more exciting, if less adaptive, world of compulsive gambling: having achieved a mature sobriety, he could gain internal pleasure and social reward by advising the governor of Massachusetts how to set up a state lottery to finance public education.

Second, over time adults gain an increasingly more experienced and perhaps a more highly evolved central nervous system. There is a real possibility that the brain continues to change in structure and complexity until age forty or fifty.[12] Until middle age, there is evidence that the brain continues to show increasing nerve insulation, or what neurologists call myelinization. In children such increasing nerve insulation is known to be important in their mental development, and so similar changes in adults may explain a fraction of the developmental shifts we see in adult ego development. Such maturation may facilitate more integrated modes of social response and help explain why, beyond mere acquisition of experience, we continue to grow mentally after twenty. True, from age sixteen, the brain shrinks a gram a year,[13] neurons die at an alarming rate, and *cross-sectional* studies suggest that the I.Q. declines from the early twenties until death. More recently, however, *longitudinal* studies of the same individuals suggest that human intelligence is stable or even increases until age forty to fifty.[14] The combination of increasing experience and a more complex brain may reduce the likelihood of the unexpected or ambiguous instinctual and external dangers that elicit immature defense mechanisms.

Maturity may not be just a value-laden ideal; it may reflect for humans, as it does in animals, a biologic reality. My developmental ordering of the eighteen adaptive mechanisms discussed in this book[15] has strong parallels with the sequential ordering of the stages of ego development proposed by Jane Loevinger,[16] and of moral development described by Lawrence Kohlberg.[17] Figure 2 and the case histories in Chapter 11 suggest that biological development may play the same sort of role in the maturation of adaptive style as it does in intellectual and moral development. By itself, biological maturity is not a sufficient cause for a given level of intellectual or ego development, but it may be a *necessary* cause. Francis DeMille's delayed transition from effeminate mother's boy into masculine insurance executive suggests such a process.

The third variable that affected adaptive maturation was the seemingly environmental effect of sustained relationships with loving people. However, biological maturation, too, is accompanied by an increasing comfort with people and a deepening appreciation of human relationships. As the lives of the Grant Study men unfolded, they revealed a process that over time thrust even the most isolated souls toward each other. Already the lives of Adam Carson, Godfrey Minot Camille, Jacob Hyde, and Herman Crabbe have provided examples of the fact that if intimacy is not achieved before thirty, then continued maturation may bring it later. There was no man in the Study *less* committed to human relationships at fifty than he had been at twenty-five. Norma Haan has suggested that within a given individual this trend toward greater interpersonal comfort may increase until age seventy.[18]

A dramatic example of the inexorable maturation of man's capacity for human relationships was provided by a Grant Study man who grew up disliking his parents. "Research in physics will be my permanent choice of career," he wrote at twenty-five. "The work I've done in physics has been the most fulfilling I have ever done." This was at a time when he had contracted a very cerebral, passionless, childless marriage to a schizoid woman — a marriage that existed more in his own mind than in reality. Fantasy was his dominant defense. At thirty, he shifted his interest in pure physics to its more humane applications — the use of cybernetics and radioisotopes in clinical medicine — and he remarried more realistically. Shortly afterward, still a scientist, he decided to go to medical school. Not until he made these choices had he ever enjoyed comfortable intimacy with anyone. By age forty, having completed his medical training, he launched himself into a new career of adolescent medicine. Although he told me friends were still not his strong point, his second marriage was as real to his wife as to him, and he loved his children. Today his work is entirely with patients, not electrons.

If inner maturation affects our modes of adaptation, what role does the environment play? First, the acquisition of suppression, anticipation, and altruism is enhanced by apprenticeship. Both as children and adults, we learn to anticipate future pain effectively only if someone first sits beside us while we learn to bear current anxiety. Follow-up studies of children suggest that early separation from parents impairs a child's capacity to postpone gratification; characteristically, children from severely disrupted homes are not adept at either anticipation or suppression. For example, deprived of stable, early love relationships, Dr. Tarrytown had little sense of time, a poor ability to plan for the future, and certainly was unable to postpone gratification.

Some men seemed unusually adept at taking in what others offered. In Chapter 7 Mayor Timothy Jefferson was cited as an example of continued growth through the evolution of mature ego defenses, and part of his continued growth sprang from his considerable capacity to learn from others. If part of any talent depends upon good teachers, part of any talent comes from a continued capacity to learn and to synthesize what others teach. To prepare for his career as mayor, Jefferson obtained two graduate degrees. He was also able to describe several mentors who had influenced him and whose lessons he had internalized, assimilated, and could now use in solving the complex task of living. Even being a Grant Study guinea pig he had put to good use. When I asked him how much trouble he had going to others for help, he replied, "The Grant Study taught me to be able to talk over problems with people. . . . Often I feel I am the receptacle for everyone else's problems; but I have developed a close relationship with one of the selectmen, and I talk things over with him."

Second, if defenses cannot be taught, they can be absorbed. For example, although Grant Study men whose heredity included mentally ill relatives per se did *not* continue to use immature defenses, the men whose environment included mentally ill *parents* did continue to use such defenses. Continued contact with immature defenses when young seemed to perpetuate their use. In contrast, Stoics like Byron, Kowalski, and Lucky enjoyed far better than average relationships with their parents, and I believe such relationships help explain why they were masters of suppression.

To an enormous, if uncharted, extent, the human ego is a precipitate of the people it has experienced. If the men did not need utterly benign childhoods in order to develop mature adaptive styles — and they did not — they did require, at crucial, if unidentified, times during their lives, close relationships with benign individuals, who could serve both as models and as positive objects for identification. During their adult lives, the critical persons associated with shifts in adaptive style were usually close friends, wives, and psychotherapists. The gradual transformation of Dr. Godfrey Camille's hypochondriasis into altruism reflects such a process. It is unfortunate that the Grant Study did not provide prospective data on the childhood and adolescent years of these men, when the internalization of relationships is even more important.

Third, in appreciating the fact that defenses evolve from less mature to more mature, it is also important to realize that the world of the adult is safer and more predictable than that of the child. An adolescent flooded with unfamiliar aggressive or sexual strivings should be less able than an experienced forty-year-old to use sublimated or altruistic behaviors in order to channel such strivings. In the same vein, the well-loved can afford to respond to object loss more maturely than a person dependent upon a single friend. Conversely, external life stresses that were sustained over time (for example, mentally ill parents or chronic illness) often facilitated maladaptive defenses and inhibited maturation; the removal of such stress permitted recovery. Callous as it may sound, Crabbe benefited from the death of his mother; he benefited also from his subsequent rediscovery of his father.

As already noted, Frederick Lion's sublimation as an editor was facilitated by living both in a relatively safe family where the members respected assertive behavior and in a country which rewards a free press. Social supports (by that I mean belonging, be it to a stable family, to a church, to a tennis club, or to a segment of society benefiting from the status quo) were strongly correlated with mature defenses.[19]

Finally, psychotherapy — broadly defined — affects shifts in defense level. Dr. Camille's psychoanalysis, Dr. O'Neill's membership in Alcoholics Anonymous, Herman Crabbe's supportive marriage, all allowed rigid defenses to be abandoned and replaced by more flexible means of coping.

In organizing defenses along a developmental hierarchy I have implied that there are moral as well as adaptive implications to human growth and development. As in the plots of Victorian children's stories, altruism, stiff upper lips, and thinking ahead led to the very material success, the love of others, and the mental tranquillity which were later used as criteria for selecting the thirty Best Outcomes. Conversely, it was precisely the defenses that led to "immoral" behavior like eccentricity, prejudice, and impulsivity that identified the thirty Grant Study men who were judged the most unpopular, irresponsible, and childish.

I have implied that the maturation of defenses, like morality, is linked both to cognitive maturation and to the evolution of impulse control. Consider the predictable changes in jokes enjoyed at different ages. They evolve from *passive aggression* (the sadomasochistic pratfall and the hilarious thumbtack in the chair) through the displacement of cartoons, puns, and schoolyard smut, to the more sophisticated *displacements* of parody and Broadway comedy, to the subtle mitigation of reality present in the adult *humor* of the *Punch* or *New Yorker* cartoon.

In order to provide evidence that this process reflects inner growth, not just socialization, and in order to demonstrate that this process is not merely the Greening of America and the shift in values between 1950 and 1970, let me review work by Jean Piaget, Jane Loevinger, and Lawrence Kohlberg.

Developmental psychologists have become increasingly persuaded that moral development and ego development appear to be a single process. Prior to the work of Jean Piaget, Freudians and Jesuits agreed that if we but gave them a child until he was seven, his subsequent moral development was assured. Jean Piaget has demonstrated that this is not the case. The embryological unfolding of the human mind continues long after childhood.[20] In keeping with this book's thesis that much of ego development comes from within, researchers who have followed in Piaget's footsteps have shown that, in Western cultures, moral development, at least in part, progresses independently of social class, nationality, and religious persuasion. Most important, moral development progresses independently of many formal efforts to teach it. As reflected by Heinz Hartmann, modern psychoanalytic theory agrees with Piaget, not Freud; adaptational maturity, not conscience, and the ego, not the externally derived superego, are the agents of morality.[21]

Jean Piaget has suggested that intellectual development recapitulates scientific evolution.[22] He has pointed out that each generation of maturing children is able to understand the laws of physical nature in the same order that they were discovered by early scientists. Piaget has made similar observations in moral development. In the ancient world Olympic gods acted out all man's projected wishes; if a man could but be as powerful as Zeus, he could do as he liked. Then, as religions matured, such apparitions were replaced by talion laws and rigid commandments (reaction formations graven in stone) against sin, which had to be internalized and never broken; man conceived of fallen angels who were to blame if he did sin. Between ages three and eight, the same process goes on in children the world over. The acting out of the Greek gods is replaced with Old Testament projection and reaction formation. Then, as children mature further, Piaget has observed that they believe that the sinner's intention is more important than the act; and as in the New Testament, the concept of mercy softens the child's eye-for-an-eye and tooth-for-a-tooth morality. In each generation children retrace the steps that led Western moralists from Mount Olympus to Mosaic law to the Sermon on the Mount.

More recently, two developmental psychologists, Jane Loevinger at Washington University of St. Louis, and Lawrence Kohlberg at Chicago and Harvard, have provided theoretical models, derived from careful empirical studies, that delineate the evolution of adaptive strategies and moral growth that accompanies maturity.[23] Loevinger and Kohlberg have built upon and extended the tentative scaffolding provided by Piaget; and they have been far more careful than I have been to respect the scientific rigors of academic psychology. More important, both investigators have paid heed to the need for confirmation of their findings across culture, sex, and social class. Recently, in a critical review, Stuart Hauser, a Harvard psychiatrist, has shown that there has been an impressive body of experimental work that confirms Kohlberg's and Loevinger's findings.[24]

Lawrence Kohlberg takes the extreme position that the maturation of morality follows "an invariant developmental sequence." His evidence suggests that "the use of a more advanced stage of thought depends upon earlier attainment of each preceding stage and that each involves a restructuring and displacement of previous stages."[25] In reviewing the astonishing evidence that Sunday schools and parental precepts have little effect on moral development, Kohlberg observes that moral conduct may be regulated more by capacity for mature reasoning than by fixed guilt feelings. He found that neurotic children, theoretically more guilt-ridden, were actually rather slower than control children in developing moral judgments. (In similar fashion, the Grant Study men who did not achieve Generativity *felt* more guilty but *were* less moral than their more mature peers.)

Although Kohlberg collected his data from a very different conceptual framework than Norma Haan's and mine, his conclusions are congruent with a developmental hierarchy of defenses. Kohlberg's sequence of morality moves from the toddler's wish to avoid guilt totally (denial) to a child's wish to conform to the system (reaction formation) to an adolescent's wish to obey the majority (suppression) to an adult's wish to respond to the needs of the community (altruism) and culminates with the sage's wish to obey the demands of his own conscience. Kohlberg suggested that mature morality includes "the ability to predict long range consequences of action" (anticipation) and the capacity to "prefer the distant greater gratification to the immediate lesser gratification" (suppression), and that both these developmental processes involve "the ability to predict the reaction of others to one's actions" (implicit in my concept of altruism). He suggests that although moral development follows a fixed sequence, the age at which any given shift occurs varies tremendously among individuals. Children with high intelligence, peer popularity, and higher social class "seemed to move through the same sequences but seemed to move faster and farther."[26]

The other developmental psychologist who has systematically studied ego development, Jane Loevinger, has suggested that as people mature they increasingly internalize their conflicts. She sees an important developmental shift occurring when the subject is able to say, "It's my problem, not yours"; in effect this implies a shift from immature to neurotic defenses. Loevinger then suggests that with further maturity there is a shift from perceiving instinctual conflicts as shameful and painful to creatively coping with them. Displacement and reaction formation become altruism and sublimation. Like Kohlberg and Piaget, Loevinger sees the development of the ego as irreversible and stage dependent.

My model and my observations suggest that ego development is far more reversible than Kohlberg's model, but my findings certainly suggest that maturity and morality are intertwined. Dr. Camille was only one of many men who could not give tangible shape to his idealism until he reached forty. A second Grant Study man had to be reminded of the fact that in his twenties he had pioneered a new means of making poison gas; at fifty, he had focused his current research upon reducing air pollution. A third man, having spent his youth calculating the blast radius of atomic warheads, rebelled, dropped out of the military-industrial establishment, and at fifty pioneered a college course in humanism.

Another difference between the middle-aged Grant Study men and themselves three decades earlier was that intention became deed: at twenty-five they often forgot to vote; at forty-seven they always remembered. To be sure, there were selfish forty-five-years-olds in the Study, but they had not behaved any better at eighteen. At eighteen, Archie Bunker would have been a Hell's Angel, not a Peace Corps volunteer. If Dr. Tarrytown sounded more idealistic at eighteen than he did at forty-five, he actually contributed more to the world in middle life.

To exploit the poetic metaphor of spiritual growth further, there is no way that we can divide and give back to the world more than we are ourselves until we have first taken other people inside. To reach full maturity we must first rediscover our parents so that, now internalized and immortal, they become a source of fresh strength. Second, we must acquire new people to care for faster than they die or move away.

In other words, to internalize and to identify is to grow. In the Study there were two brothers, one very successful, the other a relative failure. When they were young, their father left home. One brother was six and responded to the betrayal by permanently excluding his father from his life. He subsequently was unable to identify with anyone, and his life became a series of disappointments. The second brother, only four when his father left, continued to reach out greedily for a substitute. In his youth he traveled thousands of miles to rejoin his father. During his life he found three mentors and two wives — each in their own way enriched him. In midlife he has served as an influential, responsible leader of young people.

The reader may scoff at this point: How can a person, unless literally pregnant, take another person inside? Certainly psychoanalysts speak of individuals *incorporating*, *introjecting*, and *internalizing* other people; but is not that just part of the myth-making process of the Freudian imagination? A moment's reflection upon religious sacraments (e.g., taking in the blood and body of Christ through communion wine and wafer) or education (e.g., absorbing a professor's wisdom) or falling in love (e.g., she lives on inside my heart) suggests that taking the *corpora* of another person *in* is a metaphor not confined to psychoanalysts. As Dr. Adam Carson told me, "There is no question but that my father is standing looking over my shoulder and has been most of my life. I have felt the physical presence of my father day and night." After he told me that, I was fascinated that when Dr. Carson answered his telephone, his whole personality changed. Suddenly, in the role of wise counsellor, he used the same phrases and mannerisms that his father had used with the Study staff twenty-five years before. It was as if his father had walked into his son's office — into his son's body. Perhaps it was not coincidence that Carson, the middle-aged clinician, had recovered an adolescent faith in God that the young researcher had lost.

Francis DeMille provides another example of a man who discovered fresh strength when he became conscious of the presence of a strong man in his youth. In adolescence, Frederick Lion had deprecated his father; but in later life he followed in the footsteps of a dominant masculine relative on his mother's side, a man whose importance he, too, acknowledged only in middle life. Still a third man in college had denied any figures of identification; at forty-seven, when I asked him the same question, at first he again hedged and insisted that he had "never given it a thought." Then, suddenly, he revealed a maternal grandfather, "a guy who influenced me greatly . . . a sensational man, the only guy I looked up to in an unadulterated manner. He was just great!"

The men who originally denied their fathers tended to be dramatic, emotional, and flamboyant — as if to have acknowledged their fathers in adolescence would have posed too great a threat. Such men often found their eventual identities rather late in life. In contrast, more self-contained and conscientious men, men who knew what they wanted to do and did it, obsessive men like Timothy Jefferson and Henry Clay Penny who had always possessed well-formed identities, these were men who never hesitated to tell us how important their fathers were to them. Ana Maria Rizzuto, a Boston psychoanalyst, has recently elucidated the extraordinary congruence between an adult's felt and experienced image of God and the internalized aspects of his parents.[27]

In the Grant Study men there seemed to be a qualitative difference between the religion of adolescence and the religion of middle life. For centuries, over-forty butterflies have complained that under-forty caterpillars have forgotten the old religious "butterfly" verities. Perhaps the truth is that the young have never shared their elders' religion. Teenagers may not subscribe to the God of their parents; instead they characteristically hunger for some spiritual validation of their emerging identity.

Thus, if there was a modal pattern to religious involvement of the Grant Study men (and, of course, every individual was different), it was relatively high in adolescence, declined in the decades between twenty and forty, and then gradually increased again. Put differently, as the men grew older, the gods of their understanding became less important to them as surrogate Old Testament consciences and served rather as a more fully assimilated but quite invisible trusted power behind the universe, a power that catalyzed what Erikson calls "belief in the species," without which generativity is impossible.

Bill Forsythe, the state department troubleshooter, introduced to depict the defense of anticipation, illustrates the relationship between a deepening religious faith and the evolution of the life cycle. He was a man who, until fourteen, had been ritualistically religious. Like Robert Jordan in Chapter 10, Forsythe perceived religion as composed of rules, and he had followed them. Then, he began to doubt. In adolescence he gave up regular prayer; in college he gave up the church altogether. At thirty-seven, he tentatively returned to church, allegedly to give his children a sense of their heritage.

The fact was that Forsythe's return to church occurred the year after his father's death and during a year that was also characterized by intense doubts about his own efficacy in his career. In recollecting his father, Forsythe began by telling me, "We were never terribly close." Then, almost in spite of himself, he proceeded to reverse field. "I guess," he added, "I should mention my father as someone who did influence me." In adolescence and young adulthood, they had grown apart, but in his thirties, "We began to grow close together and I would look forward to serious discussions with Dad on world problems. I guess there was an attachment deeper than I was really aware of." And so, at age forty, religious faith, trust in his own professional competence, and the conscious knowledge of an internalized father became one. As with Crabbe, but with different dynamics, the death of a parent facilitated, for Forsythe, the rearrangement and reassessment of internalized values that characterize middle life.

By age forty-eight, while literally trying to hold the world together and working fourteen-hour days, William Forsythe downplayed his religious commitment. Nevertheless, he found time to become an elder in his inner-city church and to serve as director of Christian education. Despite international commitment, Forsythe attended services there every week, and now explained that one of his children had introduced him to the church. "We decided," he said, "that we had been looking for this all of our lives." At forty-nine, he wrote, "I really found a home. I've never been able to accept the divinity of Christ, but I think there is a need to reach out for some explanation for the universe and at least the possibility of a Creator." At fifty-one, he described his religious belief as deepening further. He could now admit that beginning in his early forties, religion had fulfilled a real need.

If forty-five-year-olds often returned to religion, they also increasingly assumed responsibility for holding up their end of the bargain. One subject at nineteen had been an ardent believer in Christian Science. He believed in mind over matter, in life after death, and wondered if his magical beliefs would block his becoming a doctor. By age twenty-five, he had completed medical school, but over rough spots, he would still retreat to a credo that God would take care of all; yet from twenty to thirty he virtually never went to church.

After thirty-five he became progressively more involved in religion. He no longer expected that the benign forces of Christian Science would do his work for him. He was a physician, actively involved in pioneering ghetto health care delivery. Without institutional support, he strove to improve medical care in the Chicago slums, and saw himself fighting disease as a means of fighting evil. But for him cancer was now the enemy — and such a preoccupation with cancer made a denial of death, in Mary Baker Eddy's sense, impossible. Indeed, he now sorely resented that the religion of his youth had tried to ignore death's existence, and he described intolerance for the "sweetness and light philosophy of Christian Science." He had, however, joined the congregation of a Presbyterian church.

In closing our interview, this reserved physician put his hands behind his head. Dressed in a turtleneck sweater, he was half boy-surgeon, half tough guy. He was hard, masculine, resolute, but he chose to tell me about a going away party given for him by his church. The party, he said, had really shown him the depths of people's feelings, and he added, rubbing his moistened eyes, "You're surprised to find yourself loved."

In order to illustrate that the responsibility for this surgeon's original religious immaturity lay within him and not with Christian Science, it is worth recalling the experience of Carlton Tarrytown. Not until after the death of his mother could Dr. Tarrytown finally achieve stable sobriety; and not until then could he finally internalize his mother's strong belief in Christian Science as a source of fresh strength for himself. The True Religion has yet to be revealed; but how we use our religious beliefs will reflect our maturity, our modes of adaptation, and the people who have loved us.

If the rediscovery of internalized parents was accompanied by fresh growth, often the bad had to be taken in with the good. At nineteen, one man viewed his mother as charming and powerful; he shared her intellectual enthusiasms, her hay fever and her asthma. In contrast, he saw his father as weak, distant, without friends, and beset by migraines and multiple bowel complaints. With characteristic undoing, he explained to the Study, "My father dotes on my sister, not that he doesn't like me." In reality, father and son consciously shared nothing, and at twenty-five this Grant Study man remained celibate and professionally ineffective. Like Godfrey Camille, he was forty before he completed his psychoanalysis, married, and achieved occupational competence.

After he was forty, however, his father died. Suddenly this bereaved Grant Study man began to complain of colitis and headaches, two symptoms that he had never had before but that had always characterized his father. At forty-five, in his interview with me, he revealed that not only had his baldness come "from my father's side of the family," but also much that was valuable. He now described his father as the stronger of his two parents and the owner of a marvelous sense of humor. In contrast, his previously omnipotent mother was now described as "neurotic, fearful, and not powerful." Mysteriously, her asthma and hay fever were now hers alone. A decade later, at fifty-five, this man, now a department chairman at Princeton, remains free of allergy. Occasionally he still takes medicines for his colitis and a rare aspirin for headache.

Throughout this book, themes and metaphors from the New Testament have been repeatedly linked to maturation. I worried — was I merely imposing the narrowness of my Protestant upbringing upon my understanding of development? Of course I was, and the bias would be impossible for me entirely to erase. But I have been reassured by an interdisciplinary study of "Adulthood" that appeared in *Daedalus* in 1976.[28] This issue was written by a variety of social scientists — deliberately chosen because of their cross-cultural differences both in terms of their origins and their religious and intellectual interests. They agreed that the very complexity of social order meant that, unlike animals, man must grow for decades in order to fit into his own society's mold. They observed that the Christian metaphor of the Pilgrim's Progress, depending as it does on mysterious growth within, inspired by equally mysterious forces from without, fits such a model. Regardless of their own religious orientation, the social scientists seemed to agree that the imagery of the life cycle allowed the "Christian" life with its implied potential for infinite growth to serve as metaphor. In the symposium, Erik Erikson, a scholar clearly capable of stepping outside of the parochial Christian world view, wrote that "the ethical rule of adulthood is to do to others what will help them, even as it helps you to grow."[29]

In studying the lives of ninety-five healthy men, this book has focused on their *maturation*, their *adaptive styles*, and their *external adjustment*. Undoubtedly, each of these three variables merely reflects facets of an integrated human personality. In Chapter 5 I illustrated the interrelationship between choice of *external adjustment* and *adaptive style*. In the first part of this chapter I have examined the relationship between *maturation* and the development of "mature" *adaptive styles*. Let me now summarize the association between *maturation* and *external adjustment*.

My evidence rests on Table 7, which contrasts the relative success of the Best and Worst Outcomes in negotiating the successive stages of Erikson's life cycle. (Here I am speaking once more of psychosexual, not ego, maturation.)

The Table suggests that the Best Outcomes negotiated the stages of the adult life cycle far more gracefully than those with the least successful adult adjustment. The thirty Worst Outcomes were three times as likely to have experienced childhoods that blind raters saw as uncongenial to developing the basic trust, autonomy, and initiative that Erikson suggests are the most important tasks of childhood. Their mistrust of themselves and of their universe persisted into adult life; for behavioral vignettes

TABLE 7

Differences between Best and Worst Outcomes Relevant to an Eriksonian Model of the Life Cycle

	Best Outcomes (30 men)	Worst Outcomes (30 men)
Childhood environment poor	17%	47%*
Pessimism, self-doubt, passivity, and fear of sex at 50	3%	50%*
In college personality integration put in bottom fifth	0	33%*
Subjects whose career choice reflected identification with father	60%	27%*
Dominated by mother in adult life	0	40%**
Failure to marry by 30	3%	37%*
Bleak friendship patterns at 50	0	57%**
Current job has little supervisory responsibility	20%	93%**
Children admitted to father's college	47%	10%*
Children's outcome described as good or excellent	66%	23%*
Average yearly charitable contribution	$3,000	$500

*Significant difference ($p < .03$ — a difference that would occur by chance only 1 time in 33)
**Very significant difference ($p < .001$ — a difference that would occur by chance only 1 time in 1000)

reflecting pessimism, self-doubt, and fear of sex were far more frequent in the adult lives of the Worst Outcomes. In adolescence the personalities of the Worst Outcomes were seen by blind raters as less integrated and as adults their *identities* remained less secure. The Worst Outcomes were less likely to have internalized their fathers as role models and more likely to be dependent upon their mother's external influence.

Objectively, at both thirty and fifty, the Worst Outcomes were far less likely to have mastered the task of intimacy. Their marriages and friendship patterns were barren. Finally, in middle life there were five-fold differences between the Best and Worst Outcomes in carrying out tangible tasks that indirectly reflect Erikson's platonic concept, *Generativity*. The Worst Outcomes were less clearly willing to assume responsibility for other adults. Apparently, they were able to give less to their children; for their offspring could neither achieve their father's level of academic success nor adjust to the world — socially and emotionally — as easily as the offspring of the Best Outcomes. Finally, to the extent that it can be measured in dollars and cents, they gave less of themselves back to the world.

Chapter 16

What Is Mental Health? — A Reprise

> The Normal is the good smile in a child's eyes — all right. It is also the dead stare in a million adults. It both sustains and kills — like a God. It is the Ordinary made beautiful: it is also the Average made lethal. The Normal is the indispensable, murderous God of Health, and I am his Priest. My tools are very delicate. My compassion is honest. I have honestly assisted children in this room. I have talked away terrors and relieved many agonies. But also — beyond question — I have cut from them parts of individuality repugnant to this God, in both his aspects. Parts sacred to rarer and more wonderful Gods.
>
> — Peter Shaffer, *Equus*

As I tried to report the Grant Study lives, my friends often questioned the narrowness of my conclusions. For example, how did I account for the creative artist? I would retort that Dostoevski was a one-in-one-billion long shot, and that I was basing my conclusions on 100 consecutively interviewed mere mortals. Then, after I had completed the interviews that make up the statistical conclusions of this book, I interviewed Alan Poe.

The interview was by serendipity. To gather data for a different project, I had decided to do ten more interviews. I had been in San Francisco for other reasons, and in response to my last-minute phone call, Poe had been kind enough to consent to see me. Early Sunday morning, dressed in the pin-striped suit I had brought for the opera, I trudged down Telegraph Hill to North Beach. This was a part of San Francisco that I knew about only through the Eastern press — hippies, struggling artists, alcoholics, and perhaps the last surviving members of Jack Kerouac's bedraggled band. It seemed an unlikely residence for a Grant Study man. It seemed especially unlikely for Alan Poe, whose Social Register parents had sent him to Lake Forest private schools, Andover, and finally an establishment college. As I walked through the drizzle, I wondered who I would find.

Reaching Poe's address, I climbed a dirty flight of stairs — stairs that were more like the ones I climbed in my twelve-year follow-up of heroin addicts than like any I had seen in my work on the Grant Study. I knocked on Poe's door, and a gruff, tough tugboat captain — or maybe an aging French Resistance leader — let me in.

Immediately, the fifty-five-year-old Alan Poe impressed me with his great vitality, and his receptive, piercing eyes. Only his slicked-down hair and his accent hinted of a boarding school background. (Humphrey Bogart never fully lived down the fact that he had gone to Andover either.) I looked past Poe into the humble quarters, perhaps ten feet square, that served him as office, living room, and kitchen. The kitchen caught my eye first — as primitive as a tugboat's: a sink stacked with dishes, a grimy stove, a pot of stale coffee, the sparse tin cans of food and aluminum salt shakers that might have filled the kitchen of any blue-collar bachelor. At the left of the kitchen was an oak table — solid, simple, functional — faced by a battered couch, and in one corner the surprise of a wooden chair with Poe's college crest. In the far corner of the already cluttered room was Poe's study: four feet square, a manual typewriter, several neat stacks of plain typing paper, a pile of crisp manuscript, no books — all business. It could have been a small-town newspaper office or a monk's cubicle. Then my eyes went back to his kitchen. "Well," said the tugboat captain, surveying me, "the college hasn't changed, has it?" I looked at his heavy sweater, shapeless pants, work shoes, and then at my own clothes — the banker's suit, an attaché case, and shoes shined for the opera.

Alan Poe began the interview. "I've got a bone to pick with you guys; I am a homosexual." Then, he tossed a Grant Study reprint at me. He pointed out where in my summary of the Study I had discussed delinquency, alcoholism, psychosis, and homosexuality as equivalent, albeit rare, defects among the Grant Study men. Poe was right to complain. Just that year the American Psychiatric Association had, with my blessing, *voted* that homosexuality no longer be classified a mental illness. How can anyone be voted sick or well, unless the critics of organized psychiatry are right, and mental health is just a cultural illusion?

I realized that Alan Poe was a Study member to whom I needed to listen. He chain-smoked, gulped coffee, and lectured; and I wrote down what he said as fast as I could. Poe filled me in on three marriages, an income under ten thousand dollars, and the "C" in College Soundness that he had been awarded by the Grant Study. He told me that he played no games, took no vacations, and had only grudgingly enjoyed his previous career. He abused alcohol, and his physician had noted that he was "in a very poor state of physical fitness." By criteria that I have developed so far, Poe fell in the bottom fifth of mental health. But he was one in a hundred, and so he lectured and I listened.

He asked me, "What's your definition of normality?" and then pointed out that he had been a conscientious objector during World War II. He had never regretted it; he always could articulate the reasons why, and he described how he could still equate conscientious objectors with French Resistance leaders. During World War II, he confessed, "I was the only C.O. who read *Time* from cover to cover for war news." He never doubted that the Nazis were enemies of mankind, but he felt that way about all militarists.

After the war, Poe continued to try to be true to himself. Most of the Grant Study would-be novelists had given up by thirty-five, but Poe was one of the very few writers in the Study who had persevered, and for thirty years he disciplined himself to write every day. Since his works were not published, he supported himself through a series of explicitly "moral" jobs: teaching English at inner-city schools, writing advertising copy for the Sierra Club, and always sharpening the talent that at forty-five finally began to bear fruit. In middle life, his unpublished novels had evolved into published poems, often in small West Coast literary reviews, and occasionally in the *New Yorker* and the *Atlantic*. As his rooms suggested, however, his poetry did not make him rich.

Far more problematic was the fact that Poe's three marriages had ended in divorce. "I can't stand success," he explained. Unlike Tarrytown, however, Poe had always truly loved his wives, and I never doubted for a moment that he was intrinsically a caring and compassionate man. But Poe had been in conflict about more than being a pacifist when his country was at war. In college the Study psychiatrist had been startled when Alan revealed that if another boy so much as put his arm around Poe's shoulders, it was as if someone had encircled him with a snake. Not until he was fifty, not until his third marriage had disintegrated and he had had his second homosexual affair did Poe realize who he was. "Now," he said, "I wear my yellow badge with pride." He believed that he understood how Jews and blacks, how pacifists and homosexuals really felt.

"Yes," Poe continued, "I've been kicking you guys around for a year." He wondered why we did not realize that healthy personalities could develop as much through rebellion as through conformity. He explained that he had grown up in a "WASP cocoon. . . . I had gone from private school in Lake Forest, to Andover, to college. It was all a cocoon."

At fifty, mature perhaps in the way that the cinematic version of Humphrey Bogart seems mature, Alan Poe also understood Generativity. He told me, "The kids in North Beach are in their twenties, and I act as an uncle. They even call me Uncle Alan. . . . I'm old enough to give advice and caring enough to help them get their teeth fixed."

Then, Alan Poe, who had violated every canon of health in the Grant Study, continued his lecture: "Since 1970 I've been better adjusted, happier, more creative, than at any time in my life . . . or is it just because at fifty I metabolically know what I'm going to do?" He shifted gears, paused and then almost blurted, "Let's get on to the alcohol business. . . . Can you imagine a writer without an alcohol problem? I'll give you the positive aspects. I work every day and I work hard, and by five P. M. I'm exhausted. Four to seven hours at the typewriter wears you down, your mind's under the tightest discipline. At five P. M. you take your hand off the collar and you let the 'dog' run all over the house. Sometimes you wake up with a headache, so you learn to let the dog run just so much. The dog's well exercised and in the morning you clap your hand back on the collar." In the last five years he said there were no more than five days when he had had a drink before 5

P. M., but I suspected that there were probably no more than ten days when he had been sober after dinner. "I know," he confessed, "that I'm flirting with a dangerous game." Still, for the past six months, his dominant mood had been, "Wow!"

I felt that Poe was stalked by death, suicide, and skid row, yet he lived on out of the sheer wonder of taming his powers. He saw himself as overcoming all the pain of broken relationships by his capacity to write about them. "When I get a kick in the ass, I know it will help me write. . . . You can be tremendously objective and work your way through difficulties." Thirty years before he had written to the Study, "Somerset Maugham has written that the artist is the only free man in the world — he can get the damned thing off his chest." Perhaps the sheer joy of not being trite made up for taking no vacations, for rarely enjoying his thoroughly enjoyable children, and for having loved not wisely, but too often.

Poe had also warned the Study of the paradox that I was to ponder on my way home. "You have a far bigger problem than you may realize, and a lot of old ideas just don't fit." At the same time, he had urged the Grant Study on: "This science of the total man is crucial now; it can't have blind spots." Thus, I left his apartment stunned but thinking.

Slowly, Alan Poe walked me to a cable car; and as the San Francisco drizzle fell, he told me, "I feel I'm an inherently and basically happy man." He added that he wondered how "those people felt who had not followed their inner light." Finally, he closed our interview with an anecdote of someone who, at the height of World War II, had asked Winston Churchill, "Are you of good cheer?"

I climbed on the cable car and Poe returned to his apartment, to his young gay "nephews," and to his dreams of the Nobel prize in poetry. But as I said goodbye, I felt up in the air, as a reader does at the end of Frank Stockton's short story "The Lady or the Tiger?" Toward which of the twin coliseum doors had jealous fate directed Alan? Would it be to the door that contained "The Lady," and would he ultimately gain mastery of and recognition for his poetry, or would the door he opened conceal "The Tiger," and would Poe finally lose control of his "dog" and be devoured? I did not know, but as I walked back through the fog in my respectable suit, to my respectable friend's respectable apartment, what mattered to me was that he was happy and he cared. I knew that he approached the door "in good cheer."

"Before the problem of the creative artist," Freud wrote, "analysis must, alas, lay down its arms";[1] I had to agree. Here was a man as objectively troubled as Dr. Tarrytown but whom I respected as much as Mr. Goodhart. Here was a man who at fifty-five could challenge me as he had challenged the patriotic Grant Study staff thirty years before. "If people have adjusted to a society that seems bent on destroying itself in the next couple of decades," wrote Poe as a twenty-four-year-old conscientious objector, "just what does that prove about the people?"

I felt that I needed to continue our discussion, and so when I returned to Boston, I sent Alan Poe Chapter 1. Did my treatment of Goodhart and Tarrytown allay his fears that the Grant Study might miss the boat? He wrote back. "As you know I have some disquiets . . . perhaps they would be helpful to you in writing the latter part of the book if I tried to put them down." He was right, of course, but conscientious objectors and resistance leaders often are. The letter continued:

> O.K., the data's fantastic. The methodology you are using is highly sophisticated. But the end judgments, the final assessments, seem simplistic. As I read over the material, they seem to come down to having a good income, a stable family, reasonable job satisfaction, a capacity to love, and a capacity to play. And the patient — or subject — or whatever we're calling him — either adapts to achieve those end results (and that's presumably good) or he doesn't adapt and doesn't get to those ends (and that's presumably bad). He either copes satisfactorily by mastering his life, or he limps along.
>
> Is this — honest Injun and cross your heart — the whole story as you see it? I'll bet it isn't. I sure hope it isn't!
>
> I mean, I can imagine some poor bastard who's fulfilled all your criteria for successful adaptation to life, and like maybe Charles Colson or Jeb Magruder sitting in jail and staring at the wall, or upon retirement to some aged enclave near Tampa just staring out over the

ocean waiting for the next attack of chest pain, and wondering what he's missed all his life. . . . What's the difference between a guy who at his final conscious moments before death has a nostalgic grin on his face as if to say, "Boy, I sure squeezed that lemon" and the other man who fights for every last breath in an effort to turn time back to some nagging unfinished business?

Damned if I know, but I sure think it's worth thinking about. . . .

I have two foggy concepts that you might want to churn around in the back of your head.

One I guess you would call "the celebrant sense" or that wonderful hippy word, "Wow!" . . . I get no such sense of celebration out of your portrait of Mr. Goodhart. Maybe it's there. Maybe it just wasn't a high value in your mind. But I think it's an important component in the whole adaptive process. Life needs to be *enjoyed!*

The other component of adaptation which I think needs to be considered is in my mind classified as the big discovery of my fifties. It's called by a lot of names, depending on your religious, or philosophical, or even mystical orientation. Though I call it *empathy* . . . I keep thinking about the Vietnam war. I keep thinking about those highly adaptive [Grant Study] "A-types," the "brightest and the best" of the Kennedy administration, intent on the techniques of a hard-nosed foreign policy that led us into the greatest moral, military, and political disaster of our history. What went wrong? Isn't the cardinal rule of any conflict to know your opponent? And who was the shot-caller of the opposition that Kennedy and his cohorts faced? Ho Chi Minh, and good God, you didn't need the CIA to tell you about Ho Chi Minh! You could get a perfectly good line on him by reading *Time* Magazine. Poet, chain-smoker of Salem cigarettes, equal of Stalin in the world communist pecking order, and outranking that upstart, Mao Tse Tung. As undisputed a boss of his independent power base as Tito, wily French-trained sophisticate whose idealism was as much tied up with the American Declaration of Independence as it was with Marx or Engels.

What went wrong? No lack of intelligence, or power, or will, just a mind-boggling absence of empathy. . . . Intelligence, power, and will were, without empathy, as

sounding brass and tinkling cymbals. . . . Now, don't get
me wrong. I'm not opposed to simplistic, middle-class
virtues. In fact, I rather admire them (perhaps because
I've been so bad at them), but I think true adaptation has
a larger dimension.

> Onward — and blessings!
> Sincerely, Alan Poe.

I was dumbfounded by the letter, and handed it to my research
assistant. As in the past, she counseled me wisely and simply:
"There's not much you can say about it; it's just all there."

In 1952 the Grant Study staff had tried to forecast Alan Poe's
future. "It is possible that his more conventional and quiet basic
personality will come to the fore as Poe gets mature if it hasn't
already expressed itself. Already he seems to have been subdued
by the threat [a love affair] to his marriage and possibly by other
factors such as the long struggle to gain financial security and
support his family." I was glad that Poe at fifty had evaded this
epitaph. Instead of moving to the suburbs, Poe wrote, "The older
I get, the more admiration I have for the kid at twenty you
studied so exhaustively . . . the kid who rejected big chunks of
upper-middle-class culture in which he was raised. . . . Here is a
fifty-two-year-old man who still has trouble keeping up with
him."

What the Study staff had not appreciated was that if Poe had
identified with his two conforming parents, he would have been
stifled, as were other men who continued to use reaction formation into adult life. Poe's childhood environment, after all, was
not much better than Dr. Tarrytown's. Instead, Poe never forgot
that he was a conscientious objector and a poet. His heroes remained Thoreau and Gandhi, and they would not have scored
very well on the Grant Study adjustment score either.

In general, however, the Grant Study staff had been shrewd
about Poe. In 1940, the physiologist staring at the spirograph trac-
ing of Poe's breathing pattern — and, of course, the way a gypsy
stares at tea leaves, at a million other clues, too — had written, "I
think Poe is a good example of the fact that society has a place for
unstable individuals if their instability is of a particular type."
When Alan Poe at nineteen diagnosed himself as either "manic-
depressive" or a "spoiled brat," the staff psychiatrist was smart

enough to change the diagnosis to "a rather uncontrollable sky-rocket which nobody can tame." The Study physician wrote, "If Alan can control his energy and enthusiasm, he may well become a man of eccentric but great accomplishments. He reminds me much of what Noel Coward must be!"

At fifty-five, Alan Poe still burns his candle at both ends, but not from mania or emotional illness. Ebullient energy is his way of dealing with old wounds still rubbed raw by an oppressive culture. As Edna St. Vincent Millay suggested, if such prodigal combustion is short-lived, "it gives a lovely light."

The puritan scientist in me adds the cautionary note that to use sublimation so brilliantly as to allow all the rules of biology to be waived is a long shot. Thoreaus and Gandhis are not born every minute. I had interviewed more than a hundred men before I met Alan Poe, and in the first hundred the capacity for "empathy" and "Wow" correlated with more conventional indicators of health.

The lesson here is not that we should all rush off and imitate Poe, but rather that we must ask ourselves how we can integrate Poe's passion with ourselves. The artist never insists that we live his life, only that we remember his special sense of creative potentiality. In return, the puritan in me would concede that it is not that divorce is unhealthy or bad; it is only that loving people for long periods is good.

In writing this book, I wear the blinders and I display the biases of my profession. I see human personality as evolving out of biology and inner development. I view health and disease as tangible and absolute and not relative and value-ridden. Alan Poe in particular, and sociologists in general, can have a field day with my parochialism. Is not health usually a value judgment? Does it not change from culture to culture? Perhaps health only has validity in the eyes of the beholder and is utterly relative.

"No!" I cry. Like John Keats, I, too, am a physician, and I believe that beauty and truth are one. But how to prove it? Clearly, proof requires experiment and consensus; and so this book is cluttered with statistics, comparisons, and ratings by independent judges.

But to what avail? When I say "adaptation," the sociologist will always hear "conformity" and "adjustment." (By *sociologist* I mean those who view mankind as more affected by what occurs outside than by what occurs inside.) I hope that I have under-scored the difference between adaptation and adjustment. Cer-tainly, during World War II, Lieutenant Edward Keats, flying his Thunderbolts, had conformed and adjusted better than Alan Poe in his conscientious objector labor camp. But was he really better adapted? Certainly both Lieutenant Edward Keats and Alan Poe were better adapted than Leslie Angst, who hated the safety and boredom of his laboratory *adjustment*, or Francis Oswald, who *conformed* by insisting on becoming a front-line marine only to break down in combat because he could not *adapt* to the killing. The well-adapted Byron and Lion were hardly conformists, and the badly adapted Smythe and Lamb certainly were.

Adaptation is as different from adjustment as art is different from commercial illustration. Adjustment can be viewed as a snapshot, but to view adaptation requires, at the very least, a motion picture camera. Alan Poe violated all our static concepts of mental health, but to call him unhealthy would be the same as calling a four-thousand-year-old bristle-cone pine or a wind-tortured oceanside cedar diseased.

Norman Zinberg, a sociologically sophisticated psychoanalyst, has expressed the conflict between sociology and psychiatry well: "An individual's ability to function in society depends not only on his personality but on the guidelines of that very society he lives in. Therefore, when something is psychologically wrong, the dis-order is subjective and cultural, not objective and natural, and is significantly distinct from physical illness."[2]

Zinberg anticipates the quicksand in which I found myself in Chapter 9 with the immature defenses. There I boasted that biol-ogy can separate fact from value; but that, of course, is wishful thinking. The sociologist knows that physicians often forget the interaction that occurs between subject and beholder. Indeed, immature defenses are maladaptive precisely because of this in-teraction. Similarly, in Chapter 8, whether neurotic mechanisms of adaptation led to success or disaster depended more upon the external environment than upon the individual's "health."

In extending the challenge to mental health thrown down by writers like Zinberg, R. D. Laing, Thomas Szasz, Philip Slater, and Irving Goffman, Peter Sedgwick has further pointed out how value-laden our concepts of health are. Disease, Sedgwick main-tains, is pure value judgment; it is biology applied under the dictates of social interest. "Plant-diseases may strike at tulips, turnips, or such prized features of the natural landscape as elm trees; but if some plant species in which man had no interest (a desert grass, let us say) were to be attacked by a fungus or parasite, we should speak not of a disease, but merely of the competition between two species."[3] He also reminds us, "The blight that strikes at corn or at potatoes is a *human invention*, for if man wished to cultivate parasites, rather than potatoes or corn, there would be no 'blight,' but simply the necessary foddering of the parasite-crop." Sedgwick relentlessly drives his point home: "The fracture of a septuagenarian's femur has, within the world of nature, no more significance than the snapping of an autumn leaf from its twig."[4]

How, then, can I respond intelligently to the sensible critics who will call this book "value-laden"? I can agree and try to explain why such criticism misses the point. First, adaptation does not imply morality — of course, that is a value judgment — adaptation implies *success*, and when I say success, I mean not just success in the eyes of others. Alan Poe *was* of good cheer.

Second, it is true that immature defenses, unlike leprosy and boils, disappear on a desert island; it is true that mental health, as discussed in this book, must be defined as *social success*. It is true that the objective criteria for mental health used in this book — working and loving — like the immature defenses, are not particularly important on desert islands. Nevertheless, working and loving are still the goals of society — virtually every society.

Third, I would agree with the sociologists that psychiatric labeling is dangerous. Society can inflict terrible wounds by discrimination, and by confusing health with disease and disease with badness. Alan Poe chose to be a conscientious objector and a homosexual for reasons of health, not illness. His life was badly scarred by society's response. In a different vein, James O'Neill's alcoholism was a "disease" and not the "moral turpitude" that the company for which he worked chose to call it. He was hurt, not helped, by the fact that society, his wife, and his health care system waited twenty years before giving him the label "alcoholic." When James O'Neill could wear the label "I am an alcoholic," he was on the way to cure; just as when Alan Poe could say, "I am a homosexual," he was on his way to self-acceptance. The sociologists are in error when they suggest that there is no difference between biological and social values.

Fourth, it is only in the marshaling of empirical evidence that the physician has a chance of winning a debate with the sociologist. The value judgments in this book are based on a hundred real lives followed for thirty-five years and systematically compared with each other. It is on the basis of tangible results that I insist that it is better, healthier, more beautiful, for an oyster to make a pearl from a grain of sand than to submit to the indignity of a raw, debilitating ulcer.

If I am a frail biased observer, biology is straightforward. Calluses exist and so do defenses. If you feel Goodhart's altruism healthier than Tarrytown's prejudice, then you share my values; but it is not a value to say that altruism, as a process, differs from projection, and to observe that empirically it has different social consequences. Fewer people died in Martin Luther King's empathic marches on Selma and on Birmingham than in the paranoid burning by the Inquisition of heretics and witches.

The fact that in some cultures hookworm or epilepsy are socially accepted does not make them adaptive; nor does the fact that homosexuality is classed as a disease make homosexuality a failure in a reasonable society. Empirically, alcoholism and hookworm interfere with a great many other functions. Homosexuality, or voting the straight Democratic ticket, or regularly reading the *Wall Street Journal* has relatively little to do with adaptation.

Fifth, I suspect that some sociologists' insistence upon the relativity of health borders on dissociation. Rousseau's Noble Savage and Laing's transcendent schizophrenic are idealized versions of the truth. In their denial of human pain, these images border on Marie Antoinette's carefree shepherdesses, or Stephen Foster's happy darky. To find out if someone is truly of "good cheer," one needs to ask him, and not just with a multiple-choice questionnaire.

Finally, social success, even humanely defined, *is* a value judgment, but so are the concepts of forward motion and velocity. All three — velocity, forward motion, and social success — depend on the vantage point of the observer. But if we wish to understand our own life space, all are judgments that we cannot do without.

Norman Zinberg cautions that by simplifying the world of phenomena, we cannot avoid falsifying it, and thus "the process of searching for mental health may become an end in itself. The search can be ennobling if we choose to *struggle*, but is demoralizing if we believe that the ultimate goal is an ideal society of people who will be 'healthy' all their days."[5] A senior colleague, upon perceiving how many defenses one of the healthiest Grant Study men displayed, exclaimed, "Whew, what a lot of pathology!" For a moment he forgot that adaptation must reflect the vigorous reaction to change, to disease, and to environmental imbalance.

Zinberg is right to warn us that if the concept of health is to be defined and used, caution and restraint must be exercised. Thus, in concluding this chapter it seems important that I review what some of the safeguards for the study of health may be. First, health must be broadly defined in terms that are relative and open-ended. Second, concepts of health must be empirically validated. Third, validation means special dependence upon cross-cultural studies. Finally, any student of health must remember that there are differences between real health and value-ridden morality, between human adaptation and mere preoccupation with Darwinian survival of the fittest, and between real success at living and mere questing after the Bitch Goddess Success.

What is a broad definition of mental health? Perhaps Marie Johoda, in her book, *Current Concepts of Positive Mental Health*, offers the best definition so far.[6] Freed from the constraints of having to identify specific traits in actual individuals, Jahoda lists six general features of mental health. Mentally healthy individuals should be in touch with their own identity and their own feelings; they should be oriented toward the future and over time they should be fruitfully invested in life. Their psyches should be integrated and provide them a resistance to stress. They should possess autonomy and recognize what suits their needs; they should perceive reality without distortion and yet possess empathy. They should be masters of their environment — able to work, to love, and to play, and to be efficient in problem-solving.

Although this book is written from a very different conceptual framework, it does not take a very great leap of imagination to realize that suppression, anticipation, humor, altruism, and sublimation facilitate the very abstract qualities that Jahoda equates with health, and that fantasy, masochism, acting out, projection, and hypochondriasis would interfere with every criterion that Jahoda sets forth.

In a brilliant rebuttal to Peter Sedgwick, Leo Kass, a research professor in bio-ethics and neurology, points out that health literally means "wholeness" and to heal means to "make whole." He redefines health as "an activity of the living body in accordance with its specific excellences," and then expands this definition more poetically:

"What, for example, is a healthy squirrel?" Kass asks. "Not a picture of a squirrel, not really or fully the sleeping squirrel, not even the aggregate of his normal blood pressure, serum calcium, total body zinc, normal digestion, fertility, and the like. Rather, the healthy squirrel is a bushy-tailed fellow, who looks and acts like a squirrel; who leaps through the trees with great daring; who gathers, buries, and covers but later uncovers and recovers his acorns; who perches out on a limb cracking his nuts, sniffing the air for smells of danger, alert, cautious, with his tail beating rhythmically; who chatters and plays and courts and mates and rears his young in large improbable looking homes at the tops of trees; who fights with vigor and forages with cunning; who shows spiritedness, even anger, and more prudence than many human beings.

"To sum up: Health is a natural standard or norm — not a moral norm, not a 'value' as opposed to a 'fact,' not an obligation but a state of being that reveals itself in activity."[7]

Jane Loevinger echoed the complexity of Kass's healthy squirrel when she wrote: "The more deeply one becomes involved in this area [mature ego development], the more it appears that impulse control, character development, interpersonal relations, and conscious preoccupations are indeed aspects of a single thing, so intimately intertwined that one can hardly define, much less measure them separately."[8]

To resolve the issue of values in mental illness we must also rely on the scientific method. Inoculation for smallpox has survived the test of generations. Bleeding for fevers and insulin coma for schizophrenia have proved to be merely evanescent medical fads. In somatic medicine, criteria have been developed so that people of widely varying backgrounds and beliefs can agree upon what constitutes health and disease; we need to develop the same criteria for mental health. Nowhere is the need for the rigor of experimental method more essential than in our conceptualizing and managing the immature defenses, which by interacting with the observer distort everyone's world view. The need for rational evaluation becomes especially clear in the area of criminal justice.

The most serious limitation of this book is that it fails the third safeguard. Patently, the Grant Study is *not* cross-cultural. Over and over again my credibility is undermined by the facts that the sample includes no women — and only college graduates; no blacks — and only Americans; no one born after 1924 — and only men born after World War I began. In a single study, however, the experimental method and the need for cross-cultural validation come sharply into conflict. Imagine the chaos that would have resulted had the Study focused on a thousand randomly selected human beings from the world's population over the last fifty years. How could one control for the effect of diets, pestilence, culture, war, lack of observer empathy, and even translation of emotionally loaded words?

Readers must decide for themselves when the Grant Study men reflect human beings and human wound healing, and when they merely reflect the arcane folkways of a small, perhaps unfamiliar, tribe. My own suspicion is that cross-cultural studies will show that from one part of the world to another mental health does not differ as much as we might think. Consider, for example, that the diets of a New York construction worker, of a Japanese aristocrat, and of an Australian aborigine appear extraordinarily different; but the healthy balance of basic foodstuffs in each diet that makes it nutritious is rather constant.

As a final safeguard in the study of health, healthy success must be distinguished from materialism. I must admit that the Grant Study sometimes confused the two. Focusing as it does on adaptation, this book evokes themes from Spencer and Darwin; it, too, implies that only the fittest survive. If Steven Kowalski is the model of health, is there nothing more to life than a strong offense and a stout defense? Indeed, if you cannot win, should you give up the game? Of course not!

The problem with the Grant Study sample was not so much that they were men, or favored by the social system, but rather that they were chosen for their self-reliance, and the specter of overachievement always haunted their lives. For some men, career success was bought at the price of lives of quiet desperation; and despite healthy ego function and success, healthy dependency, marriages, and vacations sometimes seemed sacrificed in the process. But remember also that frantic human activity, like the grotesque shapes of ancient but surviving trees, may be in the service of wound healing. Workaholics like Kane and Newton did well with the cards that life dealt them. Indeed, the whole point of Chapter 11 is that despite our fears career success is usually *not* associated with barren home lives.

To clarify the issue of healthy success versus materialism, a digression may be helpful. Health is not fame, nor fame health. Health is success at living, which is something very different. I have been asked what part luck played in the lives of the Grant Study men. In general my answer is that over the course of a lifetime, styles of adaptation seem to have much more effect on outcome than the insults that chance inflicted upon the men. After childhood was complete, luck and healthy development were relatively independent.

Luck and fame, however, seemed inseparable. There were four men — four of the healthiest, most ambitious and most responsible men of the Study — who were denied fame by bad luck and were by chance events prevented from reaching their potential, which was perhaps dangerously high. In a way, each of these men had something of Icarus about him, and to fly too close to the sun is always dangerous.

One of the four, a man destined to play a role in every child's history book, was pointlessly murdered before he reached his prime. Despite having a virtually perfect score on Grant Study adjustment, the most outstanding civic leader of a large city was felled at fifty by a sudden heart attack. A third man suffered the misfortune to become a college president in the aftermath of the 1967 student rebellions, the drying up of foundation support, and in the face of a series of difficult external family circumstances. At any other point in history he would have moved on to lead a major university; instead his career became stalemated. The fourth man had enjoyed a brilliant political career, one built step by step over fifteen years of hard work; it was shattered by the chance opposition of two opponents in tandem who reflected the two types of men against which he was powerless to fight. Two consecutive elections are more than most politicians can afford to lose.

Looking at each man's life up to the fatal "accident," there was only a record of unblemished success. Each man had overcome tremendous childhood or physical handicaps with healthy stoicism, suppression, and energy. Each man came from among the best adapted. Each man had enjoyed unusually warm human relationships; yet perhaps each should have been willing to settle for something closer to mediocrity earlier in their lives. I suspect that for most Grant Study men one reason that success seemed healthy is that they knew when to stop.

Chapter 17

A Summary

> All our lives long we are engaged in the process of accommodating ourselves to our surroundings; living is nothing else than this process of accommodation. When we fail a little, we are stupid. When we flagrantly fail, we are mad. A life will be successful or not, according as the power of accommodation is equal to or unequal to the strain of fusing and adjusting internal and external chances.
>
> — Samuel Butler, *The Way of All Flesh*

In the study of optimal human functioning," a leading psychologist has written, "we should also bring to light factual relationships that have a bearing on what values to pursue individually and socially."[1] What, then, are the most important lessons that I have learned from my fortuitous acquaintance with the men of the Grant Study? In observing thirty-five years of their lives, what are the principal lessons that I wish to pass on?

My first conclusion is that isolated traumatic events rarely mold individual lives. That is not to say that the premature death of a parent, the unexpected award of a scholarship, the chance first encounter with a future spouse, or a heart attack will not result in a sudden change in life's trajectory. Unexpected events affect our lives, just as a wrong or a fortuitous turn might affect a cross-country journey. But the quality of the whole journey is seldom changed by a single turning. The life circumstances that truly impinge upon health, the circumstances that facilitate adaptation or that stunt later growth — in contrast to fame — are not isolated events. What makes or breaks our luck seems to be the continued interaction between our choice of adaptive mechanisms and our sustained relationships with other people.

Although loss of a parent can severely affect the mental health of children and of adolescents, no single childhood loss seemed an important determinant in the Grant Study men's midlife adjustment. No whim of fate, no Freudian trauma, no loss of a loved one will be as devastating to the human spirit as some prolonged ambivalent relationship that leaves us forever unable to say good-bye. It was not the sudden loss of a parent as much as the continued presence of a disturbed parent, and it was not a disturbed relationship with one parent as much as it was a globally disturbed childhood that affected adult adjustment. (The depression and impoverished affect of his widowed mother in his early childhood may well have scarred Oliver Kane more deeply than her death when he was fifteen.) Preventive psychiatry will be well served if schools and community mental health agencies single out for special concern the children of mentally ill and/or alcoholic parents.

My second conclusion is that Adolf Meyer was more right than wrong when he asserted that there were no mental diseases, only characteristic reaction patterns to stress. Not that I entirely agree with Meyer; certainly, organic brain damage can produce specific disease; manic-depressive psychosis quite possibly is due to genetic defect; the human devastation produced by prolonged alcoholism may mimic disease; and ultimately schizophrenia may prove to be an inborn defect and not a failure in adaptation. But most of what is called illness in textbooks and in our diagnostic nomenclature — the neuroses, the depressions, and the personality disorders — are merely outward evidence of inward struggles to adapt to life. They reflect ongoing adaptive processes that someone has noticed and reified with a label.

In other words, most mental illness is more like the red tender swelling around a fracture that immobilizes it so that it may heal and less like the tangible biochemical defect of diabetes. If we but shift our point of view, what once seemed a neurotic phobia or loathsome prejudice becomes part of a comprehensible adaptive process. In 1856, Claude Bernard saw it clearly when he wrote, "We shall never have a science of medicine as long as we separate the explanation of the pathological from the explanation of normal, vital phenomena."[2] One of the great advances of modern surgery was to recognize that nothing could be done to hasten wound healing except to understand it well enough to learn how not to stand in the way.

Since the Middle Ages, the *rubor, calor, turgor,* and *dolor* of inflammation have not been viewed as illnesses but rather as normal human response. More recently, doctors have identified as healthy and normal the outraged white corpuscles, antibodies, capillary exudates, and nerve endings that underlie such inflammation. So it is with much mental illness and chronic misbehavior. The process of healthy inflammation needs to be understood and supported — not treated or punished.

Anxiety and depression, like blisters and fractures, become the price of a venturesome life. In daring to live and grow up, we create disparities in our inner balance between conscience and instinct, and between that precarious balance and the people we love. True, doctors can lance boils and desensitize phobias, remove cinders and anesthetize anxiety. But much of psychiatry, like much of medicine, becomes simply supporting natural healing processes.

However, in professing that much mental illness is adaptive reaction and not independent defect, I am not suggesting that doctors get out of the arena of mental health, but only that they let others in. On the one hand, I am asserting that adaptation to life is biological and that it *is* the province of doctors and not philosophers and metaphysicians. On the other hand, I am asserting that biology can be understood by everyone. Just as the patient with hypertension has the right to know how to take his own blood pressure and a pregnant woman has the right to remain conscious and to help direct the delivery room stage while she has her child, just so there is nothing special, sacred, or scary in learning about the ego's mechanisms of defense. There is much about biology that is true and can be shared.

The third conclusion of this book follows from the second. Namely, I have tried to illustrate and to differentiate eighteen basic adaptive mechanisms. I hope the reader is now convinced that defense mechanisms differ from one another and that the differences carry important implications.

The hierarchy of defenses defined in this book can be used to predict adult growth and to define adult mental health. Defenses can become the critical variables that determine whether environmental stress produces madness or "pearls." Put differently, much of the increased stress observed in the lives of the emotionally ill is a *result*, not the cause, of poor adaptation. Poor adaptation leads to manifest anxiety and depression, which in turn lowers the threshold for perceiving stress. Conversely, successful suppression always increases our tolerance of pain.

One of the great lessons that I learned from these men — one of the real lessons to be derived from the prospective study of lifetimes — is the corollary finding that the sons-of-bitches in this world are neither born that way nor self-willed. Sons-of-bitches evolve by their unconscious efforts to adapt to what for them has proven an unreasonable world. In order to love them, there are often detailed sequences of events that we need to know; usually this knowledge is lacking, even for our own relatives. Thanks to the privileged vision into men's lives which the Grant Study provided, there was no one in the Study that I did not end up liking. It was not that they were so likable, nor I so tolerant. I liked them because I understood them. So much of what we are wont to perceive as psychopathology reflects a potential healing process.

Understanding a differentiated hierarchy of defenses also allows us, even in the maelstrom of stress and emergency, to be helpful to others in a more rational manner. We should respect the mature defenses and learn to admire and nourish them. Stoicism, altruism, and artistic creativity should rarely be interfered with. Conversely, the bigot and the delinquent must be either confronted or helped; we will almost never breach the immature defenses by argument, interpretation, or punishment. Last, if we wish to succeed at psychotherapy and interpretive counseling, we must try to pick our clients with neurotic defenses — the displacement of the phobic, the isolation and undoing of the obsessive-compulsive, and the neurotic denial and repression of the hysteric. Neurotics will always change the most and be most grateful.

Admittedly, defenses are metaphorical; like gravity, they are only logically probable. However, by understanding them, the irrational can become rational and the unloved can become lovable. If we do not recognize defenses, we can become frightened by them, and we can become caught up by their contagion. Much of what is irrational and wasteful about the whole criminal justice system is that the adaptive mechanisms of the criminal and of injured society alike are not fully understood. It is so hard for us to be graceful or understanding when we are under attack, and much of the unnecessary pain in the world results from our responding to defensive behavior as incomprehensible or treating it at face value rather than understanding what lies behind.

Such understanding can only derive from accurate recognition of the defense. A contemporary illustration was provided by Martin Luther King when he recognized the fact that whites projected their own guilty anger onto blacks and then became fearful. Who can even guess the number of lives King saved by being able to articulate, "If our white brothers are to master fear, they must depend not only on their commitment to Christian love, but also on the Christ-like love which the Negro generates towards them . . . the Negro man must convince the white man that he seeks justice for both himself and the white man."[3]

Having spent ten years wrestling with the problem of the origins of defenses, I am willing to settle for a sense of wonderment at their ingenuity and a sense of pleasure at sometimes being able to understand them. I can not explain *why* specific defenses emerge and not others. In my opinion, the origin of defenses is as multidetermined as the origins of humor and art. All three require a fortuitous blend of conflict, inner strength, and earlier outside help. All require pain, talent, a receptive audience, cultural permission, and a rare mixture of identification, self-discipline, and spontaneity. Genes, parenting, close relationships, and loneliness all play their part in artistic creation, and I would imagine that the choice of an individual defense must be equally complex.

The fourth conclusion of this book is that adults change over time. If we view lives prospectively, they look different from our retrospective view of them. We were never the little butterflies we imagined. In retrospect, it is the times that change, and once an adult, always an adult. Yet if we follow adults for years, we can uncover startling changes and evolutions. We can discover developmental discontinuities in adults that are as great as the difference in personality between a nine-year-old and what he becomes at fifteen. As analogy, consider acne. In cross-section, acne presents as an incurable illness, one that for years will resist the effects of soap, diet, and the most expensive dermatologists. Viewed prospectively and longitudinally, acne becomes an illness that at twenty may magically and predictably disappear. So often is it with mental illness in the lives of adults.

But such shifts are not magical, nor do they come from without. To view lives in cross-section is like trying to understand traffic by standing in the middle of Times Square. The confusion is bewildering, and external events seem critical. The time of day, the traffic lights, rain, and adventitious accidents seem all-important. But if each car is viewed in the perspective of time, suddenly each one acquires a defined, if not fully predictable, trajectory, and seen from afar, this trajectory is governed far more by the driver of the vehicle than by the complex outer social forces that affect Times Square.

When the Grant Study was started, the hope was that it would allow prediction and that once all the data were in, college counselors could interview sophomores and tell them what they should do with their lives. This was not to be. The life cycle is more than an invariant sequence of stages with single predictable outcomes. The men's lives are full of surprises, and the Grant Study provides no prediction tables. Rather, the study of lifetimes is comparable to the study of celestial navigation. Neither a sextant nor a celestial map can predict where we *should* go; but both are invaluable in letting us identify where we *are*. Both in my own life and in my clinical work with patients, I have found that the lives of the Grant Study men provide navigational charts of the greatest utility.

Yes, I can hear the protest of many readers. Why did the Study not include people more like them? My hope is that, as the cultural anthropologists have shown us, we all can learn from well-studied, albeit unique, human samples, be they Trobriand Islanders, ancient Greeks — or Grant Study men.

The fifth conclusion made by this book is that mental health *exists*. Contrary to popular belief, lucky at work means lucky in love; lack of overt emotional distress does not lead to headache and high blood pressure but to robust physical health; and those who pay their internist the most visits are also most likely to visit psychiatrists. Inner happiness, external play, objective vocational success, mature inner defenses, good outward marriage, all correlate highly — not perfectly, but at least as powerfully as height correlates with weight. The paradox of Alan Poe is the exception, not the rule.

Not only do I now believe that mental health is tangible, but I believe that it exists as a dimension of personality. I believe that mental health exists, much like intelligence or musical ability, as a continuum; and not just as the absence of discrete psychiatric maladies. Effective evaluation of long-term therapy, especially of psychotherapy, may be better achieved by charting a patient's move along a continuum of positive external behaviors than by focusing upon the presence or absence of individual symptoms.

Our task as members of the larger society is to take pains that our culture and our own behavior enable others to play games, to achieve art, to enjoy their work. We must help others to care for their children that their children be able to love. We must ask ourselves how we can help a paranoid's projection become a novel, an eccentric's sexual fantasy become a sculpture, and a delinquent's impulse to murder evolve into creative lawmaking or into the subtleties of a *New Yorker* cartoon.

Despite its psychoanalytic terminology, this book conforms to the model of physical health put forth by the fathers of internal medicine, Claude Bernard and Walter B. Cannon. Individuals capable of homeostasis (preserving their physiological equilibrium) survive. The healthy individual is a conservative — not in the sense of being penny-pinching or "anal-retentive" but in the sense of being capable of conservation and of assessing personal costs. Hans Selye is wrong; it is not stress that kills us. It is effective adaptation to stress that permits us to live.

In closing, how do I answer the question posed at the book's beginning, "What is mental health?" Let me reply with the same parable offered by the protagonist in Gotthold Lessing's great eighteenth-century play, *Nathan the Wise*. An angry sultan had asked Nathan, on pain of death, to identify the one true religion — Christianity, Islam, or Judaism. Nathan, a Jew, gently pointed out the need to maintain a longitudinal perspective.

> *"In days of yore, a man lived in the East,*
> *Who owned a ring of marvelous worth,*
> *Given to him by a hand beloved.*
> *The stone was opal, and shed a hundred lovely rays,*
> *But chiefly it possessed the secret power*

> *To make the owner loved of God and man,*
> *If he but wore it in this faith and confidence . . ."*

Nathan then told how the ring was sought as an inheritance by each of the owner's three sons. Since he loved them all equally, the loving father gave each son an identical ring. After his death, the three sons, realizing that only one of them could have the true ring, hurried off to a judge. They demanded that he identify the lucky owner of the one true ring.

Nathan describes the judge's verdict:

> *"But stop! I've just been told that the right ring,*
> *Contains the wondrous gift to make its wearer loved,*
> *Agreeable alike to God and Man.*
> *That must decide, for the false rings will not have this power. . . .*
> *Let each one strive to gain the prize of proving by results*
> *The virtue of his ring and aid its power*
> *With gentleness and heartiest friendliness . . .*
> *The virtue of the ring will then*
> *Have proved itself among your children's children."*

References Cited

Introduction

1. C. W. Heath, *What People Are* (Cambridge: Harvard University Press, 1945), p. 4.
2. F. Barron, "Personal Soundness in University Graduate Students," in *Creativity and Psychological Health* (Princeton: D. Van Nostrand Co., 1963).
3. H. Hartmann, *Ego Psychology and the Problem of Adaptation* (New York: International Universities Press, 1958), p. 23.
4. C. W. Heath, op. cit.; E. Hooton, *Young Man, You Are Normal* (New York: Putnam, 1945).
5. Ibid.
6. E. Glover, *On the Early Development of Mind* (New York: International Universities Press, 1956).
7. F. Barron, op. cit.
8. L. Tolstoy, letter to Valerya Aresenyev, November 9, 1856, quoted by H. Troyat in *Tolstoy* (New York: Doubleday, 1967), p. 158.
9. R. R. Grinker, "Mentally Healthy Young Males (Homoclites)," *Archives of General Psychiatry* 6 (1962): 405–453.
10. L. Havens, *Approaches to the Mind* (Boston: Little, Brown, 1974).
11. S. Freud, "The Neuro-Psychoses of Defense" (1894), *The Complete Psychological Works of Sigmund Freud* (London: Hogarth Press Ltd., 1964) 3: 45–61; S. Freud, "Further Remarks on the Neuro-Psychoses of Defense" (1896), *The Complete Psychological Works of Sigmund Freud* 3: 162–185.

Chapter 2

1. J. P. Monks, *College Men at War* (Boston: American Academy of Arts and Sciences, 1951).
2. D. Cahalan and I. H. Cisin, "American Drinking Practices: Summary of Findings from a National Probability Sample; 1) Extent of Drinking by Population Subgroups," *Quarterly Journal Studies of Alcohol* 29 (1968): 130–151.
3. L. Srole, T. S. Langner, S. T. Michael, M. K. Opler, and T. A. C. Rennie, *Mental Health in the Metropolis* (New York: McGraw-Hill, 1962).
4. M. H. Oden and L. M. Terman, "The Fulfillment of Promise — 40 Year Follow-Up of the Terman Gifted Group," *Genetic Psychological Monographs* 77 (1968): 3–93; L. M. Terman and M. H. Oden, *The Gifted Group at Midlife* (Stanford: Stanford University Press, 1959).

Chapter 3

1. G. E. Vaillant, "Natural History of Male Psychological Health, II: Some Antecedents of Healthy Adult Adjustment," *Archives of General Psychiatry* 31 (1974): 15–22.
2. A. H. Chapman, *Harry Stack Sullivan* (New York: G. P. Putnam's Sons, 1976).
3. A. Freud, *Ego and the Mechanisms of Defense* (London: Hogarth Press Ltd., 1937).
4. H. Hartmann, *Ego Psychology and the Problem of Adaptation* (New York: International Universities Press, 1958).
5. E. Erikson, *Childhood and Society* (New York: Norton, 1950).

6. C. Briscoe et al., "Divorce and Psychiatric Disease," *Archives of General Psychiatry* 29 (1973): 119–125.

Chapter 5

1. S. Freud, "The Neuro-Psychoses of Defense" (1894), *The Complete Psychological Works of Sigmund Freud* (London: Hogarth Press, Ltd., 1964) 3: 45–61.
2. S. Freud, "My Views on the Part Played by Sexuality in The Aetiology of the Neuroses" (1906), *The Complete Psychological Works of Sigmund Freud* 7: 276.
3. S. Freud, "A Disturbance of Memory on the Acropolis" (1936), *The Complete Psychological Works of Sigmund Freud* 22: 239–248, at 245.
4. A. Freud, *The Ego and the Mechanisms of Defense* (London: Hogarth Press Ltd., 1937).
5. R. S. Wallerstein, "Development and Metapsychology of the Defense Organization of the Ego," *Journal of the American Psychoanalytic Association* 15 (1967): 132–149.
6. S. Freud, "Three Essays on the Theory of Sexuality" (1905), *The Complete Psychological Works of Sigmund Freud* 7: 125–245, at 238–239.
7. Ibid., p. 238.
8. S. Freud, "Jokes and Their Relation to the Unconscious" (1905), *The Complete Psychological Works of Sigmund Freud* 8: 233.
9. P. M. Symonds, *Defenses: The Dynamics of Human Adjustment* (New York: Appleton-Century-Crofts, 1945).
10. A. Freud, op. cit.
11. G. L. Bibring, T. F. Dwyer, D. S. Huntington, and A. Valenstein, "A Study of the Psychological Process in Pregnancy and of the Earliest Mother-Child Relationship: II. Methodological Considerations," *The Psychoanalytic Study of the Child* 16 (1961): 25–72.
12. E. Semrad, "The Organization of Ego Defenses and Object Loss," in D. M. Moriarity, ed., *The Loss of Loved Ones* (Springfield, Ill.: Charles C Thomas, 1967).
13. O. Fenichel, *The Psychoanalytical Theory of Neurosis* (New York: W. W. Norton & Co., 1945).
14. L. C. Kolb, *Noyes' Modern Clinical Psychiatry* (Philadelphia: W. B. Saunders Co., 1968).
15. G. E. Vaillant, "Theoretical Hierarchy of Adaptive Ego Mechanisms," *Archives of General Psychiatry* 24 (1971): 107–118.
16. G. E. Vaillant, "Natural History of Male Psychological Health, V: The Relation of Choice of Ego Mechanisms of Defense to Adult Adjustment," *Archives of General Psychiatry* 33 (1976): 535–545.
17. N. Haan, "Proposed Model of Ego Functioning: Coping and Defense Mechanisms in Relationship to IQ Change," *Psychological Monographs* 77 (1963): 1–23; T. Kroeber, "The Coping Functions of the Ego Mechanisms," *The Study of Lives* (New York: Atherton Press, 1963), pp. 178–198.
18. N. Haan, "The Relationship of Ego Functioning and Intelligence to Social Status and Social Mobility," *Journal of Abnormal and Social Psychology* 69 (1964): 594–605.
19. A. Weinstock, "Longitudinal Study of Social Class and Defense Preferences," *Journal of Consulting Psychology* 31 (1967): 539–541; D. R. Miller and G. E. Swanson, *Inner Conflict and Defense* (New York: Holt & Co., 1960).
20. G. E. Vaillant, "Natural History of Male Psychological Health, V: . . .," op. cit.
21. T. S. Langner and S. T. Michael, *Life Stress and Mental Health* (New York: Free Press, 1963).
22. Ibid., p. 156.
23. J. Piaget, *The Moral Judgment of the Child* (New York: Free Press, 1965).

24. J. H. Flavell, *The Developmental Psychology of Jean Piaget* (Princeton, N.J.: Van Nostrand, 1963).
25. L. Kohlberg, "Development of Moral Character and Moral Ideology," in M. Hoffman and L. W. Hoffman, eds., *Review of Child Development Research* (New York: Russell Sage Foundation, 1964) 1: 383–431.

Chapter 7

1. D. Hamburg and J. E. Adams, "A Perspective on Coping Behavior," *Archives of General Psychiatry* 17 (1967): 277–284.
2. I. Janis, *Psychological Stress* (New York: Wiley & Sons, 1958).
3. R. S. Ezekiel, "The Personal Future and Peace Corps Competence," *Journal of Personal and Social Psychology*, Monograph Supplement 8: 2 (February 1968), pp. 1–26.
4. S. Freud, "Jokes and Their Relation to the Unconscious" (1905), *The Complete Psychological Works of Sigmund Freud* 8: 233.
5. Ibid., p. 225.

Chapter 8

1. S. Freud, "The Neuro-Psychoses of Defense" (1894), *The Complete Psychological Works of Sigmund Freud* 3: 45–61.
2. S. Freud, "On the History of the Psychoanalytic Movement," (1914), *The Complete Psychological Works of Sigmund Freud* 14: 7–66, at 16.
3. S. Freud, *Interpretation of Dreams* (1901), *The Complete Psychological Works of Sigmund Freud* 5: 606.
4. S. Freud, "Id, Inhibitions, and Anxiety" (1926), *The Complete Psychological Works of Sigmund Freud* 20: 120.
5. S. Freud, "The Neuro-Psychoses of Defense" (1894), op. cit., pp. 48 and 52.
6. A. Leighton, *My Name is Legion: The Stirling County Study of Psychiatric Disorder and Sociocultural Environment*, vol. 1 (New York: Basic Books, 1959).
7. D. C. Leighton, J. S. Harding, D. B. Macklin, et al., *The Character of Danger* (New York: Basic Books, 1963).
8. M. Beiser, "The Lame Princess: A Study of the Remission of Psychiatric Symptoms Without Treatment," *American Journal of Psychiatry* 129 (1972): 257–262.
9. D. C. Leighton, J. S. Harding, D. B. Macklin, C. C. Hughes, and A. H. Leighton, "Psychiatric Findings of the Stirling County Study," *American Journal of Psychiatry* 119 (1963): 1021–1026.
10. G. E. Vaillant, "Why Men Seek Psychotherapy, I: Results of a Survey of College Graduates," *American Journal of Psychiatry* 129 (1972): 645–651.
11. S. Freud, "The Neuro-Psychoses of Defense" (1894), op. cit., p. 53.
12. K. Lorenz, *On Aggression* (New York: Harcourt, Brace and World, 1963).
13. I. Janis, *Psychological Stress* (New York: Wiley & Sons, 1958).

Chapter 9

1. G. E. Vaillant, "Natural History of Male Psychological Health, V: The Relation of Choice of Ego Mechanisms of Defense to Adult Adjustment," *Archives of General Psychiatry* 33 (1976): 535–545.
2. E. Erikson, *Gandhi's Truth* (New York: Norton, 1969).
3. A. Freud, *Ego and the Mechanisms of Defense* (London: Hogarth Press Ltd., 1937).

Chapter 10

1. C. G. Jung, "The Stages of Life," *The Portable Jung*, J. Campbell, ed. (New York: Viking, 1971), p. 12.
2. E. Erikson, *Childhood and Society* (New York: Norton, 1950).
3. J. Block, *Lives Through Time* (Berkeley: Bancroft, 1971); D. Levinson et al., "The Psychosocial Development of Men in Early Adulthood and the Mid-Life

Transition," in *Life History Research in Psychopathology*, D. Ricks, A. Thomas, and M. Roff, eds. (Minneapolis: Minnesota University Press, 1974) 3: 243–258; M. H. Oden and L. M. Terman, "The Fulfillment of Promise — 40 Year Follow-Up of the Terman Gifted Group," *Genetic Psychological Monographs* 77 (1968): 3–93; G. Sheehy, *Passages* (New York: E. P. Dutton, 1976); R. W. White, *Lives in Progress* (New York: Holt, Rinehart & Winston, 1957); G. W. Goethals and D. S. Klos, *Experiencing Youth* (Boston: Little, Brown, 1976).

4. J. Clausen, "The Life Course of Individuals," *Aging and Society*, vol. 3, *The Sociology of Age Stratification*, M. W. Riley, J. Johnson, A. Foner, eds. (New York: Russell Sage Foundation, 1972), pp. 457–514.

5. A. Freud, "On Adolescence," *Psychoanalytic Study of the Child*, vol. 13 (New York: International Universities Press, 1958).

6. H. Peskin and N. Livson, "Pre- and Post-pubertal Personality and Adult Psychologic Functioning," *Seminars in Psychiatry* 4 (1972): 343–353.

7. F. L. Wells and W. L. Woods, "Outstanding Traits," *Genetic Psychological Monographs* 33 (1946): 127–249.

8. D. Offer and J. B. Offer, *From Teenage to Young Manhood* (New York: Basic Books, 1975); S. King, *Five Lives* (Cambridge: Harvard University Press, 1973).

9. E. Erikson, "Identity and the Life Cycle: Selected Papers," *Psychological Issues*, vol. 1, no. 1 (1959).

10. J. Kagan and H. Moss, *From Birth to Maturity* (New York: Wiley & Sons, 1962).

11. T. M. Newcomb et al., *Persistence and Change: Bennington College and Its Students After Twenty-Five Years* (New York: Wiley & Sons, 1967); R. G. Kuhlen, "Personality Change With Age," in *Personality Change*, P. Worchel and D. Byrne, eds. (New York: Wiley & Sons, 1964).

12. R. Gould, "The Phases of Adult Life: A Study in Developmental Psychology," *American Journal of Psychiatry* 129 (1972): 521–531.

13. V. C. Crandall, "The Fels Study: Some Contributions to Personality Development and Achievement in Childhood and Adulthood," *Seminars in Psychiatry* 4 (1972): 383–398; G. H. Elder, *Children of the Great Depression* (Chicago: University of Chicago Press, 1974); R. D. Cox, *Youth Into Maturity* (New York: Mental Health Materials Center, 1970); L. M. Terman and M. H. Oden, *The Gifted Group at Midlife* (Stanford: Stanford University Press, 1959); T. Lidz, *The Person* (New York: Basic Books, 1968).

14. D. Levinson et al., op. cit.

15. E. Jacques, "Death and the Mid-Life Crisis," *International Journal of Psychoanalysis* 46 (1965): 502–514.

16. B. L. Neugarten, *Personality in Middle and Late Life* (New York: Atherton, 1964).

17. B. L. Neugarten and J. Datan (1972), as quoted in O. Brim, "Theories of the Male Mid-Life Crisis," *The Counseling Psychologist* 6 (1976): 29.

18. B. L. Neugarten, Women's Attitudes Towards the Menopause, *Vita Humana* 6 (1963): 140–151.

19. G. Winokur and R. Cadoret, "The Irrelevance of the Menopause to Depressive Disease," in *Topics in Psychoendocrinology*, E. J. Sachar, ed. (New York: Grune and Stratton, 1975).

20. G. F. Streib and C. J. Schneider, *Retirement in American Society* (Ithaca, N.Y.: Cornell University Press, 1971).

21. A. Roe, "Changes in Scientific Activities With Age," *Science*, 150 (1965): 313–318, at 318.

22. E. Erikson, *Identity: Youth and Crisis* (New York: W. W. Norton & Co., 1968), p. 138.

23. C. G. Jung, "The Stages of Life," op. cit., p. 18.

24. B. L. Neugarten, "Dynamics of Transition of Middle Age to Old Age," *Journal of Geriatric Psychiatry* 4 (1970): 71–87.
25. O. C. Brim, "Theories of the Male Mid-Life Crisis," *The Counseling Psychologist*, 6 (1976): 2–9.
26. B. L. Neugarten, "Adult Personality: Toward a Psychology of the Life Cycle," in *The Human Life Cycle*, W. C. Sze, ed. (New York: Jason Aronson 1975).
27. B. L. Neugarten, *Personality in Middle and Late Life* (New York: Atherton, 1964), p. 189.

Chapter 11

1. J. Breuer and S. Freud, *Studies on Hysteria* (New York: Basic Books, 1957).
2. L. Freeman, *The Story of Anna O.* (New York: Walker Co., 1972).
3. Ibid.
4. G. E. Vaillant, "The Natural History of Alcoholism: I, A Preliminary Report." Presented at the 1976 Annual Meeting for the Society for Life History Research in Psychopathology (Fort Worth, Texas, October 6–8, 1976).

Chapter 12

1. L. Srole, T. S. Langer, S. T. Michael, et al., *Mental Health in the Metropolis: Midtown Manhattan Study*, vol. 1 (New York: McGraw-Hill, 1962).
2. L. Luborsky and H. Bachrach, "Factors Influencing Clinicians' Judgments of Mental Health," *Archives of General Psychiatry* 31 (1974): 292–299.
3. S. Freud, "Introductory Lectures to Psychoanalysis" (1916–1917), *The Complete Psychological Works of Sigmund Freud* 16: 397–398.
4. G. H. Elder, "Occupational Mobility, Life Patterns, and Personality," *Journal of Health and Social Behavior* 10 (1969): 308–323.
5. C. Briscoe et al., "Divorce and Psychiatric Disease," *Archives of General Psychiatry* 29 (1973): 119–125.
6. G. E. Vaillant, "Prospective Prediction of Schizophrenic Remission," *Archives of General Psychiatry* 120 (1963): 367–375.
7. G. E. Vaillant, "A Twelve-Year Follow-Up of New York Narcotic Addicts: IV, Some Characteristics and Determinants of Abstinence," *American Journal of Psychiatry* 123 (1966): 573–584.
8. E. Glueck and S. Glueck, *Delinquents and Non-Delinquents in Perspective* (Cambridge: Harvard University Press, 1968).
9. H. Hartmann, *Ego Psychology and the Problem of Adaptation* (New York: International Universities Press, 1958), pp. 15–16.
10. J. Kagan and H. Moss, *From Birth to Maturity* (New York: Wiley & Sons, 1962).
11. R. R. Grinker and B. Werble, " 'Mentally Healthy' Young Males (Homoclites)," *Archives of General Psychiatry* 6 (1962): 27–75.
12. L. Luborsky and H. Bachrach, op. cit.
13. R. R. Grinker and B. Werble, op. cit.; J. Golden, N. Mandel, B. Glueck, and Z. Feder, "A Summary Description of Fifty 'Normal' White Males," *American Journal of Psychiatry* 119 (1962): 48–56.
14. F. Barron, op. cit.
15. R. Reinhardt, "The Outstanding Jet Pilot," *American Journal of Psychiatry* 127 (1970): 732–736.

Chapter 13

1. E. Siegelman, J. Block, and A. Von der Lippe, "Antecedents of Optimal Psychological Adjustment," *Journal of Consulting and Clinical Psychiatry* 35 (1970): 283–289; L. Kohlberg, J. LaCrosse, and D. Ricks, "The Predictability of Adult Mental Health from Childhood Behavior," in *Manual of Child Psychopathology*, B. B. Wolman, ed. (New York: McGraw-Hill, 1972).

2. G. E. Vaillant, "Why Men Seek Psychotherapy, I: Results of a Survey of College Graduates," *American Journal of Psychiatry* 129 (1972): 645–651.

3. T. S. Langner and S. T. Michael, *Life Stress and Mental Health* (New York: Free Press, 1963).

4. R. J. Stoller, "Symbiosis, Anxiety and the Development of Masculinity," *Archives of General Psychiatry* 30 (1974): 164–170, at 169.

5. J. MacFarlane, "Perspectives on Personality Consistency and Change from the Guidance Study," *Vita Humana* 7 (1964): 115–126, at 121.

Chapter 14

1. R. Gorney, "Interpersonal Intensity, Competition, and Synergy: Determinants of Achievement, Aggression, and Mental Illness," *American Journal of Psychiatry* 128 (1971): 436–445.

2. W. M. Kephart, "Is Sex Overrated?" *Medical Aspects of Human Sexuality* 8 (1974): 8.

3. K. Robson, "Development of Object Relations During the First Year of Life," *Seminars in Psychiatry* 4 (1972): 301–316.

4. C. W. Briscoe and J. B. Smith, "Psychiatric Illness — Marital Units and Divorce," *Journal of Nervous and Mental Disease* 158 (1974): 440–445.

5. T. R. Peskin, "Personality Antecedents of Divorce." Presented at the Western Psychological Association Symposium: Interpersonal Relationships Over the Life Span (Sacramento, California, April 26, 1975).

Chapter 15

1. J. Loevinger, "Theories of Ego Development," in *Clinical Cognitive Psychology: Models and Integrations*, L. Breger, ed. (Englewood Cliffs, N.J.: Prentice-Hall, 1969).

2. A. Freud, *Ego and the Mechanisms of Defense* (London: Hogarth Press Ltd., 1937), p. 57.

3. L. Murphy, *The Widening World of Childhood* (New York: Basic Books, 1962); G. L. Engel, *Psychological Development in Health and Disease* (Philadelphia: W. B. Saunders Co., 1962).

4. N. Haan, "Personality Development from Adolescence to Adulthood in the Oakland Growth and Guidance Studies," *Seminars in Psychiatry* 4 (1972): 399–414.

5. J. Block, *Lives Through Time* (Berkeley, California: Bancroft, 1971).

6. G. E. Vaillant, "Natural History of Male Psychological Health, V: Relation of Choice of Ego Mechanisms of Defense to Adult Adjustment," *Archives of General Psychiatry* 33 (1976): 535–545.

7. N. Haan, op. cit.

8. P. M. Symonds, *From Adolescent to Adult* (New York: Columbia University Press, 1961).

9. R. Gould, "The Phases of Adult Life: A Study in Developmental Psychology," *American Journal of Psychiatry* 129 (1972): 521–531, at 522.

10. A. Freud, "On Adolescence," in *The Psychoanalytic Study of The Child*, vol. 13 (New York: International Universities Press, 1958).

11. G. E. Vaillant, "Natural History of Male Psychological Health, II: Some Antecedents of Health Adult Adjustment," *Archives of General Psychiatry* 31 (1974): 15–22.

12. P. I. Yakovlev and A. R. Lecours, "The Myelogenetic Cycles of Regional Maturation of the Brain," in *Regional Development of the Brain in Early Life*, A. Minkowski, ed. (Oxford: Blackwell Scientific Publications, 1967).

13. R. R. Sears and S. S. Feldman, *The Seven Ages of Man* (Los Altos, California: William Kaufman, 1973).

14. P. B. Baltes, "Longitudinal and Cross-Sectional Sequences in the Study of Age and Generation Effects," *Human Development* 11 (1968): 145–171.

15. G. E. Vaillant, "Theoretical Hierarchy of Adaptive Ego Mechanisms," *Archives of General Psychiatry* 24 (1971): 107–118.

16. J. Loevinger, "The Meaning and Measurement of Ego Development," *American Psychologist* 21 (1966): 195–206.

17. L. Kohlberg, "Development of Moral Character and Moral Ideology," in *Review of Child Development Research*, vol. 1 (New York: Russell Sage Foundation, 1964), pp. 383–431.

18. N. Haan, as quoted by Margie Casady, "If You're Active and Savvy at 30, You'll Be Warm and Witty at 70." *Psychology Today* (November 1975), p. 138.

19. G. E. Vaillant, "Natural History of Male Psychological Health, V: Relation of Choice of Ego Mechanisms of Defense to Adult Adjustment," *Archives of General Psychiatry* 33 (1976): 535–545.

20. J. H. Flavell, *The Development Psychology of Jean Piaget* (New York: Van Nostrand, 1963); J. Piaget, *The Moral Judgment of the Child* (New York: Free Press, 1965).

21. H. Hartmann, *Psychoanalysis and Moral Values* (New York: International Universities Press, 1960).

22. J. H. Flavell, op. cit.

23. J. Loevinger, *Ego Development* (San Francisco: Jossey Bass, 1976); L. Kohlberg, op. cit.

24. S. T. Hauser, "Loevinger's Model and Measure of Ego Development: A Critical Review," *Psychological Bulletin* 83 (1976): 928–955.

25. L. Kohlberg, op. cit., p. 404.

26. Ibid., p. 406.

27. A. Rizzuto, "Object Relations and the Formation of the Image of God," *British Journal of Medical Psychology* 47 (1974): 83–99.

28. S. R. Graubard, ed., "Adulthood," *Daedalus* (Proceedings of American Academy of Arts and Sciences) 105, no. 2 (Spring 1976).

29. E. H. Erikson, "Reflections on Dr. Borg's Life Cycle," *Daedalus*, op. cit., p. 10.

Chapter 16

1. S. Freud, "Dostoevsky and Parricide" (1928), *The Complete Psychological Works of Sigmund Freud* 21: 175–196, at 177.

2. N. Zinberg, "The Mirage of Mental Health," *British Journal of Sociology* 21 (1970): 262–278, at 265.

3. P. Sedgwick, "Illness — Mental and Otherwise," *Hastings Center Studies* 1 (1973): 19–40, at 30–31.

4. Ibid, p. 31.

5. N. Zinberg, op. cit., p. 271.

6. M. Jahoda, *Current Concepts of Positive Mental Health* (New York: Basic Books, 1959).

7. L. R. Kass, "Regarding the End of Medicine and the Pursuit of Health," *The Public Interest* 40 (1975): 11–42, at 28.

8. J. Loevinger, "The Meaning and Measurement of Ego Development," *American Psychologist* 21 (1966): 195–206, at 200.

Chapter 17

1. M. B. Smith, "Mental Health Reconsidered," *American Psychologist* 16 (1961): 299–306.

2. C. Bernard, *An Introduction to the Study of Experimental Medicine* (New York: Dover, 1957), p. 146.

3. C. S. King, *My Life with Martin Luther King, Jr.* (New York: Avon Books, 1970), p. 116.

Appendix A

A Glossary of Defenses

Level I — "Psychotic" Mechanisms

These mechanisms are common in "healthy" individuals before age five, and common in adult dreams and fantasy. For the *user*, these mechanisms alter reality. To the *beholder*, they appear "crazy." They tend to be immune to change by conventional psychotherapeutic interpretation; but they are *altered* by change in reality (e.g., chlorpromazine, removal of stressful situation, developmental maturation). In therapy, they can be given up temporarily by offering the user strong interpersonal support in conjunction with direct confrontation with the ignored reality.

1. DELUSIONAL PROJECTION. Frank delusions about external reality, usually of a persecutory type.

It includes both the perception of one's own feelings in another person and then acting on the perception (e.g., florid paranoid delusions), and the perception of other people or their feelings literally inside oneself (e.g., the agitated depressed patient's claim that "the devil is devouring my heart"). This mechanism can be distinguished from *projection* by the fact that in the former, reality testing is virtually abandoned. It is distinguished from *distortion* by the absence of wish-fulfillment and from *introjection* in that the responsibility for acknowledged internal feelings is still projected. In toxic psychosis, *delusional projection* adaptively organizes otherwise chaotic perceptions.

2. DENIAL. Denial of external reality.

Unlike repression, *denial*, as here defined, affects perception of external reality (e.g., "girls do so got penises") more than perception of internal reality (e.g., I am not angry). It includes the use of fantasy as a major substitute for other people — especially absent other people (e.g., "I will make a new him in my own mind").

3. DISTORTION. Grossly reshaping external reality to suit inner needs.

It includes unrealistic megalomaniacal beliefs, hallucinations, wish-fulfilling delusions, and employment of sustained feelings of delusional superiority or entitlement. It can encompass persistent denial of personal responsibility for one's own behavior. It also includes acting upon, as well as thinking about, unrealistic obsessions or compulsions. In distortion, there may be a pleasant merging or fusion with another person (e.g., "Jesus lives inside me and answers all my prayers"); but in contrast to *delusional projection*, where distress is alleviated by assigning responsibility for offensive feelings elsewhere, in *distortion* unpleasant feelings are replaced with their opposites. As manifested in religious belief, *distortion* can be highly adaptive.

Level II — Immature Mechanisms

These mechanisms are common in "healthy" individuals ages three to fifteen, in character disorder, and in adults in psychotherapy. For the *user* these mechanisms most often alter distress engendered either by the threat of interpersonal intimacy or the threat of experiencing its loss. To the *beholder* they appear socially undesirable. Although refractory to change, immature mechanisms *change* with improved interpersonal relationships (e.g., personal maturation, a more mature spouse, a more intuitive physician, or a fairer parole officer) or with repeated and forceful interpretation during prolonged psychotherapy or with confrontation by peers.

4. PROJECTION. Attributing one's own unacknowledged feelings to others.

It includes severe prejudice, rejections of intimacy through unwarranted suspicion, marked hypervigilance to external danger, and injustice-collecting. The behavior of someone using this defense may be eccentric and abrasive but within the "letter of the law."

5. SCHIZOID FANTASY. Tendency to use fantasy and to indulge in autistic retreat for the purpose of conflict resolution and gratification.

It is associated with global avoidance of interpersonal intimacy and the use of eccentricity to repel others. In contrast to psychotic *denial*, the individual does not fully believe in or insist upon acting out his fantasies. Nevertheless, unlike mere wishes, schizoid fantasies serve to gratify unmet needs for personal relationships, and to obliterate the overt expression of aggressive or sexual impulses towards others. Unlike *dissociation*, fantasy remakes the outer not the inner world.

6. HYPOCHONDRIASIS. The transformation of reproach towards others arising from bereavement, loneliness, or unacceptable aggressive impulses into first self-reproach and then complaints of pain, somatic illness, and neurasthenia.

It includes those aspects of introjection which permit traits of an ambivalently regarded person to be perceived within oneself and causing plausible disease. Unlike identification, hypochondriacal introjection produces dysphoria and a sense of affliction; hypochondriacal introjects are "ego alien." The mechanism may permit the individual to belabor others with his own pain or discomfort in lieu of making direct demands upon them or in lieu of complaining that others have ignored his wishes (often unexpressed) to be dependent. It does *not* include illnesses like asthma, ulcer, or hypertension, which may be neither adaptive nor defensive. Unlike hysterical conversion symptoms, hypochondriasis is accompanied by the very opposite of *la belle indifference*.

7. PASSIVE-AGGRESSIVE BEHAVIOR. Aggression towards others expressed indirectly and ineffectively through passivity or directed against the self.

It includes failures, procrastinations, or illnesses that (initially at least) affect others more than oneself. It includes silly or provocative behavior in order to receive attention and clowning in order to avoid assuming a competitive role. People who form sadomasochistic relationships often manifest both *passive-aggressive* and *hypochondriacal* defenses.

8. ACTING OUT. Direct expression of an unconscious wish or impulse in order to avoid being conscious of the affect that accompanies it.

It includes the use of motor behavior, delinquent or impulsive acts, and "tempers" to avoid being aware of one's feelings. It also includes the chronic use of drugs, failure, perversion, or self-inflicted injury to relieve tension (i.e., subjective anxiety or depression). Acting out involves chronically giving in to impulses in order to avoid the tension that would result were there any postponement of instinctual expression.

Level III — "Neurotic" Defenses

These mechanisms are common in "healthy" individuals ages three to ninety, in neurotic disorder, and in mastering acute adult stress. For the *user* these mechanisms alter private feelings or instinctual expression. To the *beholder*, they appear as individual quirks or "neurotic hang-ups." They often can be dramatically *changed* by conventional, brief psychotherapeutic interpretation.

9. INTELLECTUALIZATION. Thinking about instinctual wishes in formal, affectively bland terms, and *not* acting on them. The idea is in consciousness, but the feeling is missing.

The term encompasses the mechanisms of isolation, rationalization, ritual, undoing, restitution, magical thinking, and "busywork." While these mechanisms differ from each other, they usually occur as a cluster. Intellectualization includes paying undue attention to the inanimate in order to avoid intimacy with people, or paying attention to external reality to avoid expression of inner feelings; or paying attention to irrelevant detail to avoid perceiving the whole. Obsessions and compulsions not acted upon are included here, although they can also be thought of as a form of intrapsychic *displacement*.

10. REPRESSION. Seemingly inexplicable naïveté, memory lapse, or failure to acknowledge input from a selected sense organ. The feeling is in consciousness, but the idea is missing.

The "forgetting" of repression is unique in that it is often accompanied by highly symbolic behavior which suggests that the repressed is *not really* forgotten. The mechanism differs from *suppression* by effecting unconscious inhibition of impulse to the point of losing, not just postponing, cherished goals. Unlike *denial*, it blocks conscious perception of instincts and feelings rather than recognition of and response to external events. If a man were weeping but forgot for whom he wept, this would be *repression;* if he denied the existence of his tears or insisted that the mourned one was still alive, this would represent *denial*.

11. DISPLACEMENT. The redirection of feelings toward a relatively less cared for (less cathected) object than the person or situation arousing the feelings.

It includes facile "transference" and the substitution of things or strangers for emotionally important people. Practical jokes, wit with hidden hostile intent, and caricature involve displacement. Most phobias, many hysterical conversion reactions, and some prejudice involve displacement.

12. REACTION FORMATION. Behavior in a fashion diametrically opposed to an unacceptable instinctual impulse.

This mechanism includes overtly caring for someone else when one wishes to be cared for oneself, "hating" someone or something one really likes, or "loving" a hated rival or unpleasant duty.

13. DISSOCIATION. Temporary but drastic modification of one's character or of one's sense of personal identity to avoid emotional distress. Synonymous with Neurotic Denial.

This can include fugues, many hysterical conversion reactions, a sudden unwarranted sense of superiority or devil-may-care attitude, and a *short-term* refusal to perceive responsibility for one's acts or feelings. It also includes overactivity and counterphobic behavior in order to blot out anxiety or distressing emotion; "safe" expression of instinctual wishes through acting on stage; and the *acute* use of religious "joy" or of pharmacological intoxication to numb unhappiness. *Dissociation* is more comprehensible to others than distortion, more considerate of others, and less prolonged than *acting out*.

Level IV — Mature Mechanisms

These mechanisms are common in "healthy" individuals ages twelve to ninety. For the *user* these mechanisms integrate reality, interpersonal relationships, and private feelings. To the beholder they appear as convenient virtues. Under increased stress they may *change* to less mature mechanisms.

14. ALTRUISM. Vicarious but constructive and instinctually gratifying service to others.

It includes benign and constructive reaction formation, philanthropy, and well-repaid service to others. Altruism differs from *projection* and *acting out* in that it provides real, not imaginary, benefit to others and from *reaction formation* in that it leaves the person using the defense at least partly gratified.

15. HUMOR. Overt expression of ideas and feelings without individual discomfort or immobilization and without unpleasant effect on others.

Some games and playful regression come under this heading. Unlike wit, which is a form of *displacement*, humor lets you call a spade a spade; and *humor* can never be applied without some element of an "observing ego." Like hope, *humor* permits one to bear and yet to focus upon what is too terrible to be borne; in contrast, wit always involves distraction; unlike *schizoid fantasy*, *humor* never excludes other people.

16. SUPPRESSION. The conscious or semiconscious decision to postpone paying attention to a conscious impulse or conflict.

The mechanism includes looking for silver linings, minimizing acknowledged discomfort, employing a stiff upper lip, and deliberately postponing but not avoiding. With *suppression*, one says, "I will think about it tomorrow"; and the next day one remembers to think about it.

17. ANTICIPATION. Realistic anticipation of or planning for future inner discomfort.

This mechanism includes goal-directed but overly careful planning or worrying, premature but realistic affective anticipation of death or surgery, separation, and the conscious utilization of "insight" gained from psychotherapy.

18. SUBLIMATION. Indirect or attenuated expression of instincts without either adverse consequences or marked loss of pleasure.

It includes both expressing aggression through pleasurable games, sports, and hobbies; and romantic attenuation of instinctual expression during a real courtship. Unlike humor, with *sublimation* "regression in the service of the ego" has real consequences. Unlike the case with "neurotic" defenses, with *sublimation* instincts are channeled rather than dammed or diverted. Successful artistic expression remains the classic example. In *projection*, one's feelings (e.g., anger) are attributed to another person. In *displacement* one's feelings are acknowledged as one's own, but are redirected toward a relatively insignificant object, often without satisfaction. In *sublimation*, feelings are acknowledged, modified, and directed toward a relatively significant person or goal so that modest instinctual satisfaction results.

Appendix B

The Interview Schedule

Below is the semistructured schedule of questions that I used to guide my two-hour interview with the men when they were forty-seven years old. Within reason, the listed questions were always asked in the same order. I took longhand notes during the interview. Whenever a question elicited a problem area in a man's life, I probed for his particular means of mastery.

I. *Work*

a. What do you do? Any recent changes in responsibility?
b. Ten years from now, where are you heading?
c. What do you like and what do you dislike about your work?
d. What for you is most difficult?
e. What job would you have preferred?
f. What are good and bad aspects about relations with boss? With subordinates?
g. How do you handle some of the problems that arise with these people?
h. Looking back, how did you get into your present work?
i. Were there people with whom you identified?
j. What work do you do outside of your job — degree of responsibility?
k. What plans for retirement?
l. Ever unemployed for more than a month? Why?
m. What will you do the first week of retirement? Anticipated feelings?

II. *Family*

a. News of parents and siblings.
b. Describe each child, their problems and sources of concern to you.
c. How do you handle adolescence differently from your parents?
d. Any deaths: first response, second response, means of finally handling feelings.
e. This is the hardest question that I shall ask: Can you describe your wife?
f. Since nobody is perfect, what causes you concern about her?
g. Style of resolution of disagreements.
h. Has divorce ever been considered? Explain.
i. Quality of contact with parents and degree of pleasure derived.
j. Which of your parents wore the pants when you were younger?

III. *Medical*

a. How is your health overall?
b. How many days sick leave do you take a year?
c. When you get a cold, what do you do?
d. Specific medical conditions and means of coping with the disability.
e. Views and misconceptions about these conditions.
f. Injuries and hospitalizations since college.
g. Patterns of use of smoking and pattern and recollections about stopping.

h. Pattern of use of medicines and of alcohol.
i. Do you ever miss work due to emotional strain, fatigue, or emotional illness?
j. Effect of work on health and vice versa.
k. How easily do you get tired?
l. Effect of health on the rest of your life?

IV. *Psychological*

a. Biggest worries last year?
b. Dominant mood over past six months?
c. Some people have trouble going for help and advice: What do you do?
d. Can you talk about your oldest friends? What made them friends?
e. Who are the people (non-family) you would feel free to call on for help?
f. What social clubs do you belong to, and what is your pattern of entertaining?
g. How often do you get together with friends?
h. What do people criticize you for or find irritating about you?
i. What do they admire or find endearing?
j. What are your own satisfactions and dissatisfactions with yourself?
k. Ever seen a psychiatrist? Who? When? How long? What do you remember? What did you learn?
l. Persistent daydreams or concerns that you think about but don't tell others?
m. Effect of emotional stress?
n. Philosophy over rough spots?
o. Hobbies and use of leisure time? Athletics?
p. Vacations? How spent and with whom?
q. Any questions raised by my review of case record.
r. What questions do you have about the Study?

Appendix C

Rating Scales

1. *Adult Adjustment Scale* (a rating from 0 to 32)

Taking the entire twenty-five-year period (from college graduation to 1967) into account, one point was assigned for each of the following thirty-two items that was true. A score of less than 7 defined the Best Outcomes; a score of 14 or more defined the Worst Outcomes.

I. Career

    a. Failure to receive steady promotion or increasing responsibility, if possible, every five years since graduation.

    b. Not listed in *Who's Who in America* or *American Men of Science*.

    c. Earned income is less than $40,000 (unless in teaching, clergy, or responsible public service or quasi-charitable work).

    d. Earned income is less than $20,000 (1967 dollars).

    e. Occupational success does not clearly surpass father's (income, responsibility, occupational status).

    f. Occupational success clearly does not equal father's.

  *g. Has not actively participated over the years in extracurricular public service activities.

    h. However prestigious in the eyes of others, his job either is not one that he really wants for himself, or over the years it has failed to match his realistic ambitions.

*Rater agreement for each item was eighty-five to one hundred percent, except for items marked with an asterisk, where agreement was seventy-five to eighty-five percent.

II. Social Health

    a. Failed to achieve ten years or more of marriage (without separation) or failed to express overt satisfaction with that marriage on two or more occasions after the first year. (Eventual divorce did not affect this item.)

    b. Divorced, separated, or single. (Exclude widowers.)

    c. Never wanted to have or adopt children. (Ignore this item if he is single due to external cause — e.g., Catholic clergy.)

    d. One-third or more of children are markedly underperforming scholastically, delinquent, or getting psychiatric care. [Subsequent data analysis showed that this question would have been useful in 1975, but in 1967, when it was asked, it correlated with nothing.]

    e. Maintained no contact with surviving family of origin, except by duty or necessity.

    f. Regularly stated that he has less than usual interest in or fewer than average number of close friends. (Subjective evidence.)

*g. Not regularly a member of at least one social club and evidence from less than two occasions that he has more than one close friend. (Objective evidence.)

    h. No regular pastime or athletic activity that involves others (family members do not count).

N.B. Items a, b, c, f, g, and h were used to separate the Friendly from the Lonely men.

III. Psychological Health

*a. For more than half of years described, did not use full allotted vacation time or spent it at home doing chores or on dutiful visits to relatives.

    b. Explicit statement that subject had missed something by being too calm, unruffled, controlled, or unemotional (at two points in time). [Like Item II-d, this item was not significantly correlated with overall adjustment.]

*c. Failure to express satisfaction with job on three or more occasions and once in the past three years.

    d. Expressed explicit dissatisfaction with job at three points in time and once in past three years, *or* had changed occupational field once or job three times since age thirty without evidence of concomitant improvement in personal satisfaction or success.

    e. Evidence of detrimental (interferes with health, work, or personal relations at home) use of alcohol, or use of sedative or stimulant drugs weekly for more than three years, or more than six ounces of hard liquor a day for three years, or use of tranquilizers for more than a year.

    f. Ever hospitalized because of mental breakdown, alcohol misuse, or "physical" illness without evidence of somatic pathology.

    g. Evidence on more than two occasions that he is chronically depressed, dissatisfied with the course of his life, or evidence that he is consistently labeled by himself or others as being emotionally ill.

    h. Has sought psychiatric help for more than ten visits.

IV. Physical Health

    a. One hospitalization or serious accident since college [Item not significantly correlated with overall adjustment.]

    b. More than two operations and/or serious accidents since college (battle wounds excluded). [Item not significantly correlated with overall adjustment.]

    c. Two hospitalizations since college (excluding those due to surgery, trauma, or physical checkup).

    d. Own estimate of general health since college expressed in less than the most favorable available terms on more than one-fourth of occasions.

    e. On the average misses two or more workdays a year due to illness.

    f. On the average misses five or more workdays a year due to illness.

    g. Afflicted with chronic illness (requiring medical care) that significantly limits activity *or* more than a month of work lost consecutively due to illness.

h. Regularly takes prescription medicine, several patent medicines, or seeks medical attention for minor medical conditions (headaches, sinusitis, allergy, skin conditions, etc.).

2. *Childhood Environment Scale* (a rating from 0 to 20)

In the 1970s research associates who were blind to the fate of the men after their sophomore year, but who were not blind to more recent theories of child development, especially Erikson's, rated the men on the adequacy of their childhoods on a 20-point scale. The only data made available to the judges were (a) the psychiatrist's and family worker's notes on the boy's reports of his home life, (b) the parents' description of their relationship with the boy, and (c) a developmental and medical history obtained by the family worker from the parents. The family worker interviewed the parents in their homes.

A score of under 6 defined the Loveless and of 14 or more defined the Lucky. The 20-point scale was as follows:

a. Infant/Childhood Problems: Feeding problems, cried a great deal, dissocial, other noted problems (e.g., phobias) — no points. An average not particularly problem-filled childhood — 1 point. No known problems to age ten, normally social and "good-natured" — 2 points.

b. Childhood Health: Severe or prolonged illness, or physical disability — no points. A childhood with minor illnesses but no severe childhood diseases — 1 point. Consistent good health — 2 points.

c. Home Atmosphere: An uncongenial home with lack of family cohesiveness, with early maternal absences, separated parents, many moves or financial hardship which affected family life — no points. An average home or little information — 1 point. A warm, cohesive atmosphere where the parents did things together in a sharing atmosphere; few moves and financial stability — 2 points.

d. Mother-Child Relationship: A distant, hostile, or absent mother; one who blamed others (i.e., nurses, teachers, etc.) for her wrong methods of upbringing; a mother who seemed either overly punitive and demanding, or overprotective and/or seductive — no points. Lack of definite information or an apparently average relationship — 1 point. A warm mother who encouraged autonomy and esteem — 2 points.

e. Father-Child Relationship: An absent, distant, hostile, or overly punitive father; one with unrealistic expectations — no points. Lack of definite information or an apparently average relationship — 1 point. A warm father who encouraged positive autonomy, helped to develop his son's self-esteem, and who participated in activities of mutual interest — 2 points.

f. Sibling Relationship: Severe rivalry and destructive relationship where one sibling consistently undermined the other, or no siblings — no points. Lack of information — 1 point. Close enjoyable relationship with at least one sibling — 2 points.

g. High School Adjustment: Marked social problems — no points. "Average" social adjustment but no competitive sports — 1 point. Social success with participation in competitive sports — 2 points.

h. Global Impression [This was the judge's overall impression of the childhood environment based on the available data]: Impression of generally negative, non-nurturing environment — no points. Predominant impression neutral — 3 points. A positive childhood which included warm sustaining relationships and an environment conducive to developing autonomy, self-esteem and initiative (one the judges themselves would have wanted) — 6 points.

Thus, each participant received a score from 0–20 points.

Interrater reliability was $r = .71$ (a statistical expression of the extent to which different raters judging the same records would agree; an r over .7 is usually deemed adequate).

3. *Objective Physical Health Scale* (a rating from 1 to 5)

In 1969 and 1974 physical exams were obtained for all of the men from their own physicians, who of course were unaware of other ratings. These examinations were almost always by internists and usually included an examination of the blood and urine, routine blood chemistries, and electrocardiogram and a chest X-ray. Each man's health was rated on the following basis:

1 = Good health, essentially normal physical exam; any positive findings reversible.

2 = Multiple *minor* chronic complaints; mild back trouble, prostatitis, gout, kidney stones, single joint problems, chronic ear problems, etc.

3 = Chronic illness without disability; illnesses that will not fully remit and that will probably progress (e.g., treated hypertension, emphysema with cor pulmonale, diabetes.)

4 = Probably irreversible chronic illness with disability (e.g., angina, disabling back trouble, high blood pressure *and* extreme obesity, diabetes *and* arthritis, multiple sclerosis).

5 = Deceased.

4. *Marital Happiness Scale* (a rating from 1 to 4)

A questionnaire (see below) was mailed to the men in 1954, 1967, and 1972 and to their wives in 1967 (and 1975 after data analysis was complete). Averaged answers to questions i, j, and k on the 1954–1972 questionnaires were used to assess "marital happiness."

1 = Marriages that were seen as "quite stable," sexual adjustment as at least "satisfying," and separation had "never" been considered. In Table 6 these were called *Good*.

2 = Marriages neither as uniformly good as those rated "1" or as bad as those rated "3."

3 = Marriages called *Bad* in Table 6. These were seen as showing, over time, "moderate weaknesses," sexual adjustment as "not as good as wished," and separation had been considered "seriously." (In the event one answer was worse, another answer could be one step better, e.g., if sexual adjustment had been considered "rather poor," then separation could have been considered "only casually.")

4 = Divorce

The actual questionnaire read as follows: In the matter of marriage adjustment, please circle the following items that seem to apply:

a. On the whole, my wife and I are: similar in temperament / different in temperament.

b. On the whole, we think and work: in the same way / differently but complementing one another / at cross purposes.

c. My wife and I disagree: never / rarely / occasionally / frequently / continuously.

d. Disagreements are usually: trivial / moderate / serious.

e. The causes of disagreements generally are: (circle one or more) my work / her work / children's raising / finances / her family / my family / house / standard of living / social circle / outside interests / personal temperament / sexual intercourse / other (state) _____.

f. Solutions generally come: easily / moderately hard / always difficult.
g. Since I have been married, I think that I have: not essentially changed / moderately changed / greatly changed.
h. I think that she has: not essentially changed / moderately changed / greatly changed.
i. How stable do you think your marriage is? quite stable / some minor weaknesses / moderate weaknesses / major weaknesses / not stable.
j. Sexual adjustment is, on the whole: very satisfying / satisfying / at times not as good as wished / rather poor.
k. Separation or divorce has been considered: never / only casually / seriously / accomplished (state circumstances).

Please comment as extensively as you wish:

5. *Maturity of Defenses Scale* (a rating from 1 to 26)

Choice of defensive style was assessed in the following manner. Each man's chart, containing roughly three hundred pages of prospectively gathered data in the form of autobiographical responses to questionnaires, interviews, summaries, psychological tests, protocols, etc., was reviewed by me. Each man's behavior at times of crisis and conflict was recorded as a vignette. Often, evidence that a vignette reflected defensive behavior depended upon subsequent follow-up. Each vignette was tentatively identified according to the hierarchy of defenses outlined in Appendix A, and the age at which the vignette occurred was also noted. Each defensive vignette was then stripped of language identifying a specific defense mechanism. For each man, about twenty such vignettes were collected (range, 11 to 34). Similar vignettes were grouped together. The clustered vignettes and a one-page summary of each man's life-style were given to blind raters (a psychiatric social worker with eight years' experience and a board-eligible psychiatrist with psychoanalytic training) who independently rated each of fifty cases. They labeled each cluster of vignettes according to the glossary in Appendix A. Each man was perceived to use an average of 5.5 defensive styles (range, 3 to 9). The raters identified three defense labels that they thought most characteristic for each man — *major* defensive styles. Other defensive clusters were called *minor* styles.

Examples of the manner in which these vignettes were organized are illustrated by the protocol of Lieutenant Edward Keats. During his life he showed two very distinct ways of handling conflicts over instinctual expression. Below is part of the summary given to each blind rater.

"The first style extended throughout all of Keats's life. His mother told the staff that as a child he 'went through a stage of being a clown, but he got over that.' At age 20 Keats looked back on his failures as funny, and he saw his 'besetting sin as procrastination.' The Grant Study staff noticed that he was chronically late for interviews, but that nobody seemed to mind. At age 30, the point at which he began to tell the staff of his discovery of hidden hostilities, he wrote 'I used to pride myself on not having any.' He also gave away his questionnaire to his psychology teacher and thus evaded answering it. Two years later he wrote, 'Sorry about last year's questionnaire. Never got to it.' Although he never sent in another questionnaire, in September 1967 he could write, 'Your good letter of last May arrived in the East, and I've not been able to get to it till now. I'll try to get the questionnaire into your hands.' He never did. At 47 he had been separated from his wife for many years, but without admitting overt conflict and without ever divorcing her. He spent seven years in graduate school, but at age 47 was still working on his thesis. His chief political activity was active participation in sit-ins."

Both the two blind raters and I agreed that passive-aggressive behavior was a *major* defense.

"A second style was evident from a briefer period of Edward Keats's life. As a teenager, although he found the human body unattractive, he was fascinated by how it worked and took pleasure in sculpture, especially of women. Shelley, Keats, and Wordsworth were his favorite poets, but until he was 30 he remained a virgin. Since he found football, at which he excelled, too aggressive, he took up flying. He wrote, 'Just being in the air is enjoyable. Two things appeal to me: shooting toward a target, and being able to maneuver a small plane at will.' At 23 he wrote home ecstatic letters about piloting fighter-bombers against the Nazis. Loathing the violence of hand to hand combat, he got exceedingly high officer rating marks and won three air medals for the aerial combat he loved. He realized, however, that had it not been for the fact that Germany was a significant enemy, he would have regarded his pleasure as selfishness." I labeled these vignettes *sublimation;* one blind rater called them *intellectualization* and the other *displacement.*

I. Scale for Rating Individual Defenses:

For each of the fifty men assessed by blind raters, each defense was rated as follows. If a defense was scored by both blind raters as *major*, the defense received a score of 5. If one rater called it *major* and the other *minor*, the defense received a score of 4. The defense was scored 3 if both raters called it *minor* or if one called it *major* and the other absent. The defense was scored 2 if one called it *minor* and the other called it absent. And the defense received a score of 1 if both raters scored it absent. The writer scored each defense 1 to 5 for all ninety-five subjects. A given defense score reflected the *number* of recorded vignettes labeled as that defense. Stoics received a 5 for suppression; Lotus-eaters received a 1.

II. Scale for the Overall Maturity of Defenses:

The men were rank ordered for relative overall maturity of defensive style by subtracting the numerical sum of the ratings for the five Mature defenses from the sum of ratings for the five Immature defenses. Ratings for the theoretically intermediate (Neurotic) group of defenses were assigned no weight. This procedure was done for the fifty men scored by blind raters and for the forty-five men scored by myself alone. (In order to convert all the ratings into positive numbers, 15 was arbitrarily added to each score. The result was a range of scores extending from 1 to 26, and men who used Mature defenses to the exclusion of Immature defenses received very low scores.)

The interrater reliability between independent raters and myself on the different defenses can be summarized as follows:

	INTERRATER RELIABILITY†	
	Combined Raters versus GEV	Rater A versus Rater B
Overall Maturity of Defenses	.77*	.72*
IMMATURE DEFENSES		
Fantasy	.53*	.15
Projection	.96*	.95*
Passive Aggression	.83*	.90*
Hypochondriasis	.84*	.87*
Acting Out	.76*	.54*
NEUROTIC DEFENSES		
Intellectualization	.69*	.44
Repression	.78*	.63*
Reaction Formation	.70*	.74*
Displacement	.63*	.41
Dissociation	.55*	−.01
MATURE DEFENSES		
Altruism	.75*	.41
Suppression	.60*	.59*
Humor	.81*	.74*
Anticipation	.91*	.75*
Sublimation	.57*	.32

†See Childhood Environment Scale for explanation of rater reliability.

*p < .001 (Rater agreement would have occurred by chance less than 1 time in 1,000.)

6. *Overall Outcome of Children Scale* (a rating from 6 to 20)

Each of the two oldest children (over 15) of each man were rated on the basis of each man's biennial description of his offspring. Raters were not familiar with any other part of the men's records. The average age of the children so rated was 22 (range 15 to 29).

The overall outcome was assessed by averaging the scores for each child by two raters for items II, III, and IV (Academic, Social, and Emotional Achievement). The total score (3 to 10) for each child was added. (If there was only one child the score was doubled.)

A total score of 6 to 10 was used to identify Grant Study men who could be labeled Good Fathers. A score of 13 to 20 was used to identify fathers who on a relative and arbitrary basis could be labeled Poor Fathers.

Interrater reliability was *r* = .78. (See Childhood Environment Scale for explanation.)

I. Father's Closeness to His Children:

1 = Very supportive, consistent interest in child, activities together, marked concern and mutual closeness.

2 = Supportive home, positive relationship, but no clear closeness (certainly not a poor or negative relationship).

3 = Not especially supportive; neglectful, though no outright rejection; no activities together, father does not *know* child; or a "supportive" father whose child consistently rejects him after adolescence.

II. Academic Achievement:
(This could not be rated in children under 18)

1 = Highly competitive college (Harvard, MIT, Radcliffe, Berkeley, Yale, Princeton, University of Pennsylvania, Cornell, Bryn Mawr, Columbia, Brown, Stanford, Wellesley, Smith, Barnard were the ones mentioned).

2 = Other four-year colleges or high standard artistic training.

3 = Junior colleges, business courses, or permanent college dropout after less than two years.

4 = Dropout or marked underachievement in high school or no college though had ability. (All had the means.)

III. Social Adjustment of Children:

1 = Many friends, popular, active, some close relationships, OK with opposite sex; *mention* by father of popularity, leadership, friends.

2 = One or more of above absent or negative, but not all (e.g., doesn't make friends easily; one or two very close friends but *no* other friendships; consistently avoids opposite sex.)

3 = Neither close friends nor many acquaintances, or consistently poor relationships (loses friends, poor marriage); also, extremely inactive in anything involving others (without physical reason) and general lack of interest.

IV. Emotional Adjustment of Children:

1 = Excellent; happy person with *no* severe extended periods of depression, crisis, or delinquency.

2 = Problems for short periods which have been overcome (e.g. troubled adolescence, etc.). Or not very happy or self-satisfied as a person, but no delinquency or "crises." Or several negative traits, though generally well adjusted.

3 = Consistently unhappy, dissatisfied, or troubled, but without serious disturbance. Lacking in ambition, direction, motivation, and rejecting of all responsibility (beyond adolescence).

4 = Severe emotional problems and sustained poor adjustment (e.g., serious delinquency, schizophrenia, psychiatric hospitalization).